# 1996–1997

## BRASSEY'S MERSHON

# AMERICAN

# D·E·F·E·N·S·E

## ANNUAL

# 1996–1997

## BRASSEY'S MERSHON

# AMERICAN
# D·E·F·E·N·S·E
# A N N U A L

## Current Issues and the Asian Challenge

Edited by
Williamson Murray
and
Allan R. Millett

**Mershon Center**
*The Ohio State University*

**Brassey's**
*Washington • London*

The Library of Congress has cataloged this serial publication as follows: ISSN 0822-1028

Hardcover ISBN 1-57488-096-9
Trade Paperback ISBN 1-57488-098-5

Designed by Merrey/Orgel Design

10 9 8 7 6 5 4 3 2 1

Printed in the United States of America

# Dedication

This edition of the *Brassey's Mershon American Defense Annual* is dedicated to the memory of our colleague and former editor of the *Annual*, Joseph Kruzel. Dr. Kruzel left The Ohio State University in 1993 to become deputy assistant secretary of defense for European and NATO policy. In August 1995, he, Ambassador Robert C. Frasure, and National Security Council Aide Col. S. Nelson Drew were killed near Sarajevo when the French armored car they rode in rolled off a narrow mountain road and into a mine field. They carried with them an American peace proposal. The following remarks were made by Secretary of Defense William J. Perry at a memorial service for Dr. Joseph Kruzel held in Columbus, Ohio, on October 3, 1995:

"In his eulogy to his brother, the humanist Robert Green said, 'In the night of death, hope sees a star.' Joe Kruzel was such a star, and his life offered hope that we can resolve the complex national security issues of our day without war.

"Joe was a cherished friend of mine, and his loss leaves an aching void in my life, but I am not alone in my feelings. One of Joe's special qualities was that he took the trouble to find out about his world. He knew policies and politics cold, but more than that—he brought a conviction and a passion to his politics. He was a primary architect for Partnership for Peace, but more than that—he was *our* partner for peace. He knew intimately the places and peoples of Europe, but more than that—he brought a warmth and vitality to his friendships with political leaders. As a result, his death sparked a flood of messages from the leaders of European countries: presidents, foreign ministers, defense ministers, and military leaders. They all knew Joe; and they all respected his achievements.

"In Albania, the government named a wing of their military hospital in honor of Joe. It was dedicated by his wife, Gail, three weeks ago. We first learned of the appalling conditions at this hospital when Gail and Lee [Perry] visited it. After hearing their report, Joe organized a team of American servicemen, drawn from the army, air force, navy, and marines, and from the South Carolina National Guard, to work with the Albanians to make that the best hospital in Albania—and they are well on the way to achieving their goal.

"The legacy that Joe Kruzel left behind really came alive for me last week, when I made a long-planned trip to Central Europe—to Slovenia, Slovakia, the Czech Republic, Hungary, and Germany. My staff referred to the trip as the Joe Kruzel Memorial Trip, because it was his brainchild—he had organized and planned it, and it was the countries that he loved, and where he was loved.

"During our visit to the Czech Republic, our Czech colleagues told us that when Joe visited Prague, he loved to go to a small restaurant, called U Kalicha. There he would drink beer with his friends from the Czech defense ministry and military, and spend hours singing Czech songs he didn't know and toasting Czech heroes he hadn't heard of.

"On the walls of the restaurant are the signatures of prominent guests. Joe's signature is there, alongside that of the Czech playwright, patriot, and president, Vaclav Havel—two men willing to put their lives on the line for freedom and peace. At our concluding meeting in Prague, the Czech Minister of Defense changed the name of the American-Czech Bilateral Working Group to the "Joe Kruzel Group"—and everyone knows what that name stands for—friendship between nations—and friendship between people.

"We ended our trip in Garmisch, Germany, visiting another legacy of Joe's genius, the Marshall Center. The Marshall Center teaches future leaders of the militaries and defense ministries of the former communist countries about the role of the military in a democracy. As a tribute to Joe, and to insure that his spirit lives on at the Marshall Center, the faculty there dedicated the auditorium in Joe's name. In the years to come, as lieutenant colonels from Estonia to Bulgaria, from Hungary to Uzbekistan, wrestle with defense transparency, parliamentary oversight, and other issues of civilian control of the military, they will have the spirit of Joe Kruzel to guide them.

"As Secretary of Defense, I had to call on my friend Joe Kruzel to take on the daunting task—to reinvigorate the NATO Alliance and to integrate the newly free nations of Europe into the security architecture of Europe. His beat was the broad swath of land from the Atlantic Ocean to the Ural Mountains. And he knew every part of it.

"But no place was more important to Joe than the war torn land of Bosnia. When Joe joined my team, he said that one of his major goals was to solve the Bosnia problem. He became so valuable to this effort that the President appointed him to a special American negotiating team. His life was cut short just as he helped to bring a new glimmer of hope to the tragedy in Bosnia.

"Joe did not intend to be a martyr for peace. But in the end, he gave his life so that others may live. This is the greatest work that God can have us do,

"I would like to close with a message for his colleagues, and a message for his family. To his colleagues—you should know that his policy initiatives have already had a remarkable degree of success; my hope is that you will preserve his memory, pursue his legacy, and persevere in his work for peace. To his family—you should know that Joe achieved something that is given to only a very few: He left the world better than he found it. My hope for you is that your pain will be relieved by the grace of God.

"To quote from Aeschylus, 'In our sleep, pain that cannot forget, falls drop by drop upon the heart; until, in our despair, against our will, comes wisdom, through the aweful grace of God.'"

# Acknowledgments

There are a number of people we have to thank for their help in putting this issue to bed. At the Mershon Center, Beth Russell as usual provided her enthusiastic support, while our assistant editors, Chris Ives and Lesley Smith, provided intelligent advice and consistent support. And we must also thank the crew at Brassey's for their clear thinking and generous support.

# Contents

# Introduction: Learning Nothing from the Past

*Williamson Murray*

This issue of *Brassey's Mershon American Defense Annual* marks the second year of our efforts to broaden the annual's focus by examining the strategic environment born from the detritus of the Cold War and the consequences that the resulting rapid changes have for American defense policy. The *Economist* has only recently (January 1996) suggested the continuing range of the potential for change in our world:

> Three or four things will happen during 1996 that between them will help to shape the way the world goes for the next fifteen or twenty years....Take, at one not inconceivable extreme, a withdrawn America, a Europe still absorbed in constitutional crochet work, a damn-everybody's-eyes Zhirinovsky Russia and a post-Deng China dedicated to the pursuit of nationalism with a China face....The only slightly likelier opposite extreme consists of a resurgent America, a group of European powers happy to work alongside America, a relatively co-operative Russia and a quiescent China.[1]

On the evidence there is *little* reason for optimism. American defense policy remains anchored firmly in a past world of the bi-polar military competition with the Soviet Union; the only new paradigm since the collapse of the Soviet Union is that of the Gulf War, which has given birth to the current buzzword, major regional contingencies. Unfortunately, that war with its six-month buildup on friendly territory has little relevance even to another contingency in the region—since *even* we cannot expect our future opponents to make mistakes on the order of those made by Saddam Hussein and his regime in the period from their invasion of Kuwait through to the onset of operations in mid-January 1991.[2]

U.S. politicians and statesmen appear less than realistic in their ability to assess the emerging political and strategic environment. If anything, they remain firmly attached to a Eurocentric *Weltanschauung*, and when their attention wanders towards the economic giants of Asia, they seem to interpret events on the far side of the Pacific through Eurocentric eyes. Finally, procurement for U.S. forces seems governed by arcane practices and influences that would, were Oliver Stone writing this article, be explained by dark international conspiracies operating near the purple water fountain in the basement of the Pentagon.

Americans appear unwilling even to call things by their proper name. Policy makers and the media characterized the slaughter of tens of thousands in Bosnia as genocide, while the U.S. government floundered in search of words to describe the slaughter of hundreds of thousands in Africa. In early 1996 the United States is deploying much of its European military power to bring peace to Bosnia. On the other hand, the United States has almost entirely receded from the ongoing crisis in Rwanda, and now Burundi, that shows every prospect of even greater slaughters as the crisis threatens to spill over from Rwanda to its neighbors. About the best one can say is that American foreign policy did not actively contribute to the slaughter of the Tutsis, as the French authorities in the region did.[3]

We cannot, of course, deal with all the ills or challenges besetting U.S. defense policy at the moment. Last year's *Defense Annual* focused on the strategic environment and the mismatch between service plans and the means at hand or foreseeable in the future. This year our focus is slightly different. We will begin with four articles that address issues fundamental national security issues confronting the United States in the world and the perception of the United States by our European allies.

The first by Robert Gaskin sets out not only the Pentagon's systemic difficulties, but the reasons why, even in a presidential election year, there is little chance for serious debates about reform much less reform itself. The second article, by Jay Young, lays out the problems within the U.S. intelligence community—problems that suggest that this costly intelligence structure with its technological capabilities cannot at the present time, nor in the foreseeable future, delineate real or emerging threats. Moreover, it is unlikely that the current intelligence community will provide policy makers with deep *analysis* of real threats even after they emerge. What we need from intelligence in the next century is sophisticated *understanding* of foreign threats, not more data. But it is the latter we will get.

The third article in this section, by Barry Watts, may be the most important the *Annual* has ever published in this editor's view: He argues that war and conflict in the next century will remain entirely Clausewitzian. Friction and its attending ambiguities and uncertainties that have always marked conflict between humans *will not* disappear. In fact, the explosion of information and data may well make war more open to uncertainties and frictions than in the past. Such a view stands in stark contrast to the claims of the "information warriors" in the U.S. military that technology will vanquish friction by the twenty-first-century. Our fourth article, by John Gooch, addresses the genesis of a growing ambivalence among our European allies towards a United States they see as possessing no rudder and no direction in a confusing and complex world.

The remainder of this issue of the *Defense Annual* will examine the emerging strategic environment in Asia—one that contains great fault lines, exacerbated by a general American ignorance of the issues and the dangers of the world's greatest continent. The commitment of U.S. troops to Bosnia will hold the attention of the American people for much of the year as U.S. "nation-building" efforts struggle to come to grips with a situation that our bureaucracy possesses neither the language skills nor historical knowledge to understand.[4]

But, for better or worse, the United States will determine Asia's direction in the next century. There already, sophisticated armaments are multiplying. There already, fundamental, irreconcilable claims exist side by side (China versus Taiwan, India versus Pakistan, China versus everyone bordering on the South China Sea, among others). There already, racial and even religious hatreds (Hindu versus Buddhist in Sri Lanka, Hindu versus Moslem in India and Pakistan, and Chinese versus Malay, among others), stewed by the past centuries, fester and simmer. And there an unprecedented economic revolution is occurring—one that is changing the world economic balance of power. For the first time since the industrial revolution, the world's economic balance is coming to rest outside the west. There are those who believe that the economic benefits of international trade, confidence-building measures, and multilateral security arrangements will combine to make Asia a healthy cooperative center of world civilization. Don't bet on it.

We have asked a number of distinguished academics to examine the Asian strategic situation. Allan Millett considers the current as well as the historical strategic interests of the United States in Asia—interests that reach back well into the nineteenth century and which will not disappear in the next century. Arthur Waldron presents a depressing view of China, Asia's new economic giant that has exploded on the world scene. It is a China that possesses little knowledge of the external world, but one that also puts forward claims to territory beyond its border that might have astounded even the cartographers of the Third Reich.

In South Asia, Stephen Cohen presents the India-Pakistan standoff; at times he has hopes for a region so far from traditional U.S. interests, but one that becomes increasingly important. Yet the weight of history, conflict, culture, religion, and communal strife should never allow Americans to forget the potential for further violence and conflict between two states so similar and yet so far apart. One of his fundamental lines of argument—quite similar to that espoused by Brian Sullivan in last year's annual—is that there is at the present time a window of opportunity for the United States to play a significant role in defusing tensions between the antagonists on the subcontinent.[5] Both agree that the attitude of benign neglect among U.S. policy makers towards the region, which has characterized so much of America's policy before, during, and after the Cold War, will contribute to the destabilizing of South Asia.

Jeffrey Grey suggests that Southeast Asia, where so many Americans bled and died two decades ago, provides the most hopeful story in Asia. The economic miracle, at least for most, is one of the more astonishing tales in the late twentieth century. Yet, there is conflict in the region, and only internal worries have limited Southeast Asian states to claims on what others hold, rather than acting on those claims. Thus far, these states have concentrated on their own internal economic growth. With prosperity comes both more to lose and the means to defend their positions. It may also bring greater ambitions against the territory of their neighbors.

So far there are only relatively modest military buildups in the region. The one regional power with substantial military capabilities, Vietnam, has come in from the cold, and no longer appears to harbor great territorial ambitions in the region. But there are worries: China has laid claim to virtually the entire South China Sea and its enormous potential in resources, and, while the Chinese can not yet enforce those claims, they will have the capabilities to enforce those claims in the near future. Moreover, local ambitions possess the potential to stir up conflict in the region. Only last year, the Indonesians laid claim to the straits of Malacca.

While India and Pakistan present difficulties, Asia's cockpit of troubles lies in Northeast Asia. There Taeho Kim presents some hope, but considerable cause for worry. North Korea, with a rapidly crumbling economy and an ideology completely out of tune with events everywhere else in the world, is one of the world's unpredictable states. The flounderings of the Clinton administration in threatening and then bribing a polity still seeking the ideological purity of Stalin's "workers' and peasants' paradise" raises the question as to whether the United States possesses either the wisdom or the stamina to provide the stability that Northeast Asia so desperately needs. For now the United States provides a modicum of glue for the region, but for how much longer? We have much to think on and not much time.

## Asia, Clausewitz, and Procurement

In the substantive portion of this introduction, I would like to turn to three subjects that suggest the difficulties that U.S. national security policy will confront in addressing the problems of the next century. It might seem as if Asia, Clausewitz, and procurement have little in common, but they do. The problems posed by Asia represent the strategic challenges that the U.S. policy-making community seems ill-prepared to address. As the work that Allan Millett and I have done on the subject of military effectiveness has suggested:

> it is more important to make correct decisions at the political and strategic level than it is at the operational and tactical level. Mistakes in operations and tactics can be corrected, but political and strategic mistakes live forever.[6]

The lack of knowledge of foreign languages, culture, and history among American policy makers lays U.S. strategy open to the dangers of strategic miscalculation on a massive level.[7] The current U.S. peace efforts in Bosnia reflect the extraordinary arrogance that only Americans with their ahistorical theories of international relations bring to the world's problems.[8] Not only do we seem to believe that we can create a multi-ethnic Switzerland out of four years of savage civil war (and all achieved in one year!), but we actually appear to believe that the temporary marriage of convenience between Muslims and Croats represents something more than a papering over of quarrels that lie deep in the murderous history of Turk, Croat, and Serb.[9] We may avoid a military and political disaster, but we cannot always count on our size and power to mitigate our ignorance. Similarly, without some coherent framework for our policy in Asia we risk bringing general instability and disaster to what will soon be the world's most important economic region.[10]

If we confront difficulties on the strategic level, there are dangerous trends within the intellectual conceptualization of the American military and its understanding of the nature of war. The once-derided intellectual conceptions of former Secretary of Defense Robert McNamara that American technological superiority and expertise will allow the U.S. military to dominate the battlefield of the future—an approach that had led to the blood-drenched fields of South Vietnam and collapse in Southeast Asia[11]—are again alive and well in the American military.

In fact, the mechanistic beliefs that American technological superiority will allow us to "dissipate the fog of war" is already a dominant theme within service cultures as well as in the joint arena.[12] Such is the popularity of such views that this author has heard a senior army general in the Pentagon announce that the army's "digitization" of the battlefield means that "Clausewitz is dead."[13] The implications of such views seem well worth exploring in this essay as well in Barry Watts' more thorough examination of Clausewitz's relevance to the future in Chapter III.

Finally, because an ahistorical American strategy may well call upon a U.S. military, prepared in a flawed intellectual paradigm, to fight with weapons that minimize America's technological advantages, it seems worthwhile to look at procurement in general and the F/A 18E/F program in particular. In an era when resources are scare, and when funding is already disappearing into the budget deficit's black hole, we might reconsider how we procure our weapons. The F/A 18E/F is a salient warning on how not to proceed.

## Asia

Last year the *Defense Annual's* introduction emphasized the lack of historical knowledge and understanding in American strategy, the combination of military power, diplomatic finesse, and historical continuities that guide the ship of state through the rough waters of international trials. Unfortunately for Americans, only history can give us some clue—no matter how opaque—as to the how the future will unfold.[14] Over the past fifty years, historians have gained a detailed, if not universal, sense of the factors that resulted in the outbreak of World War II in Europe.[15] But the origins and causes of the war in Pacific—or from the Chinese perspective, the war in Asia—remain less clear.[16] The supposed origins of the war usually boil down to simplistic incidents such as the Japanese occupation of Manchuria or the incident at the Marco Polo Bridge. In fact the causes of the war are as deep and complex as those in Europe.[17] But with our comfortable Western assumptions and our lack of languages, we look at events in the Pacific as if there were only a few incidents that determined the United States to involve itself in the course of Asian events.

Over the coming decade we may well see the same American disinterest replayed again. Only after Asia comes apart in another great conflict will the United States regain its interest. This time, given Asia's economic and political importance, the wreck would have a more catastrophic impact on the world. Where then is the heart of Asia's difficulties? In three simple words it is China, China, and China—multiple Chinas because it is not even clear which China will emerge in the first decade of the next century.

On one hand it is plausible that a combination of serious strategic mistakes, flowing naturally from the Chinese contempt for the outside world,[18] will lead China into major miscalculations of its power vis à vis even Taiwan. The inability of China's political leadership to draw a connection between means at hand and extraordinary claims,[19] suggests the possibility that the next leadership in a search for legitimacy could strike at Taiwan, or elsewhere. Such action would kill the goose fueling Chinese economic explosion, namely the massive foreign investment in South China, much of it from Taiwan.[20] A foreign policy or military defeat could have very serious political consequences, given the lack of legitimacy of the present regime. The result in political terms would be hard to calculate, but it is well to remember the impact the last Chinese collapse (in the 1920s) had on the Asian political scene—a collapse that led directly to Japan's disastrous intervention in Chinese affairs.

On the other hand, it is equally possible that a future generation of Chinese leadership, more attuned to the world, will weigh the risks and benefits of a long-term strategy—a long-term strategy according to the Asian rather than to the Western calculus.[21] In those terms China will aim at a maximum expansion of its explosive economic growth, an absorption through generous terms of not only Hong Kong, but eventually Taiwan and Singapore (*Heim ins Reich*) as well; and a gradual nibbling away at Russia's empire until the Chinese control Siberia and its enormous resources. The combination of China's population with control of Siberia would result in the creation of MacKinder's worst nightmare.

Such an empire, massive, rich, populous, and cohesive, would be a true superpower that would dwarf the pretensions of the Soviet Union and the United States during the Cold War. All the efforts of the United States, its allies in Asia, and even its friends in Europe—of doubtful utility anyway— could not restore the balance of power on the Eurasian mainland. This China would dominate the world through its economic power and the size of its population; the Asian periphery, including India, and possibly even Japan would toe the Chinese line. Europe would find itself reduced to its fifteenth century position on the periphery, while the United States would remain at sea, caught quite literally between the Pacific and the Atlantic.

The above scenarios are extreme projections of the situation in the 1990s. But whatever happens, the result is not likely to be pleasing to those who hope for a stable, pleasant world in the next century. The Clinton administration's obdurate dicta that no one in either defense or state department bureaucracies consider the implications of a hostile China for U.S. policy suggests the ostrich-like American (and British) approach that proved so successful, from the German and Japanese points of view, in the 1930s.

Moreover, whenever the national media expresses any views on Asia beyond arguing about import quotas for automobiles, they inevitably run along the lines of "don't lets be beastly to the [Chinese]."[22]

The sooner the United States confronts the Chinese with the stance that certain kinds of behavior, such as unprovoked threats against its neighbors, are unacceptable in the international arena, the better it will be for all. Such toughness might even lessen the possibility that the Chinese will make major miscalculations that could result in catastrophe for themselves and Asia. But thus far in the curious unfolding of its foreign policy, the Clinton administration has failed to take a tough line—except perhaps in regards to human rights abuses. From the Chinese perspective, the continuing American emphasis on human rights and silence on aggressive Chinese behavior in the international arena have appeared completely indecipherable.

What makes the possibility of China's appearance as a future economic and military superpower so fraught with danger is the increasing weakness of other regional powers in Asia. Russia wields only a fragment of the power that the Soviet Union brandished on the world stage. Nor have the Russian leadership and people drawn sensible conclusions from the collapse of their empire.[23] Russia's economy continues to contract; its political structure is failing to come to grips with the intractable problems confronting the nation; and the recent triumph of the nationalist and communist parties almost guarantees that the nation's leadership will refuse to address the desperate, systemic problems. Instead, regime and people will dream longingly of the days when the Soviet Union under comrade Stalin confronted a world and worked at building the "workers' and peasants' paradise."

As a result, instead of adapting and using their raw material assets to leverage a path into a modern, market economy, the Russians will flounder. Their dreams will lead them to further involve themselves in adventures like Chechnya, while the Russian military will display the same ham-handed tactics that led to the Afghanistan and Grozny debacles. As for modernization, the Russians will remain suspicious of any and all foreign influences and thereby insure that even equatorial Africa will represent a better investment. They will miss even the potential for modernizing the trans-Siberian railroad that would allow them to become the middleman between Asia and Europe and to undercut the world's seaborne trade between Asia and Europe.

Russia's present policy of friendship with China, in which the Russians are shipping their most modern weapons' technology to the People's Liberation Army, shows signs of evolving into a client-patron relationship. Meanwhile, substantial numbers of Chinese are emigrating from Manchuria to Siberia, while the Russian population, having lost Soviet subsidies to stay in the region, flocks back to Europe. De Gaulle, who alone of western leaders—

not to mention western political scientists and international theorists[24]—predicted the Soviet Union's collapse, also predicted that the Russian state emerging from the wreckage would shrink back to the Urals. On present evidence his estimate appears on the mark.

But other weak links in the Asian framework are worrisome. As North Korea enters its death spiral, the United States has been more interested in appeasement than in preparing to deter the worst case. It may be that the new North Korean leadership will lack the fanatical toughness that led Kim Il Sung to drive his armies against the south in June 1950. In fact, the ongoing interregnum suggests that North Korea will not act precipitously.

But the United States should not think that just because the Eastern European communist regimes went quietly into the dark the North Korean comrades will follow the same path. While their leadership may maintain a hold over its suffering followers into the next century, only a policy of prudence has hope of insuring that North Korea's demise will not occasion a funeral pyre for the region. What might such a policy entail? On one hand, it would demand a clear and unambiguous American military and strategic presence and commitment to South Korea. On the other, it would end the free-lunch programs that extraordinary bad behavior by the North Koreans has extracted from their neighbors and the United States. Above all, the United States can not afford to send the kind of signals the Truman administration sent in winter and spring 1950. One could, of course, argue that we have already sent the wrong message to the successors of the great leader—of an America more afraid of body bags on CNN than of a North Korea with nuclear weapons.

From an American point of view, Japan shines as the one bright spot in Asia. Whatever Japan's difficulties in adapting to the external environment or the misconceptions of Japanese as to their recent history,[25] a unique set of circumstances means that Japan needs American friendship and support more than the United States needs Japan. Japan's relative state of disarmament (one that reflects Japan's reliance on the United States), an aging population (never a recipe for national adventure), and the appearance of a significant long-term Chinese threat, all will probably push Japan towards continued reliance on the United States. The shocks that Japan has undergone this past year—the failure of its bureaucracy to respond to the Kobe earthquake, the sarin terrorists drawn from the best and the brightest of its society, and a savings and loan scandal that may dwarf even the American experience—suggest that the United States can hold the Japanese within a reasonably close and friendly framework, especially considering the Chinese problem.

But there are limits. The continued mindless American efforts to antagonize the Japanese, particularly in demanding the right to sell large American cars in the Japanese market, suggest a lack of perspective on where American long-term interests lie. Above all, any sudden and ill-considered American withdrawal of U.S. forces from Asia would force the Japanese to begin major rearmament programs, which would possibly include nuclear weapons, just to guarantee regional stability. American withdrawal might even force the Japanese to intervene on the Asian mainland with consequences that are hard to imagine. Whether the Unted States will have the courage to remain engaged in Asia is, of course, another question.

American forces and commitments allow the Japanese to maintain a relatively small military force, one that does not threaten their neighbors. Since 1953, the American commitment has kept North Korea from unleashing the benefits of the great leader's wisdom. The cost of those commitments may seem exorbitant to some, but the costs involved in a collapse of Asia's precarious balance would be so huge and strategically destabilizing on the world as to be incalculable. Better the difficulties of today than the nightmares of tomorrow. If the continuing economic explosion continues, it becomes even more important for the United States to remain engaged. American presence, as signalled by its military forces and commitments, represents the glue that holds a fragile structure together, particularly in Northeast Asia.

## Clausewitz and the American Military

In 1975 Michael Howard and Peter Paret published a new, and deeply intelligent translation of Clausewitz. The American military, particularly the marine corps and army, seized On War as a meaningful explanation for the terrible uncertainties, ambiguities, and difficulties they had confronted in the Vietnam War that they had fought from 1963 through to 1972–a conflict whose resolution was defeat. For the first time since its publication in the nineteenth century, On War came to dominate the culture and professional military education of a nation's military organizations.[26] There were, of course, other trends, such as the 1970s' edition of the army's basic doctrinal manual, Field Manual 100-5, with its heavy emphasis on a deterministic and mechanistic approach to war. But even the Weinberger and Powell doctrines—overstatements of Clausewitz' arguments on the connection between war and politics—represented a recognition of the truths in the great Prussian thinker's conceptions.

But the love affair between the American military and Clausewitz appears to have entered terminal decline. Clausewitz's uncomfortable messages—from the inseparability of war and politics to his emphasis on general friction—found an echo largely among officers who had looked over the edge into the chaos of defeat and could not avoid the implications of that vision. However, the Vietnam War experience is now almost entirely out of the officer corps of the U.S. armed forces—only a few very senior officers still on active duty bear the mental and physical scars of that conflict. Ironically, the American military are returning to the absolute beliefs in technology and system per-fectibility that so characterized the McNamara era—only this time, of course, the technology will work. There is some considerable irony in this situation, because both science and mathematics have brought forward considerable *sci-entific* support to Clausewitz's view of the world in the studies of nonlinearity and chaos math.[27] These studies underline that Clausewitz's ideas about fric-tion have a solid basis in the real world of biology and physics and that reduc-tionist approaches simply do not work in a world of complexity.[28]

It seems appropriate to let those who believe that the direction of war is entirely toward the technical to explicate their views in their own words. Admiral William Owens, the soon-to-be-retired vice-chairman of the joint chiefs of staff, has this very month (January 1996) claimed the following:

> We hear a lot about the "revolution in military affairs" these days. But what is the vision that drives thinking inside the Pentagon on the size, structure and character of America's future military forces and just how "revolution-ary" is this vision? The vision revolves around our increasing capacity to understand a military situation quickly, accurately, and in considerable detail, and to transfer that understanding with dispatch to forces that can deal with the situation with great speed, precision, and effect...Is this a mil-itary revolution? It has the characteristics of one, for it is occurring quickly, the changes in capability will be great, and the implications of the changes in military technology will extend through the U.S. military's organization, doctrine, and tactics, and *out into the nation's foreign and security policies* [my emphasis]....The revolutionary aspects of this involve what these changes will allow us to do. The emerging system-of-systems promises the capacity to use military force without the same risks as before–it suggests *we will dissi-pate the "fog of war."* [my emphasis][29]

These are indeed extraordinary claims. Even Robert McNamara might not have gone so far at the height of his dominance of the Department of Defense in the mid-1960s. In effect, Owens is a direct intellectual descendant of McNa-mara's approach to military and strategic affairs. If he is correct, then this jump forward to a system of systems represents the greatest revolution in the history of war.[30] If he is wrong, he may have initiated movement towards a cata-strophic defeat for America's military forces sometime in the next century.

We should understand that Admiral Owens' views are symptomatic of a wider phenomenon, the rejection of both the political implications of Clause-witz's arguments (see the above quotation) and the Prussian thinker's belief that friction, uncertainty, and chance have in the past, and would in the future, dominate the conduct of war by human institutions.[31] As one official in the Pentagon suggested to this author, some of the assumptions on which current military thinking is running could be characterized in the following terms: "near-perfect information on all observable phenomena; perfect linkages between sensors and shooters; no need for humans to take time to convert information into intelligence and pass it on to shooters; near-perfect battle damage assessment and follow-up strikes (should they be required); flawless, instantaneous human and technical performance in battle management and command and control; flawless, frictionless overall execution (we have repealed Clausewitz.)"[32]

Moreover, there are major efforts within the joint community to insure that the word gets down to the troops in proper form. The current draft of the chairman's instruction on the joint staff's professional military education policy makes clear that the joint staff is directing all war colleges to emphasize "Joint Vision 2010" in their educational efforts, a vision that has as "its technological foundation" the "system of systems" that will allow the American military to achieve dominant battle-space knowledge and achieve "decisive effectiveness" against our opponents.[33]

This technophilia is missing any real understanding of war as something more than a complex technological puzzle. At the end of 1995 the air force weighed in with a massive study entitled "New World Vistas, Air and Space Power for the 21st Century." The summary volume argued a consistently upbeat technological vision for America's military forces, and the air force in particular, in the next century. So linear is the thinking that the opening paragraphs tout Lanchester's basic equations (a mechanistic set of equations for estimating combat outcomes) for attrition as a theory that "has survived remarkably well."[34] Not surprisingly, the themes were thoroughly consistent with those of Admiral Owens: "The power of the new information systems will lie in their ability to correlate data automatically and rapidly from many sources to form a complete picture of the operational area."[35] Page after endless page discuss the technological marvels, the increasing sophistication of sensors, of communications, and of stand-off weapons, and the dominance of new technologies.

But nowhere in the entire document is there any discussion of what our opponents might be able to do to the United States or its military, where the money is going to come from to buy these new technologies, what the political constraints of future war might be, and especially what is going to happen in war when our opponents go about the business of trying to kill us. In the early 1980s Air Force Manual 1-1, the basic manual of the air force, went so far as to claim that the new AWACS aircraft would allow "commanders to comprehend the total air-surface battle."[36] How AWACS crews might perform under conditions of fatigue, much less combat, emerged in the helicopter shoot down over northern Iraq last year. Unless U.S. planners reintroduce some realistic parameters—namely the real conditions of war—into our technological equations, we are heading for another military disaster on the scale of Vietnam.

This author is certainly not against technology. Technology has been in the past and will certainly in the future represent a strong suit in America's arsenal of military capabilities. There is undoubtedly a "revolution in military affairs" in the wind and to ignore the enormous technological improvements and changes that are occurring would be a serious mistake. But we must not forget that as long as there are humans in the loop, there *will* be frictions, misunderstandings, and ambiguities that will insure that all military organizations will function at considerably less than 100 percent efficiency. Thus, the enthusiasm with which so many have embraced concepts such as "battlefield dominance" and "systems of systems," has considerable danger—not among the least that the United States will miss other potentially fruitful options.

These theoretical constructs (for theoretical constructs are what they are) are based neither on real world tests nor on historical analogues. Clausewitz suggests that at best theory can form "a guide to anyone who wants to learn about war...; it will light his way, ease his progress, train his judgment, and help him to avoid pitfalls."[37] Above all, "theory is not meant to provide...positive doctrines and systems to be used as intellectual tools."[38] The problem has to do with the human desire to find absolute truths about war. "Efforts were therefore made to equip the conduct of war with principles, rules, or even systems...[B]ut people failed to take adequate account of the endless complexities involved."[39] And in the end, most theories "aim at fixed values; but in war everything is uncertain, and calculations have to be made with variable quantities."[40]

It may, of course, seem pointless to quote Clausewitz to true believers, who are already arguing that "revolutionary" technological changes will allow us "to dissipate the fog and friction of the battlefield."[41] The difficulty with such arguments is that *there is nothing in the military history of the past 2,500 years that suggests this to be the case.* Nor is there anything in our most recent conflict, the Gulf War, to indicate that there was a qualitative improvement in the *knowledge* flow through the bureaucracy as opposed to the ability to collect more data.

Admittedly, in that conflict Gulf War planners and operational commanders for the most part received the information they needed, but more often than not the arrival of intelligence where it was needed reflected interpersonal relationships entirely independent of the system.[42] The fact is that U.S. intelligence had great difficulty in collating and analyzing the massive amounts of data gathered during the war. In other words they could not put a usable product in the hands of the warfighters. For substantial portions of the buildup and the conflict, the system broke down and only Desert Shield's lengthy period allowed planners and operational commanders to establish work arounds to mitigate bureaucratic inefficiencies that inhibited the ability to turn a flood of data into useful knowledge. In the future, the increasing deluge of intelligence that the information revolution *will* provide may make it even more difficult to reach meaningful decisions. In other words, the noise will drown out the message. Moreover, all the intelligence and data in the world are useless, if they arrive too late in the hands of those executing policy or operations. It is not how much information that matters, but rather how much insight one brings to the table.[43]

There are, of course, important implications from our experiences in the Gulf War. They suggest that friction in future war may not decrease. The more information that becomes available the more difficult it may be for some commanders to make decisions, at any level. After all, the Pearl Harbor and Yom Kippur surprises did not occur because there was not sufficient information available indicating that something very bad was about to occur.[44] The issue is not how much information or data about the enemy one possesses, but rather how close to an *understanding* of one's opponent one can come— how well, in other words, one understands his intentions, purposes, and will. And such aspects of our opponents will always remain incalculable in any quantitative sense. In other words, more digitized bits of data will not tell us whether our opponent will fight or surrender.[45]

In fact, the United States and its allies have actually fought and won a great information war in this century: the war of codebreaking, counterintelligence, and deception against the Axis Powers in World War II.[46] That effort suggests significant ways—as well as warnings—for how we might think about information war in the next century.[47] First, the Germans with their Enigma machines held the high end of technology; their encoding system should have been unbreakable throughout the entire course of World War II.[48] But because they believed they were technologically superior to their racially inferior opponents, they misused that superiority to such an extent that the British (and eventually the Americans) were able to break into German transmissions on a massive and coherent scale from 1940 to the war's end. Because there were indications that Allied intelligence had acquired unaccountable sources of information on German military activities, the Germans became worried on a number of occasions as to how their opponents were gaining such extraordinary intelligence. But each time, the Germans found other explanations for what was happening to them on the battlefield and in the intelligence arena.[49]

The United States may risk Germany's fate in the next century. Here we are not talking about the Iraqs of the world—although in some areas, such as weapons of mass destruction, the Iraqis did an extraordinary job of misleading and deceiving coalition intelligence. In the next century the spread of technology will insure that United States will not confront one, but rather a number of skilled technological opponents, any one of whom could manipulate the U.S. military into making major mistakes on or off the battlefield.

A portion of the writing on "information" war displays much naïvete in suggesting either that the United States or our opponents might be vulnerable to "information" strikes—an often-used example being an attack on the New York Stock Exchange. In fact, such a use of information war would be foolish. If one could reach into the heart of the U.S. economy, it would be far more advantageous to manipulate markets to one's advantage, rather than to achieve a short-term success no matter how stunning. The latter approach would alert us to both our opponent and his level of sophistication. Instead, the best use of "information" war would aim at tipping the playing field only slightly in one's favor.

This is precisely what the Allies did in World War II. In the Battle of the Atlantic, "Ultra" intelligence derived from decrypts of the Enigma machines allowed Allied naval intelligence to divert convoys around Admiral Karl Dönitz's patrol lines of U-boats.[50] Similarly, a combination of "Ultra" intelligence, the "double cross" system in which the British fed specific disinformation back to German intelligence through double agents in Britain, and a sophisticated understanding of German culture and history, and German military history and culture in particular, allowed the Allies to persuade the Nazi high command that a second major invasion would follow the Normandy landing, this one aimed at the Pas de Calais.[51]

That disinformation campaign held the German Fifteenth Army across from the Straits of Dover, while the crucial battles were fought out in Normandy. This Anglo-American success had less to do with technological sophistication than with a highly developed understanding of the strengths and weaknesses of their opponent. In effect, Allied intelligence was superior to that of the Germans because of its understanding of German language, culture, history, and even literature, not because of its superiority in technology.[52] For five years the British tilted the playing field of World War II with a skillful use of information war, and the Germans never caught on for two reasons: 1) German arrogance; and 2) the sophisticated British understanding of the German mind.

The present approach to information war and intelligence within much of the American military resembles that of the Germans rather than of the Allies in World War II. The belief seems to be that we will achieve "information" dominance over our opponents to the extent that we will see everything, while they will see nothing. Perhaps against Third World opponents, there may be some truth to such claims. But as the Vietnam War underlines, our opponents may have low-tech counters to the most modern technologies. In Somalia, in a medieval warrior culture our opponents' command and control system was so low-tech that they never came up on our screens: using the basic principle of war before modern communications, the Somalis marched to the sound of gunfire. No one had to tell them what to do.

Our opponents do not have to address us in our terms, but rather in terms more suited to their own culture and experience. And here that peculiar American contempt for history, languages, and other cultures puts us far more at risk than it does our opponents. In fact, we have little real ability to do information war in the fashion that the information warriors suggest, because Americans are too unsophisticated to manipulate their enemies as they did in World War II.[53] We do not understand foreign peoples and foreign cultures since we do not even know their languages, while our emphasis on platforms and technology may well delude us into believing that what matters in war is the number of targets serviced and not what is in the mind of the soldier or of those living in the society that supports him. The United States "won" Tet in 1968 by every quantifiable measurement, but in the current moment of our technological narcissism we should not forget that the United States also lost the war.

## Buying Junk

During the early part of the Cold War a combination of factors allowed the United States to develop numbers of superior weapons systems. On one hand it seemed that the nation provided almost unlimited funding and support for designing, fielding, and supporting new weapons. On the other, that level of funding allowed for redundant projects; as a result the appearance of a dud rarely represented a disaster, because there were usually alternatives. The air force might equip its units with inadequate aircraft like the F-101 "Voodoo" or the F-105 "Thud", but other weapons systems could and did take up the slack. Admittedly, the air force found itself in the humiliating position of having to buy the navy's F-4 "Phantom" at the onset of the war in Vietnam, but at least a superior aircraft was available.

The pressures of Vietnam War budgets and the ensuing downsizing changed this state of affairs. What the services developed, for the most part, was what they got; and if a new weapon was less than impressive then that was too bad. Even during the Reagan administration the procurement situation did not return to the bad old days of the pre-1964 period. But the ill-effects of being stuck with a less than impressive aircraft—like the B-1—were mitigated by the fact that substantial numbers of aircraft remained in the inventory which could perform the mission. The performance of the B-52 during the Gulf War is an excellent example; while B-2s sat on the ramp bleeding hydraulic fluid, the ancient "Buffs"—some as old as their crews—played a crucial role in cracking the morale of the Iraqi ground forces during "Desert Storm."[54]

All of this is about to undergo a radical change. The downward spiral of defense budgets and the continuing commitment of American forces around the world means that the Department of Defense is simply not going to able to buy at the levels to which the U.S. military have grown accustomed. What the Pentagon now buys is going to have to suffice for decades and the choices that it makes, particularly if it makes mistakes, might well close down far more attractive avenues that might be available. Consequently, every major weapons systems procurement decision the U.S. military confronts in coming years should undergo the most searching examination in terms not only of relative need—compared to the procurement of other weapons systems—but also of *the conceivable impacts that procurement now will have* on what the country can buy in the future. The defense system is not making these critical decisions in this fashion. Nothing more clearly indicates where our procurement system is going wrong than the navy's recent decision to buy the F/A-18E/F, or "Super Hornet."

On Monday 18 September navy admirals and McDonnell Douglas executives watched as the new F/A-18E/F rolled out for public display at the company's St. Louis plant. For McDonnell Douglas the aircraft represents a major triumph—one that provides jobs for 7,000 workers in the main plant and 20,000 workers with other subcontractors from no less than forty-seven of the fifty states.[55] The stakes are even higher for the navy. It aims to make the F/A-18E/F the carrier jet of the future; its long-range procurement will replace not only the older F/A-18C/Ds but also the older F-14s and A-6s. In effect, the navy is staking the future of naval aviation on the aircraft. In all the navy plans to buy 1,000 new Super Hornets to fill out its carrier decks. In addition, it is clear that the navy is mounting a major effort to force a resource-short marine corps to buy an aircraft that it does not need or want in order to bring down unit costs. The purchase of F/A-18E/F would also have a significant impact on the marines' ability to purchase other weapons they desperately need. Current estimates of the total cost of the program are nearly $80 billion, and that estimate is good only if costs stay under control.[56]

Tragically, there appears to be no justification for bringing the aircraft on board. The current program brings the E/F into the inventory at a time when the C/D is not even halfway through its usable service life. The day that the first E/F rolled out of the assembly line in St. Louis, the average C/D in navy service was only 4.5 years old.[57] The lifetime of the C/D is calculated at 6,000 hours and it is currently averaging 350 hours per year—thus it possesses a life span of seventeen years. But the Canadians are currently looking at certifying their fleet of C/Ds to 8,000 hours, *without a single structural change*. If the navy did the same, it would extend the life of the C/D fleet to 2014, nearly two decades from now.[58]

What makes the buy even more astonishing is that the Super Hornet is not as good as the F-14s and A-6s that it is replacing. It has less range and payload than the A-6 Intruder, and less range and fewer air-to-air capabilities than the F-14 Tomcat.[59] Moreover, the F/A-18E/F does not even come off well in comparison with the Soviet MiG 29, which entered service five years before the Soviet Union ceased to exist. A Canadian test pilot who has flown both the F/A-18C/D and the MiG-29 has reported that the latter was far superior—not a great endorsement for an aircraft that will meet significantly greater threats in the twenty-first century.[60] What is particularly depressing is the fact that the Super Hornet adds very little in the way of capability to the navy. It adds only fifty-sixty additional miles range to that of the Hornet, carries two additional bombs, and possesses some areas where improvements can be made—advantages lacking in the C/D.[61] However, the new Super Hornet will carry 6,000 pounds of internal fuel stored next to the engines, dramatically escalating the risks of catastrophic fire on the crowded decks of carriers.[62]

A 1993 navy study evaluated the Super Hornet against nine other aircraft. The fleet commanders in the study rated the aircraft as "poor" and "recommended cancelling the program."[63] But by then the program had gained such momentum in terms of political support—the fact that subcontractors in forty-seven states were ready to employ tens of thousands of workers obviously added to the momentum—that navy evaluations no longer counted. Moreover, the navy was paying the price for its disastrous mismanagement of the A-12 aircraft. That program had been cancelled after an expenditure of over $5 billion with nothing to show for the effort, not even a prototype. Thus, with the considerable inadequacies of the FA-18C/D, especially in range, in view and with an aging fleet of F-14s and A-6s, the navy had nothing else on the horizon. It was stuck with a most inadequate replacement.

But beyond navy mistakes the question arises as to how an aircraft with so little capability got past the Pentagon's acquisition system, which Congress has supposedly designed to prevent mistakes like the F-101 from happening. Ironically, the F/A-18E/F did not have to go through the process, because the Pentagon performed an end run around the very system that Congress had created to prevent the buying of inferior products. The Department of Defense simply called the aircraft a modification of an existing aircraft, and thus waved all requirements for serious evaluation. Actually, the Super Hornet is a new aircraft, significantly different from the older Hornet. The wing on the E/F for example is 25 percent larger and has only 16 percent commonality with the C/D wing.[64] Even more telling is the fact that the Super Hornet's airframe is 85 percent different.[65] Not surprisingly the current C/D cannot be reconfigured into an E/F, which McDonnell Douglas will assemble on an new production line that requires entirely new tooling. Finally, and depressingly, development costs for the new Super Hornet, $5 billion, are more than the costs of the original aircraft.[66]

The simple explanation for the buy is that for political and economic reasons—namely that McDonnell Douglas was in serious financial difficulty in 1991—the Pentagon, with considerable support from the Congress, scammed the system. If the E/F were to be considered a new aircraft, which it clearly is, the navy would have had to issue a Mission Needs Statement, and a Cost and Evaluation Analysis, oversight tools which the Pentagon uses to screen out inferior and unneeded systems. By claiming that the E/F was a modification to an existing airframe, the navy avoided the complex process of buying a new aircraft. Moreover, the decision to term the E/F a "modification" allowed the Pentagon to bypass safety requirements. The extra 6,000 pounds of fuel stored next to the engines should require live fire testing to determine the dangers to the pilot, but again the fact that the aircraft was judged a "modification" allowed the bypassing of such tests, because the navy had performed them on the C/D airframe. Finally, the navy did not have to build a prototype because the Super Hornet was just a "modification."

There are forces that are propelling the navy towards buying the Super Hornets now instead of waiting and testing other possibilities. The navy will in the coming decade confront considerable difficulty in manning the decks of its twelve carriers—especially considering the aging of the A-6s and F-14s. The twelve-carrier navy is an issue around which admirals have established their line in the sand, one for which they seem willing to sacrifice every other capability in their service. Some have claimed that the F/A-18E/F is "the only game in town."[67] They are wrong. Other options would be of greater benefit to the navy—and to the country. The services are already beginning work on a next generation fighter, the JAST that navy, air force and marines will use in the next century. The total buy for tri-service aircraft will be nearly 2,000 aircraft, a level of production which allow considerable economies of scale and will significantly reduce the price for advanced technology. Moreover, given the disarray in European aircraft development, it is entirely conceivable that a number of European air forces will be interested in buying in on the JAST program.[68] Participation of the RAF alone, which will be confronting the aging of its airfleet early in the next century, would help in reducing costs.

Ongoing risk reduction programs and a pipeline in the F-22 research and production data should result in the JAST being an aircraft far superior to the Super Hornet at a lower price tag—and the new aircraft will most likely be stealthy. This seems a far superior option than fielding the E/F which is nothing more than an expensive overhaul of an aircraft design rooted in the 1970s–one that lost out to the F-16 in the fly off in the air force's light-fighter competition. Moreover, cancellation of the F/A-18E/F would free both the developmental monies needed to keep the U.S. lead in aircraft technology and undoubtedly pay for some aircraft production when the JAST is ready. The JAST *can* be accelerated by diverting money from the E/F program; there are no less than $3.2 billion available in Fiscal Year 1996 dollars.[69]

Until the JAST can come on line, the F/A-18C/D could continue in low rate of production to insure that carrier decks remain full. The contemporary C/D is a significant improvement over the Desert Storm aircraft. It uses the Nighthawk infra-red targeting system to drop laser guided bombs, a capacity the aircraft did not have five years ago. In addition, the GBU 24 stand-off land attack missile has significantly expanded the combat range of the C/Ds. The F/A-18C/D is also the lead aircraft in developing the Joint Stand Off Attack Weapon which will give it even greater ability to strike at extended ranges.

Ten years from now, the life span of the F/A-18C/D will still only be thirteen years; it seems impossible that we would be embarking on purchasing an aircraft that represents little significant improvement over what we now have. But we are. There is, of course, little chance that the present administration or any possible successor will have the toughness to cancel a program that the country quite simply does not need. But the United States is going to pay a price for that piece of casual, ill-thought-out political expediency. The Congress and the Pentagon are going to saddle the navy's pilots with an aircraft of declining utility well into the second decade of the next century, and we may well subvert the marine corps ability to do its mission in the next century. And finally and most important, the United States is going to defer substantially the design, testing, and procurement of an aircraft that all three services need. But the Pentagon and the Congress will not have to pay the price. Young men and young women, presently in their diapers, may pay in 2015 for our piece of casual political expediency, a price that has nothing to do with dollars or jobs.

## Conclusion

Through the centuries America's isolation from the world has allowed Americans a certain dispassion and casualness in thinking about the world. Such attitudes have resulted in a national ignorance of foreign languages, cultures, and histories. But today's world thinks and acts from very different cultural and historical backgrounds—a world that speaks in many tongues. The failure of our government, our institutions, and our military to understand or deal with that world could have terrible consequences. We face a difficult world with difficult choices; paraphrasing Wolfe's phrase shortly before he conquered Quebec, strategy and military policy represents "an option of difficulties." We must learn to make hard choices and the longer we wait the harder those choices are going to be.

# Chapter 1

# The Great 1996 Non-Debate on National Security

*Robert Gaskin*

For a decade and half, presidential candidates have relegated major national security issues to the back burner. The last serious presidential debate over national security occurred during the 1980 election when Ronald Reagan capitalized on President Jimmy Carter's record in the defense and foreign policy arenas. The 1980 presidential debates and, eventually, the election turned on the public perception of American weakness. A series of events shortly before the election had created an indelible impression of this state. In 1979, the Soviet Union boldly invaded Afghanistan while the United States stood by. That same year, Iranian revolutionaries seized the U.S. embassy and created a cancerous sore by holding large numbers of Americans hostage. But the knockout punch was a disastrous series of errors that occurred when a U.S. force blew itself up in the Iranian desert during an ill-conceived, fatal attempt to rescue those hostages.

During the 1980s, debates over national security issues in national elections focused on weapons-related issues integral to the Reagan defense buildup. Occasionally, the "sacred cow" of readiness that had haunted Carter surfaced, but this time in the hands of Democrats who opposed the Reagan administration's defense policies. In 1982, the Democratic fact book for Congressional candidates charged that Reagan's push for more expensive weaponry had actually degraded day-to-day readiness.[1] Similar charges again appeared in the 1984 election, but in neither case did they become major campaign issues.

The 1992 elections featured no serious debates over either national security strategy, policy, forces, or programs. Aside from boilerplate rhetoric in his campaign speeches, presidential candidate Bill Clinton focused on a single noun—change! His strategy deliberately ignored foreign policy and national security issues and zeroed in on a floundering economy, which he considered to be President George Bush's greatest weakness. "It's the economy stupid" became the mantra of Clinton's campaign.

During the 1994 Congressional elections, neither party highlighted defense issues in their political strategy. Republican House candidates did insert a plank into the "Contract With America" that emphasized several national security issues, but there was almost no counterfire from Democratic candidates. Thus, in yet another national election there was no debate on national security issues. And for a variety of reason this pattern is likely to repeat itself despite the fact that there are systemic, serious problems with the state of U.S. defenses.

## Defense "Revitalization"

Five years after the Soviet Union dissolved, on the eve of another presidential election, the United States finds itself still spending a quarter of a trillion dollars a year for defense, nearly 85 percent of Cold War levels. However, unlike the Cold War era when a national consensus existed as to America's national security priorities, most Americans have not the slightest notion as to why the United States spends so much on defense. Nor do many in Congress. This phenomenon is occurring at a time when a struggle is underway in Congress to bring a runaway national deficit under control by cutting popular social programs. The soaring national debt now exceeds $4.6 trillion, 70 percent of annual gross domestic product.[2]

The Republicans tried to build a new consensus on defense during the 1994 off-year elections by inserting a defense plank in the now famous "Contract With America." They charged that the president had gone too far with reductions and that the nation must restore its eroding defenses. The National Security Restoration Act (H.R. 7) embodied major defense provisions in the Contract; however, in the end this legislation took a back seat to a number of economic, social, and political issues higher on Republican agendas.[3] In truth, H.R. 7 did not aim at addressing the most pressing national security issues confronting the nation. Instead, the legislation rested on a solid base of partisanship. It focused largely on a set of polarized issues that provided a launching pad for attacking the administration and Congressional liberals.

U.S. participation in UN peace-keeping efforts was a juicy target. H.R. 7 would have restricted U.S. involvement in such unpopular UN operations by placing a host of caveats and restrictions on U.S. participation.[4] However, the real motive behind such provisions had more to do with scoring points on the administration's failures in Somalia and Bosnia. Quite simply, they made good politics. The second major theme of H.R. 7 dealt with strategic missile defense, or the lack thereof. While this issue was worthy of attention, again, the basic motivation was politics. Republican strategists believed the administration's move to limit Reagan's dream of a national defense against nuclear missiles to one limited only to the defense of U.S. forces involved in regional wars was a serious error. In simple terms, the Clinton defense strategy apparently believed that defending Seoul was good, while defending Omaha was bad. The Republicans strongly disagreed with such logic.

But aside from political hype about "restoration," these two issues had little to do with rebuilding U.S. defenses. In fact, the current American military is not weak, not run down, not shattered, and not "hollow." True, America's military posture has shrunk steadily over the past decade. The defense budget for Fiscal Year 1996 is the eleventh (inflation adjusted) decline in U.S. military spending. In addition, by 1998, the United States will spend 35 percent less on its military than it did during the peak year of Reagan's buildup in 1986. By the end of the decade, defense spending will likely amount to less than 3 percent of gross domestic product, the lowest such percentage since before Pearl Harbor.[5] But while American forces have shrunk, our peer competitors have disappeared. In election year 1996, America stands as the world's only superpower, a nation possessing great military power, able to dominate, deter, and defeat potential aggressors around the world.

The real issue is not whether a smaller military should return to the size of Reagan's military force; everyone realizes that is a non-starter. The real issue is whether the current size of U.S. military forces is excessive, given the lack of a clear threat, and more importantly, should this issue surface in the 1996 campaign?

## Is Smaller Better?

For forty years following the Korean War, defense planning and budgets remained generally constant. Large, sudden changes in the size and composition of U.S. military forces were infrequent. The U.S. had a clearly identified opponent, and its weapons, tactics, doctrine, and strategic outlook addressed that threat. While Mao's China decreased as a threat in the 1970s, most

Americans understood that the Soviets and their Warsaw Pact allies represented the greatest danger to American security throughout the Cold War. In short, for four decades the U.S. had a threat that determined its strategy, budgets, and its force composition. The routine of strategic planning became a given for nearly all military professionals. American military officers would have considered what happened to the vaunted Soviet war machine in 1990 inconceivable only a few years earlier. In fact one can argue which military the turn of events surprised more, the Soviet or the American.

Early efforts by the Bush administration to deal with the new situation were clumsy and naive. The Pentagon's 1992 draft Defense Planning Guidance dreamed of a range of improbable scenarios—such as an attack on Lithuania and Poland by Russia and Belarus—to justify the current force.[6] However, the draft leaked, and an embarrassed Secretary of Defense Richard Cheney quickly backtracked. Today, America's defense forces rest on Secretary Les Aspin's Bottom-Up Review, which conceived of fighting two, nearly simultaneous, major Iraq-sized regional wars. The strategy does not name the aggressor nations, but clearly they are understood to be Iraq and North Korea. Less clear is whether such predictable adversaries could ever live up to the Pentagon's expectations. Moreover, even if they did, is the American military currently still too large in a world of minor threats?

Although they suffered a disastrous defeat in 1994, Congressional liberals will undoubtedly question current levels of defense spending throughout the 1996 election campaign. They will argue, with some logic, that given the absence of a definable threat, the United States should not commit so much of its national treasure to its military establishment. Their arguments, however, are not really new. They represent a carbon copy of earlier rhetoric that called for smaller, less sophisticated forces and much lower levels for defense spending, to free money for social programs. In reality, their voices are advocates of increased social spending at the expense of defense programs. As the old saying goes, the more things change, the more they remain the same.

Still, the question remains: is the U.S. military too large considering the absence of a clearly definable threat? Serious thinkers began furiously debating the issue four years ago. They received encouragement from Democrat Les Aspin, then the intellectually inclined Chairman of the House Armed Services Committee. Much of Aspin's thinking wound its way into Clinton's campaign and, not surprisingly, Aspin received the job of Secretary of Defense. On 6 January 1992, Aspin delivered a visionary paper before the Atlantic Council calling for a basic rethinking of U.S. national security policy. In his view, the Bush-Powell "Base Force" was a product of Cold War thinking, generally unsuited to a new era. Aspin saw the Base Force as a temporary hedge in case the Soviet threat somehow suddenly reappeared.[7] While he saw this as a dim possibility, he saw other dangers moving into the strategic vacuum left by the Soviets.

More importantly, Aspin raised the notion of how the United States should define "threats" to its national security. He chided the then chairman of the joint chiefs of staff, General Colin Powell, for his assertion that "we no longer have a threat to plan for" and that the Base Force was "no longer a threat-based force."[8] Aspin also disagreed with former Secretary of Defense James Schlesinger for advocating the same idea. Schlesinger had just argued in *Foreign Policy* that the basis for U.S. military strength should "not simply be the response to individual threats, but rather that which is needed to maintain the overall aura of American power."[9]

Aspin, however, argued that just because America's Cold War opponent, the Soviet Union, had disappeared, there was no reason to discard threat-based planning as Powell and Schlesinger suggested. He went further by suggesting a set of newer, non-traditional threats, such as the spread of nuclear weapons, terrorism, regional thugs, and drug traffickers. More importantly, he identified Saddam Hussein and Iraq as the prototype for post-Soviet threat planning.[10]

Twenty-one months later, as Secretary of Defense, he unveiled his Bottom-Up Review as a notional, threat-based tool for shaping and sizing U.S. forces. He envisioned having to fight two major regional wars (again, based on the Iraqi model) at nearly the same time. Thus the Bottom-Up Review reshaped the Pentagon's planning to focus on multiple, near-simultaneous regional wars instead of a single global conflagration with the Soviet Union and its allies.

Three years after the Bottom-Up Review's debut, liberals continue to reject such thinking; they argue that both Cheney's Base Force and Aspin's Bottom-Up Review force are far stronger than actually needed to address the current international scene. These arguments are perhaps best represented by a report in the August 1995 edition of the Bulletin of Atomic Scientists which argues for greater cuts in military forces, modernization, and budgets.[11] The report's rather linear arguments rested on force and military spending comparisons between the United States and its most likely adversaries in the developing world.[12]

Other organizations that argue for lower defense spending attack the size of the Pentagon's budget for force modernization. The Center for Defense Information has consistently has called for lower defense spending and argues that the Pentagon should forego spending the estimated $546 billion needed for modernization by simply upgrading current weapons systems in the inventory.[13] Left unsaid in such arguments is how the services would eventually replace current weapons. Upgrading indefinitely is apparently the preferred solution.

Former Assistant Secretary of Defense Larry Korb continues this line of criticism by focusing on the costs of maintaining current defense forces compared to the levels of other nations. He seconds the logic of the Atomic Scientists and argues that it does not make sense for the U.S. to spend $262 billion in 1995 which represents approximately 37 per cent of the combined military expenditures of every other nation in the world. Our NATO allies' spending on defense for 1995, for example, comes only to $150 billion.[14] More significantly, he claims, if we look at all the potential threats combined—Iran, Iraq, Libya, Syria, North Korea and Cuba—their combined military budgets amount only to approximately $15 billion.[15]

Korb and most liberal critics of current defense spending use the year 1980 as their index. Thus, they are able to complain that in 1995 the United States will pay more for defense, about $15 billion in inflation-adjusted dollars, than it did in 1980 at "the height of the Cold War."[16] Unfortunately for their case, 1980 was a bad year. That year America's armed forces were in a weak state due to a decade of under-investment that followed the U.S. withdrawal from Vietnam. The chief of staff of the army, General Edward C. "Shy" Meyer, referred to his own army as a "hollow force." Even Carter realized that things had gone too far, and proposed higher defense budgets for Fiscal Year 1981. In summer 1980, press reports in America's newspapers suggested the possibility of a military in collapse: "half of all combat aircraft unready...only six of the navy's thirteen aircraft carriers and ninety-four of 155 air squadrons ready for combat...F-15s with only a day and a half of air-to-air missiles."[17] Given these statistics, one cannot make a case that 1980 was the height of the Cold War. If anything, it represents the bottom of investment in defense for the entire Cold War and the deplorable condition of U.S. forces became a winning issue for Reagan.

Predictably, those on the Republican right do not agree with Korb and other liberals. Presidential candidates Lamar Alexander and Phil Gramm pledged to stop the decline in defense spending. Former Secretary of Defense Casper Weinberger, speaking to the National Policy Forum in May 1995, stated that the Clinton cuts in defense were "virtually disarming America."[18]

Perhaps these opposing views could have been sufficiently addressed had the Republicans convened the House blue ribbon panel called for in H.R. 7. Such a group might have been able to examine the fundamental assumptions of the Bottom-Up Review as well as the Pentagon's strategic planning. It might eventually have recommended some of the adjustments called for by

Korb and other critics of defense spending. But unfortunately, the blue ribbon panel became a casualty in the opening days of the 104th Congress. On 27 January 1995, Secretary of Defense William Perry testified before Congress and complained that the proposed panel would "usurp [my] responsibilities."[19] Astonishingly, the newly elected Republican majority accepted his claim. Thus, the Pentagon's Bottom-Up Review stood unchallenged by the 104th Congress throughout 1995, and indeed, stands as the administration's platform on defense for the 1996 elections. So the current debate has crystallized around the Bottom-Up Review; between those who think the United States spends too much on defense, and those who not only defend the review, but argue that Clinton defense budgets for FY 1996-2001 are inadequate to support it. One thing is certain. Given the fiscal reality of the need to balance the federal budget against that fact that the United States will likely spend approximately $1.7 trillion dollars on defense during that period, a national debate on defense spending is badly needed. But will such a debate occur? At this time, the prospect appears most unlikely.

First, a Republican opponent who believes that current levels of defense spending are inadequate will challenge Clinton; Senators Bob Dole and Gramm as well as ex-Governor Alexander fall in that category. Second, given political trends and the impending retirements of Democrats in Congress, the 105th Congress will most likely be even more conservative than the present Congress. Liberals are bailing out in droves, led by such icons as Patricia Schroeder and Bill Bradley. Third, if the polls are accurate, America is becoming more conservative and less supportive of liberal positions, which further weakens the liberals' political leverage in arguments over the level of defense spending. Fourth, and most important, defense spending does not exist in the abstract. Jobs and political power are at stake. The reality is that each and every year, Congress pours forth a vast largesse in the form of defense appropriations. Politics aside, defense procurement remains a powerful inducement to vote for the status quo on national security. Pentagon procurement has enormous political and economic consequences. In the FY 96 defense budget, defense procurement is down nearly 70 per cent from the peak levels of the Reagan years. Yet, even in that reduced state, it still accounts for nearly 70 percent of all government buying.[20] That's power.

For these reasons, there will, unfortunately, be no serious debate on defense spending during the election, except in the most isolated of circumstances. Certainly liberals like Barney Frank and Ronald Dellums will rail against the current "excessive" defense program in their local races. However, they are from districts that are overwhelmingly liberal/Democratic and where they are unlikely to be seriously challenged by conservative Republicans. As for the rest of America, House and Senate challengers and incumbents who believe that the Pentagon should cut jobs at local bases and with local military contractors because the United States spends more on defense than the rest of the world will move on to positions as schoolteachers, lawyers, bankers, and state legislators after the election. The winner, who favors a strong defense, buying more from the local defense contractor and keeping the local military base open will proudly take his/her seat in the new 105th Congress. So the answer is this: No, smaller is not better, at least not in 1996.

## The Hollow Farce

Following the November 1994 elections, victorious Republicans became excited over an issue that had received little attention throughout the campaign—the readiness of America's military to go to war. The brouhaha started with an army report on 15 November 1994 that three active army divisions had declined to a readiness state of "C-3," a condition that implied that they were only "marginally ready" to go to war, at least according to the Pentagon's Status of Resources and Training System.[21] The announcement was especially embarrassing to the administration, for only a few weeks before, then-Deputy Secretary of Defense John Deutch had publicly stated that the U.S. military were "more ready and capable than they've ever been."[22]

The press, which has always used the readiness issue to generate sales, predictably had a field day. On the day after the army's announcement, *The Washington Post* ran a story that featured Secretary of Defense Perry's admission that the army's combat readiness was overstated.[23] Newspapers across the land took their lead from the *Post* and ran similar stories. Representative Floyd Spence (R-SC), the prospective chairman of the House Armed Services Committee, made the state of U.S. military readiness a major issue in the public statements leading up to the February 1995 hearings on the defense budget. Senator John McCain (R-AZ), a highly respected member of the Senate Armed Services Committee, joined him in a crusade. McCain was not only a former military aviator, squadron commander, and Vietnam POW, he was also an authority on readiness, by having published two reports, "Going Hollow," in 1993 and 1994 that chronicled troubling trends in this area.

Three weeks after the announcement about the three marginally ready army divisions, on 5 December, Spence released a report entitled "Military Readiness, The View From the Field." He assembled anecdotal "evidence" that convinced him that there was clear evidence of a "long term systemic readiness problem."[24] The "other body" in the Senate had been equally busy.

On the same day that Spence released his report, Senators McCain and John Warner (R-VA) wrote Clinton to complain of "the litany of readiness problems disclosed in recent weeks."[25] In media interviews, McCain expressed his discomfort with reports he had received from field commanders about the deterioration of readiness in U.S. forces. Service chiefs and regional commanders-in-chiefs (CINCS) testified that "unless something changes...they are going to be near the edge of serious problems in readiness."[26]

The Republicans' strategy was clear. Paint the Clinton administration as being grossly neglectful of America's defense needs and having given the country a military much like the one Reagan inherited from Carter in 1981. Republicans aimed to convince America that its military forces were well on the way toward becoming the demoralized, drug-soaked, mentally handicapped, under-equipped military of a decade and a half earlier where 60 per cent of all aviation squadrons, divisions, and ships received ratings of marginal or non-combat ready.[27]

Rhetoric is one thing, proof is another. Only forty-eight months earlier, U.S. forces had trounced Iraq, then the fourth largest military power on earth, in the most one-sided military victory of the twentieth century. In fact, the mismatch between the U.S.-led coalition and Iraq was hardly a war; it was more like, as General Chuck Horner suggested, beating a tethered goat.

Still, the administration responded to Congressional rhetoric. On 9 February 1995, Perry assured the Senate Armed Services Committee that military readiness was his *number one priority*. "Today, the department, the Joint Chiefs, the CINCS, and I are watching readiness more closely and in more ways than at any time that I can remember."[28] But Perry also refuted most of the extreme Congressional statements on the subject. He argued that forces deployed overseas or standing by for deployment were at unusually high historical levels of readiness.

Eleven days after Perry's testimony, Representative Spence countered by kicking off House hearings on 22 February. He declared: "looking beyond the present...the future readiness of today's force is unquestionably in jeopardy."[29] But Congressman Dellums had had had enough. The day of the hearings, following Spence's opening comments, he leaned forward and quietly asked the four service chiefs if there were systemic readiness problems or a collection of year-end shortages. After much paper shuffling, *not one of the chiefs* testified that his service had a "near-term" readiness problem. They suggested rather their *real concern was about "long-term readiness,"* or modernization.[30]

The chiefs based their conclusions on a high-level report released by the Defense Science Board task force eight months earlier. The task force chairman, former army chief of staff General Meyer, disagreed that there was a near-term, readiness problem. His report admitted that "pockets" of readiness problems did exist, but that these resulted from the ongoing turbulence of change and defense downsizing.[31]

Senator McCain now shifted his focus to the problem identified by the chiefs—long-term readiness. In February 1995, McCain released a report, signed by four respected four-star generals, including former air force chief of staff, General Charles Gabriel. The report found that the services were doing a credible job maintaining short-term readiness, but complained that the front-loading of the defense budget to maintain near-term readiness would eventually produce a force equipped with aging and obsolete weapons.[32] McCain thought that "the Administration got a bum rap on the three divisions."[33] And he was right. The fact that these divisions were C-3 was not militarily significant, because they were reinforcing divisions, purposely maintained by the army at lower levels of readiness. In addition, the army had scheduled two of the three divisions for elimination in the near future, so naturally, they had not exhibited the same readiness as front line units. Meanwhile, long-term readiness, or modernization, emerged as the real problem as 1995 progressed. During Senate Armed Services Committee hearings on 27 April 1995, the chiefs again maintained that short-term readiness was not a problem and forcefully reiterated the point that their real concern was deferring modernization to fund short-term readiness.[34]

Many of the current short-term readiness problems resulted from the Bush and Clinton administrations' penchant for committing U.S. forces to unexpected—and unbudgeted—contingencies, including Rwanda, Haiti, Cuba, Kuwait, Somalia, and Bosnia. Because there was, and still is, no line item in the Pentagon's budget to fund such operations, the Pentagon had to pay for them out of its operations and maintenance accounts. And because the Pentagon is forbidden to touch certain of these accounts (such as civilian pay, recruiting, and health benefits), the only accounts that are "safe" to drain funds from for unplanned operations are depot maintenance, training, and other force support accounts, the very funding that supports near-term readiness.[35]

In reality what has happened is that the military does not have a readiness problem so much as it has a cash flow problem. If Congress would provide a "readiness" line the defense budget, the Pentagon would possess the financial protection it needs to preclude the robbing of training and maintenance accounts to pay for unbudgeted contingencies. However, such a line in the defense budget would lessen Congressional influence regarding such random, politically sensitive missions. Thus, there is no chance of such an approval. In essence, the Pentagon's operations and maintenance budget is a hostage to presidents who favor an activist agenda for humanitarian and other non-military operations, and those in Congress who desire to control presidential zeal through the cumbersome, time-consuming, politically-weighted supplemental appropriations process. Such political games with the lives of U.S. fighting men and women represent a key issue that could and should be raised by candidates. They should challenge the current Congressional practice of not funding such operations until months after they have begun.

What serious candidates should consider is a fiscal mechanism that avoids annual fights over the Pentagon's supplemental spending. One possibility would be for Congress to establish a Readiness Authority that the Pentagon could draw on with Congressional approval. Limits could exist to satisfy Congress. Dr. John Hamre, the Pentagon Comptroller and former staffer for Senator Sam Nunn, has proposed to limit such authority to the last two quarters of the fiscal year. In addition, the Pentagon could only draw on the fund for items directly related to readiness, and then only with Office of Management and Budget's approval. Finally, the supplemental process and the defense rescissions in other accounts would repay such authority.[36]

The second issue that candidates need to raise concerns the issue that the service chiefs keep alluding to—long-term readiness, or modernization. Since 1985 military procurement has fallen nearly 70 percent in constant dollars. This is partly a result of the downsizing that has continued over the last five years, and partly results from the fact that the Soviet threat no longer exists. Still, one must begin replacing obsolete equipment at some point. The $39.4 billion acquisition budget for FY 1996 has reached the low point. For FY 1997, it will begin climbing and then go nearly vertical on cost charts, soaring to $67.3 billion by 2000. But even that rise may not be fast enough. In October 1995 JCS chairman, General John Shalikashvili, sent his boss, Perry, a glum budget assessment that recommended a 50 percent increase in defense procurement over the next twenty-four months. His assessment recommended speeding up procurement programs by two years to peak in 1998 instead of 2000.[37] However, even with a sudden 47 percent increase over the FY 1996 procurement budget, many experts do not believe that funding will be available for the administration's ambitious modernization programs. The Defense Budget Project, hardly a conservative organization, recently published an analysis of the FY 1996 Pentagon budget which strongly questions whether "the administration's proposed force structure of 1.45 million active duty military personnel and 893,000 reserve personnel could be adequately modernized over the long term within procurement budgets of this size."[38]

Moreover, there is another problem with the administration's modernization plans. The Pentagon plans to pay for modernization with cost savings in two major areas: acquisition reform and base closing. Unfortunately, acquisition reform has slowed to a snail's pace, while base closings have taken far longer and cost more than anyone imagined. In fact, the closings are costing instead of saving money, at least over the period of procurement ramp-up. Expressing the Pentagon's disappointment, Ted Warner, assistant secretary of defense for strategy and resources, recently admitted that the Pentagon has erred in projecting savings.[39]

So, if the savings are not likely to pay for new weapons, and it is unlikely that Congress will pump more money into acquisition budgets at a time when the drive to balance the Federal budget really hurts, is the Pentagon's modernization strategy realistic? Are hard choices at hand? Should the Pentagon prioritize rather than cave in to service modernization plans?

These are crucial questions for the next election, but unfortunately, there will be no readiness debate in the 1996 campaign. First, the Readiness Authority fund has no constituency. It is such an abstract issue that it is unlikely to fire Americans' passions—unless, of course, their sons, brothers, or daughters die on some foreign beach because they run out of gas or ammunition. Congress does, and will continue to, hold the cards. So for the time being, the Pentagon will balance its training and maintenance needs against the agenda of an activist administration hoping to save the world, restore democracy, build nations, and keep the peace.

As for long-term modernization, Congress will do what it always does; it will fund the Pentagon's programs as long as they remain reasonably well managed and do not draw fire from the *New York Times*. When procurement money gets tight, Congress will stretch, rather than cancel, programs. After all, jobs are at stake. The modernization issue remains too obscure at the present time to become an issue for this election. Despite the fact that the Pentagon and Congress will make decisions in 1996 that involve hundreds of billions of dollars in future acquisition costs, the squeeze between a balanced federal budget and futuristic weapons systems will not occur until early in the next century. For now, it remains a free ride for the candidates.

## Dark Visions

Senator Richard Lugar (R-IN) is a worried man. He has stated categorically that he believes that terrorists will use nuclear weapons against the United States before the decade ends.[40] He is the only candidate for the presidency to make this an issue for the 1996 campaign. His page on the World Wide Web spells out his belief that the leakage of nuclear materials and technology from the former Soviet Union represents the greatest threat to U.S. national security.[41] He is not alone. Senator Sam Nunn (D-GA) also agrees that global proliferation of materials, components, and weapons of mass destruction constitute the greatest threat to not only the United States, but the world.[42]

Many academics are also growing more fearful for the future. In 1993, Samuel Huntington presented a gloomy world where the competitors embarked on global conflicts that eventually threatened the end of human life. He did not believe that the industrialized West could long co-exist with the Slavic culture led by Russia. He also thought that the world's dominant religious cultures, such as Islam, Hinduism, Shintoism, and Confucianism would also eventually fight it out on the global stage.[43]

In looking at the future, Paul Kennedy also sees worldwide strife and war in the next century. In his *Preparing for The 21st Century*, he suggests that the major battles will occur between the West and the Third World. He believes that hopeless poverty, population explosion, and resource shortages will produce a hatred and ever-deepening hostility towards the developed nations.[44] Given the views of some of America's most distinguished political and academic thinkers, it is astonishing that few candidates for the Senate, the House, or the presidency, view the situation with similar alarm. As a result, one of the crucial issues relating to U.S. national security will receive only marginal attention as America prepares to enter the next century. But while political candidates may view such issues with skepticism, world events suggest their attitudes are seriously out of touch with a chilling reality.

On 20 March 1995 the Japanese cult, Aum Shinrikyo, attempted to murder thousands of innocent commuters in the Tokyo subway system with crudely made dispensers of home-made nerve gas. Fortunately, the cult made a mistake in its preparations. That mistake, combined with clumsy dispersal devices, resulted in only twelve deaths instead of tens of thousands. More importantly, it was not the first time the cult had tried to kill with its home-brewed arsenal of nerve gas. On 27 June 1994 it had attacked the city of Matsumoto, Japan, again with nerve gas, possibly as a dress rehearsal for the March 1995 attack. Seven died and over five hundred were seriously injured, many of whom remain in comas.[45]

Amazingly, this first attack received virtually no attention in the United States. Kyle B. Olson, an expert on proliferation and terrorism, visited Japan three months after the incident and was "astonished by his own discoveries."[46] He concluded that a terrorist attack had taken place and that the group had used nerve gas. Olson also concluded that for the first time organized terrorists had demonstrated not only the will to use chemical weapons against civilians, but the *ability* to so do. And he did not think that Matsumoto would be the last attack; in fact he believed it was only the opening salvo of a larger effort. He was right.

Following the cult's Tokyo attack in March 1995, Japanese police, already shadowing the cult, conducted over 500 raids on over 300 locations. They arrested hundreds of cult members. While many feel the Shinrikyo threat is now over, the truth may be otherwise. No one really can calculate the potential threat from the remaining cult members. It still possesses enormous financial assets, has thousands of members, and continues to articulate a virulent anti-western and anti-government ideology.

The ease with which this powerful and influential cult assembled a host of deadly weapons and associated technologies is especially disturbing. More troubling, prior to the 20 March attack on the Tokyo subway, not one single U.S. intelligence agency viewed Aum Shinrikyo as a threat.[47] One wonders how competent America's vaunted intelligence network really is at protecting U.S. national security, when a fanatical cult with billions in financial resources, operates with brazen openness in one of the richest countries in the world and receives no notice from our intelligence community.

Aum Shinrikyo had the resources and technical know-how to make its own nerve gas. However, in today's world, terrorists do not need to make chemical warfare agents. They can simply buy them from the desperate citizens of the successor states that were members of the former Soviet Union. Russia's chemical weapons storage facilities are in such a bad state that the potential for theft is extraordinarily high. Recently, the Russian army chief of staff, General Mikhail Kolesnikov, admitted that security measures at those sites were "inadequate." His chief concern was that since the Soviet Union's breakup, not only is Russia's chemical stockpile vulnerable to theft, but now every terrorist knows the location of most of those sites. It's now all a matter of public record.[48] But those who steal or divert Russia's chemical weapons are more likely to be Russians themselves rather than foreign terrorists. Last year the KGB placed General Anatoly Kuntsevich, a high-ranking chemical weapons expert, along with many of his co-workers under house arrest for allegedly stealing and then selling 1,800 pounds of chemical weapons in 1993 and again in 1994—materials they supposedly were guarding.[49]

Again, as with the Shinrikyo cult, it is unclear how vulnerable Russia's chemical stockpile really is. Moreover, Western intelligence agencies are unsure who is doing the stealing, and who is doing the buying. What we do know is that America remains vulnerable to an attack by terrorists using such weapons. While the military has the resources and training to counter the chemical threat, not so the rest of America. In fact, it is unlikely that terrorists would target the U.S. military; instead civil society provides the best targets.

Chemical weapons are not the only danger leaking from the former Soviet Union. Smuggling of nuclear weapons components and bomb-grade fissile materials is on the rise as well. The demise of the Soviet empire has created enormous opportunities for states or terrorists who seek nuclear materials, weapons, or components. U.S. experts warn that America simply has not awakened to this new proliferation danger—one completely beyond imagination only five years ago. The problem? Huge cracks have appeared in Russia's security system. During the Cold War's four decades, the Soviets guarded their nuclear weapons and production complexes with a very effective, regimented system that had strong political authority. Extraordinary oversight and a system of redundant checks and balances guaranteed that nuclear materials remained under tight control. Today that system has collapsed.

With the breakup of the Soviet Union, the military, which guards these weapons, confronts hard times with little pay, inadequate food, reduced manning, and dreadful living conditions for dependents. Moreover, the status of the military has fallen as well. Not surprisingly, such conditions have bred corruption. In a recent report, the U.S. Department of Energy suggests that approximately 3,000 officers have been caught and punished for engaging in "questionable business practices, and forty-six generals and a host of lesser officers face criminal charges."[50] In 1992 alone, the Russian ministry of defense admitted 4,000 cases of conventional weapons theft. In 1993, it got worse; nearly 6,500 cases were reported.[51]

The desperate situation confronting the military is the much same with scientists working in Russia's nuclear production facilities. Today they have less prestige, fewer perks, and in many cases, are making less money than common laborers. A recent directive from Russia's Ministry of Atomic Energy best illustrates the cash squeeze on personnel at nuclear production facilities. The directive warned that they had to market their goods and skills in the civilian economy to stay in operation.[52] Ironically, that access has been made easier by the very arms control treaties designed to reduce nuclear dangers. Under the Strategic Arms Treaties negotiated between the United States and the former Soviet Union, both countries are now dismantling approximately 2,000 nuclear weapons per year. However, while destroying the weapon itself is relatively easy, the disposal of nuclear warheads is not a simple matter. A growing mountain of nuclear cores of enriched uranium and plutonium represents a terrorist's dream. Russia must guard nearly 120 tons of plutonium and 1,200 tons of bomb-grade, highly enriched uranium.[53] Worse, they have

absolutely no idea how much of this deadly material the Soviet Union produced during the Cold War.

After the dismantling of the missiles, the nuclear materials are transferred
from the shaky but stronger security of the military to the appallingly lax
oversight of the civilian-run Ministry of Atomic Energy. Some U.S. experts
suggest that, because things are so bad with that ministry's security, all
weapons dismantling should stop until control is restored.[54] As the weapons
are destroyed, the nuclear materials move through eleven time zones where
the potential for theft is high.

Between 1989 and 1995 the Russians have consolidated the number of
weapons storage sites from 600 to approximately 100, but security and
weapons accountability procedures for most of these facilities remains poor.[55]
According to Dr. Thomas Cochran, Senior Scientist for the Natural
Resources Defense Council and an expert on nuclear weapons, "U.S. government officials and support contractors who have visited some of these
facilities can give you hair-raising accounts of lack of physical security at some
of these places. Given the lack of security, it is not surprising that quantities
of weapons-usable fissile materials have already been stolen."[56]

The evidence mounts that fissile materials are finding their way out of
the former Soviet Union. U.S. sources point to five major cases of nuclear
smuggling over the last four years. Three involved small amounts of highly
enriched uranium, but more ominously, the other two involved over "100
grams of plutonium."[57] Another report indicates that during 1993 Russian
security forces foiled eleven attempts to steal uranium and over 900 other
attempts to gain entry into nuclear facilities to steal nuclear documents.[58]
Between 1991 and 1994, the German government reported over 700 cases
related to nuclear smuggling,[59] while the Central Intelligence Agency now
lists thirty-one cases of seizures by the German police in just the first half of
1995.[60]

In August, 1994, Bavarian police arrested three men at Munich airport
for attempting to transport several hundred grams of lithium 6, which can
produce tritium, and nearly twenty ounces of weapons-grade plutonium and
uranium. They had flown in from Russia, where German authorities believe
they had obtained the material from a nuclear weapons laboratory.[61] Four
months later, police in Prague intercepted a Czech nuclear scientist and two
friends from Belarus and Ukraine. They were carrying over six pounds of
highly enriched uranium in the back seat of a Saab, along with a huge cache
of Russian documents.[62]

In 1991, three months after the collapse of the Soviet Union, Congress
wisely created the Nunn-Lugar Cooperative Threat Reduction program to
improve fissile Material Protection, Control, and Accounting in the former

Soviet Union. Senators Nunn and Lugar pushed the legislation to address this dangerous situation. They were convinced that securing the thousands of weapons and tons of fissile material was a priority that America could ill afford to miss. To date, Nunn-Lugar's "chain of custody" assistance has provided quick, physical security improvements—primarily for weapons in temporary storage and transit across Russia.[63] In conjunction with Nunn-Lugar's other programs, these measures represent a success. However, Nunn-Lugar's achievement in strengthening the security and control of fissile materials is less satisfactory. Unfortunately, the U.S. response to the precarious situation has become mired in bureaucracy and political infighting. Congress can pass laws, but the administration has to act, and the Russians have to cooperate. Therein lies the problem.

The Clinton administration moved slowly to reduce the bureaucratic tangle in Washington which had hamstrung the efforts to deal with the unclear situation. For example, the funding for improving Russia's accounting and protection of fissile material was in the Department of Defense, while the experts were in the Energy Department. Worse, neither department had authority to negotiate with the Russians—that belonged to State Department diplomats, who lacked the expertise required for the task.

If that were not bad enough, negotiating and installing Material Protection, Control, and Accounting improvements at Russian weapons facilities proved near-impossible because of suspicions on both sides. Russia's Ministry of Atomic Energy, led by the cranky and eccentric Victor Mikhaylov, steadfastly refused to allow U.S. experts access to classified weapons-material facilities without reciprocal arrangements. Elements within the U.S. military were justifiably nervous about granting such reciprocity to America's old foe. The result was gridlock. Fortunately, there has been limited progress of late. Because the Department of Energy has finally received its own Material Protection, Control, and Accounting budget, it no longer has to beg a reluctant Pentagon for program funding. One initiative in particular, the Department of Energy's Lab-to-Lab program, has become the centerpiece of cooperation between Moscow and Washington over protecting fissile materials. This program built on the professional congeniality between scientists at U.S. and Russian nuclear weapons labs to develop systems themselves, effectively bridging the customary gap between the Pentagon and the Ministry of Atomic Energy. Led by an agreement between Secretary Hazel O'Leary and Mikhaylov in June 1995, the two agencies have finally begun to institute modest control and security improvements for hundreds of tons of weapons-grade materials at *all* of the 100 key facilities. The bad news is that pitiful funding from Congress will stretch the program out over nearly a decade. The Department of Energy has secured only $70 million in its FY 96 budget for this new program, which may increase slightly to $90 million in 1997. However, despite the paltry funding, these developments do represent a significant change, both in priority and action within the U.S. and Russian governments.

Several dangers remain, not the least of which is from home. Since 1993, Congress has attacked the very program it created. In 1995, the House of Representatives criticized the "non-defense" aspects of Nunn-Lugar and tried to cut nearly half the Pentagon's requests, which had remained level from the previous year. Projects specifically targeted for removal from the budget included a central fissile storage facility that had been painstakingly designed over the last two years. The Senate was less critical, but still proposed cutting over $40 million from the requested budget.

Congress' short-sighted actions may make good politics, but they do real harm to America's national security. The $400 million requested for 1995 Cooperative Threat Reduction programs represented less than .2 percent of the entire Defense Department budget. By comparison, the Pentagon has spent approximately $35 billion on programs associated with the Strategic Defense Initiative, without a single system yet deployed.[64] This represents nearly twenty-nine times all the money appropriated for Cooperative Threat Reduction programs since they began in 1991. The issue that confronts voters in 1996 is whether the United States should ramp up a minuscule Cooperative Threat Reduction budget to better match resources to the threat. Today, this country spends approximately $800 million a year to guard its own inventory of nuclear materials. Unfortunately, it spends less than $100 million to help Russia keep track of a much larger mountain of bomb grade material.[65]

Perhaps, when American citizens are pulling themselves out of the radioactive crater created by the first nuclear terrorist strike within the United States, they can at least take comfort in the fact that they are defended from Russian missile attacks.

Regarding the issue of terrorism, there was some promising political movement in early 1995 to address that potential threat. On February 9, 1995, the Clinton administration introduced a bill, the *Omnibus Counterterrorism Act of 1995*, aimed at countering terrorism on U.S. soil. Some of the more significant provisions of the proposed law were:

1. International terrorism would become a federal crime. Under the current law, terrorists cannot be charged with specific acts of terrorism. It would address the situation where the terrorists who bombed the World Trade Center could only be prosecuted with laws designed to convict people who damage buildings.

2. The law would allow the FBI more power to prevent groups from making financial transactions, if the government thought they would be used for acts of terror.

3. The law would allow the government to deport people designated as terrorists and prevent the outrageous re-occurrence of what happened with one of the bombers of the World Trade Center. The mastermind, Ramzi Ahmed Yousef, simply strolled through U.S. customs at Kennedy Airport with an Iraqi passport and asked for political asylum. Under U.S. law he had the right to appear before a judge, so he was released onto the streets of Manhattan where, over the next six months, he planned the Trade Center bombing before eventually fleeing the United States as the smoke cleared in downtown New York City.[66]

Two and half months after Clinton introduced his counterterrorism legislation, a disgruntled group of ex-militiamen blew up the Murah Federal Building in Oklahoma City with a huge fertilizer bomb. Politicians went crazy. Both the House and Senate swiftly moved on the counterterrorist legislation. Barely three weeks after Oklahoma City on 9 May 1995, President Clinton, sensing the political winds, added muscle to his legislation by proposing the *Antiterrorism Amendments Act of 1995*. Among its proposals was a controversial amendment to allow the military to "disarm and disable" individuals suspected of possessing chemical or biological weapons. This provision would invalidate a portion of the 118-year-old Posse Comitatus law that restricts the military from taking part in civil law enforcement. Two weeks later on 25 May, the House moved. Representative Henry Hyde (R-IL) introduced H.R. 1710, aggressive legislation that included legal powers for law enforcement officials tasked to fight terrorists on U.S. soil. Moving rapidly, the Senate, barely a month later, passed its terrorism legislation, S. 735.

Unfortunately, the legislation was in trouble in the House. Despite the fact that the House legislation finally cleared the Judiciary Committee on 20 June, it never reached the floor for a vote. It never will, since the votes are not there. The terrorism legislation was stymied by an unusual, but powerful, coalition of liberals and conservatives. Conservatives feared a greater role for the military in law enforcement, while liberals, backed by groups such as the American Civil Liberties Union, worried deeply the law's potential for eroding civil liberties, and its provision of greater powers to wiretap and to access to private records.

Ironically as for finding nuclear terrorists, the legislation would not have gone nearly far enough. The point that Congress missed is that it is more important to keep the means of terrorism out of the hands of terrorists rather than to catch them once they are here. America is simply too porous. Currently, there are 301 points of entry into the United States. Yet there are only 10,000 customs inspectors, and not one of those agents has the training to spot or detect nuclear materials. Every day some 1.25 million people arrive in the United States along with billions of cargo tonnage. Nevertheless, fewer than 5 percent of these entries are physically inspected. Even if the United States possessed more inspectors, and more arrivals were physically scrutinized, such improvements would do little to address the nuclear smuggling problem. There are *no* sensors at present capable of detecting nuclear materials at any U.S. port of entry. Moreover, current technology is only capable of detecting nuclear materials at distances of thirty to 300 feet—and then only if the materials are not shielded.[67]

Politics has also tied up the best means of dealing with terrorists who might use chemical weapons against the United States. Senator Jesse Helms (R-NC) wants to combine three foreign government agencies into the State Department, but Senate Democrats are blocking the effort. In response Helms is preventing the Chemical Weapons Convention from reaching the Senate floor for ratification unless he gets his reorganization plan. Helms' irresponsible behavior is, thus, blocking a powerful tool for dealing with a dangerous situation. According to U.S. intelligence, roughly two dozen countries have the ability to make chemical weapons. They believe that the Chemical Weapons Convention is the best means available to fight terrorists who would use such weapons against a civil population. So far, only forty-two of the required sixty-five nations have ratified the far-reaching treaty, but American leadership is vital. Experts say that unless the United States takes action soon, others are likely to lose interest in the issue.

This issue and the ones relating to leakage of nuclear materials are unlikely to receive a hearing in campaign '96. The threat is too amorphous and too theoretical to concern most Americans. Moreover, the threat has no real constituency outside of a few government agencies and interest groups. It does not resonate among the voters in mainstream America because it does not yet threaten them or their families. But the real reason the issue of terrorism will be ignored during the coming elections is that 1996 will represent a titanic struggle between the Democrats and Republicans for power. The major political focus will revolve around balancing the budget in seven years and whether Republican actions to accomplish that goal have met the approval of the voters. Nuclear leakage, chemical weapons for sale, terrorists on the loose are all real dangers, but until they represent a clear and distinct threat, apparent to most Americans, politicians will focus on other issues.

Only a direct attack by terrorists using such weapons will awaken Americans from their lethargy. Many, like Senators Lugar and Nunn, believe that will be the inevitable result. One thing is for certain. The stakes are considerable and time is running short.

## The Iron Rice Bowls

Members of Congress are usually judged whether they affect the lives of constituents in a positive or negative fashion. An unproductive Congressman does not keep his/her job for long. The easiest and most quantifiable index of effectiveness for senators and representatives is how much money they funnel back into their state or district. This practice is not new, and has long been called "bringing home the bacon," "pork-barrel spending," or just plain "pork." Oftentimes, pork-barrel spending addresses real needs; but in many such cases politically motivated spending generates projects or programs where none existed before.

This practice of diverting or adding funds to the home district is as old as democracy. It is very effective in political terms. Steven Levitt, an economist at Harvard, recently documented the impact of just how much it helps, and how expensive each vote is. He found that members of Congress who bring home the pork win by large margins. However, he also found that in the average district, an additional $100 dollars in pork-per-capita only gains an incumbent approximately 2 percent more votes. This is because influencing voters by pork barrel spending is less focussed and therefore inefficient when compared to outright bribery. Levitt computes that the average pork-barrel cost per vote is approximately $14,000.[68] At those ratios, it takes lots of federal money to feed the political appetites at home.

Since defense spending, even in lean years, accounts for such a large percentage of discretionary spending, it is not surprising to find that the barons of Congressional pork have always belonged to one of the four defense authorizing and appropriating committees/subcommittees in the House and Senate. In a macro sense, pork-barrel spending looks harmless. But, while the money does go for weapons and defense projects, the long-term damage to coherent national security is insidious. More often than not, Congressional pork replaces, diverts, or cancels programs that have a higher priority and fill real, not created, needs.

For over forty years, Democrats have dominated at least one house of Congress. During that time, the pork-barrel spending by members of defense committees became legendary. Capitol Hill still remembers that when Senator John Stennis (D-MS) served on the Senate Armed Services Committee, Washington pundits joked that the state of Mississippi would probably sink into the Gulf of Mexico if any more ships were built there. It is no accident that Stennis and his powerful colleague in the House of Representatives from South Carolina, Mendell Rivers, have ships named after them.

While the 1994 Republican campaign contained a pledge to revitalize national security, it did not specifically address pork-barrel spending. However, statements by incoming Republicans certainly gave hope that wasteful habits of the Democratic defense barons would end. Shortly more than a week after the 1994 election, Representative Robert Livingston (R-LA), future chairman of the House Appropriations Committee, stated emphatically that "we are going to be re-evaluating every program, every rice bowl that the Democrats have built up over fifty-sixty years. There are going to be a lot of them that are going to be kicked over...[Democrats] have entrenched themselves and their friends and their fancy programs. The American people are going to find out where the special interests are."[69] To a skeptical public it appeared that the Republicans were finally going to get tough with pork, and in particular, with defense-related pork.

Unfortunately, judging by the conduct of the defense appropriations and authorizing committees, nothing has changed. Both House and Senate added approximately $7 billion in new spending to Clinton's FY 1996 defense budget for weapons the Pentagon has professed not to want. In particular, the House spent $533 million as a down payment for twenty additional B-2s. These additional aircraft could eventually cost the Pentagon $38 billion, money diverted from other accounts if the program goes forward.

Whether the air force needed twenty more B-2s was not at issue. In fact, one could make a good case for the additional bombers. A 1984 RAND study stressed that additional B-2s would allow the air force to field a *smaller* bomber force due to the B-2s greater effectiveness. BDM, an analytical organization that does work for the Pentagon, stated in a 1994 report that "of all modernization options, additional B-2 procurement provides the greatest impact on bomber force effectiveness." Moreover, on 4 January 1995, no less than seven former Secretaries of Defense came out strongly for the additional bombers in a letter to President Clinton.[70] The real issue, however, is affordability.

Since the high costs associated with additional B-2s would eviscerate planned modernization programs across the spectrum of the four services, there was little choice from Secretary Perry's perspective. While estimates for twenty more aircraft were not firm, they varied anywhere from as little as $15 billion to $38 billion, depending on who was asked, what assumptions one made, and whether one included other expenses like life-cycle costs.

Politicians do not necessarily have to ponder trade-offs and opportunity costs as does the Secretary of Defense when they load on money for new weapons. However, the fact is that for each new B-2 purchased, the Pentagon must give up something else. Economists refer to this phenomenon as opportunity costs. For example, if one assumes that the Pentagon could purchase twenty additional B-2s at the low estimate of $15 billion, and further assuming that the defense budget does not increase to absorb the added costs, then it is easy to make straight-line calculations on what one would have to sacrifice in modernization programs to pay for the additional bombers. According a former staffer for the Senate Armed Services Committee, possible trade-offs for twenty additional B-2s could be:

- 178 F-22s ($89 million each)
- 63 C-17s ($251 million each)
- 757 F-16s ($21 million each)
- 360 C130Js ($44 million each)
- 293 F-18E/F ($54 million each)
- 443 V-22s ($36 million each)[71]

Such logic is rarely persuasive to members of Congress who have a higher priority: keeping the folks at home happily employed. It is no accident that in 1995 large numbers of liberals in the House, folks for whom spending a dime on defense is akin to taking food from the mouths of starving children, joined conservatives in an effort to increase spending on the additional B-2s. That is why one found Maxine Waters (D-CA) joining "B-2 Bob" Dornan (R-CA) in voting to stuff an additional twenty B-2s into the defense budget.

Looking at the money added by both House and Senate for new weapons, one once again can recognize the pork-barrel phenomenon. For example, only six states accounted for nearly $4.6 billion of the $6 billion in new spending. They are in order: 1) Mississippi, 2) Louisiana, 3) California, 4) Missouri, 5) Washington, and 6) Texas. Each state had multiple members on either the Senate or House authorizing or appropriating committees or subcommittees. Senators who sat on either the appropriations or the armed services committees got $4.1 billion of the additional money, or 81 percent of all add-on spending.[72]

Perhaps nowhere does the pork stand out as starkly as in the millions the Republican Congress added for military construction projects the Pentagon never requested. Again, the Republicans' actions were strikingly at odds with their initial rhetoric. In early June 1995, Representative Joel Hefley (R-CO), the new Republican Chairman of the House National Security Subcommittee on Installations and Facilities, told a reporter that the practice of adding military construction projects to their districts had ended. According to Representative Hefley, the rules for this budget cycle would be, "If the Pentagon did not ask for it, we will not fund it."[73] Not surprisingly, new money appeared. Despite the fact the administration asked for $10.7 billion in military construction, or a huge increase of 20 percent over FY 1995, Congress piled on nearly $500 million more for add-on projects.

Again, as with the add ons for unrequested weapons systems, the lion's share of add-on funding went to the home states of committee members. Of the thirty-one states represented on the House National Security Committee, twenty-eight received add-on projects.[74] More than 80 percent of the total amount added, $564 million, went to the members' home states. Of the eighty-seven unrequested projects, forty went straight to the home district of sitting committee members. Non-committee members did not fare as well. A paltry 7 percent of all add-on money went to districts not represented on the national security committee.[75]

Not all members of Congress have climbed aboard the pork-barrel express. McCain has consistently proven to be a thorn in the side of Congressional porkers. In a series of scathing opinion pieces in America's most influential newspapers, the senator argued that every dollar for pork is a dollar less for real defense. On 9 March 1995 he stated his hopes in the *Wall Street Journal* that the wasteful special interest spending of his colleagues in the Senate would raise the ire of Americans in that it "threatens the very security of the United States."[76] Again in fall 1995, McCain attacked Senate pork barons in the *Washington Post*, charging the Republicans of attempting to squander $4.1 billion of the $7 billion added to the Administration's request on "unwanted, needless projects."[77]

McCain has focused on the real issue: *how* the defense budget is spent is more important than *how much* is spent. It makes little sense to McCain to spend billions on Seawolf submarines or B-2s, if those programs snuff the life from higher priority projects. McCain believes that if Congress aggressively tackled pork, it could free up nearly $8 billion for defense programs that the services badly need.[78]

Despite McCain's Quixotic crusade against Congress' irresponsible behavior, the pork issue will never surface in the 1996 political campaigns because the very voters who should be outraged are the ones being bribed. Voters will not view this issue from a national perspective. After all, what McCain calls pork is really about *jobs* with the local defense contractor, *jobs* building construction projects on local military bases, and *jobs* refitting ships at the local ship yard.

McCain assumes that the best way to fight such irresponsible Congressional behavior is to put the spotlight on wasteful spending habits, in effect shaming Congress into reform. He believes that once the public knows what is really going on, Congress will cease its irresponsible behavior. Taking their cue from the senator, the national news media, Washington think tanks, and influential civic groups have all launched "anti-pork" crusades with annual reports regularly grounded on McCain's shame-based assumption. Unfortunately, such efforts will likely not pay off. After all, it matters little to voters from the great state of Massachussets if their fellow Americans in Maine, Georgia, and California are outraged because Senator Kennedy brings home billions in add-on defense contracts. As the old saying goes, "incest is relative." So it is with pork.

## Conclusion

National polls show that most Americans do not want to dismantle the defense establishment built up during the Cold War. There are no public calls for large cuts in defense; nor are there pressures to withdraw from our alliances in Europe and Korea. Moreover, Americans back the president's aggressive agenda for peace-keeping, so long as current operations in Haiti and Bosnia do not turn sour. Essentially, the public appears content to leave national security issues in the hands of elected politicians. Judging from the past three years of the Clinton administration and one year of a Republican Congress, drastic changes are not in the cards. The drawdown is about over, a new modernization binge is about to begin, and defense spending is finally about to start climbing after over a decade of steady reductions.

Yet the issues raised here are important, and the public should know that the country is ignoring or delaying crucial policy choices to maintain a deceptively placid status quo. With the coming free-fall in discretionary spending on the horizon, Americans will eventually have to challenge the current priorities for defense spending. Politicians' cries for defense "revitalization" need to be recognized as the political sound bites they are. Spending a few billion more on defense than the administration requests is not a clarion call for revitalization. Instead, voters need to look to see what is not happening. For example why has Congress not seriously examined the administration's Bottom-Up Review, the foundation of America's current defense strategy. If, indeed, it has as many flaws as its critics claim, it does not make sense to continue pumping money down a "bad hole." After all, it is the Bottom-Up Review that drives the current force structure and spending levels. The Republicans were absolutely on target to call for a blue ribbon review of defense strategy and policy in their "Contract With America." Unfortunately, they backed off from an aggressive review without a whimper when a feisty Secretary of Defense called their bluff.

Americans need to hear from their representatives, and those who challenge them in the 1996 campaign, why America maintains forces to fight two major wars nearly simultaneously and why this country is about to spend hundreds of billions of dollars building an array of new and sometimes questionable weaponry. In most cases, one can make a good case for the Pentagon's new modernization program. In others, questionable weapons systems like the Navy's F/A-18E/F need to be more seriously examined.

Politicians should tell Americans why this country's fighting forces need to be kept at Cold War levels in near-term readiness at the expense of longer-term priorities. Voters, in turn, need to cut through political hype. The fact is that with the Cold War over, the military can relax readiness levels for units with a lesser priority. This country is no longer toe-to-toe with another superpower. Thousands of nuclear missiles, bombers, tanks, ships, submarines, and fighters no longer threaten the Western alliance. Instead the United States faces a new strategic environment that contains a host of embedded potential foes, none of whom can match U.S. military power. Yet for some politicians, readiness remains the "sacred cow." Readiness is not free. Needlessly keeping the entire military structure quivering for instant action drains funds from other areas with equal or greater importance, such as modernization and sustainment.

Voters should also be aware that Congress is not paying attention to the real dangers of terrorism which might have the potential to unleash nuclear or chemical attacks on the United States. The traditional approaches to keeping the proliferation of weapons of mass destruction under control are no longer meaningful because of the leakage of weapons, components, and materials from the former Soviet Union. Whether the United States should significantly increase funding for the Cooperative Threat Reduction programs should be an important issue in the 1996 campaign. Unfortunately, because most Americans judge a four dollar increase in Medicare premiums more important than placing strong safeguards around tons of plutonium and uranium in the Russia, they will ignore this issue.

But the world will not go away. Things are happening that bode ill for the future. On 23 November 1995 Russian hazardous materials specialists carefully removed a container from a Moscow park, one placed at the location two weeks earlier by Shamil Basayev, a Chechen rebel leader. Inside was an batch of highly radioactive cesium. Basayev wanted to demonstrate that he could place such materials any place in Russia as part of a Chechen terrorist campaign: Russian authorities certainly heard the message. This raises a question. If Chechen separatist guerrillas can actually demonstrate the ability to poison population centers in Russia with radioactivity, what does it suggest about the potential for destruction by a well-financed and organized group of terrorists in the United States when equipped with a small portion of the dangerous materials piled up all over Russia? Interestingly, the story about

Basayev's chilling demonstration rated only a short mention on Page 34 of the *Washington Post*.[79] Page 1 that day discussed issues the Post decided were more important than nuclear terrorism in the heart of Moscow—issues such as the death of Izzy Cohen, the founder of Giant Food, a debate about Washington D.C.'s General Hospital, and Republican divisions on environmental issues.[80]

Terrorism is a danger that our elected leaders need to deal with. There were plenty of reminders in 1995, a year that saw the cult attack on Japanese commuters with homemade nerve gas, a handful of disgruntled cranks blow up a Federal building with a crudely constructed fertilizer bomb, conviction of a group of Middle Eastern religions fanatics for blowing up the World Trade Center in Manhattan, and a demonstration by Chechen guerrillas proving that they had the ability to terrorize Russia with radioactive materials. Yet, Congress cannot summon the votes to pass legislation to improve the ability of America's law enforcement agencies to deal with terrorists.

If Republican efforts to balance the budget are successful, the result will significantly slow the growth of entitlements and other popular discretionary spending programs. The first law of political dynamics will eventually place pressure on those in Congress who favor robust levels of defense. This is the debate that so far has not taken place, primarily because the pain of the coming budget reductions has not hit home yet. That is one reason why 1996 will not be the year for a fruitful debate on national security issues.

In the 1980 election, when the Soviets were running amok in Afghanistan, when top U.S. commanders derided the very ability of the forces they command, when the incompetence of the American military was revealed on CNN following Desert One, Americans finally decided that they had had enough and chose a tough-talking president and sent the incumbent back to his peanut farm in Georgia.

But Jimmy Carter did not lose because events overwhelmed him. He lost because he had not been paying attention to America's real national security needs. Instead, he had focussed on a range of domestic and economic issues popular with the domestically-oriented Democrats. Ironically the same fate awaits the current crop of complacent Republican and Democratic politicians who refuse to discuss the emerging new dangers: their own greed, a military force based on an unworkable strategy, and the spending of tens of billions for weapons that do not measure up. They, like Jimmy Carter, may suddenly be consumed by a groundswell of angry voters for their complacency. Until then, politicians will continue, in the immortal words of Kiffin Rockwell, a pilot in the legendary World War I Lafayette Escadrille, to "fly along, blissfully ignorant, hoping for the best."

Chapter 2

# Reengineering U.S. Intelligence

*Jay T. Young*

T he end of the Cold War has proved traumatic for the U.S. intelligence community, especially the Central Intelligence Agency (CIA). Since 1994, CIA has endured the exposure of a damaging traitor at the heart of its supposedly elite Directorate of Operations (DO). Although complete details of Aldrich Ames' treachery remain classified, he undoubtedly destroyed a carefully constructed network of well-placed human sources in the Soviet national security bureaucracy just as the regime began to disintegrate. Had the USSR, like many ailing empires before it, tried to delay or reverse history's verdict through some desperate military venture, the absence of these sources could have had catastrophic consequences. Instead, his unmasking has revealed an arrogant, insular institutional culture in the Directorate of Operations indulgent of mediocrity (or worse) among insiders and hostile to external criticism. Subsequent revelations that senior Agency leaders passed information from suspected Soviet double agents to policy makers during the 1980s, and that Directorate of Operations personnel in Guatemala protected brutal sources of limited intelligence value in that country's notoriously murderous military, have reinforced the need for major change in a culture clearly disconnected from reality.

In addition, CIA's analytical arm, the Directorate of Intelligence (DI), has not escaped criticism over the past two years. Many policy makers and analysts inside and outside of Washington claim that the CIA failed to foresee the Soviet collapse. According to Senator Daniel Patrick Moniyhan, perhaps the most notable (and widely quoted) Agency critic, "The CIA failed in its single overriding mission which was to chart the course of Soviet affairs." As result, Moniyhan, who has called for the Agency's elimination, and his supporters assert that the Directorate of Intelligence's overestimation of Soviet strength led the U.S. to squander billions on unnecessary defense spending during the 1980s.

The major national agencies that form the core of the intelligence community, CIA, the Defense Intelligence Agency (DIA), and the National Security Agency (NSA), emerged during the Cold war to monitor and assess the Soviet threat. Not surprisingly, the USSR's collapse has prompted a reexamination of the purpose, size, and structure of a community whose budget now totals some $28 billion and which contains numerous civilian and military organizations with bloated staffs and overlapping responsibilities. This reexamination is not, however, occurring in a vacuum. Almost the entire Federal bureaucracy, including cabinet-level departments and large programs, has come under increased Congressional and public scrutiny. Even President Clinton, a Democrat whose failed 1994 health plan reflected his party's traditional penchant for large, Federal programs, declared in his 1996 State of the Union address that, "the era of big government is over."

This trend reflects the revolution in the business world that has occurred over the past decade—a revolution which has now reached the Federal government. Faced with a global competitive environment of unprecedented intensity and rapid technological change, American industry has undergone a vast restructuring that has included traumatic personnel reductions, organizational changes, and process overhauls of every area from manufacturing to customer service. The aim of this (as yet) unfinished revolution has been to enhance competitiveness by enabling companies to focus on those "core competencies" that provide maximum value to their customers. Several distinct intellectual phases have driven this revolution; one recent and highly influential one, "reengineering," stresses using advanced technology to transform corporate processes. Most recent management thinking, however, has emphasized that corporate leaders must accept rapid change as a constant and continuously question their organization's most cherished assumptions.

Recent U.S. corporate experience offers useful guidance for reengineering an intelligence community whose organization and culture, like that of American business in 1980, remains firmly rooted in the past. The immense national security bureaucracy of the Cold War, of which the intelligence community is one (albeit important) part, was often ponderous and unimaginative in meeting the challenges posed by the environment that spawned it. It is even less ready for a future strategic landscape marked by multiple threats of varying intensities and origins, continuing technological change, and prolonged budgetary restrictions. Fashioning an intelligence community more appropriate to this situation requires, above all, a sophisticated understanding of what real value secret intelligence can provide in an information-besotted-world. It also demands a willingness to learn from the corporate world's mistakes by refusing simply to slash the size (while expanding the responsibilities) of the current, inadequate structure, and then calling it reform. Real reform demands a complete rethinking and overhaul of the mission, products, processes, and especially culture of the community.

The continuing importance of intelligence in the post–Cold War era underscores the need to accelerate radical change. Ethnic violence and separatism, the spread of weapons of mass destruction, instability caused by economic and technological change, the growing power of international organized crime, and the rise of new centers of power in Asia are perhaps the most important hallmarks of what is, and likely will remain, a highly fluid strategic environment. To be sure, the technological capabilities that have been a traditional core competency of the Anglo-American intelligence community will remain critical to assessing many of these problems. Nonetheless, as Bosnia and other recent crises have demonstrated, many post–Cold War intelligence issues will demand the sustained attention of analysts whose understanding of regional cultures, histories, and politics is second to none. In a world that places a premium on analytical skill, any reengineering of the intelligence community must ensure that its human capital is adequately nurtured, periodically augmented, and wisely employed.

## The Commercial Information and Organizational Revolution

The pace of technological change and increased international competition have brought great change to business over the past fifteen years. On one level, the new, information-based economy has elevated the role played by certain individuals. In a global economy overwhelmed by information, analytical skill has become a critical competitive discriminator. In most advanced economies, those who know the best sources of information (many human), who add value through seasoned judgment, and who disseminate intelligence to clients in a timely fashion, dominate the marketplace. In the business world, this new analytical elite are the industrial analysts at major brokerage firms or specialist consultancies. Their prognoses on specific companies and predictions on broader trends receive instant media attention and influence huge securities transactions. Such individuals are probably the most highly paid analysts in the world, since on their expertise rides the fate of countless investors. Not surprisingly, brokerage firms and consultancies provide star analysts with huge salaries and, just as importantly, the freedom to study their subject in detail and arrive at conclusions unhindered by meddlesome bureau-cratic delays.[1]

On a broader scale, corporations and organizations throughout the indus-trial world continue to undergo radical restructuring in response to rapid changes in technology and the competitive environment. For example, increased automation of industrial processes has cost jobs, while boosting pro-ductivity. Processes that require extensive manual input come in two cate-gories. The first includes assembly or manufacturing jobs that machines can not yet perform; or low-skill service jobs such as retailing and telemarketing. The other category includes those high-value occupations that involve ana-lytical judgment, technical expertise (e.g. research and development), or cre-ative skill (entertainment/advertising). Companies initially had difficulty recognizing this dichotomy. Financial executives (still dominant in too many U.S. companies) oversaw much of the initial reengineering work undertaken by firms desperate to increase efficiency in the face of the Japanese onslaught. Consequently, most efforts to "reengineer the corporation" sought to control costs by ruthlessly slashing personnel and overhead. Many companies, how-ever, soon discovered that they lacked sufficient skilled personnel to imagine and develop innovative new products—a phenomenon known as "corporate anorexia." Moreover, the chaos caused by such "slash and burn" efforts at reor-ganization produced rock-bottom morale among the remaining employees. [2]

The thrust of corporate reengineering has changed—at least among most innovative companies. Many seek first to determine what constitute their strategic technologies or competencies and then, through increased invest-ment or new technology, how to leverage these capabilities into new prod-ucts and markets. Such thinking requires real strategic analysis and greater technological literacy than the simplistic "bean counting" that underlay so many early restructuring projects.[3] The process of identifying these compe-tencies also helps pinpoint what companies can safely outsource without jeop-ardizing their competitive advantages. Thus, the most efficient companies in today's business world understand the basis of their competitive advantage, value key employees, invest in improving strategic technologies/competen-cies in anticipation of new market trends (while outsourcing other, less crit-ical skills), and maintain sufficient organizational flexibility and personnel depth to adjust to unexpected threats.

Still, though corporate leaders now can identify core competencies and determine the basis of competitive advantage, ossified and insular corporate cultures often inhibit implementation of innovative strategies. Long-established institutional attitudes and deeply ingrained values are difficult to change even with radical reorganizations, process reengineering, and personnel reductions. Sometimes, the scale of change required is so immense that even top executives who intellectually understand the challenge shrink from assuming responsibility. Others are unwilling to understand the intricacies of their company's culture and identify elements that represent significant barriers to change. Deeper cultural issues, especially the importance of transforming recruiting, training, and personnel attitudes often remain unresolved.

The reason for discussing the revolution in management style and philosophy that has marked the 1980s and 1990s is that the American intelligence community confronts similar challenges to those confronted by U.S. business in 1980: a bloated bureaucracy, products irrelevant to new consumer requirements, comfortable assumptions, a lack of vision, *and* a strategic environment that has undergone *radical* change. And similar to the American business world of 1980, the culture of the intelligence community remains hostile to fundamental change.

## The Intelligence Community and the End of the Cold War

The collapse of the Soviet Empire led to immediate calls for vast cuts in Cold War national security bureaucracy. The large, Washington-based intelligence agencies have taken their share of such cuts which, according to one source, will lead to a 25 percent reduction in personnel by 2000.[4] Growing public dissatisfaction, however, with the government as a whole has also led to large cuts in non-national security agencies and programs. The Republican Congress is seeking even deeper reductions in long sacrosanct (and expensive) entitlement programs, while prominent Congress members, notably Ohio's John Kasich (R. Westerville), are calling for deeper reductions in national security programs. Thus, the likelihood of further cuts remains high.

Too often, however, the debate about downsizing has duplicated the first stage of the reengineering craze that swept the business world in the 1980s. Congressmen eager to prove their dedication to attacking public waste have moved to cut personnel and abolish organizations without first trying to understand what goods and services government can best provide or how best to transform the Federal bureaucratic culture. Cuts in the intelligence community reflect such tendencies. As with the military, the current intelligence structure is a smaller version of the large, duplicative, and expensive organization spawned by the Cold War. Some centralization and rationalization has occurred or is underway. For example, CIA Director, John Deutch has accelerated a long overdue formation of a central imagery tasking and analysis organization (the National Imagery Agency) that will perform many of the same functions for overhead imagery that the National Security Agency (NSA) has for signals intelligence (SIGINT) since the early 1950s. Prior to this change, the intelligence community contained multiple, and often competing centers of imagery tasking and analytical exploitation. According to the CIA, this organization should be operational by 1996 and its existence should alleviate problems faced in the Gulf War in securing timely and relevant imagery products for combat organizations. Nonetheless, few other significant structural changes have occurred in the four years since the passing of the Soviet regime. Aside from simple bureaucratic inertia, the delay probably stems from a desire to wait for the Aspin commission's report on the intelligence community. This report, due out in mid-1996, will address what the "roles and missions" of the intelligence community should be in the post–Cold War era. To date, however, there has been no indication on the commission's thinking.

In the meantime, an expansion of responsibilities has accompanied cutbacks in personnel. Many in the Clinton administration came to power convinced that the Soviet Union's collapse had produced a Fukayama-esqe "end to history" and that the national security bureaucracy should now focus on more "relevant" functions, such as support for the United Nations, monitoring environmental issues, and helping U.S. industry become more competitive in international trade. Thus, while keeping basic national defense policy and its structure intact, the administration has heaped numerous "new age" requirements, environmental, economic, and other "transnational" issues, on a shrinking intelligence bureaucracy. In some cases, a radical reorientation of post–Cold War intelligence priorities was indeed necessary. For example, some "transnational" issues, such as the growing power of international crime cartels, possess genuine national security implications (e.g. smuggling of weapons of mass destruction and destabilization of friendly governments). In other cases, however, increased requirements levied on CIA, in particular, for mundane economic information, have distracted analysts from following more important issues on which the community can provide unique insights.

## Strategic Competencies of the Intelligence Community

Any reassessment of the roles and missions of the intelligence community must begin with an understanding of the key competencies of intelligence services. What real value does the community's collection and analytical resources deliver? What structural, technological, and cultural changes may be necessary to ensure the continued functioning of the community. The following sections describe six key functions that the intelligence community, whatever its structure, must perform to provide effective support to the formulation and conduct of U.S. grand strategy into the next century.

As illustrated by the historical development of intelligence during the twentieth century, they represent those critical capabilities that any great power's intelligence service must perform well in order to provide political and military leaders with the most accurate and actionable intelligence analysis, and to neutralize the efforts of hostile services. These functions are: collection, warning, estimative analysis in support of national security decision making, support to warfighters/military policy makers, counterintelligence, and conduct of covert action. Each section also assesses the current intelligence community capability in providing products and services stemming from these core competencies and highlights areas that require reform or adjustment.

## Collection

Collection is the most basic function of intelligence. Intelligence services incapable of delivering the most complete and timely data possible are wasting taxpayer dollars. Technical collection has long been a core competency of the Anglo-American intelligence community. The large, complex, and successful effort to collect and exploit Axis communications during World War II established a foundation of excellence expanded upon during the Cold War. The organization of the National Security Agency (NSA) in 1954, which combined the diverse organizations conducting signals intelligence collection and analysis, and the close postwar links between NSA and its British counterpart, Government Communications Headquarters (GCHQ), have ensured that Western decision makers and military commanders have received excellent SIGINT.[5]

The challenge posed by the closed, totalitarian societies of the Soviet Union and Communist China, as well as the danger of miscalculation in the nuclear age, prompted the United States to undertake high priority projects to develop advanced imaging systems. From the U-2, to the early Corona reconnaissance satellites, through to current advanced imaging satellites, U.S. technical capabilities have remained unmatched. During the tense years of the early Cold War in particular, imaging systems provided early indications of dangerous military deployments (Cuba 1962) and permitted greater understanding of the weaknesses of Soviet armed forces. More recently, imagery warned of the Iraqi military buildup opposite Kuwait and supported the planning and conduct of the subsequent Coalition campaign against Saddam's forces.[6] As was apparent during the Gulf War, imagery product has not always reached consumers in the field in a timely fashion or in the most appropriate format. As they had during earlier crises, classification problems, bureaucratic rivalries, unsuitable formats, and communications deficiencies within the Washington intelligence community often kept field commanders from receiving imagery data quickly enough or in the most useable form—a situation that establishment of the National Imagery Agency may help correct.

No power can now match the range and technological sophistication of the U.S. imagery and SIGINT collection platforms. During the Gulf War, these capabilities, and Iraq's inability to obtain similar information or deny such intelligence to its opponents, substantially bolstered Coalition military effectiveness. Maintaining this advantage through continued research and development of new space-based and terrestrial systems, as well as supporting analytical software and equipment, must remain a high priority. Yet, obtaining consensus on this priority may become more difficult. Many of the analytical challenges of the new era are less suitable for technical exploitation and, as budgets shrink, the urge to cut research and development programs will become harder to resist.[7]

Major research cutbacks, however, could erode this traditional core competency of the Anglo-American intelligence community. As Iraq's extensive deception effort to conceal its development of nuclear, chemical and biological weapons demonstrated, knowledge of current U.S. technical surveillance capabilities has become widespread and the United States will confront increasing instances of such *maskirovka* (deception) in coming years. Finally, if the military arena is indeed undergoing a Revolution in Military Affairs (RMA) based on advances in information collection and processing capabilities, then major powers will increasingly consider possession of satellite reconnaissance and advanced intelligence capabilities essential to the effectiveness of their military forces. A U.S. failure to build on its current advantages could thus prove disastrous if potentially hostile powers eventually close the gap.[8]

Collection of human source intelligence (HUMINT) presents a different set of problems. Save for some spectacular examples such as Col. Oleg Penkovsky, KGB defector Oleg Gordievsky, and the Polish general staff officer, Col. Kuklinski, evidence of HUMINT's value is generally unavailable. In contrast, problems associated with the recruitment of human sources, for which CIA has the major responsibility within the intelligence community, surface with enough regularity to provoke numerous calls for the U.S. to abandon the odious practice of running agents. Reactions to recent revelations about an unsavory CIA military source in Guatemala, who may have been involved in the murder of an American citizen, illustrate the intense unease many in the United States feel about espionage operations. This discomfort is not confined solely the press or academe. One former director of State Department Intelligence, who is also an OSS veteran, recently commented that the U.S. should abandon all human espionage. As CIA Director from 1977–1980, Stansfield Turner's aversion to HUMINT and almost religious faith in technical collection systems prompted him to gut the Operations Directorate. [9] Although less consistently reliable than technical intelligence, HUMINT remains indispensable. As this author can attest from his own experience in the CIA, well-placed human sources can provide intelligence that technical means cannot match. As an analyst at CIA during the 1980s, this writer had to assess the prospects for a fanatical, rapidly growing insurgency in a remote part of a major country. Limited technical collection capabilities in the region, its relatively low priority at the time, and the difficulties faced by technical systems in providing insight on problems of this type, heightened the value of the excellent human sources recruited by the enterprising station chief and his staff. Repeated warnings by CIA and others about the deteriorating situation ultimately led Washington to provide much needed, if relatively discreet, assistance to the embattled government. Significantly, agents are not the only human sources that can provide valuable information. Even defense attachés, despite their status as official spies, can develop highly useful contacts in local militaries. Moreover, the CIA's National Resources Division, which debriefs U.S. businessmen with dealings in foreign countries for knowledge of important foreign technical developments, is another critical source of such intelligence.

HUMINT's importance is likely to increase in the next century. Weapons proliferation, international crime cartels, and regional ethnic tensions raise challenges that are often less susceptible to technical collection efforts. In addition, many countries are now well aware of the capabilities of U.S. imagery satellites and may be able to take increasingly effective measures to deceive or deny collection by them. As illustrated by Iraq's brilliant, multi-layered deception effort to prevent discovery of the scale of its nuclear weapons program, totalitarian states in particular can organize efforts that will defeat the most advanced technical sensors.[10] Unfortunately, obtaining HUMINT from such regimes can be equally difficult.

CIA should remain the principal collector of HUMINT for the intelligence community. Its extensive experience in this realm, despite periodic (and sometime spectacular) lapses in efficiency, make the agency a logical choice to remain the focal point of U.S. HUMINT efforts. CIA's operating methods will, however, have to undergo substantial change to meet the intelligence challenges posed by international crime syndicates, "rogue" states such as Iraq, and other post–Cold War problems. Although case officers working under diplomatic cover, the foot-soldiers of the Cold War espionage war, will remain useful in certain locales and circumstances (e.g. tracking diplomatic and military developments in Europe), CIA must make increased use of non-official cover (NOC) agents. NOCs, who pose as businessmen and other professionals, lead a stressful and often dangerous life, since they must work full time at their demanding cover job while also attempting to recruit agents or obtain information—all without diplomatic cover. Aside from the obvious physical and emotional attributes, NOC work demands technical expertise, language proficiency, and, in many cases, a different cultural and educational background than that of the white, middle-class males who presently make up the bulk of the Directorate of Operations' (DO) ranks. Increased use of NOCs would not only provide an enhanced capability to collect vital intelligence on post-Soviet era issues, it would also help transform the DO's clubby culture by introducing large numbers of highly-trained, results-oriented individuals less tolerant of intellectual mediocrity and bureaucratic time-serving.

Increased use of NOCs, however, will also bring new challenges. The agency, which often remains unwilling to share information with local ambassadors about what its case officers are doing, must work even more closely with the State Department to insure that NOC actions, if compromised, do not come as a total surprise to U.S. diplomats and endanger larger foreign policy objectives. Greater employment of NOCs will also require more elaborate tradecraft and sophisticated communications capabilities so the agency can contact and receive reports from, and, if necessary extract, agents in sensitive positions. In short, larger numbers of NOCs in the Directorate of Operations' ranks will force a general tightening up of administrative and field procedures that can only enhance the clandestine service's effectiveness.

Aside from intelligence produced by clandestine sources, analysts now face a rising tide of open-source information. The community has always integrated open-source reporting, often from the CIA's Foreign Broadcast Information Service, into its products. Now, however, the information revolution and the collapse of the Communist Bloc have resulted in a profusion of sources that possess considerable intelligence value. In addition, the new demands on the community, especially in the economic realm, have also increased the requirement to monitor open sources. According to CIA spokesmen, the Washington agencies are confronting the problem: an interagency committee is presently assessing those open sources of sufficient interest to scan regularly.[11] However, the real answer to the flood of open-source information lies in narrowing analytical focus and leaving the assessment of most "non-traditional" issues, for which open sources provide most of the useful information, to the private sector or other government agencies.

## Warning

Warning of near-term events or actions that could pose significant dangers to U.S. interests remains a central mission of the intelligence community. The CIA's origins stem from the greatest warning failure in American history: the attack on Pearl Harbor. The agency's creators, aware that modern weapons had reduced warning time while increasing the threat, sought to avoid a nuclear-age repetition of the Japanese strike. Despite this rationale for its creation, however, CIA and the other intelligence agencies have a mixed record on warning, perhaps because of a surprisingly ambiguous attitude towards its significance within the community.

Examples of such warning failures in the post-1945 era are numerous: they include the North Korean attack on South Korea in 1950, the Soviet deployment of missiles in Cuba, the invasion of Czechoslovakia in 1968, the 1973 Arab attack on Israel, and the fall of the Shah. The reasons for these failures resulted from a combination of the following problems: wishful thinking about the other side's intentions, lack of understanding about significant changes underway in local politics or culture, a lack of well-placed sources, or successful deception by the adversary. On other occasions, policy makers burdened by other concerns or unwilling to accord the CIA's analysis the significance it deserved, simply refused to listen. Recent accounts of the days immediately prior to Iraq's invasion of Kuwait indicate that the CIA's National Intelligence Officer (NIO) for Warning, as well as DIA's alert center, accurately forecast a full-scale attack. Nonetheless, high-level decision makers at State, Defense, and the National Security Council, distracted by events in Europe, and lulled by a bizarre belief that Iraq represented a bulwark against Iranian fanaticism, were reluctant to acknowledge the seriousness of the situation.[12] The CIA's accurate prediction in 1990 of the violence that would follow Yugoslavia's breakup, apparently made over vehement objections from the State Department, also received little or no attention among top policy makers.

Intelligence officers cannot make American leaders listen to what they do not want or have time to hear. Nonetheless, a reassessment of the community's own attitude toward warning might increase the likelihood that policy makers will pay more attention to warnings it issues. For too long, the warning issue, at least within CIA, has suffered from low institutional prestige, which has translated into limited influence with policy makers and the CIA's own senior managers. For example, in a recent book on the Gulf War, the authors note that the position for Warning at CIA has long been a bureaucratic Siberia for unconventional individuals such as the 1990 incumbent, Charles Allen. Convinced that Iraq intended to overrun Kuwait, Allen faced hyper-cautious CIA senior managers wary of his outspoken views, and a pre-occupied Bush administration which was reluctant to accept the seriousness of Saddam's intentions. Moreover, the authors also correctly observe that the intelligence community largely viewed warning as a technical problem of monitoring the readiness of Soviet strategic strike forces.[13] Thus, it is unsurprising that so many post-1945 intelligence failures have involved wars or revolution outside Europe. In short, the challenge posed by a focus on warning of the most dangerous, but least likely, occurrence, has led to an ossification of thinking about other dangers and threats.

Warning is both a short- and a long-term problem. Short-term warning obviously focuses on issues of immediate concern, such as whether Country A will attack Country B or if Country C is in danger of a coup. On the other hand, long-term warning seeks to identify dangerous trends in a country or region that may threaten U.S. interests so that analysts can prepare policy makers to recognize the emergence of significant future problems. At present, no clear significant threat lurks on the horizon against which the U.S. can base its security planning. This situation is reminiscent of the nineteenth century since even during the 1920s, Japan's ambitions and military power remained of concern at least to U.S. naval strategists. Without a clearly defined threat, warning will recede even further in importance among intelligence priorities or become excessively focused on short-term problems.

In fact, warning should probably receive more, not less attention, simply because the present international environment is so volatile. Where and when significant threats may emerge is still unclear and may remain so for some time. Thus, the community's focus in warning analysis should probably be longer-term. This probably calls for closer integration of the warning function with both the National Intelligence Council (NIC)—or perhaps a redefinition of the council's charter to provide a larger role in warning—and with analysts following regional issues. Moreover, the intelligence agencies must make warning duties a prestigious and competitive assignment sought after by the best people and provide analysts working warning problems the freedom to challenge assumptions on key issues. Perhaps such "institutionalized Bolshevism" might have provoked earlier questioning about the 1989 National Intelligence Estimate that concluded Iraq would cause no trouble for at least three years.[14] In short, a redefined, and expanded concept of warning must be a critical "core competency" of the intelligence community.

## Estimates, Analysis, and National Security Decision Making

Intelligence community analysts have one overriding purpose: support for decision making. They are not scholars at universities engaged in seminal research nor are they reporters rushing to beat the competition. Nonetheless, many managers and analysts, especially at CIA, have all too often viewed themselves as both. For example, the growing volume of news information and the rapidity of its dissemination have led to constant fears in the CIA of being scooped by the press.[15] By the early 1990s, much of the intelligence community's current production, especially CIA's, was not only unimaginative but consciously imitative of the press. Stylistic and content limitations in the most widely disseminated intelligence publication, the National Intelligence Daily (NID), as well as the need to coordinate its contents with other Washington intelligence agencies, resulted in an increasingly bland publication of limited utility. Although the CIA has now added a daily publication on economic issues at the behest of the Clinton Administration, it is still unclear that either the format or substance of daily intelligence products provides any significant insights beyond those found in the press.[16]

In longer-term research, CIA analysts have confronted many structural and procedural barriers that have often led to poor and/or untimely products. Until recently, the Directorate of Intelligence's research production process reflected the worst features of both academia and government bureaucracy.[17] For example, the main criteria used to judge an analyst's performance was not the accuracy of his or her analyses or the timeliness of delivery but rather the number of lengthy papers produced each year. "Publish or perish" was as much a factor in the life of a Directorate of Intelligence analyst as in that of any assistant professor. Despite the pressure to publish, CIA forced papers to go through numerous layers of review, which blunted analytical sharpness and guaranteed late arrival. By its nature, intelligence work forces upon organizations and individuals a degree of insularity and clannishness unmatched in almost any other government or private-sector organization. Still, largely as a result of the Congressional hearings on intelligence community activities during the 1970s, the CIA in particular became increasingly suspicious of and isolated from many of its customers. Too often, agency managers limited contacts between analysts and policy makers for fear that a junior, and less politically astute, analyst might reveal something a Congressional committee could use to embarrass the Agency. As a result, the Directorate of Intelligence turned inward to such a degree that by the early 1990s, many of its analysts were working on research papers of limited concern to policy makers already deluged by information from other sources.

Overseen by the CIA's National Intelligence Council, the process that produces National Intelligence Estimates (NIEs) is even more cumbersome than that of regular Directorate of Intelligence offices. Unlike Directorate of Intelligence papers, NIEs must undergo sustained review by the intelligence community. Although not all NIEs harbor the fuzzy judgments their detractors have claimed—the 1990 estimate on Yugoslavia is a good counterexample—the process produces too many papers whose finely hedged judgements and overlong, academic format limit their usefulness (and appeal) to policy makers. In fact, the intricate NIE process seems increasingly anachronistic.

First, current and future generations of policy makers appear even less inclined than their predecessors to read lengthy documents. Moreover, they will not assign a mystical level of significance to the fact that NIEs represent the august judgment of the intelligence community.

To contend with mounting criticism of its analytical products, the agency instituted serious reforms in the early 1990s under DDI Doug MacEachin (1991-1993). MacEachin formed a commission consisting of senior analysts and managers to study the problem. The commission met with consumers, analysts, academics, industry consultants, and others. Consumers told it that CIA papers were heavy on opinion and background, and far too light on important facts and descriptions of the sources supporting the analysis. Based on these comments, MacEachin attempted to reform the production process by eliminating some layers of review and even a few managerial positions, reducing the numbers and types of formal products analysts must produce, and increasing the use of briefings. He also introduced a system of "tradecraft" for analysts to bring more methodological rigor and added consumer value to Directorate of Intelligence products. Analytical "tradecraft" involved stating clearly for policy makers the facts, findings, and analytical "linchpins" supporting the agency's argument on a particular issue.[18] Joseph Nye, who headed the National Intelligence Council from 1993-1994, also made some useful changes. These included reducing the number of NIE's produced and providing policy makers with summaries.[19] Thus, the agency has recognized the need for change and is attempting to overhaul its rigid, often unimaginative production process. What is not clear is whether CIA Director Deutch will sustain the pace of change. Moreover, such changes represent only a starting point for more fundamental cultural and organizational transformation that the agency requires.

Reform of the CIA (and elsewhere) will fail unless policy makers rethink the community's analytical focus. Even before the Soviet Union's demise, the explosion of open-source information, along with growing concerns about declining U.S. competitiveness and other "non-traditional" security issues, resulted in significant new tasking for the intelligence community. This trend accelerated under the Clinton administration which arrived in power convinced that the Soviet collapse had left international trade as the only real battleground. Since the many economists who hold its top positions believe that the Japanese/French neomercantilist model of support to trade and industry holds the key to long-term prosperity, this administration has asked the intelligence community for significant "competitiveness" information on industrial technology, foreign economic strategies, and similar issues.[20]

Most commentators have concluded, however, that the role government intelligence can play in helping U.S. industry remains limited. Reporting from secret sources on selected issues such as trade negotiating strategies and industrial espionage is probably the most effective support. Yet such efforts can be problematic as recent U.S. intelligence efforts in the economic realm indicate. Paris easily exposed an amateurish CIA scheme to retaliate against France for attempts to steal U.S. corporate secrets. This operation, and a more extensive effort to obtain information about Japanese trade strategies during an important round of trade talks, jeopardized relations with two key allies, revealed sources and methods, and provided little or no useful intelligence.[21] In addition, American corporations have displayed little interest in government intelligence as opposed to more traditional forms of Federal assistance such as export credits, price supports, and tax and regulatory relief. Finally, most major companies are already well aware of what their competitors are doing and, less consistently, what technological challenges they confront. If they require additional information, numerous private sector consulting and information firms already provide services tailored to business needs.[22]

Similarly, it makes little sense for the intelligence community to duplicate economic analyses done in the private sector. It, or other government organizations, such as the Treasury or Commerce Departments, should seek out the best private sector reporting and integrate it into government products. In general, the economic work done by the intelligence community should focus on the political-strategic ramifications of issues such as the prospects for and impact of economic reform in Eastern Europe, or the ongoing financial problems in Japan. To be sure, insightful analysis of such problems requires extensive understanding of many economic issues. Nevertheless, the intelligence community can add unique value to its assessments only by approaching such issues from a different perspective (and with different sources) than private sector analysts or other government agencies provide.

The Clinton administration's obsession with trade issues, "the arms control talks of the new age" as one Washington official dubbed them, threatens to dilute the value of secret intelligence. At present, the intelligence community is trying to provide too much intelligence on too many subjects to too many people. Quality coverage on all subjects will suffer until this or another administration recognizes the importance of a distinct analytical focus and a more select customer base. With regard to analytical focus, those issues more closely related to traditional definitions of national security must remain the intelligence community's top priority. First, issues such as nuclear and chemical/biological weapons proliferation, modernization of China's armed forces, and political instability, for example, in Russia and the Middle East, truly threaten U.S. national interests since they concern potential matters of war and peace. International trade is not war and the fate of the American polity does not rest on the number of Toyotas that enter the United States in a given year. Moreover, the intelligence community's technical collection systems and analytical expertise allow it to provide consistent support on these issues rather than on economic competitiveness. Secret intelligence serves best when it focuses on those key elements of national power—socio-political, economic, technological, and military—in current or potential adversaries who might pose threats to U.S. strategic interests worldwide.

The Defense Department is the other major source of intelligence analysis and its efforts also require tighter focus. According to a recent estimate, the number of military intelligence analysts dwarfs the analytical contingent at CIA: 13,000 vs. 1,500.[23] Aside from specific service-related technical or targeting tasks, these analysts prepare analytic briefings and papers on topics such as military technology, order of battle, operational and doctrinal developments, and military leadership. Large numbers of these analysts work in Washington at DIA and other joint and service-specific components. Others staff joint and specified commands, or work at recently created centers for service intelligence in Dayton, Ohio, (air force), Charlottesville, Virginia (army), and Suitland, Maryland (navy). One of the main problems in the military intelligence community lies in the vast inter-service duplication. Analytical components at various theater and national organizations churn out products on identical or near-identical subjects mainly to justify continued funding for their staffs.

In addition, as a recent panel at Georgetown University on the future of U.S. intelligence observed, the quality of much military intelligence is poor and its relevance often questionable.[24] For example, the military intelligence community, especially in Washington, produces large numbers of paper studies, either too general or esoteric to be of much use to the main military customers: warfighters. Moreover, many military analysts produce reports on political and even economic issues that are usually pale imitations of those done by civilian agencies. Recent budget cuts have reduced manpower levels throughout the services and at DIA but military intelligence needs further major reorganization and rationalization to perform the core missions discussed below.

## Support to Warfighters and Defense Policy Makers

Ideally, military intelligence should serve its customers in two basic ways. The most obvious is the provision of detailed and timely information and analysis to forces preparing for or engaged in combat. Intelligence, however, also has an equally important role in peacetime. It must maintain and update basic information (order of battle, target data) on potential adversaries, support efforts to reshape doctrine, evaluate technological developments, conduct war planning, and anticipate new threats.

These latter functions are especially important now since no major challenge has yet appeared, while rapid technological change continues. Led by the Pentagon's Office of Net Assessment, long one of the few innovative analytical centers within the government, many military officers now speak of a Revolution in Military Affairs (RMA) built largely around information technology and precision strikes.[25] The Gulf War provided ample evidence of the effectiveness of military forces using advanced precision-guided weapons and supported by space-based and terrestrial intelligence collection platforms. Even with these advantages, Allied intelligence had significant gaps: coalition forces never destroyed a mobile Scud launcher, nor did intelligence ever pick up the scale of Iraq's program to build weapons of mass destruction. Moreover, detailed information did not always bring greater understanding. Before the war, U.S. intelligence analysts vastly overrated Iraqi capabilities, which some analysts equated to an Arab version of the Waffen SS. Nonetheless, the scale and role of information technology led many analysts to see the Gulf War as a transitional conflict between large-scale twentieth century conventional warfare and a still hazy twenty-first century "face of battle." What is clear is that achieving some form of "information dominance" will be essential to victory in the future. As the *Gulf War Air Power Survey* noted, "the rapid collection, processing, and exploitation of information is likely to become even more important in future war than it has been in the past... taking the place, perhaps, that the contest for geographical position has held in previous conflicts."[26]

In this technological transition, military intelligence has several important tasks. First, it must follow foreign developments (civilian and military) in information technology, precision-guided systems, stealth technology, and weapons of mass destruction. Moreover, military intelligence analysts must understand how changes in doctrine, force structure, and strategy may indicate that a potential adversary has integrated technology and operational concepts to the point of substantially increasing its military effectiveness. This calls for more subtle and sophisticated analysis than the simplistic "bean counting" approach that characterizes so many military assessments.

Analysts must also avoid "mirror imaging" that imposes U.S. concepts on other nation's strategies. The CIA's belief that the Soviet Union had accepted Western notions of deterrence led analysts to discount the purpose and impact of Moscow's military buildup. In the wake of the Gulf War, future adversaries, especially some regional powers, may develop strategies that mix local concepts of warfare (e.g. irregular or small unit operations) with selected high technology weapons to inflict maximum casualties on U.S. forces. Others may seek simply to deploy a sufficient arsenal of nuclear, conventional, or biological weapons, to discourage the United States from interfering. In contrast, emerging great powers such as China may deploy armed forces similar to those of the most advanced Western countries relatively quickly, especially if they can purchase or develop advanced technology. In either case, the U.S. military must not find itself in a situation similar to that of 1990 when it discovered that the national database on Iraq was virtually non-existent. U.S. military intelligence needs to insure that it tracks regional threats with sufficient rigor and maintains the organizational flexibility to reallocate assets quickly when unexpected contingencies occur. Finally, in an era of rapid change, U.S. military planners must integrate the latest and best intelligence into doctrinal discussions, wargames, and exercises where new force structures and operational concepts are under examination. A clear understanding of foreign military and technology developments may prevent a turn down a doctrinal blind alley which could lead to unpleasant surprises on some future battlefield.[27]

The Gulf War also suggests that as force levels shrink, and information's centrality to warfare increases, military organizations will have to train more combatants to use and understand intelligence. One of the major problems faced by all services in the Gulf was the lack of qualified individuals to support intelligence operations. Personnel shortages, as well as technological limitations, hindered the flow of timely and relevant intelligence to many units, especially air wings.[28] Two solutions exist. First, the military must expand the numbers of those who understand the value of intelligence and can manage collection, interpret the product, and know where in the bureaucracy to go for critical information. In a shrinking force structure, this could mean either that there will be intelligence specialists or that individuals from other specialties receive cross-training. The military may also need to make increased use of reservists for intelligence-related tasks. Many reservists work in high technology industries where they receive constant exposure to systems integration and technology management issues. Since continued manpower constraints are likely, however, development work must accelerate on automated systems capable of fusing data from multiple sources and providing actionable products directly to front-line units. Analogies exist today in the commercial world. For example, commercial consultants now provide customers such as power companies and television stations with near-real time weather data (including Doppler radar and satellite images) on both local and national weather conditions. Subscribers purchase PCs, software, and a satellite dish to receive the contractor's signal. They also pay a monthly subscription fee for which they receive highly customized data, and speak directly with staff meteorologists at the contractor's headquarters. Many such companies no longer employ professional meteorologists since the available data is so complete and timely that the need for on-site expertise has almost entirely disappeared. Something similar—customized packages for specific theaters/units with fused data fed directly to the user and with instant access to specialists in a central location—may obviate the need for large numbers of intelligence specialists at all locations.[29]

The military must also train more intensively for intelligence support during wartime. The *Gulf War Air Power Survey* suggests that managing the high volume of data and servicing numerous daily requests for intelligence support overwhelmed many intelligence staffs during Desert Storm.[30] Such problems also highlight the need for intelligence to assume a higher profile in military exercises. Computers can now generate the message traffic, requests for analytical support, and collection management problems that replicate a wartime intelligence environment.

Continued socio-political constraints on U.S. strategy also reinforce the importance of integrating intelligence into military operations. Edward Luttwak has observed that most Western democracies, for reasons such as declining birthrates, or growing sensitivity about the use of force abroad, are increasingly unwilling to accept casualties, even with all-volunteer militaries.[31] This hesitancy also extends to inflicting casualties on the enemy, as illustrated by the military's fears about public reaction to collateral damage during the Gulf and Bosnian air campaigns. Such socio-political constraints demand that intelligence on enemy intentions and capabilities, as well as intelligence that supports targeting of friendly weapons, be ever more precise. This requires not only the continued development of technical collection systems but intensified peacetime training.

## Counterintelligence

The Aldrich Ames case illustrated the vast counter-intelligence (CI) problems in at least one major intelligence agency. The Ames debacle reflects the CIA's unique cultural problems, in particular the Directorate of Operations' willingness to tolerate mediocrity (or worse) among its case officers. In most corporations, the system would probably have prevented a demonstrated drunk and incompetent not only from achieving a significant position but from remaining with the organization long enough to inflict serious damage. In addition, the paranoid delusions of James Jesus Angleton had introduced into CIA culture an almost knee-jerk reaction to CI that lasted almost twenty years after his ouster. Angleton's persecution of innocent CIA personnel in his quest to uncover the "monster plot" of world Communism convinced many at the agency that excessive zeal for CI issues was *prima facie* evidence of mental imbalance.[32] CI duties became a dumping ground for unwanted officers, such as Ames. Moreover, CIA security, like much of the intelligence community, placed too much faith in the technological promise of the polygraph (which Ames managed to pass). Like the German intelligence services, which thought that Enigma's technological sophistication made it impossible to break, agency security officers became too complacent about the CI utility of polygraphs.

Ames' unmasking led to sanctimonious editorials and articles questioning the significance of spies and their information. It is now clear that the agency had recruited some high-level sources inside Moscow's military and scientific communities and that Ames destroyed a network painstakingly constructed over years. We do not yet know what impact the loss of these sources may have had on the agency's analytical effectiveness during the waning days of the Soviet Union, but the loss indicates how damaging even one, well-placed traitor can be to an agent network, as well as to the *strategic* importance of having a competent CI capability. Historical examples of CI's strategic significance are numerous. During World War II, effective CI enabled Britain to "turn" almost every agent sent into the UK by the Germans and feed false information back on Allied troop movements and military plans. On the other side, lack of imaginative CI (and effective Allied security measures) never led the Germans to question seriously their communications' security. In the post-war era, the immense damage done to Britain's Secret Intelligence Service (SIS) by the Philby debacle stands as another example of the strategic impact of poor CI.

The agency has initiated some reforms in the wake of the Ames debacle but more far-reaching changes are necessary. According to agency spokesmen, the CIA now keeps personnel and security records together (banned before because of privacy considerations) to facilitate the rapid spotting of potential problems. Director Deutch has also increased the institutional status of CI by appointing a new ADDO for Security, and establishing a CI staff integrated with the FBI.[33] Following a major review by an independent commission, the Pentagon has also begun to overhaul its security procedures through rationalization of the clearance process and reducing the number of billets that require access to classified information.

Two further changes, however, need to occur. The first is organizational. Congress should consider a distinct counterintelligence service similar to Britain's MI5. Given the institutional aversion within the CIA to counterintelligence and the traditional animosity between the FBI and the agency, this may be the only way to ensure that CI receives the prominence it deserves. Since the new agency's relationship to the CIA and FBI, as well as its authority over the military, would require precise definition, such an approach will cause considerable bureaucratic difficulties. Still, such a radical change may be necessary to reinforce the importance of CI to those long accustomed to downplaying or ignoring it, as well as to obtaining a staff of dedicated professionals focused *solely* on CI issues.[34]

Yet even major organizational change will not address the CI problem adequately unless CI itself receives a consistently higher priority and status in the minds of the many intelligence professionals who still view it as an unpleasant, police-like function. In a country rightly wary of allowing government too much leeway in investigating individuals, tensions between personal rights and CI requirements will always exist. Nonetheless, the bias against the "CI mentality" within the community must end since, as discussed above, sloppy CI can have disastrous strategic consequences. Efforts to combat this bias can include more training and education, which might raise CI's prestige among officers and attract higher caliber personnel to CI duties. CI processes themselves should receive detailed scrutiny. Perhaps more emphasis on creative investigative techniques that better mesh targeted field investigations with electronic searches and place less emphasis on heavy-handed methods such as the polygraph might prove effective.

## Covert Action

Although it currently accounts for only some 3 percent of the CIA's budget and has represented a small portion of the community's activity, covert action is certainly the most controversial mission of U.S. intelligence. According to one recent commentator, covert action has four distinct aspects: 1) Political Action; 2) Propaganda; 3) Paramilitary Activity; and 4) Intelligence Assistance.[35] Almost all Cold War presidents have seen covert action as a useful tool when conventional diplomacy has failed and military action remains too costly. This was especially true in Latin America from the 1940s through the 1980s, where the United States used its intelligence services as a substitute for the marines whenever possible. In general, the United States used covert action to support friendly governments and attack hostile ones. Three of the most controversial uses of covert action occurred in Latin America: the Guatemala coup of 1954, support to anti-Castro insurgents, and the paramilitary efforts against the Sandinista government during the 1980s. This last project was remarkable in size since the agency organized one of the largest (some 15,000 men) and best-equipped insurgent armies in Latin America since the Mexican Revolution. Since these efforts provoked intense hostility in the region, each was probably of dubious ultimate value in securing America's long-term strategic aims. Moreover, in the case of Nicaragua, the U.S. program provoked a major domestic political crisis.

Yet, covert action has also enjoyed success. Clandestine support of democratic forces in Western Europe, in conjunction with Marshall Plan, helped stabilize that area during the austere and uncertain days of the late 1940s. The most spectacular success took place nearly forty years later when, in the waning days of the Cold War, CIA-orchestrated support to the Afghan resistance, especially delivery of Stinger hand-held SAMs, helped increase the burden of Soviet empire to the point that Gorbachev made withdrawal from Afghanistan a top priority. Moreover, the unpopularity and cost of that war helped to erode the faith in the regime's legitimacy, while further crippling Moscow's economy.

Covert action has, of course, been an instrument of great power politics for centuries. That the world's greatest power should retain such capabilities is evident except perhaps to members of the political extremes. The need for clandestine capabilities to influence events may not be as important as during the struggle against communism, but it will not disappear. Moreover, the CIA should probably retain responsibility for covert action because it has both the personnel and the experience in organizing and running such operations. The ineptitude of some agency paramilitary ventures suggests, however, that the Pentagon should play a larger role in managing such activities. Nonetheless, as Ernest May and others have noted, deep-seated ambivalence about covert action in U.S. culture, as well as the difficulty in maintaining secrecy in an open society, suggests that covert action is a tool only for exceptional circumstances such as neutralization of a terrorist group attempting to obtain nuclear weapons or aid to peoples struggling against invasion against a hostile power, as in Afghanistan.[36] In addition, bipartisan support (through the intelligence committees) must be a precondition for launching any major covert operation. Perhaps the most effective covert action of the Cold War era, aid to the Afghan guerrillas, began under a dovish Democratic administration and concluded under its hawkish Republican successor. If the danger is clear enough, agreement will probably exist.

## Organizational Challenges

The following analysis of structural reform for the intelligence community rests on two assumptions. First, in the absence of a clearly defined strategic threat to the United States, defense spending will shrink over the next five years. Second, despite recent cutbacks and the increasing importance of intelligence to military operations, the intelligence community is still too big. Measured cuts, in conjunction with a reallocation of intelligence "roles and missions," can bring both needed economies and higher value products.

The intelligence structure of the next century should retain CIA to support the Executive Branch and Congress. Like any bureaucracy, CIA has and always will have institutional biases and interests. Nonetheless, the record of military and State Department intelligence analysis during the Cold War underlines the importance of maintaining one intelligence organization free from the pressures of analytic objectivity inherent in any policy-making bureaucracy. Still, as discussed earlier, CIA should focus its analytic efforts on those regions and issues of long-term U.S. interest and avoid becoming overburdened with extraneous tasking it cannot effectively carry out. In addition, like the best corporations, it must make greater use of videoconferencing and other advanced information/communications technologies that permit links to policy makers across the spectrum of government. CIA should also accelerate cuts in its still bloated staff which contains too many unnecessary support organizations and senior managers with too little to do. Its core staff should consist of the best regional and technical experts the government can afford. Finally the Agency should also have a culture that encourages regular contacts with outside consultants and academics who possess competing viewpoints on the more obscure issues or regions that may suddenly become important.

The role of DIA requires reassessment in any reorganization of intelligence organizations. DIA remains an odd combination of CIA-clone and Pentagon step-child. From its inception, service politics never allowed it to realize Robert McNamara's goal of becoming a truly combined defense intelligence organization staffed by high quality personnel.[37] Instead, it evolved into another well-entrenched Washington agency that competes with CIA and delivers products of questionable value to both its military masters and non-military consumers. The CIA (which has performed military analysis of foreign armed forces) and DIA (which does no small amount of political and economic analysis) have increasingly come to resemble each other. Stung by criticism of its effort during the Gulf War, Director Deutch, a former Assistant Secretary of Defense, has established offices led by general officers to improve coordination with the military. To what degree the CIA, as opposed to a more effective DIA, should undertake this role remains questionable.[38]

In fact, there is no need for two national-level assessment organizations with so many overlapping responsibilities. One solution might be to transform DIA into a smaller, more focused agency to provide military-related support to task-oriented groups (organized around policy, technology, or warfighting issues) in the Office of the Secretary of Defense, the Joint Staff, and unified/specified commands. In wartime, its personnel would perform special analytical tasks in support of theater commanders and oversee the flow of intelligence to field commanders. In conjunction with any reorientation of the DIA, however, the Pentagon should undertake a thorough audit of theater and service intelligence staffs to ensure they are providing unique support and not merely duplicating work done elsewhere. In general, such staffs should have a strict focus on targeting, order of battle, and technical issues in their area of responsibility.

Any reform effort must also strengthen the position of the Director of Central Intelligence (DCI). Few would now dispute that the DCI's limited authority over the intelligence community, the bulk of which remains under Pentagon control, results in poor coordination and planning, needless arguments, and wastage of tax dollars. A recent study suggested some important reforms to produce a more streamlined and effective leadership for the whole community. The first would end the distinction between national and tactical program budgets and consolidate both under DCI control. "Technology," the Georgetown report states, "has blurred if not eliminated," the distinction between tactical and strategic systems.[39] Thus, the National Security Agency, the National Reconnaissance Office (NRO), and the new National Imagery Agency under consideration, would come under the DCI as opposed to the Pentagon. The report also recommends that the DCI remain head of CIA where, as the president's chief intelligence advisor, he can oversee clandestine operations and preparation of analysis. Giving the DCI more control over resources now controlled by the Pentagon would provoke howls of outrage in the Department of Defense. Yet, rationalization of the DCI's authority would permit him (or her) to become a more effective advisor to the president and ensure a more effective allocation of resources among community components.

## The Culture Problem

The greatest change that must occur within the intelligence community is cultural. The recasting of corporate culture is the by far the most difficult part of any reengineeering process: no amount of reorganization and refocusing can succeed unless the culture itself undergoes dramatic transformation. The most successful examples of organizational renaissance in industry are those where dynamic leaders have altered cultural patterns through dramatic overhauls of incentive programs, hiring and firing practices, and training courses. Nowhere is the need for such change more apparent than at CIA, whose cultural peculiarities have become glaringly apparent.

Flaws in the Directorate of Operation's culture permitted an incompetent drunkard like Ames to destroy some of the CIA's most sensitive sources. The agency then compounded the impact of Ames' treachery by passing intelligence from double agents to top U.S. policy makers without informing them of the possible compromise.[40] Director Deutch is attempting to change that culture. For example, his appointee as the Director of the Directorate of Operations has moved larger numbers of DI officers into managerial posts as a start. The CIA also claims it is tightening procedures for recruiting and running agents so that the Directorate of Operations will no longer allow sources with dubious background and doubtful ability to remain on its payroll indefinitely. Moreover, Deutch took a step forward by dismissing or demoting those officers whose incompetence led the Guatemala station to protect numerous, and often brutal, military sources who had long lost any intelligence value.[41]

Further reform, especially in training and selection, remains necessary. Deutch's program of change, however, may already be off course. Some reports suggest the agency has placed unrealistic limitations on recruitment following the Guatemala incident such as forbidding contact with *any* individuals suspected of human rights violations.[42] Unfortunately, many of the most valuable human intelligence sources will usually lack advanced Ivy League degrees or deeply held democratic convictions. Instead of trying to keep unpleasant people from becoming U.S. sources, Deutch and successors should ensure that future CIA officers have *intellectual* skills that match the courage and *savoir faire* traditionally possessed by Directorate of Operations personnel. In short, the DO needs a recruitment and training program dedicated to raising the highly uneven quality of its officers, whose educational levels and cultural sophistication vary from exceptional to abysmal. More creative attempts to lure a wide variety of recruits, such as unique training opportunities stressing languages and development of cultural expertise, and more intensive recruiting at top universities nationwide, can help transform the DO's ossified culture.

The intelligence analysis arms of CIA and DOD are in equal need of a cultural transformation. Analytical success, whether in support of policy makers or warfighters, demands flexibility and independence sorely lacking in most bureaucracies, not just those of the intelligence community. Successful corporate reengineering removed superfluous managerial layers and eliminated redundant functions to focus resources on critical tasks and provide individuals the freedom to perform effectively. These individuals, however, must themselves possess the intellectual skills and substantive training to make best use of new opportunities.

The culture of CIA's Directorate of Intelligence (DI) is difficult to define. Like its predecessor, the OSS's Research and Analysis group, much of the DI's culture resembles that of a college faculty, since many CIA analysts are either ex-academics or graduate students who failed to find a job. Understandably, they have often looked to the academy for their intellectual inspiration. In contrast, many other DI recruits, especially during the major expansion of the 1980s, lack advanced academic training and much understanding of foreign cultures, languages, and history. Many younger DI military analysts often do not possess either military experience or any grounding in military history and strategic theory. Historically, the CIA has made it difficult for analysts to improve their skills: it has consistently limited their opportunities for further academic study or sabbaticals. Finally, it has provided its personnel with one of the worst array of training courses of any government agency.[43]

Bizarre management practices have also hindered DI analytical effectiveness. From its inception, the agency has undervalued regional expertise. Analysts move from one regional office to another with relative frequency, a factor that greatly hinders development of any substantive depth. In addition, new analysts often take over accounts about which they know little or nothing since their academic training and experience may have been in a totally different discipline or area. Personnel practices have sought to develop competent generalists whom management can shuttle from position to position, on the assumption that an intelligent individual can quickly become conversant with most issues by "reading in" with message traffic and previous publications upon taking over a new assignment. To be sure, some can meet this challenge but most flounder badly. Too many DI branches contain a small (and perhaps dwindling) cadre of substantive experts and a larger number of non-specialist, career analysts and inexperienced junior personnel.[44]

As most clearly demonstrated by the DI's performance against the USSR, this culture has produced a highly uneven analytical performance. The agency's record is not as universally poor as recent critics, such as Senator Moniyhan, have charged. Recently declassified estimates on Soviet military power indicate that CIA provided much needed balance to highly alarmist assessments of Soviet strategic capabilities by air force intelligence in the late 1950s and early 1960s. Moreover, by the late 1970s, the agency was well aware of many Soviet economic weaknesses and in publicly available analysis stated that Moscow's arthritic command system would face major problems in the coming decade.[45] A 1994 Harvard Study, based on declassified estimates from the 1980s and interviews with senior DI analysts, indicates that by 1989, the agency's views on the Soviet Union's economic, nationality, and political problems were pessimistic enough to cause the National Security Council to establish a "top secret planning group" to examine the possibility of a Soviet collapse. By early 1990, the agency raised the possibility of a hardliner coup against Gorbachev.[46] Thus, although the evidence is not complete, elements of CIA's Soviet analysis, especially during the regime's death throes, were probably more incisive than its critics have claimed.

Still, the debit side of the ledger is extensive. The CIA failed to recognize the scale of the nuclear and conventional buildup launched by Moscow after 1965. Its faulty analysis stemmed from a fundamental misunderstanding of Moscow's military doctrine, especially the Soviet view of deterrence. U.S. military intelligence was generally more astute in estimating the size of the buildup and its impact on Soviet capabilities. Although in the 1970s the agency recognized that the Soviet economy was experiencing substantial problems, a reliance on faulty economic models produced consistent over-estimations of the economy's size, and an underestimation of the damage Moscow was inflicting on itself with massive military spending.[47] Like the academic Sovietologists from whose ranks it often recruited, the Office of Soviet Analysis (SOVA) downplayed emigré reporting in the 1970s and 1980s—reporting which pointed to much greater Soviet political and economic problems.

Moreover, like their academic counterparts, SOVA analysts failed to examine deeper societal issues until the early 1980s. For example, only in 1984 did SOVA establish a branch to examine problems such as bureaucratic ineptitude, crime, and alcoholism, and their impact on societal cohesiveness.[48] Consequently, SOVA underestimated two major trends that eroded the basis of Soviet power: the rise of nationalism and the growing loss of confidence among Soviet elites about the regime's legitimacy and economic viability. In short, SOVA analysts were too reflective of mainstream academic thinking about the USSR. Their shortcomings mirrored a failure of analytical imagination (often combined with intellectual dishonesty and wishful thinking) that characterized most Western academic analyses of the Soviet Union as well as the agency's own analytical rigidity and reluctance to tap unconventional sources of information and expertise.[49]

As with the Directorate of Operations, ensuring analytical excellence at CIA in the post-Cold War era requires a concerted effort to transform the Directorate of Intelligence culture. The community must recruit, develop, and train the best people it can find. Matching private sector salaries, especially in an era of fiscal restraint, is probably not possible, but CIA can offer additional incentives. It should recruit top talent by offering educational inducements (intense training in languages, regional culture, technology), opportunities for increased responsibility, access to senior policy makers, and flexible working arrangements that offer opportunities for publishing articles or books, teaching courses, and going to conferences.

Analyst training in particular must receive higher priority than it has in past. Once again, the private sector paradigm is useful: the most progressive corporations have established comprehensive training programs for their staffs that employ internal and external resources. In a world of rapid change, organizations must have analysts who are constantly upgrading their knowledge. This "learning organization" must, by definition, eschew the isolationism and arrogance that often characterized the old intelligence community, especially CIA.[50] Moreover, analysts must be free to make tough calls and deal directly with their customers. Ideally, a future national intelligence organization would resemble less a bureaucracy than a collection of highly talented individuals linked with each other, their consumers, and outside sources of expertise, in a loose structure that permits a dialogue on key issues. Measures of effectiveness in such an environment would depend less on formal publications and more on intangibles such as responsiveness, and the ability to deliver unique insights supported by facts.[51]

Military intelligence faces a different cultural challenge. Traditionally, the prestige of intelligence within service cultures has been relatively low. Most officers still see intelligence as a support function for the "real" marines, soldiers, sailors, and airmen who drive tanks, sail ships, or fly aircraft. One reflection of this attitude has been the inconsistent quality of DIA's analytical staff. As an organization whose institutional legitimacy the services have consistently questioned, DIA has never attracted the best intelligence personnel. Intelligence components fighting for respect and resources within their own services have refused to send their best to DIA. The Pentagon's recent emphasis on jointness and post-Cold War attempts to consolidate functions, have superficially given DIA more power and prestige. The agency remains, however, one of many competing military intelligence organizations: it is unclear whether additional spending and responsibilities, as opposed to the more precisely defined mission suggested earlier, will improve the quality of its products and services.

In fact, a thorough overhaul of military culture is necessary to accommodate the position intelligence requires in an era of information-dominated warfare. Clearly, further reorganization and rationalization (e.g. elimination of duplicative analysis staffs, curtailment of unnecessary production, better use of reservists), as well as more creative training, are necessary to enable military intelligence to support warfighters and perform crucial peacetime tasks more effectively. What the military must also do, however, is to raise the prestige of intelligence within its institutional cultures. Simply assigning more people or spending more money will not accomplish such a change. Improving the institutional status of intelligence may also require mandatory, baseline intelligence training for all officers, whatever their specialty (much as army officers on the make today have to go to Ranger school). Intelligence officers also require more intensive training in U.S. doctrine and military capabilities. The intelligence arms must, like the CIA, shake off their own insularity and work more closely with their operational counterparts. In short, during the interregnum we may now be entering before the emergence of another great power threat, intelligence may struggle to emerge as a co-equal with more traditional combat arms much as armor and the air services did during the 1920s and 1930s.

## Conclusion: The Reengineering Imperative

The end of the Cold War presents an ideal opportunity to reshape the nation's intelligence community. Like their counterparts in the commercial world, who found that Japanese competition and the pace of technological development had re-written the rules of business, the Soviet Union's collapse offers intelligence reformers the opportunity to effect far-reaching change. They should not hesitate to draw from the experiences of U.S. corporations. First, wholesale personnel cuts and abolition of organizations may play well in the media and with taxpayers eager to starve the bureaucratic beast in Washington. Nonetheless, without a coherent strategy including a thorough re-thinking of the products and processes that support its core capabilities, the intelligence community will likely emerge from any reform effort as a smaller, less efficient version of its current inadequate self. Properly conceived, reform can achieve significant cost reductions and result in more effective organization. The current structure contains so many redundancies that measured cutbacks, reorganizations, and rationalizations are clearly possible. Moreover, opportunities for tighter analytical focus, especially through elimination of collection and analysis requirements on economic, environmental, and other issues better done elsewhere, are also numerous. Concentration on those issues where secret intelligence can deliver unique value can also support personnel reductions and greater efficiency. In addition, more creative use of external sources can compensate for manpower reductions and enhance value through added insights and competitive analysis.

Yet, in making the community more relevant, reformers should not assume that we have entered a world in which democracy's inexorable march has now relegated most international issues to the status of trade disputes. More likely, we are in a transitional, highly fluid period between the Cold War and a more multipolar, and possibly more dangerous, era populated by a combination of major new powers, and a more nebulous collection of terrorist and criminal groups. Thus, reformers should hesitate before making major changes in the community's structure and priorities to support missions unique to this transitional era, such as peace keeping. To be sure, the establishment of organizational, technological, and intellectual flexibility that permits rapid reaction to contingencies during this period is important. Even more crucial, however, is ensuring that U.S. intelligence can provide unmatched support to decision makers wrestling with traditional problems of great power politics, especially if, how, when, and where to use military force. History is by no means a perfect guide, but it is the only one we have in trying to divine the future. If anything, the end of the Cold War has led not to history's demise but its resuscitation. We may expect that in the future, the U.S. and its allies, who currently face no major international challenge, will confront one or more major hostile powers. Thus, reform of the intelligence community must ensure that Washington can anticipate the emergence of such powers, monitor their activities, and, if necessary, confront and neutralize the threats they present.

## Chapter 3

# Friction in Future War*

## Barry D. Watts

### The Once and Future Problem of General Friction

Since the end of the Cold War, there has been growing discussion that technological advances in the means of combat will produce fundamental changes in how future wars will be fought. A number of observers have suggested that the nature of war itself will be transformed. Some proponents of this view have gone so far as to predict that these changes will include great reductions in, if not the outright elimination of, the various impediments to timely and effective action in war for which the Prussian theorist and soldier Carl von Clausewitz introduced the term "friction." Friction in war, of course, has long historical lineage. It predates Clausewitz by centuries and has remained at least a factor in combat outcomes right down to the 1991 Gulf War. Thus, in looking to the future, a seminal question is whether Clausewitzian friction will succumb to the changes in leading-edge warfare that may lie ahead, or whether it reflects more enduring aspects of war that technology can but marginally affect. It is this question that this essay will address.

---

* Editors' note: This article represents a substantial condensation of a longer essay due to the space limitations in the *Brassey's Mershon American Defense Annual*. While we made every effort to retain the heart of the argument, we had to cut three whole sections and much other material.

The earliest known use of the term "friction" to "describe the effect of reality on ideas and intentions in war" by Carl von Clausewitz occurred in a 29 September letter to his future wife, Marie von Brühl, less than three weeks before France defeated Prussia in the twin battles of Jena/Auerstädt in October 1806.[1] By the time Clausewitz died in 1831, his original insight regarding friction's debilitating effects on the campaign of 1806 had grown into a central theme in the unfinished manuscript his widow published as *Vom Kriege (On War)*.[2]

American military officers today most often refer to Clausewitz's unified concept of a general friction as the "fog and friction" of war.[3] The diverse impediments to the effective use of military force that those with military experience instinctively associate with this phrase are generally acknowledged to have played significant roles in all the wars since Clausewitz's time. Even in a conflict as pervaded with advanced weaponry as the 1991 war in the Persian Gulf, there was no shortage of friction at all levels—tactical, operational, strategic, or, even, political. Indeed, close examination of Desert Storm suggests that the frictional impediments experienced by the winning side did not appreciably differ in scope or "magnitude" than those encountered by the Germans during their lightning conquest of France and the Low Countries during May 1940.

This historical persistence of friction, despite vast changes in the means of war since Clausewitz's time, suggests that his concept reflects more than a transitory or contingent feature of continental warfare during the Napoleonic era. Yet, as we think about war in the next century, nothing precludes us from wondering whether the scope or magnitude of Clausewitzian friction may change. Some within the U.S. military suggest that foreseeable advances in surveillance and information technologies will sufficiently lift "the fog of war" to enable future American commanders to "see and understand everything on a battlefield."[4] Nor are military officers alone in this view. In a six-month evaluation of a possible "Military Technical Revolution" by a Washington think tank, participants concluded that "what the [Military Technical Revolution] promises, more than precision attacks and laser beams, is...to imbue the information loop with near-perfect clarity and accuracy, to reduce its operation to a matter of minutes or seconds, and—perhaps most important of all—to deny it in its entirety to the enemy."[5]

These forecasts raise at least three first order questions about Clausewitz's concept of general friction. First, is it likely, contrary to what Clausewitz might have thought, that general friction does not represent an inherent feature of the violent interaction between contending political entities that we call war? Second, even if friction is an enduring, structural feature of combat, can technological advances appreciably reduce the aggregate frictions experienced by opposing sides in future conflicts? Third, do either wars since Clausewitz's time or foreseeable advances in the means of waging future wars demand major modifications in the original concept? Or alternatively, how might Clausewitz's concept change if interpreted in light of contemporary knowledge—particularly from the standpoint of disciplines such as evolutionary biology and nonlinear dynamics?

To establish a common baseline for discussion the next section of this essay reviews the evolution of friction in Clausewitz's thought. The discussion will then clarify and extend the taxonomy of Clausewitz's mature concept.

The next step in the argument is to subject this baseline understanding of general friction to the test of empirical evidence. What does the Persian Gulf War suggest about the persistence of Clausewitzian friction as recently as 1991? Further does friction's role in that conflict provide any grounds for concluding that its potential role or "magnitude" has appreciably diminished since World War II?

Having examined friction's role in past wars, the remainder of the essay addresses its prospective role in *future* conflicts. The discussion from this point on aims at building a case for three conclusions. First, the prospects of eliminating general friction appear quite dim because friction gives every evidence of being a built-in feature of combat. Second, whether technological advances in the means of combat can appreciably reduce friction's overall magnitude for one side or the other is less important than whether such advances facilitate being able to shift the *relative* balance of friction between opponents more in one's favor. Third and last, recasting Clausewitz's concept in contemporary terms is a useful step toward better understanding its likely role in future war regardless of what one may conclude about the possibility of either side eliminating its frictional impediments altogether.

Since we have no direct evidence about future conflicts, the case for these judgments will have to be indirect. Arguments for friction's undiminished persistence in future war will, therefore, have to be constructed on the basis of related structural limitations in other areas. For example, the inaccessibility to central economic planners of all the information needed to run a national economy more efficiently than market forces driven by a myriad of individual choices reveals an economic "friction" comparable to that inherent in the conduct of war by military institutions. Moreover, the limitations built into mankind by biological evolution provide sources of general friction that seems likely to persist as long as the human race does. Finally, the contemporary understanding of nonlinear dynamics suggests how nonlinearities built into combat processes can render the course and outcome of conflict unpredictable in the long run by repeatedly magnifying the effects of differences between our constructs of unfolding military operations and their actuality.

## Clausewitz's Development of a Unified Concept of General Friction

From first use in 1806 to the final revisions of *On War*, friction was among the conceptual tools that Clausewitz employed in his efforts to understand the phenomena of war. When Clausewitz first invoked the term "friction" in a letter written in the field with the Prussian Army, his aim was to voice his growing anxiety over the resistance that his mentor, General Gerhard von Scharnhorst, was encountering to any all-out, bold, or well-conceived employment of Prussia's military potential to avert defeat by the French.[6] Hindsight fully justified his anxiety. Prussia's defeat at Jena/Auerstädt destroyed the army created by Fredrick the Great and reduced Prussia to a French satellite.[7] Yet, when Clausewitz first used *Friktion*, he could only guess the outcome of the campaign. Thus, this first reference to friction in its historical context refers to the powerful resistance to sound decisions and effective action that developed *within* the Prussian Army itself before the catastrophe occurred.

Over the next six years Clausewitz expanded the original notion, identifying other sources for the vast differences that he and Scharnhorst saw between theory, plans, and intentions in war and war as it actually unfolds.[8] By 1811, for example, one of Clausewitz's lectures at the *Kriegsakademie* mentioned two distinct sources for "the friction of the whole machinery": "the numerous chance events, which touch everything, and...the numerous difficulties that inhibit accurate execution of the precise plans that theory tends to formulate."[9] The latter source—internal resistance to precise plans—recalls the type of friction first mentioned in Clausewitz's 1806 letter. But the other source—the play of chance—represents a significant exposition of the original notion. By April of the following year, shortly before he resigned his Prussian commission to switch sides and oppose both his own monarch and the French in their 1812 invasion of Russia, he had pushed the concept further. In an essay Clausewitz sent to his pupil, the crown prince of Prussia, he now listed eight major sources of the "tremendous friction" that makes even the simplest plans and actions so difficult to execute in war: 1) insufficient knowledge of the enemy; 2) rumors (information gathered by remote observation or spies); 3) uncertainty about one's own strength and position; 4) the uncertainties that cause friendly troops to exaggerate their own difficulties; 5) differences between expectations and reality; 6) the fact that one's own army is never as strong as it appears on paper; 7) the difficulties in keeping an army supplied; and 8) the tendency to change or abandon well-thought-out plans when confronted with the vivid physical images and perceptions of the battlefield.[10] Although the list lacks the conceptual clarity exhibited by Clausewitz in his unified conception of general friction in *On War*, it goes well beyond the letter of 1806 and represents Clausewitz's first systematic development of friction, including its positive as well as negative aspects.[11]

Undoubtedly the difficulties and frictions he experienced with the Russian Army in 1812 and over the course of the last three years of the Napoleonic wars "strengthened his already pronounced realism," and thereby reinforced his intellectual passion to find a comprehensive way to "distinguish real war from war on paper."[12] In the unfinished manuscript published as *On War* —a work that "almost completely" occupied his last twelve years[13]—friction became Clausewitz's central theoretical concern. As one commentator has noted, it "runs through the entire work."[14] The thrust of the opening chapter—the only one of 125 chapters that Clausewitz judged complete on his death—highlights friction's pivotal role.[15] In response to the chapter's title, "What is War?", Clausewitz attempts to abstract war's essence from its pure concept by establishing the properties that war must have. Reflecting on the concept, he concludes that war is the use of force to compel the enemy to do our will. From this *theoretical* conclusion, it is only a short step to the equally theoretical implication that, since war is an act of force, "there is no logical limit to the application of that force."[16] In the sixth section of Chapter 1 ("MODIFICATIONS IN PRACTICE"), however, Clausewitz juxtaposes this implication of pure theory with the empirical fact that in the real world "the whole thing looks quite different."[17] He then examines the validity of this empirical modification of war's abstract essence in a series of short sections whose titles alone indicate the inadequacy of any purely theoretical conclusions about war: "7. WAR IS NEVER AN ISOLATED ACT...8. WAR DOES NOT CONSIST OF A SINGLE SHORT BLOW...9. IN WAR THE RESULT IS NEVER FINAL...10. THE PROBABILITIES OF REAL LIFE REPLACE THE EXTREME AND THE ABSOLUTE REQUIRED BY THEORY...11. THE POLITICAL OBJECT NOW COMES TO THE FORE AGAIN...12. ANY INTERRUPTION OF MILITARY ACTIVITY IS NOT EXPLAINED BY ANYTHING YET SAID." The last section introduces the problem of the suspension of activity often observed in actual war, and in response sections 13–20 emphasize the crucial role that imperfect knowledge and chance play in making "the whole thing look quite different." With this difficulty in hand, Clausewitz concludes: "In short, absolute, so-called mathematical factors never find a firm basis in military calculations. From the very start there is an interplay of possibilities, probabilities, good luck and bad that weaves its way throughout the length and breadth of the tapestry."[18]

The pattern of argument, then, is one of contrast between military theories, plans, or intentions and war as it actually is. The role of general friction in Clausewitz's theoretical writings must be understood in this context. To repeat the oft-cited definition given in Chapter 7, Book I of *On War*: the unified concept of general friction alone "more or less corresponds to the factors that distinguish real war from war on paper."[19] The diverse sources of general friction are the things that render action in war "like movement in a resistant element" and "span the gap between the pure concept of war and the concrete form that, as a general rule, war assumes."[20] From Clausewitz's first use of the term friction to his final revisions of the manuscript we know as *On War*, friction was unquestionably among the conceptual tools he employed to grasp the phenomena of war. Friction was not simply a notion Clausewitz toyed with from time to time. Rather, the idea of 1806 grew over the course of more than two decades into a theoretical concept that lies at the heart of his mature approach to the theory and conduct of war.

## Clausewitz's Mature Concept of General Friction

The account of friction in *On War* contains two interlocking difficulties: the absence of a reasonably exhaustive taxonomy of general friction's various components; and Clausewitz's confusing use of the term "friction" to refer both to the unified concept as well as to one of general friction's sources. The easiest way to clarify, much less extend, his original concept is to resolve these difficulties, and the place to begin is with what Clausewitz calls "the atmosphere of war." The first book of *On War* offers two lists of the various things that coalesce to form the atmosphere of war:

| *Chapter 3, Book I:* | *Chapter 8, Book I:* |
| --- | --- |
| 1. danger | 1. danger |
| 2. exertion | 2. physical exertion |
| 3. uncertainty | 3. intelligence |
| 4. chance[21] | 4. friction[22] |

What do these lists represent? Ignoring for the moment the discrepancies in the last two places of both lists and the confusing occurrence of "friction" in the second, the obvious answer is that these lists detail various elements or sources of general friction. This interpretation can be readily confirmed by observing that *On War* unambiguously identifies danger, physical exertion, intelligence, and chance (construed as the countless minor incidents that one can never foresee) as sources or components of friction in the inclusive sense of the unified concept that distinguishes real war from war on paper.[23]

Next, can the apparent discrepancies in the third and fourth places be resolved? The easiest way to begin answering this question is to consider first Clausewitz's detailed descriptions of danger and physical exertion as sources of general friction. A close reading of Chapter 4 in *On War*'s first book, titled "On Danger in War," reveals that the phenomenon at issue consists of the debilitating effects that the threat of imminent death or mutilation in battle has on the ability of combatants at every level to think clearly and act effectively. Physical exertion is much the same. The extraordinary physical demands of combat impede clear thought or effective action. For a sense of what danger and exertion have meant even on late twentieth century battlefields, the reader needs look no further than the searing account of the battles fought by two air-mobile infantry battalions of the 1st Cavalry Division in the Ia Drang Valley against three North Vietnamese regiments in November 1965; or, for an equally riveting narrative drawn from armored combat, the reader might consider Avigdor Kahalani's description of the Israeli Army's Battalion 77 on the Golan Heights in October 1973.[24]

Turning to "intelligence" versus "uncertainty," *On War* initially explains the former as "every sort of information about the enemy and his country— the basis, in short, of our own plans and operations."[25] But Clausewitz turns quickly to the uncertainties and imperfections that pervade the information on which action in war unavoidably rests. Among other things, imperfect knowledge of a combat situation can lead to mistaken judgments on whether to act at all.[26] The seeming discrepancy between the third items in the two lists is, therefore, more apparent than real. Perhaps all that one needs to add from a contemporary perspective is that in light of the fundamental role played by uncertainty in fields like quantum mechanics and information theory, uncertainty is the deeper, more fundamental concept of the two and seems the preferable term.

What about "chance" versus "friction" at the end of both lists? Here the discrepancy is more substantive. The opening paragraph of Chapter 7, "FRICTION IN WAR," seems to emphasize the unified conception of general friction. It focuses on the overarching or inclusive concept of friction, not on one of general friction's components. By contrast the second and fourth paragraphs—and all of the third save for the opening sentence—focus on friction "in the narrow sense," which Peter Paret interprets as "the impediments to smooth action produced by the thousands of individuals who make up an army."[27] How might one understand these divergent aspects of general friction? Friction in the narrow sense is certainly a robust source of resistance to effective action in war. But it is not at all obvious that one can identify this source of friction with chance in the sense of unforeseeable accidents, the play of good and bad luck, that run throughout the tapestry of war. Chance is unquestionably a legitimate source of general friction in its own right, and seems distinct from friction in the narrow sense.

This analysis suggests that we replace Clausewitz's four-item lists of friction's sources with a composite one containing five components:

1. Danger's impact on the ability to think clearly and act effectively in war;

2. The effects on thought and action of combat's demands for exertion;

3. Uncertainties and imperfections in the information on which action in war is unavoidably based;

4. Friction in the narrow sense of the internal resistance to effective action stemming from the many men and machines making up one's own forces; and

5. The play of chance, of good and bad luck.

Yet is even this taxonomy of general friction complete? If one construes the general concept as all the disparate things that distinguish real war from war on paper, it is not difficult to find other important and distinct sources of general friction in *On War*. Consider, once again, Clausewitz's argument in his first chapter as to why the actual conduct of war falls so far short of the maximum possible application of violence implicit in the theoretical concept. One of his reasons concerns the spatial and temporal limitations on employment of military force in the Napoleonic era: "WAR DOES NOT CONSIST OF A SINGLE SHORT BLOW." In an age of intercontinental, thermonuclear weapons, these *physical* limits may be considerably less than in Napoleon's day. Nevertheless, physical limits remain even with thermonuclear weapons, and to these physical limits one must add the *political* constraint of war's necessary subordination to policy. In the final analysis, the reason why the United States and the Soviet Union did not use nuclear weapons during the Cold War was that policy makers on both sides came to realize that an all-out nuclear exchange could serve no useful end.[28] Thus, physical and, above all, political limits to the unrestricted use of military force offer another source of general friction.

One can cull at least two more sources of general friction from the pages of *On War*. In Book II, which discusses the theory of war, Clausewitz emphasizes the unpredictability of interaction with the enemy stemming from the opponent's independent will.[29] The last source of friction in *On War* lies in Clausewitz's injunctions in Book VIII that the *means* must be suited to the *ends*.[30] Perhaps the most telling twentieth century case is the U.S. intervention in Vietnam. While the widely accepted view that the war was unwinnable entails a degree of determinism seldom warranted in human affairs, neither the U.S. Army's firepower intensive, "search and destroy" approach, nor the incremental bombing of North Vietnam, could build a viable South Vietnamese nation. The critical point as Scharnhorst said of the War of the First Coalition, was that "one side had everything to lose, the other little."[31]

With these three additions one can reconstruct Clausewitz's "unified conception of a general friction [*Gesamtbegriff einer allgemeinen Friktion* ]" as follows:

1. danger;

2. physical exertion;

3. uncertainties and imperfections in the information on which action in war is based;

4. chance;

5. friction in the narrow sense of the resistance within one's own forces;

6. physical and political limits to the use of military force;

7. unpredictability stemming from interaction with the enemy; and

8. disconnects between ends and means in war.

This taxonomy clearly goes well beyond customary interpretations of *On War*. It suggests a view of general friction closer to what Clausewitz might have reached if he had lived long enough to revise *On War* to his satisfaction.

This essay began with three questions about Clausewitzian friction. 1) Is it a structural feature of war or something more transitory? 2) Even if friction cannot be eliminated altogether, can its magnitude for one adversary or the other be substantially reduced by technological advances? 3) What might Clausewitz's original notion look like if formulated in the language and concepts of contemporary disciplines like nonlinear dynamics? While we are not yet far enough along to offer full answers, the reconstruction of Clausewitz's general concept suggests some preliminary observations. Regarding the first question, Scharnhorst and Clausewitz's staunch refusal to accept that any theories, systems, or principles of war could eliminate chance suggests that, in their view, friction was a built-in, structural feature of violent conflict between nation states. From the lowest-ranking soldier to generals and field marshals, friction was a force with which combatants on both sides had to cope.

Yet, turning to the second question, Clausewitz himself suggested "lubricants" to ease the "abrasion" or resistance that friction caused for one's own military operations. *On War* mentions combat experience, maneuvers sufficiently realistic to train officers' judgment for coping with friction, and the genius of a leader like Napoleon as viable means of reducing general friction within one's own forces.[32] The German general staff system's emphasis on individual initiative and judgment, for which Scharnhorst deserves considerable credit, constituted an institutional lubricant to general friction. And there are at least hints in *On War* that elements like chance could provide opportunities to exploit friction's "equally pervasive force … on the enemy's side."[33] Thus, Scharnhorst and Clausewitz evidently believed that the relative balance of friction between two opponents could be manipulated to one's own advantage, even if they were skeptical about driving up enemy friction as opposed to reducing one's own.

As for the third question, friction, like Clausewitz's notion of center of gravity, was undoubtedly borrowed from Newtonian physics via Kantian concerns about how physics was possible. *On War* invokes the mechanistic image of an army as a machine whose internal friction "cannot, as in mechanics, be reduced to a few points."[34] Nonetheless, it is evident from our final list of general friction's sources that, over time, his unified concept moved increasingly away from its mechanistic origins. Indeed, not one of the entries in the reconstructed taxonomy is inherently mechanical. Moreover, all, including chance, ultimately reduce to phenomena that affect the ability of human beings to think clearly and act effectively in war. Consequently, general friction may have more in common with twentieth-century fields like nonlinear dynamics and neo-Darwinian syntheses of evolutionary biology than first meets the eye.

## The Undiminished Persistence of General Friction in the Gulf War

Has general friction remained a continuing feature of war since Clausewitz's time? If so, is there any evidence that the "magnitude" of its influence has changed appreciably in recent decades? A minimalist response would simply note that military history since Napoleon has consistently and strongly confirmed the persistence of general friction. Such a minimalist response, however, will not satisfy those lacking either first-hand experience with military operations or in-depth familiarity with military history (particularly twentieth-century military campaigns). Nor does it offer any insight into the possibility that the "magnitude" of general friction's influence on combat processes may have changed. Operation Desert Storm provides an obvious case study through which we might address these questions. First, it is the most recent, large-scale conflict available. Second, coalition forces employed many of the most technologically advanced military systems in existence, including satellite communications and reconnaissance, direct-attack and stand-off precision-guided weapons, as well as stealth aircraft. Third, the author, having led the operations and effects portion of the Gulf War Air Power Survey, arguably has as good a grasp as most on the events that occurred during the forty-three day campaign, particularly in the air.[35]

At the tactical level of the air campaign, even a cursory examination of day-to-day operations suggests that general friction was a consistent feature of the war. Aircrews had to cope with equipment malfunctions, inadequate mission planning materials, lapses in intelligence on targets and enemy defenses, coordination problems between strike and support aircraft (including a number of F-111F sorties aborted due to aircraft being unable to find tankers for prestrike refueling[36]), target and time-on-target changes after take-off, unanticipated changes in prewar tactics, adverse weather, a lack of timely bomb damage assessment, and, in many wings, minimal understanding of what higher headquarters was trying to accomplish from one day to the next. None of these problems were new in 1991. Indeed, the author personally experienced virtually every one of them flying F-4s over Vietnam during 1967 and 1968.

Two examples should suffice to substantiate friction's seemingly undiminished pervasiveness at the tactical level during Desert Storm. After the initial three days of actual operations (17–19 January), coalition air commanders began to shift all low-level bombing operations to medium altitude to minimize losses to Iraqi low-altitude air defenses.[37] While this decision did not appreciably affect the accuracy of laser-guided bombs delivered by F-111Fs or F-117s, it substantially degraded the visual-bombing accuracy of platforms like the F-16 and F/A-18 as pilots began releasing their unguided bombs from altitudes well above 10,000 feet.[38] Since F-16 and F/A-18 pilots predominately employed unguided munitions, this restriction severely limited their ability to hit targets such as bridges, fiber-optic cable junctions, or dug-in Iraqi armor until the restriction against low-altitude employment was lifted at the beginning of the coalition's ground offensive. Thus, the combination of coalition sensibility to losses, coupled with the impracticality of eliminating more than a fraction of the Iraqi low-level anti-aircraft defenses, unexpectedly and seriously impeded the bombing accuracy of coalition aircraft. During the Vietnam War, most air-to-ground bombing was done manually or with very early computerized bombing systems. As in 1991, staying high enough to avoid losses to low-altitude AAA systematically degraded bombing accuracies.

Adverse weather, which Clausewitz explicitly associated with friction in *On War*, offers another unambiguous example of the frictional impediments to the execution of plans and intentions in Desert Storm.[39] Weather substantially disrupted operations, especially in the early days of the air campaign and during the ground offensive at the war's end. On the second and third nights of the war, more than half of the planned F-117 strikes aborted or were unsuccessful due to low clouds over Baghdad. On the second day of the ground campaign (25 February 1991), weather forced the cancellation of all F-117 sorties.[40] So disruptive were the cumulative effects of adverse weather that the coalition's head air planner, (then) Brigadier General Buster Glosson viewed weather as his "number-one problem" and, by implication, as a greater impediment than the Iraqi Air Force.[41] Similar assessments of weather's disruptive or frictional influence on air operations can be found as far back as World War II. In reflecting on the Combined Bomber Offensive against Nazi Germany during 1943–1945, Major General Haywood Hansell observed in 1972 that "weather was actually a greater hazard and obstacle than the German Air Force."[42]

Tactical-level friction was unquestionably far worse on the Iraqi side. If coalition air forces found themselves knee-deep in "tactical frictions," the Iraqis drowned in them. In air-to-air combat, the Iraqis suffered thirty-three losses in exchange for the single coalition fighter believed lost on the first night.[43] So quickly did the Iraqis lose control of their own airspace that over the forty-three days of fighting, they are known to have mounted only two air-to-surface attack sorties against coalition targets, and a Saudi F-15 shot down both of the Mirage F-1s involved prior to weapons release.[44] The domination of coalition forces is, if anything, even more apparent in sortie comparisons: by the end of Desert Storm, coalition fighter and bomber crews had flown over 68,000 shooter sorties in comparison to considerably less than 1,000 for the Iraqis.[45] In fairness, the Iraqi Air Force was not designed to deal with an adversary as large and as capable as coalition air forces, nor did it seriously attempt to contest control of the air. Instead, Iraqi airmen seem to have hoped to impose some losses on their opponents, while riding out coalition air strikes, if not the war, inside their hardened aircraft shelters.[46] Imagine, then, the shock—and friction—imposed on Iraqi squadrons when over the night of 22/23 January coalition aircraft began taking out individual shelters with laser-guided bombs.[47]

Coalition air power imposed a similar shock on Iraqi ground forces. Saddam Hussein had not planned to rely on his air force but, instead, to bank on

his army to inflict so many casualties on coalition ground units that his enemies would not be able to stand the pain. His model of future combat was the
kind of bloody ground battle of attrition that had dominated the Iran-Iraq
War.[48] When in late January 1991 Saddam ordered the probing attacks that
precipitated the Battle of Khafji, his premise was that Iraqi ground forces
could move at night, a view that proved disastrously wrong over the night of
30/31 January. When an E-8 Joint STARS (Joint Surveillance Target Attack
Radar System) detected two Iraqi brigades on roads in Eastern Kuwait moving south, coalition air power inflicted such devastating destruction that both
units halted before they could even reach the Saudi border.[49] Further, while
the inability of Iraqi ground forces to move at night was a tactical issue, it had
profound implications for Iraqi strategy. In retrospect, Saddam's only viable
military option after Desert Storm began was to force an early start to the
ground war before coalition air attacks exhausted his own troops. That this
gambit failed in late January and was never attempted again underlines how
much coalition air power dominated the military outcome and illustrates that
unexpected frictional impediments can have operational and strategic consequences as well. This last point suggests that the impact of friction on the
Iraqi war effort was not only far higher than on the coalition's at the tactical
level, but at the operational and strategic levels as well. In this sense, general
friction's manifestations go far to explain both the failure of Iraqi strategy in
the Gulf War and the lop-sided military outcome. These observations should
not tempt the reader to conclude that coalition forces encountered little, if
any, friction at the operational and strategic levels. Although coalition friction was certainly less at these levels as well, it was by no means absent.

Consider coalition efforts during the Persian Gulf War to destroy Iraq's
nuclear program. The coalition's publicly stated goal of promoting the "security and the stability of the Persian Gulf" provided the political basis for trying to eliminate this program with military means.[50] By the eve of Desert
Storm, destruction of Iraq's nuclear, chemical, and biological warfare capabilities, including research, production, and storage facilities, had become an
explicit objective of the air campaign.[51] Indeed, U.S. Central Command's
operations order for the campaign identified these capabilities as one of Iraq's
"three primary centers of gravity."[52] Destruction of Iraq's nuclear program was
primarily a postwar rather than a wartime objective since coalition air planners and intelligence correctly believed that the Iraqis could not yet field even
a crude nuclear device. Targeting of the program in Desert Storm aimed,
therefore, to inflict sufficient destruction on nuclear-related facilities that Iraq
would need many years to reconstitute a viable nuclear development effort.[53]

This seemingly straightforward targeting problem foundered not only on
inadequate intelligence about individual targets but, more importantly, on

coalition misunderstanding of the target system as a whole. The problem went deeper than the failing to identify even half the geographic locations containing nuclear or nuclear-related facilities by the war's end.[54] By the late 1980s, most observers in the West believed that the Iraqi nuclear program had gone dormant after the Israeli destruction in 1981 of the French-supplied *Osirak* reactor under construction at Al Tuwaitha. The truth of the matter was quite different. As international inspectors discovered after the Gulf War, the Iraqis had responded to the Israeli attack by restructuring their program to minimize its vulnerability to accurate bombing. The decision that fundamentally transformed the program was to shift their efforts to developing enriched-uranium, rather than plutonium, weapons, thereby eliminating dependence on reactors for weapons-grade material.[55] Far from abandoning their nuclear aspirations in 1981 the Iraqis embarked on a clandestine, lavishly funded, and highly redundant program.[56] Deception of International Atomic Energy Agency inspectors, extensive concealment and dispersement, compartmentalization, the use of middlemen and front companies to import needed elements, and, even, construction of decoy facilities formed portions of a national-level program.[57] These efforts to hide their intentions from the outside world succeeded: through the final days of Desert Storm, the true *nature* or *functionality* of Baghdad's nuclear program was not suspected by coalition commanders and military planners, much less grasped.

As a result, coalition air forces were unable to target the Iraqi nuclear program effectively during Desert Storm, much less destroy it. Even with laser-guided bombs, aircrew still have to know where to aim and at what they are aiming. To compound the frictional impediments further, the Iraqis displayed a surprising capacity to evacuate, disperse, and hide program elements, including nuclear material, once the campaign began.[58] The upshot was that while Desert Storm halted Iraqi work on nuclear weapons, inflicted some damage, and caused the dispersal of many program elements, coalition bombing failed to achieve the objective of eliminating Iraq's nuclear program. The crux of this failure, moreover, lay in classic manifestations of Clausewitzian friction; coalition failure to grasp the nature of the target system reinforced by prodigious Iraqi efforts to conceal its nuclear ambitions from the outside world. Admittedly, the magnitude of the coalition's military success by 28 February 1991 created a postwar situation in which perhaps the most intrusive compliance regime imposed on a sovereign state since the postwar occupations of Nazi Germany and Imperial Japan eventually achieved the goal of limiting Iraq's nuclear threat. But what one cannot deny is that general friction prevented coalition forces from achieving their stated operational and political goals regarding Iraq's nuclear-weapon program during the war.[59]

A similar fate befell the coalition's operational goal of "destroying" Iraq's Republican Guard, identified by the theater commander, General H. Norman Schwarzkopf, as a primary center of gravity for Saddam's regime. Despite U.S. Army doctrinal emphasis on synchronization, the timing between the marine-led holding attack in the east, whose objective was to reach Kuwait City, and the multi-corps "left-hook" from the west, which aimed at destroying the Republican Guard, was substantially out of "synch" in execution. Third Army's VII and XVIII Airborne Corps were to take "seven to ten days" to execute the left hook and destroy the Republican Guard, whereas the Marines, more cognizant of actual Iraqi capabilities after the fighting at Khafji in late January, replanned their attack to reach Kuwait City within three days and, in the event achieved their objective.[60] To make matters worse, when the coalition ground offensive kicked off at 0400 on 24 February, Third Army initially stuck with its plan to delay the advance of its heavy units for twenty-four hours.[61]

As early as 0840 on the opening day of the ground offensive, however, Schwarzkopf received reports of Iraqi demolitions in Kuwait City indicative of withdrawal preparations and called Lt. Gen. John Yesock, Third Army Commander, to obtain his views on scrapping the original timetable and attacking early with heavy forces.[62] They moved the attacks by VII Corps up to 1500 on the 24th. As darkness approached on 24 February, VII Corps commander, Lt. Gen. Frederick Franks, after consulting with his divisional commanders, elected to stop the advance until daybreak.[63] Regardless of the reasons for the delay, the decision did not reflect the theater commander's intent. As the Third Army historian noted later, "a gap had begun to open between the tactical operations Franks was fighting in the field and the operations Schwarzkopf envisioned in the basement of the Ministry of Defense."[64] This frictional gap widened as the ground war unfolded. Indeed, by the fourth day of the campaign Schwarzkopf "did not know where his leading forces actually were."[65] This single gap between intentions and reality in the Gulf War explains much about why coalition ground forces failed to destroy Iraq's Republican Guard despite the immense tactical success of the coalition's 100-hour ground offensive.[66] Another critical incidence of friction bearing on the outcome was the gap between the coalition ground commanders' belief that the Iraqis would stand and fight and actual enemy's behavior: beginning on the night of 25/26 February, the Iraqis began a wholesale withdrawal.[67]

These two frictions were compounded by others. The coalition's ground offensive occurred during some of the worst weather of the campaign. Because none of the Iraqi armored and mechanized units ended up fighting from the positions they had occupied prior to 24 February, considerable uncertainty developed within XVIII Airborne and VII Corps as to their locations by 26

February.[68] Further, there was no time in an operation that ended in 100 hours to calibrate the accuracy of reports from those doing the fighting. More crucially, the difficulties in coordination between ground and air, especially on 27 February, undermined the effective use of air power to prevent the escape of the Republican Guard and armored forces. In spite of a rapidly changing situation, army commanders stuck to their original plan of destroying Republican Guard heavy units by smashing headlong into them with a multi-divisional phalanx of armored and mechanized units rather than first encircling the Iraqi forces and then destroying them at leisure.[69] The army's operational concept, which emphasized synchronization between units aimed at presenting no flanks, was a doctrinal preference quite at odds with the battlefield practice of leading World War II armored commanders such as Heinz Guderian, Hermann Balck, George Patton, and John S. Wood.[70] As such, the preference for synchronization exemplifies friction in the narrow sense and harks back to Clausewitz's original usage of the term in 1806.

The picture that emerges of the coalition's ground offensive, then, is one of multiple frictions, often worsening as the offensive unfolded. From this perspective, the *cumulative* balance appears more than adequate to explain how and why coalition commanders failed to achieve their operational objective of destroying the Republican Guard. Schwarzkopf implied after the war that his intention had been to inflict sufficient damage on Republican Guard forces so that they would no longer represent "a threat to any other nation."[71] The return of U.S. forces to the Gulf when T-72-equipped Republican Guard forces that had escaped destruction in 1991 again menaced Kuwait in October 1994 provides compelling evidence that Schwarzkopf's command failed to achieve this objective.

In sum, scrutiny of Desert Storm indicates that Clausewitzian friction persisted at every level. Even for the coalition, general friction had operational and strategic consequences, not merely tactical effects. Moreover, none of the specific frictional impediments encountered—from adverse weather and faulty intelligence to the U.S. army's infatuation with synchronization—would be unfamiliar to Clausewitz.

What about the overall magnitude of general friction in 1991 compared to that in earlier conflicts? The most revealing "quantity" would be the differential between coalition friction and Iraqi friction. However, especially at the operational and strategic levels, no overall metric for estimating such a quantity obviously exists. Merely describing such a metric—even if just in qualitative terms—would be hard given the likelihood that frictional imbalances between opponents could fluctuate considerably over the course of a campaign. Very likely, estimating the relevant quantities would be even harder in specific historical cases—especially for purposes of comparisons spanning decades. Nonetheless, it seems reasonable to suggest that the frictional differential between victor and vanquished in 1991 was not appreciably different from that experienced by the opposing sides in the *blitzkrieg* campaign of May 1940. Both produced lop-sided victories in which the winning side's friction was palpably less than the loser's. Yet, in each case, friction at the operational and strategic levels also left the winning side short of what it might have achieved: in 1940 some 338,000 Allied troops escaped from Dunkirk harbor and the surrounding beaches to fight another day, much as happened with elements of the Republican Guard in 1991.[72] Thus, over the half century spanning 1940–1991, it seems likely, on the evidence, that friction has not only persisted, but persisted relatively undiminished in magnitude.

## The Inaccessibility of Critical Information

Granting that Clausewitzian friction prevented coalition forces from achieving important operational-strategic goals despite Desert Storm's lopsided outcome, why should one take the next step and infer that technological advances in the future will be unable to find any enduring solution to the historical problem of friction? The direct evidence just presented of general friction's evidently undiminished persistence as recently as 1991 is of little avail regarding friction's *future* role under the premise of technological progress. Direct empirical evidence from wars still to be fought, after all, is unobtainable. Nonetheless, one can find evidence in fields as diverse as economics, evolutionary biology, and nonlinear dynamics for suspecting that many real-world processes, including physical ones, can exhibit structural unpredictability.[73] Since this sort of inherent unpredictability is part and parcel of what Clausewitz subsumed under his unified concept of a general friction, confirmation of similar, if not related, unpredictabilities in fields far from war would begin to build a case for the conclusion that Clausewitzian friction will persist regardless of technological progress. Of course, direct evidence and arguments cannot underpin a case grounded on the ubiquity of unpredictable processes. Like evolutionary biologists, who cannot directly observe the workings of natural selection, we shall have to rely on *indirect* arguments.[74] The first of these indirect arguments arises from considering the inaccessibility of critical economic information.

The initial argument for general friction's robust persistence in the future stems from the distribution of information within very complex systems such as market economies or the earth's biosphere. In both cases, even fundamental information regarding the underlying adaptive processes (or adaptations) is, for all practical purposes, inaccessible at particular places and times.[75] Comparable levels of information involved in the orchestration of combat within any reasonably large volume of "battlespace" exhibit precisely the same inaccessibility due to their distribution in space and, especially, time. Even granting the enormous advances in information systems and related technologies expected to occur in coming decades, the temporal distribution of critical information bearing on the conduct and effectiveness of military operations alone seems sufficient to ensure not only the future persistence of general friction, but to raise doubts about the possibility of reducing its overall magnitude and impact.

One place to begin building a case for this conclusion is the work of the economist Friedrich von Hayek. Hayek was perhaps the twentieth century's greatest champion of the extended, spontaneous order of human cooperation that constitutes market or capitalist economies. Over a career spanning six decades, he became the foremost critic of socialist economics. He argued that ultimately the aims and programs associated with centrally directed economies were "factually impossible to achieve or execute [and] ... logically impossible."[76] At the core of his mature economic philosophy lies the notion that the market represents an evolutionary process of discovery (or adaptation) whose primary function is the gathering and processing of dispersed, unsurveyable information:

> Modern economies are vastly complicated. Somehow they must process immense quantities of information—concerning the tastes and incomes of consumers, the outputs and costs of producers, future products and methods of production, and the myriad of interdependences of all of the above. The task of gathering this information, let alone making sense of it, is beyond any designing intelligence. But it is not beyond the market, which yields "spontaneous order" out of chaos.[77]

In other words: "Modern economics explains how such an extended order can come into being, and how it itself constitutes an information-gathering process, able to call up, and to put to use, widely dispersed information that no central planning agency, let alone any individual, could know as a whole, possess, or control."[78]

How could the exquisite order of the market have arisen spontaneously without being designed and consciously directed by human reason? In Hayek's view, the first step in this evolution was the development of "several property, which is H. S. Maine's more precise term for what is usually described as private property."[79] The emergence of "several property" in primitive human groups, the details of which are now lost in prehistory, was "indispensable for the development of trading, and thereby for the formation of larger coherent and cooperating structures, and for the appearance of those signals we call prices."[80] In turn, the development of trade, which Hayek identified as a precondition of the emergence of Egyptian, Greek, and other ancient civilizations, depended on the freedom of traders to profit from the use of privileged "information for purposes known only to themselves."[81]

Given these "reconstructions" of how market orders most likely emerged, how could such a structure gather and process information inaccessible to any single individual or group?

> Much of the particular information which any individual possesses can be used only to the extent to which he himself can use it in his own decisions. Nobody can communicate to another all he knows, because much of the information he can make use of, he himself will elicit only in the process of making plans for action. Such information will be evoked as he works upon a particular task he has undertaken in the conditions in which he finds himself.... Only thus can the individual find out what to look for, and what helps him to do this in the market is the responses others make to what they find in their own environments....The market is the only known method of providing information enabling individuals to judge comparative advantages of different uses of resources of which they have no immediate knowledge and through whose use, whether they so intend or not, they serve the needs of distant unknown individuals. This dispersed knowledge is *essentially* dispersed, and cannot possibly be gathered together and conveyed to an authority charged with the task of deliberately creating order.[82]

This "*essentially* dispersed" economic information is distributed in time as well as in space. Humans will adapt their economic actions through the extended order "not only to others distant in space but also to events beyond the life expectancies of acting individuals."[83] Some of the information that the extended order gathers and processes only comes into existence when individuals confront particular choices in particular circumstances. Other elements, especially those having to do with long-term consequences, will occur later in time because of the subsequent contingent choices made by others. Just as combat commanders can choose among alternative courses of action, individuals can react in more than one way to economic signals whenever they like and at times of their own choosing. In the marketplace, therefore, "unintended consequences are paramount: a distribution of resources effected by an impersonal process in which individuals, acting for their own ends (themselves also often rather vague), literally do not and cannot know what will be the net result of their interactions."[84] Moreover, the consistent failure throughout the present century of centrally directed economies to achieve economic performance comparable to that of the extended market order underline that these are consequences one must take seriously.[85]

Hayek's outlook reflects a keen appreciation of the fact that there are "limits to our knowledge or reason in certain areas."[86] He points to the marginal-utility theory developed by W. S. Jevons, Carl Menger, and others, with its stress on the "subjective" nature of economic values, as having produced a "new paradigm" for explaining how structures can, and do, arise "without design from human interaction."[87] This new paradigm in turn rests on "the discovery" that economic events cannot be entirely explained "by preceding events acting as determining causes" due to the role of later interactions.[88] The result is not to suspend causality. However, the temporal inaccessibility of key economic information means that detailed predictability is lost.

This same pattern of "*essentially* dispersed" information plays a crucial role in evolutionary biology. An example would be the search for the female who is the most recent direct ancestor, in the female line, of every human being alive today. Scientists have christened her the Mitochondrial Eve because, since the mitochondria in our cells are passed exclusively through the female line, all the mitochondria in everyone alive today are direct descendants of her mitochondria.[89] However, because her offspring could, whether by accident or a lack of evolutionary fitness, have all died off, Mitochondrial Eve "can only be *retrospectively* crowned."[90] Her status as the closest direct female ancestor depends not only on contingencies in her own time, but on those in later times as well. Thus, her status, like all events associated with the demarkation or emergence of species, was "invisible at the time it occurred."[91]

In both economics and evolutionary biology, then, the distribution or dispersal of critical information in both space and time sets limits on what one can know at any given point of time. Sufficiently complete information to eliminate major uncertainties about the future is not possible in economics and, almost certainly, in biological evolution through natural selection.[92] While these parallels to the frictional uncertainties that confront combatants in wartime cannot, in and of themselves, establish similar limits in combat, nonetheless, the awareness of such limits in other highly contingent processes suggests the *possibility* that the same is true in regard to war—even future war.

Is there any empirical evidence that confirms this conjecture? In retrospect, only now do we know how much the coalition planners did not know during the Gulf War. Only the intrusive UN inspections *after* the war revealed how thoroughly Iraq's nuclear program had escaped destruction during Desert Storm. In the same vein, revelations in August 1995 concerning Iraqi preparations in December 1990 to employ biological agents revealed that there were fundamental facts about that campaign that were neither known nor knowable outside of Saddam's inner circle and selected military units for several years after the war.[93] To see the essential contingency of such issues, consider the following possibility. If the Iraqis had destroyed all the physical evidence (including documents) regarding their biological warfare capabilities, and if everyone involved had gone to their graves without talking, the information that surfaced in 1995 following the defection of some of Saddam's closest associates would, one day, have become unrecoverable.

For those unpersuaded by these first two cases, consider a third example: the temporal contingency of determining whether coalition forces had imposed sufficient destruction on the Republican Guard by 28 February 1991 to preclude their being used to threaten Iraq's neighbors. By mid-1993, more than two years after Desert Storm, this question had become a subject of heated debate.[94] Yet the question was not unambiguously decidable by Western observers until October 1994, when Republican Guard heavy units equipped with T-72s that had survived destruction in 1991 deployed again to threaten Kuwait. The resolution of the uncertainty depended on Iraqi actions more than three years later, thus exemplifying the essential temporal dispersion of critical knowledge about military effectiveness.[95] Since there can be no guarantees that such temporal dispersion of equally elementary knowledge about the result of particular military actions will not recur in the future, the most plausible conclusion is that such dispersion will continue to be a feature of future war. If so, then Clausewitzian friction seems likely to persist as well.

The distinction between explicit and tacit knowledge offers additional support for this viewpoint. As articulated by Michael Polanyi, *explicit* knowledge refers to meaningful information available for entry into databases and information systems. *Tacit* knowledge, by contrast, encompasses the implicit information and processing capabilities that humans possess by virtue of their genetic endowment and biological development, cultural background and upbringing, and cumulative individual experiences.[96] Such knowledge is—in an important sense—not directly accessible, although it can be drawn upon implicitly in appropriate contexts. Thus, "tacit knowledge" refers to human capabilities to know or sense more than can be explicitly told or specified.[97] A military example would be the tacit understanding of how fellow aircrew or flight members will likely react to unexpected combat situations. Such information is usually accumulated by regularly flying and training with the same individuals. Military organizations such as squadrons, wings, and air divisions generally contain considerable amounts of information, although widely dispersed among individuals, difficult (if not impossible) to enumerate in detail, and generally called into use only in concrete circumstances or instances of organizational activity. The Israeli Air Force's domination of its Arab adversaries from 1967 through 1982 suggests that the right kinds of tacit knowledge can provide military organizations with major long-term advantages over adversaries and competitors. Dysfunctional tacit knowledge, on the other hand, can have quite the opposite effect, as Scharnhorst discovered in the final weeks preceding Jena/Auerstädt. These points not only illuminate the roots of friction in the narrow sense that originally led Clausewitz to coin the term, but suggest a basic argument for general friction's future persistence as a continuing factor in war.

The inaccessibility of critical information involved in combat processes, arising from the essential dispersion of that information in space and time, argues that at least two sources of general friction we listed earlier—uncertainties in the information on which action in war depends, and friction in the narrow sense of resistance to effective action within one's own forces—will persist. Advances in information technologies may reduce spatial dispersion of explicit knowledge. Perhaps related advances can even render some portions of tacit knowledge explicit, although one suspects, given how much of the brain's information processing is both dispersed and inaccessible to consciousness in any direct or real-time manner, that much tacit knowledge will remain so.[98] Nevertheless, temporally dispersed information and irreducibly tacit information present clear limits to how much of all that combatants might like to know can actually be gathered together and explicitly grasped. Hence the prospects for one opponent or the other to reduce substantially the frictions arising from the dispersed information and tacit knowledge embedded in human organizations seem dim. These conclusions can be supported without appealing directly to the occurrence of similar phenomena in Hayek's extended market order and evolutionary biology. Yet the resemblance across all three areas does not seem merely accidental.

## Evolutionary Biology as a Source of Friction and Exemplar for Military Theory

The above discussion on evolutionary biology has opened the door to the possibility that the spatial-temporal inaccessibility of certain information implies that human beings and their institutions can neither eliminate some degree of uncertainty about the higher-level effects of future combat interactions, nor substantially reduce the magnitude of such uncertainties beyond the limits set by dispersed information and tacit knowledge. This section has two aims: first, to consider evolutionary biology as a source of general friction in its own right; and second, to explore whether evolutionary biology may offer a better model for a "scientific" theory of war than quantitative sciences like physics.

Darwin's core evolutionary thesis in *The Origin of the Species* (published in 1859) was that the rich diversity of living species making up the earth's biosphere had come about "chiefly through the natural selection of numerous successive, slight, favorable variations; aided in an important manner by the inherited effects of the use or disuse of parts; and in an unimportant manner, that is in relation to adaptive structures, whether past or present, by the direct action of external conditions, and by variations which seem to us in our ignorance to arise spontaneously."[99] While Darwin's original theory contained large gaps that "have only recently begun to be properly filled in," the modern neo-Darwinian synthesis is about as secure as any scientific theory ever has been or could be. True, vigorous controversies remain in evolutionary theory, not the least of which is how self-replicating molecules initially emerged. Nonetheless, these controversies are matters of "just science," meaning that no matter how they turn out they "will not undo the basic Darwinian idea."[100] As the well-known paleontologist Stephen Gould observed in 1994: "Natural selection is an immensely powerful yet beautifully simple theory that has held up remarkable well, under intense and unrelenting scrutiny and testing, for 135 years."[101] An instructive indicator of just how secure core Darwinism (the minimal theory that nonrandom survival of random hereditary changes guides biological evolution in adaptively nonrandom directions) is Richard Dawkins's 1991 argument that it is the only known empirical theory capable, even in principle, "of solving that most difficult of problems posed by life anywhere in the universe, namely, the problem of the existence of adaptive complexity."[102]

Given this understanding of evolutionary theory, how might it support general friction's relatively undiminished presence in war? Consider both Clausewitz's and this author's lists of friction's sources. Occupying the first two places in all three are danger and war's demands for physical exertion. These are straightforward and noncontroversial sources of friction, especially at the tactical level. Nevertheless, there is evidence that their combined effects on human beings in ground combat establish a practical limit on how long individuals can sustain continuous operations without risking precipitous declines in their effectiveness. Further, because this limit—about four days—has not changed over at least the past 130 years, it appears rooted in human cognitive and physical limits built in by evolution.

The most recent evidence of this "human" limitation surfaced during the final fifteen hours of the coalition's ground offensive during Desert Storm. As the Third Army historian later wrote, these closing hours witnessed a number of events that "were indicative of the larger problem of friction in war."[103] These events included VII Corps' failure to capture the road junction near Safwan in accordance with Schwarzkopf's desires, as well as the fact that VII

Corps stopped in place at 0130 hours on 28 February 1991 rather than continue its advance until 0800, the official time for the end of offensive operations. One can easily identify the immediate cause of these lapses. Key individuals in the chain of command had had little sleep since the ground campaign started and were approaching physical and mental exhaustion; gaps were opening up between where friendly units actually were and where higher echelons thought they were; and, the clarity of communications, up and down the chain of command, was eroding in the press of events. However, one can push the analysis deeper, and that is precisely what the Third Army historian did in reflecting on what occurred during the ground offensive's final hours:

> Douglas Southall Freeman notes that, during the American Civil War, "in the Army of Northern Virginia the men could stand almost anything for four days, but the fifth day in almost every instance they would crack." When judging the apparent unraveling of tight control on the night of 27–28 February by men who had had little rest for four days of movement and combat, one may well remember Freeman's warning: "Beware of the fifth day...." Interestingly enough, Major General Rupert Smith of the 1st U.K. Armored Division began issuing written, rather than oral, orders to avoid confusion due to fatigue on the part of the sender and the receiver.[104]

The Third Army historian attributes the loss of tight control to fatigue, and fatigue directly recalls war's demands for physical exertion, one of Clausewitz's sources of general friction. When such exertions occur in war, though, the companion friction stemming from human lives being at stake—including one's own—is probably impossible to separate. For participants in sustained combat, the risk of death or mutilation is constant and compelling. Yet, even for high level commanders like Schwarzkopf, danger makes itself felt in terms of their personal responsibility for those under their command. Bad decisions can get their own people killed unnecessarily, and this all-too-visceral pressure can, and does, impose its own friction.

The fact that coalition forces appear to have run up against the same four-day limit on sustained operations experienced by the Confederate Army during 1862-1865 suggests that enduring human limitations are involved.[105] Such psychological and physical limitations are not as constant or precise across diverse individuals and groups as the temperature at which water freezes. And coherent operations have been sustained over longer periods than four days by ensuring combatants and leaders rest whenever possible.[106] Nevertheless, the underlying psychological and physical limitations appear to be every bit as real as the regularities in sciences like physics and to rest ultimately, in the environmental circumstances of the late Pliocene, some 2–3 million years ago, that gave rise to the emergence of the genus *Homo*. It is worth adding that human cortical tissue developed in these evolutionary conditions "to facilitate action," particularly with respect to courtship and reproduction, not abstract thought.[107]

There are, then, finite limits, grounded in biology and evolution, to human capabilities to receive sensory data, integrate that input with prior experience and information, reach plausible decisions about what to do, and act upon those decisions.[108] Any time the demands of combat force participants beyond those limits, friction manifests itself. As many fighter pilots can attest, the stresses of combat will quickly constrain sensory input. Danger and physical exertion will also degrade orientation in a combat situation, precipitate poor decisions, and produce slow, ragged, and even flawed execution. The consequences of such effects seem potentially as severe in the future as they have been in the past. Indeed, short of "reengineering" *Homo sapiens* at the genetic level, it is difficult to see how one might reduce—much less eliminate—the *potential* adverse effects of exceeding these inherent biological limitations so long as humans and their purposes remain an integral part of war.

Biology, therefore, confers relative permanence on at least some of the sources of friction in war. The *potential* of danger and exertion to impede effective military operations will always be there, just beneath the surface. Realistic training and actual combat experience can, as Clausewitz suggests, do much to limit their effects. However, like interrelated human potentials for sex and aggression that evolution has programmed in *Homo sapiens*, the potential for a determined, capable adversary to push human combatants beyond their biological capacities for effective observation, orientation, decision making, and action seems an inherent, deeply programmed limitation.[109] From this evolutionary perspective, technological solutions *per se* are almost certainly not possible so long as we remain human.

The theory of biological evolution has another implication for our thinking about Clausewitzian friction. The evidence so far presented suggests the following propositions could form the basis of a reasonably comprehensive theory of war and conflict:

*Proposition I:* War is a violent, two-sided contest of opposing wills dominated by Clausewitzian friction.

*Proposition II:* Outcomes are highly contingent, and the various indirect effects or second-order consequences arising from a campaign or war may not be knowable until sometime after the conflict has ended.

*Proposition III:* In combat, from moment to moment, it is the *differential* between the levels of general friction experienced by the two sides that matters most.

*Proposition IV:* So long as human purposes, frailties, proclivities, and limitations remain an integral part of war, Clausewitzian friction will retain the potential to make the difference between success and failure.

The salient observation about these four observations for present purposes is that they are neither readily nor obviously amenable to the kind of quantification that enables tides or the positions of the planets to be precisely predicted indefinitely into the future. Only Proposition III offers any hint of a quantifiable, predictive relationship. But even in this instance some overarching metric for measuring the absolute level of friction experienced at a given moment by each side would be needed, and no such metric has yet been discovered. In fact it seems open to doubt whether such a universal metric is possible other than in a qualitative or conceptual sense.

By contrast, Isaac Newton's famous second law of motion was originally formulated as: "*The change of motion is proportional to the motive force impressed; and is made in the direction of the right line in which that force is impressed.*"[110] The simplest version of this law is expressed by the scalar relationship $F = ma$, where $F$ is the impressed force, $m$ is the mass of the object subjected to the force, and $a$ is its acceleration. This form of law expresses a precise quantitative relationship because force, mass, and acceleration are all physically measurable quantities.

As the biologist Ernst Mayr has emphasized, physicists since Newton have been strongly (and arrogantly) inclined to see these sorts of quantitative, predictive laws as "co-extensive with science."[111] By implication, this attitude led many in the so-called "hard" sciences to the prejudice that evolutionary biology is somehow not a full-fledged empirical science on a par with the Newtonian synthesis, or is at best a protoscience still awaiting its Newton. The reason is that the principles of evolutionary biology established by Darwin and his successors are more like the four qualitative propositions just proposed about the conduct of war than a quantitative law like $F = ma$.[112]

Is the identification of science with quantitative, predictive laws defensible? To reiterate the point made in the opening paragraphs of this section, evolution by means of natural selection is arguably the best confirmed theory in the history of science. Newtonian mechanics is not an exception since, strictly speaking, the relativistic mechanics of Albert Einstein supplanted the Newtonian synthesis early in this century, and the emergence of quantum mechanics during the 1920s later upstaged both Newtonian and relativistic mechanics. As a result, a major implication of Darwinian theory is to show that one cannot regard explanations as unscientific and "unsatisfactory" when they do not contain quantitative laws, "or when they are not such as to enable the event in question to have been predicted."[113] Moreover, even the most quantitative of empirical sciences, physics, is not thoroughly quantitative at its roots. As the mathematician and physicist Henri Poincaré rightly argued, the scientist's selection of which facts to pay attention to out of the practically infinite number of knowable facts, while by no means capricious or random, ultimately rests on qualitative judgments such as simplicity, repeatability, and beauty that defy quantification.[114] Last but not least, Poincaré's most far-reaching contribution to mathematical physics was, arguably, the creation of topology, a branch of mathematics that permits the *qualitative* analysis of dynamic systems.[115] Topological methods enable one to obtain information about the global behavior of a dynamic system by constructing a geometric picture that is "totally inaccessible from the classical bash-out-a-formula viewpoint."[116]

Two points follow from these observations. First despite its heavily nonquantitative and nonpredictive character, evolutionary biology is as legitimate an empirical science as anything in physics. Its lack of quantification arises from the contingency and diversity of the phenomena with which it deals. Second, for this very reason, evolutionary biology would appear to be a better paradigm for an overarching theory of war than, say, quantum physics. Regardless of how one feels about the detailed content of any of the four hypothesis offered above, they do illustrate the kind of qualitative, empirically refutable propositions that an adequate science of war would require.

## Nonlinearity and a Modern Taxonomy for General Friction

We have deferred nonlinearity to the end to avoid burdening the exposition any earlier than necessary with a "hard science" concept that various readers may find unfamiliar or alien to the subject at hand. Clausewitz, himself, though, was not the least shy about appropriating concepts like friction and center of gravity from the physics of his day to illuminate the study of war. Furthermore, in the winter of 1992/1993 Alan Beyerchen argued persuasively that Clausewitz himself not only perceived war "as a profoundly nonlinear phenomenon...consistent with our current understanding of nonlinear dynamics," but that the predominance of a linear approach to the analysis of war "has made it difficult to assimilate and appreciate the intent and contribution of *On War*."[117] This author's experience also has been that attempts to apply the ideas of nonlinear science to the study of war continue to meet resistance, if not incomprehension, for precisely the reason Beyerchen cited: the widespread predominance of linear modes of thought.

What is nonlinear science about? The core ideas are not hard to describe. Nonlinear dynamics arise from repeated iteration or feedback. A system, whether physical or mathematical, starts in some initial state. That initial state provides the input to a feedback mechanism which determines the new state of the system. The new state then provides the input through which the feedback mechanism determines the system's next state, and so on. Each successive state is causally dependent on its predecessor, but what happens to the system over the course of many iterations can be more complex and less predictable than one might suppose. If the nonlinear system exhibits *sensitive* dependence on initial or later states, then at least three long-term outcomes are possible: (1) the system eventually settles down in some single state and remains there despite further iterations (long-term stability); (2) the system settles on a series of states which it thereafter cycles through endlessly (periodic behavior); or, (3) the system wanders aimlessly (so-called "chaotic" behavior). In the third case, detailed predictability of the actual state of the system can be lost over the course of a large enough number of iterations.

The "mathematics of chaos" that has been used since the early 1960s to explain this understanding of nonlinear dynamics can easily be demonstrated using a personal computer or a programmable calculator to explore a simple nonlinear equation such as the "logistic mapping," $x_{n+1} = kx_n(1 - x_n)$.[118] Depending on the choice of the "tunable" parameter $k$, the logistic mapping exhibits all three of the long-term outcomes—stable, periodic, and chaotic behavior—just described. Unfortunately those uncomfortable with mathematics and computers are easily deterred by such investigations even though, for the very simplest nonlinear functions, the requisite calculations do not require more than the arithmetic of real numbers. Granted, the amount of repetitive number crunching involved in any serious exploration demands machine assistance, and one does have to be meticulous about the number of places to the right of the decimal point to which calculations are carried. Still, the mathematics of elementary nonlinear functions like the logistic mapping are readily accessible to anyone willing to invest a modest amount of time and effort.

The underlying mathematics aside, nonlinearity has a crucial role to play in completing the case for the proposition that general friction will persist more or less undiminished in future war regardless of technological advances. Specifically, the role nonlinearity plays is to close the door once and for all to the belief that one can attain, even in principle, the full predictability of the "clockwork" universe advocated most persuasively during Clausewitz's lifetime by the mathematical physicist Pierre Simon de Laplace.

The idea that one could completely predict the subsequent motions and effects of physical phenomena on the basis of their earlier states was first argued at length in the 1750s by the Jesuit priest Roger Boscovich.[119] However, Laplace, more than anyone else, seemed to make good on this heady promise. Using the improved calculus developed by various colleagues, Laplace was widely perceived to have "removed all the known errors from, and explained all known anomalies in, the Newtonian cosmology and physics."[120] Whereas Newton had never been fully convinced of the stability of the solar system, which he suggested might require some divine correction now and again,[121] Laplace claimed to have proven "that every known secular variation, such as the changing speeds of Saturn and Jupiter, was cyclic and that the system was indeed entirely stable and required no divine maintenance."[122] Laplace also completed the theory of tides and solved another of Newton's problems, the deduction from first principles of the velocity of sound in air. His unbroken string of triumphs in removing the anomalies in Newtonian mechanics led him to conclude that the universe is deterministic in the spirit of Boscovich. "Given for one instance," he wrote, "an intelligence which could comprehend all the forces by which nature is animated and the respective situation of the beings who compose it—an intelligence sufficiently vast to submit these data to analysis—it would embrace in the same formula the movements of the greatest bodies of the universe and those of the lightest atom; for it nothing would be uncertain and the future, as the past, would be present to its eyes."[123] On this view, predictive, mathematical laws strictly determine the universe's operation down to the most minute details and the smallest particles. The world is quite literally a giant clockwork. Regardless of human ignorance or shortcomings in such matters, mathematical laws leave nothing to chance, not even combat outcomes or the emergence and evolution of biological life on Earth.

The difficulty with this Laplacian outlook is not, of course, its plausibility or appeal. Early in the twentieth century most physicists accepted "Laplacian determinism" as a well-established scientific fact, and many still do today. The problem is that the universe we inhabit is not broadly or universally deterministic in the sense Laplace meant—not even in disciplines like physics and mathematics. There are processes like the Earth's tides and solar eclipses that are periodic and hence, predictable and rectrodictable. However, there are processes such as weather that are so sensitive to the slightest perturbations or differences in initial conditions that detailed predictability disappears over time spans as short as a few days.[124] While nonlinear processes such as weather prediction are "deterministic" in the restricted or narrow sense of being causally determined, they exhibit long-term unpredictability which is inconsistent with "Laplacian determinism." At best, these sorts of highly nonlinear processes harbor occasional islands of predictable behavior within a sea of unpredictability.

This untidy situation reared its head early in the development of Newtonian physics. During the drafting of the first edition of *Principia Mathemat-*

*ica*, Newton ran into difficulties moving from the problem of two bodies mutually attracted to one another by gravitation, which he easily solved, to the problem of describing the dynamics of many such bodies.[125] In the summer of 1694 he returned to this problem in the form of the dynamics of the moon moving about the earth, which in turn was orbiting the sun (the three-body problem).[126] Once again, though, Newton's achievements fell short of his aspirations. In retrospect, Newton's difficulties with the irregularities of lunar motion are wholly understandable. As we now know, the three-body problem "does not admit a general analytic solution."[127] So Newton's renewed efforts in 1694–1695 to find such a solution to the "inequalities" in the moon's orbit were doomed to failure, just as they had been in 1685–1686 when he was laboring to complete the first edition of *Principia Mathematica*. The problem he labored to solve was literally impossible to solve.[128]

Again, Laplace thought he had proved that the observed perturbations of the planets were periodic rather than cumulative: they would "repeat themselves at regular intervals and never exceed a certain amount," thus substituting dynamic stability for divine intervention.[129] But mathematicians no longer consider Laplace's proof of the stability of the solar system rigorous, and "all attempts to make it so have failed."[130] Indeed, recent evidence indicates that Pluto's orbit and the solar system as a whole appear to be unstable or chaotic on time scales of 4 million–20 million years.[131] The first individual to recognize that the three-body problem included unstable or nonperiodic behavior was Poincaré. In an 1890 essay he showed that a gravitational system involving only three bodies would not universally give rise to predictable or periodic motion. Specifically, in the case of an idealized form of the three-body problem in which the third body is vastly smaller than the other two, Poincaré discovered motion so complex and irregular—"homoclinic tangles" to use the technical term—that he did not even attempt to draw the corresponding figure.[132] This "chaotic" behavior is "fundamental"; neither "gathering more information," nor processing it better, will eliminate the unpredictability.[133]

Since the early 1970s, scientists have confirmed empirically the kind of chaotic or unpredictable behavior—the essence of nonlinear dynamics—in a wide range of phenomena, including electronic circuits, mechanical and electromechanical systems, hydrodynamics, acoustics, optics, solid-state physics, biology, and even ecology.[134] Nonlinear behavior, it seems, is ubiquitous in the real world; pockets or areas of chaos infect a wide range of physical phenomena, and within those "chaotic regions" detailed predictability is lost. In this sense, chance abounds within substantial regions of the natural world.

What bearing does this discovery have on friction in future war? Clausewitz wrote of war that no other human activity "is so continuously or universally bound up with chance" and compared it to a game of cards in its sensitivity to chance.[135] He believed chance could not be eliminated from conflict. He also identified chance as an explicit source of general friction, although he did not (and could not) explain how small differences from what is expected or predicted could turn success into failure and vice versa. What the empirical fact of nonlinear dynamics does is to explain how such small differences or "chance" occurrences of "the kind you can never really foresee" can give rise to long-term unpredictability.[136] Laplace believed that human judgments about chance and probability were simply a result of ignorance. In many cases, including games of chance like cards, he felt that humans simply do not know enough, or have inadequate time to predict the outcomes. Expressed in the language of nonlinear dynamics, Laplace's presumption was that human ignorance prevents us from eliminating tiny differences between our representations of phenomena and their actuality. If, however, one cannot eliminate these small differences even in principle, then nonlinear dynamics explain how global or macroscopic unpredictability arises from the structural dynamics of iterated feedback—particularly when the feedback function exhibits, in at least some part of its domain, extreme sensitivity to initial or later conditions. Since there is increasingly compelling evidence from a number of fields, especially mathematical logic and physics, that any coherent or formal system we develop "to represent or deal with large portions of reality will at best represent or deal with that reality incompletely or imperfectly," it appears that these mismatches cannot be eliminated.[137] Consequently, the existence of nonlinear systems confirms Clausewitz's deepest insights on the nature of combat processes and the fundamental role of chance in those processes. It also suggests that unforeseen and unforeseeable differences in initial or later conditions—which, on present evidence, cannot be wholly eliminated even by Laplace's "vast intelligence"—allow us to subsume chance within the framework of nonlinearity.

Clausewitz insisted in *On War*'s second book that the basic nature of two-sided interaction between opposing sides was bound to make interaction unpredictable.[138] Nonlinear dynamics in general, and recent mathematical research aimed at determining if nonlinear effects arising from "mathematical chaos" could be demonstrated in a simple computer model of land combat in particular,[139] reveal how inspired Clausewitz's observation was. In nonlinear systems, iterative feedback can so magnify the smallest differences, including those stemming from human decisions, as to render combat outcomes *structurally* unpredictable. In other words, while technological advances might temporarily mitigate general friction, they could neither eliminate it nor substantially reduce its potential magnitude.

With these insights, we can now reconstruct general friction in modern terms. The hypothesis underlying this reconstruction is that general friction ultimately arises from three elementary sources: human beings and their purposes, the spatial-temporal inaccessibility of key information in military affairs, and the unpredictability of nonlinear dynamics. This hypothesis suggests the following list of general friction's sources as a late twentieth century alternative to the eight "Clausewitzian" sources enumerated earlier:

1. constraints imposed by human physical and cognitive limits, whose magnitude or impact are inevitably magnified by the intense stresses, pressures, and responsibilities of actual combat;

2. informational uncertainties and unforeseeable differences stemming, ultimately, from the spatial-temporal dispersion of information in the external environment, military organizations, and the brains of individual participants; and,

3. the structural nonlinearity of combat processes which can give rise to the long-term unpredictability of results and outcomes by magnifying the effects of unknowable small differences and unforeseen events.

At least three observations should help motivate and explain this reconstruction of general friction. First, this revised list is shorter than those previously offered. The reason is that the reconstruction focuses on the most fundamental or elementary sources of friction. Derivative sources, such as poor intelligence or human reactions to the imminent threat of death or mutilation are clearly implied, but need not be called out separately.

Given the emphasis that Clausewitz and his mentor Scharnhorst placed on chance, it may be surprising to see chance, too, reduced to a derivative source of friction. In this case, however, a more accurate characterization would be that chance has been spread across all three of general friction's sources. Both human participation and the distribution of information in war give rise to unpredictable differences—uncertainties that *cannot* be eliminated. When nonlinear processes magnify these differences, they render large-scale results unpredictable and thus give rise to ever-greater differences that in turn feed back into nonlinear processes. From this perspective, chance is rendered pervasive, but, once again, without letting go of causality.

Second, the reconstructed list of friction suggests a way of dealing with a recurring objection to the entire concept. The objection, which has been consciously ignored to this point, is that a unified concept of general friction embraces so much of war that it does not provide a precise instrument for analyzing the phenomena at issue. If we return to the notion of general friction as the entire panoply of factors that distinguish real war from war on paper, Clausewitz's reason for pulling so diverse a collection of factors together under a single concept is clear: general friction was the bridge between war in the abstract and war in reality. Still, the objection suggests that some parsing of his unified concept into separable-but-fundamental components could prove fruitful. Whether the three proposed in this section will do so remains to be seen. However, constraints on military operations stemming from the physical and cognitive limits of human participants, uncertainties rooted in the spatial-temporal distribution of the information on which action in war is unavoidably based, and the unpredictabilities inherent in nonlinear dynamics seem more precise and, potentially, more promising as conceptual tools than any of the decompositions of general friction provided earlier.

Third, the principal merit of the late-twentieth-century recasting of Clausewitzian friction proposed in this section is the transparency it gives to friction's place in military affairs. Human limitations, informational uncertainties, and nonlinearity are not pesky difficulties that better technology and engineering can eliminate, but *built-in, structural* features of the violent interaction between opposing groups that we call war. Why? Because at least one of the root sources of Clausewitzian friction lies, when all is said and done, not in the weapons we wield but in ourselves. The presence of humans in the loop—with all the diverse frailties, physical and cognitive limits, purposes, and decisions which their presence and participation entail—alone seems sufficient to render Clausewitzian friction impossible to eliminate entirely and, in all likelihood, extraordinarily difficult to reduce greatly in any permanent sense. At the same time, human participation cannot be isolated from the spatial-temporal distribution of information on which combatants act, and those actions, in turn, involve processes that can be highly nonlinear. As a consequence, general friction's *potential* to *dominate* outcomes seems likely to persist regardless of the changes technological advances bring to pass. On this reconstruction of Clausewitz's concept, therefore, general friction arises, to paraphrase Roberta Wohlstetter, from fundamental aspects of the human condition and unavoidable unpredictabilities that lie at the core of combat processes.[140]

## Implications for the Future

The notion about future war that we set out to examine was the possibility that foreseeable advances in sensor technologies and information systems may (or will) enable the side exploiting them more effectively to eliminate the "fog of war" while turning the opponent's systems into a "wall of ignorance."[141] Implicit in this view is the presumption that "knowing everything that is going on" in a volume of battlespace is a problem that techno-logical advances will eventually "solve" once and for all.[142]

Better weaponry, like superior training or operational concepts, can cer-tainly provide leverage for shifting the relative balance of friction in one's favor, especially against an adversary lacking comparable means. The poten-tial that the Joint STARS demonstrated during the Gulf War to enable the coalition commanders to track "coherent" vehicular movement on the ground was truly breathtaking. However, driving one's own friction to zero while, simultaneously, rendering the enemy's effectively infinite is *not*, at its core, a technical problem.

In the first place, even in an "information-rich" environment, there is only so much that any human can absorb, digest, and act upon in a given period of time. The greater the stress, the more individuals will ignore or mis-represent data, mistake and misconstrue information, and the greater will be the prospects for confusion, disorientation, and surprise. Second, the spatial and, especially, the temporal distribution of information relevant to decisions in war means that many key pieces will remain inaccessible at any given time and place. Those who have held senior positions in corporations or military services need only reflect on how much they did not know about what was taking place in their *own* organizations to appreciate the reality of informa-tion being temporally or spatially inaccessible. Third, the empirical fact of nonlinear dynamics, when coupled with unavoidable mismatches between reality and our representations of it, reveals fundamental limits to prediction, no matter how much information and processing power technological advances may eventually place in human hands.

To push the implications of these three points further, the ways in which friction will manifest itself in future conflicts, too, undoubtedly involves human foibles, inaccessible information, and nonlinear dynamics. No matter how much technological advances may constrain general friction in some areas, the evidence and arguments mounted in the second half of this essay suggest that it will simply balloon in others—usually in ways we cannot pre-dict. Technological innovation in the means of combat introduces novelty into warfare, and the indirect effects and second-order consequences of nov-elty are never predictable with any high degree of certainty. Who among IBM's executives genuinely foresaw in the early 1980s that personal comput-ers would so rapidly erode the company's traditional mainframe business that "Big Blue" would post a $5 billion loss in 1992, lay off tens of thousands, and lose forever its dominance of the industry?[143] Who could have predicted that the main benefit the Israelis would find in their early battlefield experience with remotely piloted vehicles would turn out to lie in fixing their own forces rather than enemy targets?[144] And who would have guessed that the invention of the postbox would contribute to women's liberation by enabling young women to post letters to their sweethearts without parental knowledge?[145] The social consequences of technological innovation are especially hard to predict and war is, after all, a social enterprise.

Looking ahead to how friction might manifest itself in future conflict, one should also consider the susceptibility of "digitalized battlespace" to subtle forms of misinformation and deception. The more the U.S. military embraces digital networks and synthetic environments, the greater will be the potential for subtle manipulation of our "situation awareness" by a sophisticated adversary, to say nothing of our own ability to confuse ourselves with an overabundance of "information." Indeed, it is entirely possible that the application for information technology to war will expand considerably the potential for deception. Similarly, the more "transparent" battlespace becomes, the more human participants may feel pressured to make life-or-death decisions in shorter and shorter time spans. Hence, there appear to be good reasons to expect that wholesale introduction of state-of-the-art information technologies into future war, far from eliminating friction, will simply give rise to new and unexpected manifestations.

Yet, despite all that has been said, might one not still hold out for some overall reduction in the magnitude of friction as advanced sensors and information systems make greater inroads into the conduct of military operations? Such a question is hard to answer definitively, given the lack of any universal, quantitative metric for gauging either side's absolute level of friction. Even at the tactical level, where considerable quantification is possible, direct measures of aggregate friction on either side do not exist. Thus, the question demands quantifiability where it has neither existed nor seems possible. One can measure the temperature or mass readily enough, but social utility and the second order consequences of wartime decisions are another matter entirely.

What might be some of the more salient implications of general friction's relatively undiminished persistence in future war for military theory? First, there has been some resurgence of anti-Clausewitzian sentiment since the fall of the Berlin Wall in 1989. Martin van Creveld has argued that because future wars will be low-intensity conflicts waged by non-state actors against whom the "modern regular forces" of states like Israel, Britain, Russia, and the United States are "all but useless," the age of large-scale, conventional warfare on the Clausewitzian "trinitarian" model appears to be "at its last gasp."[146] This view, whatever its merits, does not really touch the subject of this essay, general friction. Indeed, van Creveld himself recognizes that "inflexibility, friction, and uncertainty" will continue to apply to future warfare, even if war's new form resembles more closely the primitive conflicts preceding the Peace of Westphalia in 1648.[147]

The second point concerns what a scientific theory of warfare might be like. The four propositions we advanced earlier in the paper are not such a theory, although they represent a plausible start. The wholesale reconstruction of Clausewitz's original concept in the preceding section of this essay suggests that starting there would be a good idea since the three "frictional" components highlight some of the more enduring features of real war as opposed to war on paper. Emphasis on these "structural" features stemmed, of course, from the great clarity Clausewitz and Scharnhorst had concerning what actually occurred on the battlefields of their day. In this sense, their theoretical emphasis on friction, particularly as reconstructed in the previous section, was as legitimately scientific as Darwin's notion of evolution of biological species by means of natural selection.

Third, it is easy at this stage to clarify friction's place in Clausewitz's thought. On the one hand, we have not spared the Prussian soldier and theorist. Where his thinking about friction and related matters warranted correction, extension, or revision in light of later knowledge and military experience, the author has made such changes without hesitation. On the other hand, Richard Simpkin suggested in 1985 that friction was, to his mind, "Clausewitz's most important contribution to military thought."[148] It turns out that retired U.S. Air Force Colonel John Boyd had reached the same conclusion by the spring of 1982 based on his willingness to connect Clausewitzian friction with the second law of thermodynamics.[149] At a minimum, this essay has underlined how the central unified concept of general friction was to Clausewitz's understanding of war.

This essay, however, had a more ambitious goal—to make the case that general friction will continue to be central to future war regardless of technological changes in the means of combat. Perhaps the single most important theme woven into the tapestry of the argumentation for this view is the realization (Proposition III above) that it is the *differential* between the two sides' levels of general friction that matters most in combat outcomes. If what counts in real war is not the absolute level of friction that either side experiences but the *relative frictional advantage* of one adversary over the other, then the question of using technology to reduce friendly friction to near zero can be seen for what it is: a false issue that diverts attention from the real business of war. Even comparatively small frictional advantages can, through nonlinear feedback, have huge consequences for combat outcomes. Such relative advantages, morevoer, hinge fundamentally on: 1) constraints imposed by human physical and cognitive limits; 2) informational uncertainties and unforeseeable differences stemming from the spatial-temporal dispersion of information in the external environment, military organizations, and the brains of individual participants; and 3) the structural nonlinearity of combat processes. One may or may not choose to gather these diverse structural features of combat and war under a single, unified concept of general friction, as Clausewitz did. Nonetheless, they seem destined to remain the root sources of one side's relative frictional advantage over the other even in the age of so-called information-based warfare. Consider, after all, how much would have to be overturned or rejected to conclude otherwise. Among other things, one would need to overthrow nonlinear dynamics, the fundamental tenets of neo-Darwinian evolutionary biology, the second law of thermodynamics, and all the limiting metatheorems of mathematical logic, including Kurt Gödel's famous incompleteness theorems and Gregory Chaitin's extension of Gödel's work to demonstrate the existence of randomness in arithmetic. No small task indeed!

# Rethinking the "Ould" Alliance: Europe and the United States after the Cold War

*John Gooch*

## Introduction

T he 1990s will be a crucial decade for Europe. Indeed, although mercifully not replicating the violence and turmoil of the years 1910–1920 and 1940–1950, they may well be no less significant in redefining the structures and patterns of international relations at the start of the third millennium. Two sets of events—the disappearance of the Soviet Union and the continuing development of European integration—have together unfrozen a world in which the relation to a now non-existent third party predominantly defined the relationships among the states of Europe. In the new order, common interests will be harder to find. Nevertheless, the search for such commonalities will determine what replaces the structure built to service the North Atlantic Alliance. It will also determine how, and how far, the United States will interact with the new Europe.

## The European Security Environment

For the United States, the Cold War made the definition and determination of its European policy a relatively simple matter. The Soviet Union represented a demonstrable threat to America's interests: one at the same time strategic and ideological in character. Indeed, so intertwined were the two facets of Moscow's politics and action that Americans had a hard time in disentangling them. In a bipolar world of nuclear confrontation, America's national interests were clear. On the one hand, the defense of free peoples against the insidious threat to democracy from indigenous Communist parties defined the ideological arm of U.S. foreign policy in Europe and Asia. On the other, the prospect of the resources of Western Europe falling to the Soviet Union through force or atomic suasion defined its strategic aim. The United States countered the twin challenges of Soviet power with a policy of containment effected through NATO. The United States linked itself to Europe for purposes that were easily definable and readily intelligible (at least to those not predisposed to distrust America *per se* ) by an "Atlantic bridge" whose existence suited all parties.

Starting in 1989, the Cold War's order collapsed with unexpected rapidity. Demolition of the Berlin Wall, unification of Germany, disintegration of the Warsaw Pact, Soviet retreat from the eastern satellites, and the disintegration of the U.S.S.R in 1991 consigned containment to history. For some commentators, this disappearance of the past in a precipitous and comprehensive manner demands reconstruction of Europe's security and foreign policy. As one commentator has remarked, "The circumstances which made the [wartime and post-war Anglo-American] alliance a central aspect of American foreign policy and enabled it to become a central theme in British foreign policy, have now gone."[1] Now that the *casus amicae* had gone, the need for NATO's old defense machine had gone with it. The question then, upon which there is no unanimity in Europe or America, is whether there are other potential threats to Europe's future which, although not directly comparable to the Soviet Union, are sufficient to justify a renewed and a revitalized relationship between Europe and the United States.

The unlamented departure of the Soviet Union from the international scene is not, of course, the only way in which Europe's circumstances have altered. To claim such would freeze the Cold War into arctic immobility.[2] Chaos has replaced order. The political reconfiguration of Europe after the collapse of the Soviet empire has created a zone of instability in Eastern Europe which presents new and more complicated challenges than did any of its predecessors. For Western Europe, developments in this region are critically linked to its general security interests: for the United States such links seem less obvious, and, to some extent, nonexistent. The distance between the interests of a post-Cold War America and Europe's other crisis area, the North African/Mediterranean arc, appears even greater, since the threats it presents are predominantly domestic and result from illegal immigration and drug-trafficking. The disappearance of a common and universal threat has led to the emergence in Europe of actual and potential dangers which are not so general and direct as to command U.S. involvement in their resolution. Nonetheless, they are sufficiently disturbing to make that involvement highly desirable to many Europeans.

The political and economic integration of Europe presents yet another set of issues which a future European security structure must accommodate. The Maastricht process, bounded by the first Danish referendum in June 1992 and Germany's accession in October 1993, checked the pace at which the more enthusiastic wished to cement the European community. For the moment, the path to progress lies in widening, and not deepening, the community. Denmark's admission on the basis of its nonparticipation in Union decisions and actions which have defense implications raises the question of the institutional inter-relationship between NATO, the European Community, and its defense arm, the Western European Union. Similar developments in the future will lead to a more complex Europe. They will force the participants to sort out the present alphabet soup and develop a more coherent security architecture to replace the multitude of institutions currently involved in devising and executing policy.[3] Less prominently publicized, but no less important, are the economic relations between the European community and the United States. The concluding stages of the Uruguay round of GATT well illustrated the potentially divisive nature of economic issues. There exists in Europe a sense that a turning point is at hand in a relationship which has been as much adversarial as amicable.[4]

As well as highlighting the social and ethnic forces which communism's break-up unleashed, the war in former Yugoslavia encapsulates the problems inherent in developing a new security order in Europe. From the moment when the European Community first interceded in June 1991, its approach has been uncertain and its councils undecided. Initially an activist France sought to utilize the Western European Union as the arm for military intervention, only to be blocked by Britain. In a series of policy and directional changes thereafter, initiative passed to the UN and to NATO, divisions opened between Germany and France, and the use of force to back UN resolutions developed only reluctantly and hesitantly. Critics found the early stages of the imbroglio "procedural, ahistorical, moralistic," and claimed they opened up a leadership vacuum.[5] More broadly, the wretched European performance has highlighted the shortcomings of present security and political structures. "The war in the former Yugoslavia has shown that neither the collective defense system of NATO nor the economic integration of the European community has been truly relevant to this crisis."[6] So far, so bad, perhaps, though in August 1995, the fact that the Luftwaffe participated in UN-sanctioned air operations over Bosnia suggests the possibility of deeper European cooperation in this collective security venture.

The war in the Balkans has displayed several unique characteristics. For the first time, the UN has managed a crisis in Europe and, for the first time, NATO has used its forces in a collective military operation "in-area." Perhaps most importantly, the war has thrown into relief the fact that some of the more important problems in shaping a new pattern for European security derive from the posture and politics of the United States.

## Losing Direction? The United States in Post–Cold War Europe

Until 1940, the United States kept the world at arm's length. Although willing to participate in some nonpolitical programs, it remained outside the League of Nations and made its own somewhat idealistic and impractical proposals to deal with Nazi and Fascist aggression by quarantining the culpable powers. However, the Axis drive for world hegemony drew the Americans into direct intervention in European affairs, and Stalin kept them there. The logic of that involvement grew directly out of America's delineation of its national interests. The foundations of the construct were the physical survival, independence, and freedom of the continental United States.

To achieve this, the U.S. had to prevent hegemonic control of regions of the globe which were of geostrategic or economic importance and whose independence helped secure American well-being. The superstructure of the edifice was the requirement to protect and extend the liberal values embodied in the American politics. In this respect, America's attitude towards Western Europe during the Cold War was little more than a continuation of its stance during World War II.[7]

During the Cold War, the notion that American security was closely interlinked with European security was axiomatic. For Atlanticists it still remains true, though the threat has altered. Where once they postulated a hostile hegemon, they now identify an unstable Europe as the danger to interests which they more often than not define vaguely or even tautologically.[8] The three main areas of concern involve the relationship between NATO and Russia, the new role of a powerful Germany, and the scope of the transatlantic alliance. In seeking to square this circle, neo-Altlanticists find themselves returning to NATO as the rock upon which to anchor European-American friendship.

NATO's proponents see the organization as the solution to several American dilemmas. The first derives from the growth of an integrated Europe free from the Soviet threat and therefore from the need for an organization in which the United States has such a strong presence. One commentator has identified the dilemma thus:

> In order to continue to reliably "tie in" Germany, European integration should really be promoted. The Europe which would then emerge, which would also be integrated in terms of its security, would be capable of engaging in conflict with the USA and perhaps threatening American interests.[9]

In reiterating an American commitment to Europe—and therefore to NATO as both a symbol and instrument of that commitment—even neo-Altanticists acknowledge an erosion of the essential points in the special relationship as well as the increasing importance of the Pacific rim to the United States. Yet arguing in favor of European integration "so long as it remains open and congenial," they also express American fears that an integrated Europe will inevitably emerge as a competitor.[10]

Statements of the manifest need for American leadership almost invariably accompany calls for a European renewal based in whole or in part on expansion of NATO. Apart from the value of addressing a resounding call to a nation manifesting signs of abandoning its fifty-year internationalism and retreating to North America under a banner of "America first," such calls derive from the presumption that "the prosperous and democratic part of Europe is having tremendous difficulty in coming to terms with the continent's new problems." There is, according to such views, "no single European country with the resources or acceptance from its partners to organize the effort."[11]

Proponents of NATO see that organization as possessing the strength to supervise change in Europe. Its continued existence fills what would otherwise be a security vacuum, the inevitable consequence of the necessarily slow process of revitalizing "essentially Cold War institutions."[12] Its virtues are twofold. First, by tying the United States into Europe, NATO allows German armament to remain at levels which the community finds acceptable. In this context, an American departure would carry the possible corollary of some form of German nuclear armament to assume its share of the common defense. Secondly, it safeguards Europe by committing the United States to an anti-Russian coalition, should one ever become necessary. Thus, NATO is the best hedge against war with Russia and the less likely possibility of war among Western and Central European nations, since it preserves America's role as a "defensive balancer" and creates a focus for western coordination.[13]

NATO's future within the new European order raises fundamental questions. The first is how far NATO should expand eastward to secure Europe's stability. The NATO nations agreed on expansion in principle in January

1994. The most obvious candidates for membership are the Visegrad countries (Poland, Hungary, the Czech Republic, and Slovakia). Their supporters,
however, have failed to explain satisfactorily how this expansion would avoid
sufficient anxiety in the Ukraine to drive that country back into the Russian
orbit. Thus the question of where to draw NATO's eastern border remains
unresolved.

The second, interconnected issue relates to the future of Europe's other
security and political mechanisms. The notion of a "twin-track" approach to
the European problem has much to commend it. The need for steps to meet
Russia's legitimate security needs and to ensure that future European structures do not threaten those interests is self-evident. Indeed, those who oppose
NATO expansion to Poland point out that any such move would depart from
the pattern established after 1987 wherein no modification to Europe's security arrangements has occurred without Russian consent.[14] The favored
options in a "twin-track" approach include some or all of the following: a special security treaty between Russia and the West, expansion of NATO following the Partnership for Peace, an expansion of the European Union with
a revitalized Organization for Security and Cooperation in Europe as an
umbrella organization, and possible roles for the North Atlantic Cooperation
Council.

"The absence of a longer-range design for Europe," according to Zbigniew
Brzezinski, "can deprive the alliance of its historic *raison d'être* ."[15] Insofar as
institutional architecture constitutes a design, what emerges from many of
these proposal is a cat's cradle, some filaments of which are stronger and some
parts of which are more tenuously connected than others. One element
which seems particularly suspect to some North American NATO enthusi-
asts is the Western European Union. The reason is obvious: the Western
European Union provides Europe with a common military arm independent
of U.S. influence. Assistant Secretary of State for European and Canadian
Affairs Richard Holbrooke has argued that the Union should only develop as
long as it does not impinge on NATO. He has also suggested the necessity of
breaking the "layers of ambivalence, confusion, complacence, and history
that inhibit reforms," something the Clinton administration has signally
failed to do. Nor does the two-track, multi-institutional process put forward
to maintain America's leadership in Europe offer much likelihood of resolving the dilemmas resulting from the Soviet Union's demise.

## President Clinton's Problems

One of the striking features of the debate about Europe's future security organization is the call by many Americans for leadership in a country which seems unwilling to lead—their own. If Europe is to grant American claims to leadership, the necessary precursor is that the United States sort out its own goals and its foreign policy in ways that would command transatlantic confidence. At present, there is too much ground for European doubts to permit the creation of anything like the Cold War model of a NATO with the United States at its hub as the anchor of Europe's security machinery.

Clinton's problems are by no means entirely of his own making. Like every incumbent in the White House, he is to some extent the prisoner of circumstances. Not the least of these is the legacy of his predecessor. Skeptical of "the vision thing," George Bush displayed little in his foreign policy. Veering from globalism in 1990-1991 to unilateralism in 1992, Bush ended up with a "values-free" foreign policy, which amounted to no foreign policy at all.[16] Inheriting nothing, Clinton's own proclivities determined that nothing would replace it; rather, restricting vision to the domestic arena, he opted for an often confusing and sometimes contradictory pragmatism in foreign policy.

Political opposition also constrains the president. The election of Republican majorities to the 104th Congress of the United States produced that party's "Contract with America" and a subsequent drive to reduce U.S. overseas obligations, particularly to the UN. Republican proposals would effectively end U.S. financial backing for many UN peace-keeping operations.[17] The force of political opposition to the UN drew from Clinton his Presidential Decision Directive 25. That directive spells out a series of conditions that would have to be met before the United States would participate in any peace-keeping operations. Presidential Decision Directive 25 also announced that the United States would not support a UN standing army and would not earmark specific U.S. military units for service with the UN.

The directive was clear evidence of Clinton's need to bend with the wind of Republican isolationism. One must not under-rate the force of that isolationism. House Speaker Newt Gingrich has put forward what Arthur Schlesinger, Jr., has called the "Orwellian" National Security Revitalization Act which would cut more than $1 billion from America's current contribution to UN peace keeping and control the president's power to approve new peace-keeping missions. "The effect, should the bill be enacted into law would be to eviscerate the American role in collective security."[18] Senate majority leader Robert Dole's Peace Powers Act similarly claims to restrict the president's capacity to contribute American money and lives to UN efforts.

Congress appears to be in a mood ugly enough to lead to America's repudiation of the very internationalism that created the United Nations in San Francisco in 1945. Where Roosevelt once promised not to send American boys to fight in foreign wars, Dole now proclaims the nation's unwillingness to tolerate American casualties "for irresponsible internationalism." Far from declining, neo-isolationism threatens to become a major issue in the coming 1996 presidential election. On the right, Pat Buchanan espouses a form of "fortress-America" isolationism, which is even more extreme, and more visceral, than that of either Gingrich or Dole. With much of his domestic agenda in ruins, Clinton may well feel the need to run with the hounds, if he is not to be hunted by them.

Clinton's problems in forging an agenda for Europe result in part from the consequence of the intermixing of foreign and domestic affairs in American politics. The president made a deliberate choice on the presidential campaign trail in 1992 to amalgamate the two elements together to create a weapon with which to attack the incumbent president. "In this new era," Clinton declared, "our first priority in foreign policy and our first domestic priority are one and the same: we must revive our economy."[19] In part, Clinton's approach reflected what is a growing degree of distrust of Federal government felt by a significant number of Americans. In part, too, Clinton's ambivalence towards foreign policy springs from an all-too-honest recognition that America is not the world power it once was—an admission that may be true, but may not be the whole truth.

In choosing between conflicting roles for the United States in Europe—the lone superpower, the global balancer, the conciliator and facilitator—the Clinton administration has allowed itself to be influenced by its perception of the United States as "the shrunken superpower." A Samson now shorn, the United States must concentrate on revitalizing its economy before it can contemplate wider commitments. Such a perception leads to a redefining of the extent of America's commitments. So said Under-Secretary for Political Affairs Peter Tarnoff in May, 1993. Despite rapid reaction by State Department spin-doctors to reassure the alarmed that the United States had no intention of abandoning its position of leadership, both Secretary of State Warren Christopher and the president himself have reiterated similar messages on a number of occasions.

However, 'Declinist' interpretations of America's great power status have been vigorously challenged, and there is no reason for doubting that the United States remains the strongest single entity in the world. Paradoxically, as remarked earlier, one of the more potent challenges to that position comes from the prospect of an integrated Europe with interlocking economies. In the meantime, however, no rival of the U.S. seems in a position to challenge.

Japan is undergoing a period of financial retrenchment and internal doubt, the Pacific rim economies remain very much in the process of development, and Russia has far to go before it can unlock the oil, mineral, and timber resources of Siberia. Whether the United States wishes to redevelop its leadership role in Europe is very much a matter of *its* choice: this, of course, rests in turn upon the relative priorities given to domestic and foreign concerns. Clinton is to some extent compelled to opt for a domestic agenda, but he is also personally inclined to do so. It may not be the right choice—it certainly is not the right choice for a power which has aspirations to lead the process of reorganizing Europe's security order—but the opportunities to follow another path diminish with every step towards the 1996 presidential election.

The international actions of an administration that propounds the primacy of domestic politics, that puts economics to the fore, and that opts for a policy of multilateralism to share the burdens of world leadership have not been reassuring. Clinton has displayed a tendency to react pragmatically and has emphasized diplomacy and sanctions over military force. There is perhaps a measure of unintended wisdom in this. Peace keeping is an activity which demands skill in low-intensity warfare, while the U.S. Army has made this mission the least of its priorities. The Powell doctrine, propounded by the former chief of the joint chiefs of staff, emphasized swift and massive use of force and equally swift withdrawals. This approach is not calculated to remedy deficiencies in low-intensity war. At one level, the United States should stand aloof from peace-keeping operations until its military develops some necessary expertise.

But even under Clinton, the United States has not avoided direct military interventions, as its record in Somalia and in Haiti bears witness. Over and above the performance of the U.S. military, these episodes reveal a dismal descent from the heights of liberal humanitarian rhetoric to crude political fixing. In the case of Haiti, General Raul Cedras, accused of extensive human rights crimes, escaped from his sins into a comfortable exile. In Somalia, an American military aircraft flew General Aideed, responsible for the murder of a number of UN peace keepers, to a conference to resolve the crisis. To a watching world, the lessons of Somalia and Haiti are that the United States has learned "the art of the deal."[20] While this strategy has allowed Clinton to escape from several holes, Europeans do not see this kind of practice as a suitable basis for partnership with, or leadership of, their continent.

For Europeans, the Clinton administration's record in Bosnia gives most pause for thought. Here American policy has swung right across the spectrum and back. After first claiming that it had no national interests in the conflict, the United States then invoked powerful shibboleths: human rights, preservation of state sovereignty, and maintenance of territorial integrity. First willing to contemplate the use of force in a unilateral context in the Balkans, the administration abandoned that notion when it realized that the American people were likely to balk. Peace plans have been rejected and deals broken. At present the two sides have agreed to the Dayton Accords in which a Bosnia-Hertzegovina federation holds the larger share of the territory while a Serb republic holds the smaller. Both entities would have the right to establish special relationships with neighboring countries (Croatia and Serbia respectively); both are to hold elections, respect human rights, and allow freedom of movement. However, if the peace actually works, it will be a consequence of NATO's air and artillery strikes on Serbian positions surrounding Sarajevo, and not of the superior merits of third-party mediation over military intervention. As such, it will be a disguised defeat for U.S. policy; or, to be more accurate, a success which owes less to American influence than to European power wielded on behalf of the United Nations.

How valid is the Clinton administration's claim to leadership in Europe in the light of such experiences? While domestic and international difficulties have forced the president into a pick-and-mix brand of multilateralism, the accompanying stop-go diplomacy betokens a deep uncertainty in foreign policy. As one commentator has noted, "even a benign interpretation of the administration's inconsistence could not obscure [its] record of indecision."[21] A less benign observation is that the president "has demonstrated that he is unwilling to defend military values whose violation he had described as the most serious crimes of the past few decades."[22] Divided deeply politically between neo-Altlanticists and neo-isolationists, lacking an established and agreed-upon agenda of national interests, practicing pragmatism in diplomacy while preaching idealism, the United States today lacks every one of the foundations on which it might build a persuasive policy for the new European and world order.

# Europe and the Architecture of Security

If America currently finds itself in difficulties, so too does Europe. Alongside the political currents generated by European integration, specific events—the break-up of the Soviet Union, continuing war in the former Yugoslavia, and emerging instabilities in Eastern and Central Europe—have created new security dilemmas. In contemplating them, Europe not only has to consider the costs and benefits of maintaining a strong American presence in Europe through NATO but also the likely outcomes of defining a common foreign and security policy, the development and redefinition of the Western European Union, and the security implications of an enlarged European

Union. The elements of a new security organization lie on the table like pieces of a jig-saw puzzle; the issue is whether—and how—to fit them together or to accept that there is no need to design a new structure because the security challenges do not require it.

There is much to be said for making NATO the core of any new security arrangement. American participation, even at the more modest level envisaged by the Clinton administration, reduces the costs to the Western European nations of defense. NATO represents, proponents claim, the best hedge against the ambitions of a resurgent Russia. The value of extended deterrence, in other words, will hold good even though the Cold War which generated it has ended. By the reverse token, without U.S. participation through NATO, Western European security guarantees to protect Central European states from Russia are far less credible.[23]

Western Europe's interest in maintaining collective and multilateral security through NATO extends beyond the threat a renascent Russia might pose. A French commentator has noted five possible scenarios: direct threats to the territorial integrity and security of European states; spillovers from areas of instability; direct challenges to the functioning of the international system (such as the Iraqi invasion of Kuwait); threat to overseas allies or possessions; and a return to "a competition for national power and influence between European states which had reverted to essentially national security and defense policies."[24] NATO may not even possess the capacity to meet these varied problems, but it does embody the transatlantic strategic coupling which would permit the use of American resources in Europe's defense, as well as providing the focus for organizing a U.S.-European security relationship.

A further argument for the preservation of NATO is that it enables the collective provision of military assets which otherwise would not be available at all, or that would have to be extensively and expensively duplicated. During the Gulf War, when American lift was not available, NATO's own shortage of air transport resulted in the need to hire Antonov transports from the Soviet Union to deploy mobile forces to Turkey.[25] AWACs, Hawk and Patriot missiles, and NADGE radars all come under direct NATO control in peace and war and would have to be extensively replicated if NATO disappears. Thus, the costs alone in *materiel* of discarding NATO would be high.

Maintaining NATO, and with it American involvement in Europe, has other advantages for those who prefer to eschew "architectural speculation" in favor of concentrating on the security challenges that Europe confronts. The United States is the only state that can effectively deploy large-scale rapid-reaction forces. In a word, it adds practicality as well as credibility to European defense. By obviating the need for a nuclear-armed Germany, it contributes to nonproliferation, an activity in which it plays a vital orchestrating role in respect to the necessary array of export policies, rewards, and sanctions required to buttress the Non-Proliferation Treaty. Thanks in large measure to the U.S. presence, NATO can exercise both control and deterrence over the nuclear environment. "NATO and American engagement remain essential to the management and development of a viable arms control regime in Europe, and they remain essential to the protection of adequate nuclear deterrence in the period of ambiguity."[26]

Critics of NATO as a structure for developing and reconciling defense and security issues suggest that the organization carries the stigma of Cold War victories in Eastern Europe and a whiff of American hegemony in Western Europe. They argue that the alternative through which Europe can develop an independent unified security structure, and one towards which America manifests some caution, is the Western European Union.[27] Maastricht reinvigorates the Western European Union as a player in the process of European integration. Its membership will soon include other European NATO and European Union countries, with neutrals admitted as observers. The Western European Union is developing its common operational role through such instruments as its planning cell (which became fully operational in April 1993), meetings of chiefs of defense staffs, and closer military cooperation. The Western European Union has made much progress in the last two years in developing its institutional and operational dimensions. Participating nations have identified deployable forces and defined the purposes for which they might be used. Members have also addressed the question of when and in what circumstances the Western European Union could act without the authorization of a UN Security Council resolution. Finally, they have delineated the status and rights of associate members who are not parties to the Western European Union Treaty (Norway, Iceland and Turkey).

Nevertheless, the Western European Union displays considerable shortcomings. These operate on two levels: the political and the practical. Politically, the different member states have kept different national interests and different perceptions of common security problems. These differences revealed themselves most clearly during the Yugoslav crisis, when NATO proved a more acceptable and effective support instrument for UN peacekeeping activities. Practically, the Western European Union does not yet have the means to match the resources of NATO—those chiefly of NATO's strongest member, the United States—effectively in complex military operations. In the words of one expert commentator, "The development of a real European capacity to act collectively is probably still some way off."[28] Such capacity may well come. In the interim, Europe took some heed of Bush's warning in February 1991 that the construction of a European defense caucus could damage the Atlantic Alliance. The Western European Union now moves ahead on the basis of recognizing the Atlantic Alliance as a body whose decisions are paramount over its own, while under the Maastricht treaty it develops and implements European Union decisions with defense implications. Beyond this lies the common defense which might in time result from the common foreign and security policy. Presently standing as the European pillar to complement NATO, the Western European Union nevertheless contains the seeds of independence, just as it contains the seeds of division.

## The European Triangle: France, Germany and Great Britain

Revision of the roles and functions of the Western European Union is the inevitable and inescapable concomitant of further European integration. Seeing European military structures as rivals to NATO and as military levers against American interests, the United States remains suspicious of Franco-German attempts to revise the role of the Western European Union. Europe is no longer America's junior partner in security issues: it pursues its own policies and has to an extent "relativized" the American role both in Europe and NATO. The nature of this development is, however, not the outcome of a process of recognizing and catering to generic issues. As Europe emerges from an era of American preponderance, its most important members display differences in outlook that could reconfigure the political map. The United States should—and no doubt will—pay close attention to the aims and anxieties of the European triangle; its own actions will have some role to play in the outcome.

Despite long-standing French suspicions regarding American intentions within NATO, changes in the post-Cold War system have dictated a need to reappraise France's role within that institution. That reappraisal is taking place within the context of changes in the external European environment which are not necessarily congenial to France and in a domestic environment in which Jacques Chirac's victory has ended a period of cohabitation between a left-wing president (Mitterand) and a right-wing prime minister (Balladur), thus opening up the possibility of a more dynamic foreign policy. In deciphering French attitudes towards NATO, "one should never forget that their basis is largely founded on domestic as opposed to external, political rationales." It is certainly true that in relativizing NATO and the Western European Union, France must respond to new external developments.[29]

France's preference for intensification over enlargement of the European Community—deepening rather than widening—has for the time being hit the buffer of public hesitancy. Enlargement is now at the head of the European agenda, and it poses a particular threat to French interests, for it presents a newly-unified Germany with the opportunity to develop, or redevelop, a powerful sphere of interest. "Paris believes, therefore, that an eastward enlargement of the European community would automatically be accompanied by an increase in German influence."[30] This is one potentially powerful counterforce to future development of the Franco-German joint brigade which the two powers established in 1992. Another is the option of intersecting the Bonn-London alignment and so depriving Germany of the capacity "to play the British card" against France.

In responding to the new security agenda, President Chirac is likely to keep the Western European Union at the core of his European policy. As prime minister under Mitterand, he closely associated himself with the Western European Union's relaunch in the 1980s. Moreover, the timespan allowed to the original Western Union (fifty years) runs out in 1998. The expiry date offers scope for renewing the Western European Union and possibly integrating it more closely with the European Union. France may also choose to build on the fact that the Eurocorps has been placed at the service of the Atlantic Alliance in order to bring France back fully into the NATO fold. France's experiences in the UN/NATO operation in the former Yugoslavia may provide further fillip to this move, although national differences over policy in this region (for example, with Germany over its swift recognition of Croatia) could produce a realignment of forces in Europe. The prospect of a modified form of Gaullism is perhaps reinforcing France's obduracy in resuming nuclear testing on Muraroa atoll.

France's ultimate aim may, thus, be to build up the institutional strength of the Western European Union while pursuing greater involvement in NATO. This coincides with the notion, to which the United States is likely to have to reconcile itself, of a stronger European Union defense community which complements rather than supersedes NATO. By resting that policy on a Franco-German axis, recognizing Germany's claim to a seat on the UN Security Council, and "treating Germany as a true political equal," France may facilitate stable relations with Russia.[31] However, the implications of Franco-British cooperation in Bosnia suggest that there also exists the possibility of a new bilateral relationship within Europe which would have implications for the United States in its NATO policy.

During the Cold War, Germany was Europe's frontline state. While the urgency of the Soviet threat has greatly diminished with the Soviet Union's retreat and disappearance, Germany's security concerns remain considerable.

Geography has placed the German nation at the center of Europe. Politics has put her on the border of a region racked with ethnic and religious strife. Thus the central objective of German security is the preservation of stability in Europe. Behind this objective lies a concept of security which includes nonmilitary as well as military threats: in the event of serious disorder or economic distress in Eastern Europe and the collapse of a presently fragile order, Germany would be the first recipient of waves of refugees. Germany has need, therefore, to shape the European security agenda; to achieve its goals, it must adopt a leadership role which does not render its actions ineffective or unacceptable by reawakening the ghosts of the past. Thus, the Germans are, and must be committed to, European integration. Indeed, Christoph Bluth suggests that Germany's "commitment to Western European integration has possibly been the most fundamental principle of West German foreign policy after the Second World War."[32] To achieve their goals, the Germans have adopted an approach to the issues of domestic and European security which one commentator has characterized as "polycentric steering."[33]

On the one hand, Germany remains committed to NATO and to an American presence in Europe. As well as countering trends towards neoisolationism emerging in the United States, NATO offers Germany a general nuclear guarantee and a political reassurance against the emergence of a Russian threat. For a state which has renewed its renunciation of nuclear weapons, such a guarantee remains essential until such time as Britain and France can offer a continuing substitute—if such a time ever comes. At the same time, German perceptions of the need for a pan-European system of collective security, deriving directly from their position as the outlier of Western Europe, move them towards support for the Organization for Security and Cooperation in Europe as the best mechanism for meeting the security needs of Eastern Europe, securing the levels of economic cooperation necessary to rebuild the economies of the former communist countries and bringing together the United States and Russia.

A third arm of Germany policy, which provides another powerful reason for Germany to adopt the mantle of integration, is the gradual rebuilding of its national military capability. Fifty years of antimilitarism have built a popular barrier to German military activism which will take much time to remove. Nevertheless, the instabilities which Germany seeks in part to overcome by institutional integration may also require both the capability and the willingness to project national force as part of a multilateral action. Admiral Ulrich Weisser, head of the German Defense Ministry's Policy Planning Staff, has stated that "the use of military power may have to be possible and occasionally necessary, for a just cause." He has also argued that Germany must cease to be a "net importer of security" and become instead an exporter of it.[34] The German courts have recently decided whether the German constitution needs to be amended for the Bundeswehr to operate outside NATO territory in the government's favor in July 1994. That decision unlocked the legal gates to extended military action, and the Luftwaffe's involvement in UN/NATO-authorized air action in Bosnia may prove to be another significant milestone on the path back to normality for the German state.

Germany's geographical location creates security needs which it shares with the rest of Europe, and even the United States, but which it feels particularly sharply. The nation's economic power provides the motor for competition with those same powers. Already it is possible to detect "a new assertiveness and a certain renationalization" in German politics.[35] The Clinton administration has shown a distinct preference for a Washington-Berlin axis in much of its European security policy. If Germany is to develop a leadership role in Europe commensurate with its needs and status, this must come in the context of integrative and collaborative architecture. Incautious American bilateralism forced on Germany—perhaps designed to balance out a London-Paris axis—could do as much as anything else to upset the apple cart.

Perhaps the least secure American avenue is Europe is that of the "special relationship" with Britain. British officialdom stresses the need to retain NATO since that organization offers a tried and tested forum for the discussion of security issues and embodies through its integrated military structure "essential transatlantic military links." Yet British officials acknowledge that the challenge lies in managing a greater role for security and defense with the Western European Union while maintaining NATO as "the essential framework underpinning European security."[36] Lurking beneath these architectural issues—the lobster-pot on the seabed of British politics—lies the question of whether the special relationship has had its day and the time has come for Britain to enter into full partnership in Europe. Uncertainties about the United States, for reasons outlined above, join hands with conceptions of Britain's interest in the post-Cold War, post-colonial, world to create a powerful argument for a repositioning of the United Kingdom.

"Declinist" conceptions of America suggest that Britain would be well advised to move out of the American orbit, as the United States supposedly has no will to remain a European power, no vision for a post-Cold War Europe, and no finance to contribute. The United States in the 1990s, in the Declinist view, resembles Britain at the end of the Second World War: an "overstretched and economically faltering superpower."[37] To this way of thinking, the rationale for Britain's continued interest in the "special relationship" derives from a mixture of nostalgia and myopia. In clinging to the United States, Britain is "looking forward to its past," while at the same time attempting to justify a wayward policy over Europe, where its true future lies.

The once-trumpeted kinship between English-speaking peoples has now disappeared as the differences between Britain and American have widened. At the same time the conflictual tendencies of the United States, evident in its policies towards Libya, Iran, and Iraq, make it as much a potential cause of instability as a gatekeeper of order.

In support of this view is the proposition that changes in the new world order mean that the circumstances which underpinned the "special relationship" have all changed and that it has therefore lost its raison d'être. Germany is once again the largest country in Europe, and the Baltic, Balkans, and the Southern flank all represent urgent security issues. Faced with a situation in which the emerging European order, and especially the issue of Central European stability, are crucial to British interests, it is difficult to define a coherent national interest that is distinctive to Britain. Indeed, such is the seriousness of the common problems of Eastern Europe that they "must be the first priority for British foreign policy-makers in the next few years."[38] If this conception holds more than a germ of truth, then sooner or later, British foreign policy will have to adjust to the realities of global change in the 1990s.

The fact that the United States, while still reliable as a partner in Europe, may be less willing to become involved on Europe's borders lends weight to those who see the future of the United Kingdom as lying in the Western European Union rather than in NATO.[39] Limited though nuclear power may be, and outdated though the tactical and military rationales underpinning British and French nuclear deterrents may appear, nuclear capability remains of paramount importance in a world in which Russia stands as the most potent threat to European stability. Britain and France are the only European powers to posses that capability: deploying it in the collective interest through the Western European Union offers Britain the opportunity to lead the way in formulating a post-Cold War nuclear strategy. Further, an Anglo-French axis, built partially on the foundations of a shared willingness to execute military action in circumstances such as the Bosnian imbroglio, offers a means for Britain to control an ever-stronger Germany.[40] Thus France might serve Britain better as a partner in Europe for the 1990s than the United States.

## Through a Glass Darkly...

Contemporary debate focuses more broadly on America's relationship with Europe, rather than specifically with Britain. This is a reflection of the physical change of western interests brought about not only by disintegration in the Soviet Union and Yugoslavia, and by German reunification, but also by the continued move towards an integrated European community. While the "special relationship" enjoyed a renaissance under Margaret Thatcher, it lies lifeless on the periphery of Clinton's concerns. Indeed, the basic foundations of any such relationship have started to disintegrate. America increasingly looks to the Pacific for its economic future. Its political elite is no longer exclusively white and Anglo-Saxon, nor does it necessarily share enduring European traditions. As Christopher Coker argues, for the United States the "special relationship" is perhaps only useful to maintain some control over the speed and type of European integration, while maintaining a position of influence as it enters a period of decline. Similarly, it offers British politicians a reason to ignore the lack of direction over Britain's role in European integration. While lower-level political contacts may well flourish and work effectively, this can no longer justify the "special relationship" as a focal point of high politics.

Clinton's posture towards Europe, and the development of American foreign policy since 1992 has reinforced such an attitude. While ostensibly seeking a flexible Europe with a strengthened NATO, American policy lacks the political will to pursue any agenda. American vacillation over Bosnia, the continued reinterpretation of its interests to accommodate events (both welcome and unwelcome), and Clinton's chosen preference for domestic and economic matters leaves little ground for focus on a specific transatlantic relationship. The sense that Clinton no longer controls foreign policy as a result of the 1996 presidential campaign, or can effectively cope with the domestic debate over America's international role further compounds such feelings. Not only is the administration embattled by the Republicans in Congress, there is also evidence of divisions between the State Department and the Pentagon. Foreign policy making seems as fragmented as ever. Whilst there is still scope for hopeful developments (such as Clinton's avowed multilateralism), America has struggled to approach the obvious contradiction between an integrated Europe as a security structure and an integrated Europe as an economic competitor. Thus, so far, Clinton's foreign policy has lacked resonance and coherence.

Europe's future is difficult to discern, since it will result from the intermeshing of many variables. Not the least of these is national policy. A significant proportion of the Western European electorate remains skeptical of what they see as the submerging of national identity in, and surrendering of sovereignty to, a new, supranational Europe run by bureaucrats in Brussels. As ever, politicians must educate their peoples, if they are to carry them along the path to a wider, and ultimately deeper, integration of Europe.

The new thinking to be done in the transition to a new order must encompass the fact that a transatlantic disassociation, although possible, is not likely, and that the new era will not inevitably be one of peace and cooperation. The development of policies and the design of architecture through which they are to be effected must go hand in hand. The former demands the clear articulation of national interests which must be shared. In this respect, Europe is drawing ahead of the United States. America must make up ground, if it is to play a leading role in the future. The latter demands that those charged with security produce a system for tomorrow's needs, not one that caters to the world of yesterday. In all this, America's Cold War outlook—its juxtaposition of allies and adversaries, its propensity to see international policy in terms of a manichean struggle between good and evil, its manifest destiny to lead those it terms its partners, and its preference for grand designs within which to conduct its affairs—will likely prove to be a grave handicap.

## Chapter 5

# The United States and Asian Security

*Allan R. Millett*[1]

The walls of Kwangsong-bo citadel tower above the Yomha straits that separate the island of Kanghwa-do from the headlands at the mouth of the Han River. Built by the Korean kings of the Yi dynasty in the seventeenth century to block Japanese invasions and to provide a safe haven from rebellious subjects, Kwangsong-bo citadel dominates a fortification system of three forts, linking walls, and an artillery redoubt. The royal complex of palaces and temples includes other fortifications, most rebuilt and restored during the reign of President Park Chung Hee, (1961–1979), but Kwangsong-bo is special. It is the place where the first American servicemen died in combat in Korea.

Under the pretext of avenging the destruction of the American merchantman, *General Sherman*, in 1866 and the execution of the largely Asian crew, a U.S. naval squadron sailed for Korea in May 1871 from its rendezvous at Shanghai, China. Under instructions crafted by the State Department and its minister to China, Frederick P. Low, the punitive expedition of five ships with 1,230 sailors and Marines, commanded by Rear Admiral John Rodgers, reached Korean waters later the same month. Thinking that the Korean negotiators they had met on 1 June had permitted them to explore the Yomha channel, Low and Rodgers sent two gunboats and four launches up the narrows the next day. Perhaps as a result of a translating error, the Korean batteries opened fire, just as they had on a French expedition five years earlier. Rodgers' warships returned the fire with gusto, but in eight days of intermittent bombardment the American admiral saw that he could not silence the Korean batteries without capturing the forts. On 10 June an American landing party of 651 sailors and Marines, supported by naval gunfire, attacked the Kwangsong-bo forts. They seized two positions without serious resistance, but Governor Oh Chae Yon and his younger brother, Oh Chae Sun, made a stand at Kwangsong-bo citadel with their courageous, but poorly armed garrison of around 260 soldiers. In the heat and dust of late morning, 11 June 1871, the American landing party stormed the citadel amid a deluge of cannon balls, musket balls, spears, and stones and annihilated the Korean garrison, almost to the last man. Today, only the graves of the brothers Oh are marked; their soldiers rest under seven Korean burial mounds, guarded by shrines and a site for purification.

The American victory, represented by fifty captured banners and 481 obsolete brass cannon of varied calibers, did not come without cost. The first of eleven casualties, Private Daniel Hanrahan, USMC, an Irish immigrant, died early in the charge, and Landsman Seth A. Allen perished in the charge over the parapet. Near Allen, the first man through the breach, Lieutenant Hugh W. McKee, USN, took a bullet and spear tip in the groin and upper thigh. He died that night on board *Colorado*, Rodgers' flagship. Having "avenged" the insult to the U.S. flag and considering the hull damage to *Palos* and *Monocacy* caused by running aground in the Kanghwa-do shoals, Rodgers ordered his squadron back to China. He buried his dead at sea.[2]

One hundred and twenty-three years later, but less than two hundred miles east of Kanghwa-do, the most recent American combat death in Asia occurred on 17 December 1994. Confused or careless during a routine orientation flight along the DMZ, CWO-2 Bobby W. Hall II and CWO-2 David M. Hilemon, Army helicopter pilots in the 501st Aviation Battalion, Eighth Army, flew their OH-58C "Kiowa" helicopter into the North Korean air defense zone. Blasted by one SA-7 surface-to-air missile, the "Kiowa" crashed inside North Korea, killing Hilemon. That Hilemon is only the latest U.S. fatality, but not the last, seems a safe bet.[3]

If a democratic nation measures its vital national interests by the blood of its servicemen and the treasure and mourning of its citizens, then the deaths of McKee, Hanrahan, Allen, and Hilemon link a historic U.S. commitment to the fate of Asia. Since 1899 when American troops once again began fighting Asians in Asia, the United States has lost over 190,000 combat dead in three major wars and a number of other pacification campaigns and punitive expeditions. These combat deaths outnumber the total combat fatalities suffered by the American armed forces in the defeat of the Third Reich (185,000) between 1941–1945. If these sacrifices in American lives represent a tragedy or failure of policy, then they represent a catastrophe of major proportions for the United States, not to mention the millions of Chinese, Koreans, Japanese, and Filipinos who have fallen to American arms since the Rodgers Expedition visited Kanghwa-do. The historical evidence, however, suggests otherwise.[4]

Regardless of the state of American relations with Europe or individual European states, which have swayed between collective security and isolationism, which really means only an absence of binding diplomatic ties, the United States has had an enduring fascination with Asia, especially China, Japan, and Korea, since the merchantman *Empress of China*, carrying New York ginseng, put into Canton harbor on 30 August 1784. Like most enduring American foreign commitments, the Asian connection depends upon an uneasy mix of free-trade economics, reciprocated cultural imperialism, strategic considerations however tenuous, religious conviction, bureaucratic zeal, the search for cheap but controllable immigrant labor, a missionary ardor in spreading "progressive" Western learning through transplanted educational institutions, romantic journalism, sheer adventurism, and the impact of charismatic individuals with access to policy makers, government or private. To separate these factors into categories of cause and effect, of means and ends, is impossible. At best the course of Asian-American relations is as muddy as the Yangzi and tortuous as the Great Wall.[5]

The aftermath of the Rodgers Expedition offers a good example of how unpredictable events can be in just one Asian nation and over a short period of time. Eleven years after the Rodgers Expedition sailed away with its trophy cannons and banners, and without firing another angry shot, the United States signed the Treaty of Amity and Commerce at Chemulp'o (modern Inchon) in 1882 with the willing participation of King Kojong's court. The U.S. received the privilege of conducting formal diplomatic relations with Korea, using Korean ports for trade and to refit ships, and enjoying limited commercial activities in Korea under the court's protection. Britain, Russia, Italy, and France soon negotiated similar treaties with Korea. The Hermit Kingdom, "the land of the Morning Calm," opened its gates to the West.

Nevertheless, the Korean experience in the last years of the nineteenth century provides a cautionary tale to Western pundits. This change in Korean policy did not represent a sudden conversion to Western values—only a desperate attempt to preserve Korean national independence in the face of renewed Japanese imperialism. In 1875 the Japanese succeeded where the French and Americans failed. When Korean soldiers in a Kangwha-do fortification fired at a Japanese survey party, the Japanese Navy responded with shellfire and a landing assault that destroyed the Korean redoubt. Under the pretext of further punitive action against the Koreans for firing on the *Unyo*, a Japanese squadron of six vessels and a regiment of special landing troops occupied Kanghwa-do until the Koreans agreed to grant special commercial privileges and protections in the Treaty of Kanghwa-do, February 1876. Not only did the Koreans then turn to the Western nations for countervailing influence, exercised for Britain and the United States by Methodist and Presbyterian medical and educational missionaries, but the Kojong court sought military and diplomatic protection from the Manchu Empress Dowager Ts'u Hsi. By 1905, after Japan had defeated both China and Russia in war and cowed the United States with its aggressive modernity, Korea had shifted from hermit to captive.[6]

Korea's unhappy experiment in drawing Western nations into a shifting regional balance between China (fading) and Japan (resurgent) reflected only another chapter in East-West politics that one might date with Alexander's assault on the Hindu Kush in 327–326 B.C. The more direct lineage to Western guns, books, and trade goods begins with the explorations and exploitations of the Spanish and Portuguese in the sixteenth century, followed shortly by the Dutch, English, French, and finally the Germans and Americans. The sprawl of Western maritime trade and naval expeditions spread throughout the Pacific. The Royal Navy, for example, discovered that Botany Bay and Kealakekua Bay did not open quite the same doors to wealth and fame, even for Captain James Cook. Watching the march of European influence up the coast of China, Japan turned from the useful but irritating manipulation of declining European colonial powers and the Catholic Church to embrace the Meiji Restoration and the best technology and military practices of Britain and Germany. Like the Koreans, the Chinese sought protection abroad and, after the Revolution of 1910, looked to Russia—even the Soviet Union—and Germany for capital as well as advisors, military and bureaucratic. Britain, playing the "Great Game" in Central Asia, signed an alliance with Japan in 1902, which concerned the United States, now the colonial governor of the Philippines, dropped by Spain in a postwar treaty in 1898. Germany fell heir to other Spanish islands in the Pacific and established a major enclave on the Shandong peninsula, China. From Afghanistan to Japan, only one nation, the kingdom of Siam, remained independent, because of Western inability to agree on the division of spoils, European exhaustion in the process of imperialism, and a favorable geographic position between the British Raj and the French *mission civilatrice*. All Asian nations became pawns in a great power global competition. A regional hegemon, Imperial Japan, a jackal on the plains of world power, stood ready to pounce on European leftovers.

Two world wars, a world depression, and the Cold War rewrote the politics of Asia and, by extension, most of the Pacific islands west of the international dateline. Much has changed by the dying decade of the twentieth century, but in the future rest the perils of the past. European imperialists—

at least those in uniforms and striped pants—are gone, dumped from power by the ravages of two world wars. Quaint outposts like Macao and Hong Kong remain, but not for long. A list of twice-liberated nations (first from the Europeans, then from the Japanese) includes a roll call of South and Southeast Asia: Myanmar, Malaysia, Singapore, Indonesia, Cambodia, Laos, Vietnam, and the Philippines. India and Pakistan left the British Empire and each other. In their own unique fashion Australia and New Zealand have held both Britain and the United States at arm's length. The Taiwanese emerged from fifty years of Japanese rule—then faced another fifty-year struggle to throw off a rightist regime imposed by mainland Nationalist refugees.

Divided by a civil war in 1945–1953, the two Koreas at least stand apart from China and Japan. The Republic of Korea still values its alliance with the United States even if the threats from China and the Soviet Union have receded, for North Korea (the Democratic People's Republic of Korea) remains a military threat and the Japanese cultural and economic rivals. Unchanged, too, are the regional and communal tensions brought by the end of colonialism, the Cold War's course and conclusion, economic competition in a global market, reduction of Russia to a sub-regional power, and a love–hate relationship with the United States. In North Asia the question is whether China and Japan will open another round of their centuries-old competition to prove the superiority of their cultures. The fact that one nation is still nominally Communist and the other a capitalist, multi-party democracy is less important than the fact that the *han* and the *yamato* peoples remain essentially unchanged in their cultural values. Confucius is more important than Marx in China, while Shintoism remains a cultural and political force in Japan. China is already a nuclear power, and Japan could easily be one if left to its own devices. The same applies to the two Koreas.

Having divested itself of almost all of its political and military ties with the Philippines and now embarked on a halting reconciliation with Vietnam, the United States has displayed little interest in playing the same role in Southeast and South Asia that it has in North Asia. Its concern, however, about the future relations of China, Japan, and Korea forces it to pay some attention to the rest of the region. The newly-independent nations of the Malay Barrier and the southeast corner of Eurasia do not wish to fall under the domination of either China or Japan, the former by force of population and military power, the latter through financial and economic imperialism. Although American repudiation of the legitimacy of the Republic of China (Taiwan) is a cause for alarm, Southern Asians do not fear excessive American activism, given the U.S. experience in Vietnam. Yet American military power (even in small commitments) might prove decisive in a crisis in which air and naval power are more important than large armies and protracted conflict. The most deeply engaged external power in Asia, the United States is the big brother that younger brothers seek to unleash in the face of their self-defined bullying neighbors. Britain once played this role along the Malay Barrier—and Australia has assumed some of its burden in places like Brunei and Singapore—but the United States is the only nation powerful enough to make a difference in a major crisis. One example should suffice. When, in 1977, the Carter administration, bloated with anti-imperialist conceits, announced that the U.S. 2nd Infantry Division would leave South Korea, the news set off a shock wave in the region. Chinese and Japanese protests against such a drastic alteration in the *status quo* produced a hasty change of policy, if not of heart, in Washington since the Carter administration remained unhappy with the autocratic regimes of Park Chung Hee and Chun Doo Hwan. Being courted, however, as an ally of a kind does not answer the question of whether the much-wooed Columbia should continue the courtship into the twenty-first century.[7]

## The United States and the Future of Asia: The Security Dimension

The latest official definition of America's "national security strategy," itself an awkward term that further confuses ends and means, is that the United States seeks 1) to protect itself from foreign military threats, 2) to bring about important reforms in the national and international economic system that will enhance American economic growth and the distribution of wealth in the United States, and 3) to promote democracy, interpreted to mean the weakening of autocratic regimes whatever their philosophical base. (One wonders what, for example, Saudis and Singaporeans think of the latter goal.) The United States aims to advance none of these goals by war or the threat of war, but rather by deterring others from using force through "engagement and enlargement" in bilateral, multilateral, and international associations and agreements. The Clinton administration pledges to apply its principles everywhere; that is, to makes no distinction by geographic area or to establish any priorities among its goals.[8]

Foreign policy problems and crises carry with them special contextual factors. Peace in Rwanda does not bear the same significance as peace in the Republic of South Africa, although both require coming to grips with militant African tribalism. Since the end of World War II the United States has tried to stitch together a global foreign policy, but in reality it has dealt with problems in terms of five regions: North America and Europe from the

Atlantic to the Urals; the Middle East from Morocco to Afghanistan; Asia-Pacific from Pakistan to Russian Siberia; Central and South America; and Sub-Saharan Africa. The first three regions have vied almost equally since 1945. Eurocentric politicians trumpet the importance of NATO and the restoration of a "good" Germany, but forget that the United States recognized Israel in 1948 and saved the Shah of Iran in 1954, while reforming Japan and intervening in the Korean War. In strategic terms, of course, the Soviet nuclear missile force and the forward deployment of the Red Army in East Germany gave European affairs an edge, but that edge crumbled with the Berlin Wall.

Of the many reasons that U.S. policy makers cite, with mantra-like conviction, for deterring major interstate war in Asia, economics occupies pride of place. At one time strategic considerations—such as the role of American forces and bases in a global war with the Soviet Union—received equal billing, but the Straits of Tsushima, the Sea of Okhotsk, and the thickness of Soviet air defense systems on the Kamchatka Peninsula have faded from the screen in most discussions of Asian security affairs. The sudden development of Chinese-American intelligence cooperation in the 1970s has also disappeared. At the other edge of the spectrum, conversations about combating rural-based insurgencies in the Philippines and elsewhere have shrunk into isolated corners of the special operations community, which is rarely special or communal. One hesitates to say that the United States has learned its limitations in combating "people's war," but it may be so. The U.S. military may do well in some special operations, but such efforts are small and hurried—not the sort of patient commitment that pacification requires and which must rest on the indigenous political and military leadership.

The strategic focus is upon conflict that will interrupt the current trade patterns. Such a conflict is the war between states which endangers maritime commerce, threatens the factories and ports of Asia, involves the potential disruption of oil shipments, and represents a threat to the region's urban managers and workers. All analysts know the economic numbers. The Asia-Pacific nations are America's major trading partners; the region has the fastest climbing rates of economic growth; and Asian nations seem to offer the greatest promise of escalating productivity, principally through the exploitation of cheap, obedient labor, and skillful management. The difficulty with the economic argument is simply that it works principally for the benefit of Japan, the only nation whose involvement in the American economy as both producer and consumer is essential to America's well-being. Japanese willingness to help fund the deficit spending of the federal government through the purchase of government securities is also not inconsequential leverage on American policy.[9] Yet should Japan's economic role dictate America's security policy in Asia?

Japan has its champions in the United States, and these Nipponophiles usually base their arguments on a realpolitik of trade, not on arguments that Japan and the United States share common cultural values. European-Americans have made their peace with Japanese-Americans, who have proven their loyalty thrice-over, but the former still view the Japanese people as the architects of Pearl Harbor and the deserved recipients of two nuclear weapons in 1945. No doubt such views fail to show much understanding of Japanese politics in 1945, but not much has happened since 1945 to disabuse Americans of the notion that Japan may be capitalist, entrepreneurial, and technocratic, but it is not democratic. Driving a Honda will not necessarily make an American a fan of Japan, even after the World War II veterans take their arguments to a Higher Court. However, the debate over just who is America's most adept pupil in Asia continues, passed now through three or four generations.

The Sinophiles are making a concerted effort to portray China, whatever its government, as the most deserved recipient of American support. The massacre of democratic demonstrators in Tiananmen Square dampened their argument, but it is again gathering force as the memories of Chinese oppression fade and anxiety over the fate of China after the death of Deng Xiaoping mounts. Yet the possibility of conflict over the scheduled absorption of Hong Kong is real, and the pretense that Taiwan is simply a "lost province" of mainland China is even more bothersome, since the Republic of China is rich, well-armed, and determined to shape its own destiny after a century of colonial thrall at the hands of the Japanese and the Guomingtang. That Taiwan now holds the greatest concentration of disposable world currencies gives it potential leverage that it has not yet exploited. The difficulty with the Sinophile position is that the United States no longer needs China to contain the Soviet Union, and the accompanying development of economic and non-governmental institutional ties, while strong, has not developed sufficiently to give China an edge over Japan in either State Department or Congress.[10]

Korea, unified or not, is the Asian "wild card." South Korea has several advantages in winning the hearts and minds of Americans. First, it has emerged as a serious economic rival to Japan in automobiles, electronics, construction, shipbuilding, heavy equipment, machine tools, consumer goods, and athletic equipment. The Koreans also have legitimate claims to special consideration for their victimization by American policy decisions, their massive conversion to Christianity, their reverence for American higher education, and their record as a constant ally, a loyalty matched only by Israel. The Koreans see themselves as the Irish or the Jews of Asia, and the simile is not far-fetched. Americans love underdogs—including Jews and Irishmen—and might well view Korea as the North Asian nation of choice when it comes to security commitments and security ties, especially after the final passing of Korean general-presidents. Significantly, the last ambassador to Korea was the CIA station chief in Seoul while the current ambassador is a former university president and Methodist missionary. Korea's commitment to democracy is debatable, but the provincial and city elections of 1995 suggest some diffusion of power.

American foreign policy decisions, especially those that risk war or produce war, are not determined by the calculus of policy-insiders, however compelling their expertise. American public opinion—expressed by European-Americans, Hispanic-Americans, and African-Americans—will eventually influence the level of sacrifice the United States will endure for its own and some Asian nation's survival. The United States has fought two post-colonial wars in Asia and the comparative experience is instructive. The U.S. government claimed the first war, in Korea, was essential to the security of Japan, but the second was not. The first involved a nation (South Korea) with historic ties to the United States. Its president, Syngman Rhee, spoke English, gained a doctorate at Princeton University, married an Austrian, and practiced a dedicated Protestantism. Ngo Dinh Diem spoke French and Vietnamese, was a practicing Catholic, and had virtually no knowledge of the United States and U.S. values. American operatives plotted against Syngman Rhee, but they helped overthrow and murder Ngo Dinh Diem in 1963. This uncomfortable history has a point. The United States has an effective tie with North Asia that it does not have with Southeast Asia. If it has any special leverage in India and Pakistan, it rests on nothing more than fragile conceptions of a balance of power, the "containment" of China, and some small cultural and economic investments. Pakistanis noticed that American military and economic interest in their country faded rapidly after the Soviets left Afghanistan. Nothing in Islam and Hinduism strikes a spark in the American imagination to the degree that the ordeals of the Sino-Asian Christians do. Americans view immigrant Pakistanis and Indians as the highly-educated refugees of the British Empire, while Southeast Asians have won some sympathy for their struggle against communism. For the first time Americans elected a Korean to the House of Representatives in 1994. How long will it take for the Asian-Americans to include a Vietnamese or a Hmong tribesmen in elective office? Is there a potential Filipino politician who can compete with Hispanic-Americans whose family roots are in Cuba, Panama, El Salvador, or Nicaragua? Thus, North Asian consideration will shape American policy toward Asia, and Southeastern Asian countries had better address their security problems through regional associations and the United Nations.

The demographics of the American electorate suggest that Asian policy makers cannot depend upon an American constituency to press their case for

American protection, at least not in the same way Israel has depended upon American Jewry to argue its case in the United States. The 1990 census provides the numbers. Of 250 million-plus Americans, 200 million identify themselves as white or European. There are thirty million African-Caribbean-Americans, seven-plus million Asian-Americans, two million native Americans, and nine million people who define themselves in ethnic terms that do not match the standard categories. Hispanic-Americans, who number twenty-two million, identify themselves by language and culture, not by race and are scattered in every category of ethnicity. Among Asian-Americans, the North Asians (Chinese, Japanese, Koreans) number approximately three million and the south Asians and Indians (their ranks swelled by Filipinos) around four million. The immigration patterns (legal immigration, that is) show no special advantage for North Asians, who were admitted in about equal numbers with Russians, Vietnamese, and Filipinos. The largest number of legal immigrants are Mexicans, and there is no doubt in the Immigration and Naturalization Service that illegal Hispanic immigration numbers are in the hundreds of thousands each year. No ethnic-national group except the Mexicans enters the United States in numbers above 100,000. Numbers alone then are inadequate to give Asian-Americans political leverage; they must depend upon targeted influence, money, their considerable business and professional success, and their ability to create multi-racial coalitions of support, a considerable challenge for people with a heritage of communal, homogeneous insularity. If left to their own devices, however, the political leaderships of their ethnic Asian homelands have repeatedly proven that they do not understand that political practices at home do not translate into the American political environment. Thus, participation of Asian-Americans is essential to any pro-Asia lobbying.[11]

The first challenge is to interest the American people in any foreign policy issue. A national New York Times /CBS News Poll in August, 1995 found that Americans listed foreign policy concerns tenth among their immediate political concerns. Less than 4 percent of those polled thought that foreign policy was the nation's most pressing problem. The Chicago Council of Foreign Relations conducted a more detailed survey of views on American foreign policy which found that opinion leaders and the public agreed that only a small (10 percent) proportion of the challenges facing the United States in 1995 concerned foreign policy. The public did not see foreign policy among the top ten public policy issues, and opinion leaders ranked foreign policy issues only tenth among their concerns. Of the foreign policy issues the opinion leaders and public did think important, only the containment of nuclear proliferation had clear support. Supporting military alliances and maintaining national military power has ambivalent support at best.

As the issues narrow specifically to Asia, the public is more alarmed than its leadership by Japanese economic competition and Chinese arms modernization. A majority of opinion leaders do not regard either development as a threat to U.S. vital interests, but a majority of the public does. The public and leaders agree that China and Japan should be a high concern for American policy makers but for very different reasons and neither constituency provides clear guidance on how the U.S. might synchronize economic and security issues. After a sharp drop in support for defense spending and alliance commitments, U.S. opinion leaders agree that the current defense policy is sound. They support the commitment to defend South Korea from North Korean attack. Only 39 percent of the public holds the same view. These significant disparities between leadership and public positions are the most striking of the Chicago Council's findings. The only thing they have in common is a deep distrust of the current government's conduct of foreign policy and the emphasis upon domestic problems. Even if one understands that the degree of public response to foreign policy issues is crisis-driven, the champions of "engagement and enlargement" face a tough selling task, and they will require the support of diplomats who represent Asian interests.[12]

Of the estimated twenty-three million war-related civilian and military deaths in the world over the period 1945-1992, fourteen million were Asians. One crucial point is that Asia has been the most dangerous and deadly place in the world since the end of World War II and requires global attention, especially given the scale of potential and real Asian nuclearization. Another significant trend is the growing capacity of Asian nations to wage modern warfare and to do so with a real prospect of success against every nation in the region except the United States. Imagine a Chinese-Japanese military combination directed at Russia and bent upon recovering the "lost lands" seized from them by Russian military forces since the 18th century. Or consider the air-naval capability in the hands of China in the 1990s and imagine not just how the Chinese might deploy these considerable forces around the Spratly Islands—now occupied by five different countries—but in the Gulf of Tonkin, the Straits of Formosa, and the Yellow Sea. It is one thing for Americans to caution against military confrontations with the Chinese in Asia, but the Chinese can now take Asia well out beyond their coastline, and they even have an admiral, Liu Huaqing, who sounds like Alfred Thayer Mahan or Sergei G. Gorshkov. One can apply the same calculus to Japan, where the political sea state has started to shift with the suicide of the Liberal Democratic Party. Whatever the existing provisions of the "Peace Constitution," its interpretation and application rests in Japanese—not American—hands, and American public opinion is now more favorable to Japanese military activism than at any time since World War II.[13]

Both China and Japan have initiated world-class military programs that represent the same sort of gross spending and share of national spending associated with Britain, France, and Germany and only slightly below that of the United States and Russia. Japan's budget is public knowledge: its defense expenditures are in the $50-plus billion range or just over 1 percent of Japan's $4.5 trillion gross domestic product. The traditional measures of defense spending and socio-economic investment show a progressive, modern, and underarmed Japan, which is ranked by one respected source as the seventh most "happy nation" in the world. What is more suggestive is that Japan possesses one of the most heavily capitalized military establishments in the world; Japan's spending is $111 million a year per soldier, a level of investment only surpassed by the United States ($129 million a year per service person) and some special cases like Switzerland and Saudi Arabia. (France, Britain, and Germany all spend less than $100 million a year per service person.) In other words, the Japanese Self Defense Force is in a class by itself in Asia in terms of modernity and its air and naval capability. The Chinese figures are much more elusive, but China is clearly the only other major regional military power. No one really knows what the productivity of the Chinese economy is, but various estimates put gross domestic product between $500-plus billion and $1 trillion. The official Chinese position is that defense expenditures consume less than 2 percent of gross domestic product and represent the equivalent of $17 billion for the 1995 defense program. No independent analyst takes these figures at face value. Depending on the method of calculation and the correction of categories assigned to defense spending, responsible estimates by national governments and international organizations range as high as $62 billion a year. The most recent analysis done by the International Institute for Strategic Studies estimates Chinese expenditures for military programs at $28 billion for 1994. With both nuclear weapons and large (if unevenly modernized) conventional land, air, and naval forces, China clearly rates as a major military power.

Unlike the United States, Japan and China do not have full-spectrum armed forces, capable of global power projection, but their power projection needs are regional, not global. For example, they do not need major investments in aircraft carriers if the base structure of the Chinese Air Force and the Air Self Defense Force allows their air forces to perform maritime missions, much as the Luftwaffe and the Soviet air force did in World War II. Another example of cost-effective investments with regional consequences would be the continued expansion and modernization of the Chinese and Japanese submarine and mine warfare forces. Such forces would be far more dangerous to the U.S. Navy than anything it faced in the Persian Gulf, especially with added land-based air threats. As the Imperial Japanese Navy learned in World War II, the straits and passages of the Pacific rim offer unparalleled opportunities for relatively low-cost naval operations. Submarines and mines stand a greater chance of success than the current capital ship of the region, the missile-firing fast surface attack ship or craft. Whatever the Chinese and Japanese might develop for air and naval warfare, the same capabilities are not beyond the power of most other Asian nations, given some patience and technological investments. Although it has started from a low level of investment, such modernization is already underway: since 1985 defense spending throughout Asia has increased 44 percent while it declined in North America and Europe.[14]

Another contextual concern in Asian security affairs is that the Asian nations have little experience or precedent in dealing with security issues within the framework of international organizations, permanent alliances (with attendant political and military institutions), negotiated security agreements like arms control regimes, confidence-building measures, information exchanges, and almost any sort of multilateral association. In other words, Asia has no NATO-analog, no CSCE-equivalent. Its recent history is one of colonialism and imperialism, not a history of consultation and peaceful accommodation. The first step in a new departure from the Cold War alliance system in Asia was the establishment of the ASEAN Regional Forum (ARF) in 1993 and its first meeting in 1994. This forum includes every nation with Asian-Pacific security concerns east of Myanmar except France and North Korea. The Asian nations are also probing participation in United Nations peace-keeping expeditions. The success of the peace-keeping operation in Cambodia offers one positive example of Asian military multilateralism.

The last major strategic consideration is the potential sources of conflict in Asia, at least conflict so disruptive that it takes on regional and global significance. Two sources of conflict have largely disappeared: wars of national liberation and revolution against the colonial powers and their native collaborators and the global competition between the United States and the Soviet Union, which may not have caused wars but certainly transformed them in Korea and Indochina. By one authoritative count, there are twenty-eight *continuing* regional conflicts over sovereignty, legitimacy, and territory in which the contestants have already shed blood. Another assessment identifies nine on-going conflicts in Asia, seven of them essentially civil wars, among twenty-eight global wars. The same assessment predicts a war over the Spratly Islands and believes another Korean war and India-Pakistan war are not unlikely.

The conventional wisdom of Asian specialists in the 1990s is that ethnic and revolutionary conflicts are now less likely than interstate conflict, but such civil wars are seldom fought without active or potential foreign intervention. Could the communal warfare in Sri Lanka and Kashmir continue without the tacit or active support of the Indian government for the Tamils and the Pakistanis for Moslem Kashmiris? Whatever the source of communal conflict within the current state borders of Asia, one cannot ignore these conflicts simply because the opponents have limited military capability or a constrained operating environment. The one dependable lesson of the twentieth century is that local conflicts have a way of escalating into larger wars, a fact to which the Serbians, for example, might bear witness. The Balkanization of Asian conflicts already underway is a development that the members of the ASEAN Regional Forum cannot disregard. The possibility that Bouganville may secede from Papua New Guinea may not send tremors throughout the Pacific rim, but what might happen if a coup d'etat in the court of Kim Jong Il became a civil war within the borders of North Korea? Would the South Koreans simply wait out the battle and disarm refugees, as did the French at the end of the Spanish Civil War? Similar scenarios provided the political assumptions for many NATO command post exercises and REFORGER deployments. There is no reason to assume U.S. armed forces should forget that bit of their history.[15]

## The United States Armed Forces and Asian Security

The questions of how much force the U.S. should apply to protect and advance American vital interests in Asia, however defined, and when that force should be applied have bedeviled every American president since Herbert Hoover. Until the 1990s, global security considerations dominated policy, since almost every crisis had some potential bearing on the rise of fascism, the Cold War, and containment of the Soviet Union and the People's Republic of China. Such considerations also had relevance (and still have) in dealing with security concerns in North Asia, but they always had more limited appropriateness throughout the rest of the Asian-Pacific region. Since the end of the Vietnam War in 1975 and the post-Mount Pinatubo withdrawal from the Philippines, South Asia occupies less and less U.S. attention. The present structure and location of the some 350,000 American service personnel assigned to the region (100,000 in forward deployments) reflects that "two Asias" strategy which has inherent problems in any contingency from minor humanitarian missions or civilian evacuations to major regional conflicts. The best that one can claim for the problems faced by the Commander in Chief, U.S. Pacific Command (CINCPAC), is that Pacific Command (PACOM) is at least now focused on the China-Korea-Japan-Russia cockpit, and not elsewhere in the region.

Assuming that strategic nuclear deterrence holds in North Asia under the American umbrella, the worst case/most likely contingency becomes a war between the two Koreas, which carries with it the potential for escalation in terms of additional participants (China, Russia, Japan) and expanded geographic destructiveness from North Korea's intermediate range ballistic missiles. The United States has to seek a quick, successful solution to a second Korean war. That solution must be imposed rapidly, a lasting lesson of 1953, even if the eventual political result might be limited, even to the continuation of two Koreas. Short of initiating its own nuclear war against Pyongyang, the United States faces strategic and operational conditions more demanding than those it met in the Gulf because it must consider the vulnerability of its principal ally, the Republic of Korea, and the existence of 16-plus million Korean hostages in the Han River Valley.[16]

Even working on optimistic assumptions about strategic warning time and the pace of mobilization, U.S. armed forces would be hard-pressed to put an expeditionary force of 500,000 (or a Gulf War equivalent) into the Korean theater in time to spare south Korea an invasion and to reinforce the Korean armed forces and the one U.S. Army infantry division and the two wings of Seventh Air Force now on the peninsula. The principal early-war American contribution would be air power: additional air force composite wings deploying to Korea (assuming the availability of bases) and the employment of carrier-based naval aviation. Marine corps tactical aviation can be land or sea-based and would come from Japan and Hawaii. The first available ground forces are likely to be the III Marine Expeditionary Force, which has troops afloat, as well as stationed on Okinawa (Japan) and Hawaii. This force can use the equipment prepositioned aboard logistical ships (which must unload in a safe port) now held in the Indian Ocean and the western Pacific. I Marine Expeditionary Force (California) could also augment the force. The principal army reinforcing headquarters is I Corps (Ft. Lewis, Washington), which has only the 25th Infantry Division (Light), currently stationed in Hawaii. Other army divisions must come from Alaska or the continental United States, but they, too, can draw on army maritime pre-positioned equipment that is also forward deployed.

Although moving men and material to a theater almost as distant as the Gulf poses serious problems, the real difficulties come in Korea itself. Assuming that ROKAF and USAF tactical aviation can retard a North Korean advance into the Han River Valley under conditions in which terrain and weather limit air power, the Commanding General, Combined Forces Command, a U.S. Army general, must decide whether he can hold south of the 38th Parallel with the South Korean Army and his token reinforced American division. If not, how long must he wait for the marines and army's I Corps and at what cost? If he receives authorization to conduct operations north of the 38th Parallel with ground forces (a decision that took three months in 1950), how and where does he introduce an American field army for such a task? (The South Korean Army, especially after intense defensive operations, probably could not meet this challenge.) What risk is there of Chinese or Russian intervention, even if much reduced from 1950? Even if the Korean government wants to press on with the war, would Japan allow the United States to wage war from its national territory as it did in 1950-1953 when it had no choice and, in fact, profited from its participation as an unsinkable logistical center. Would Japanese air and maritime forces act to deter Chinese and Russian intervention? Given that the military capabilities of all the potential belligerents are much greater than they were in 1950, the risk of miscalculation carries with it a potential level of destruction outside Korea that has not been experienced since 1945.

One promise of the Clinton administration is that it will not mortgage nonmilitary issues, especially trade relations, to strategic concerns in dealing with China, the two Koreas, and Japan. One serious issue is neither nonmilitary nor exactly strategic, and that is the impact of American garrisons in Korea and Japan upon domestic, nationalist civilian politics in both countries. Host-nation support agreements for peace and war impose financial burdens on South Korea and Japan that some national politicians find unacceptable, while Americans use property in both countries that is attractive for commercial and residential development. The explosive social interaction between U.S. service personnel (who are not only young, but now integrated by race and gender) and North Asians (who despise drug use, alcohol abuse, American manners, crimes of passion and carelessness, and off-post entertainment districts) only serves to exacerbate the problem. The American response to such complaints is seldom satisfactory; it encourages black-marketeering, the hiring of foreign nationals who give little service in peace and may give none in war, and onerous restrictions upon law-abiding American service personnel. The other approach is simply to reduce the number of service personnel in Japan and Korea. The services might instead lessen the tension created by forward-deployed tactical units by changing force structure, not numbers. The U.S. might replace its 2nd Infantry Division, for example, with an additional aviation assault brigade and a heavy artillery brigade.

The marines on Okinawa might return to the western United States, but their equipment and war reserves (like the brigade set now stored in Norway) could remain in the region, but in Korea, not Japan. The forces kept in the theater could be predominately tactical aviation units and logistical/command elements, which means that the American garrisons would consist of older, wiser, more stable personnel, many of whom might choose to stay in the region for personal and family reasons. The public reaction in Japan to the rape of a teenage Okinawa girl in September, 1995 was the largest mass demonstration against American military presence on the island since World War II. The protest marchers focused not on the crime rate (actually declining) but upon other daily annoyances: the noise of aircraft and artillery, obstruction of roads with military convoys, traffic accidents, and restricted land use. With fewer troops to support, economic benefits from the American garrisons on Okinawa have contracted with the crime rate and thus reduced the leverage of Okinawan employment.[17] The difficulty is that diplomats fear any change in the forward deployment status quo will be destabilizing, while military leaders fear that any combat troops withdrawn from north Asia will simply disappear from the troop list. Neither concern is unjustified, given the erratic behavior of Congress on issues of readiness and conventional force structure. Not coincidentally, the state of Hawaii does not love its military installations as it once did, another political influence on Asian-Pacific military planning.

Another trend of American military behavior in the region is the reduction of large-scale exercises, which cuts expenses and host-nation social tension, but limits field testing. "Team Spirit" in Korea may soon be only a memory, with "Cobra Gold" in Thailand soon to follow. A better means of presence may be short, smaller unit (e.g., battalion task forces) deployments on specific exercises with host-nation forces for combined training that includes live firing, fire support coordination, and operations in inhospitable terrain, not in short supply along the Asia-Pacific rim. The redeployment of the Australian armed forces to Australia's northern states offers a new opportunity for desert, mountain, riverine, and jungle warfare training and the creation of a base structure (like a similar investment in Saudi Arabia in the 1980s) that would allow American forces to influence strategic events along the whole Malay Barrier and the Indian Ocean. Just as Canada served as NATO's great training ground, Australia might perform a similar role for multinational forces associated with the ASEAN Regional Forum.

The American armed forces have many options in executing a strategy of "engagement and enlargement" for Asia and the Pacific islands. These tools include the permanent stationing of defense representatives abroad, exchanging high-level visits by defense officials and senior officers, military talks, bilateral and multilateral conferences, joint exercises, the extension of education and training assistance, arms sales, and port visits. By 1995 the United States has had some sort of military contact with thirty-one Asian-Pacific nations, and it had no contact with only one, North Korea. The other two bastions of military isolationism are Myanmar and Vietnam, with the latter due to come in from the cold. Foreign aid plays only a small role in these relationships. The United States extends only one-fifth of its global public assistance ($8 billion in 1994) to Asian-Pacific nations. Global foreign military sales (goods and services purchased by foreign countries through the Department of Defense) under contract in 1994 amounted to $33 billion worldwide, of which $9.15 billion went to Asian countries. Two-thirds of this sum represent arms sales to Taiwan ($6.2 billion) with Japan a distant second ($1.4 billion). Only one Asian nation (the Philippines) in 1994 received foreign military assistance (grants and loans), $150 million of a $6.6 billion program in which Egypt and Israel received $5.3 billion. Appropriations for international military education and training (which means foreign nationals training in the United States or at U.S. installations abroad) dropped 50 percent in FY 1995 from $42.5 million to a pathetic $21.5 million. CINCPAC's share fell from $5.5 million to $2.84 million. This inattention to the future of combined operations, for which both the Department of State and Congress bear responsibility, is inexcusable.[18]

Just as America is paying less attention to Asia so, too, are Asian nations less interested in cooperation with the United States. Only a threat equivalent to the Soviet Union in its Cold War days would bolster U.S. deterrent leverage in the region, especially in North Asia. Even if the U.S. faces trying times with South Korea and Japan, it should continue to tilt towards its postwar allies, not the dangerous and unpredictable People's Republic of China. The most immediate challenge is for the United States to pull North Korea's nuclear fangs, but to do so in a collaborative relationship with South Korea and Japan. While this immediate crisis will absorb much diplomatic attention, the United States should make Asian contingencies the rationale for an enhanced program to develop a robust theater missile defense system. Both China and North Korea have well-developed missile development programs and each enhancement produces increased range and accuracy for those missiles, missiles which could be used for military or population attacks with conventional or unconventional warheads. The Gulf War is instructive on how politically unsettling and strategically threatening a theater missile threat can be, a threat that the United States cannot meet credibly with the threat of nuclear retaliation alone. A crash program in theater ballistic missile defense would also engage the electronics industries of South Korea and Japan, with a range of beneficial results for American and Asian technological advances. Such a program would be a dramatic proof of America's dedication to its principal Asian allies.[19]

The other American initiative is well-advanced in principle: the extension of nuclear arms control and non-proliferation to Asia. The developing arrangement with North Korea to substitute trade, economic aid, and other power sources for missile weapons material represents an effort to keep one nuclear genie bottled, but India and Pakistan offer a higher order of challenge since neither of them is a signatory to the Non-Proliferation Treaty. Nor are they as isolated and desperate as North Korea. Even though the recent publicity of the nuclear business of South Africa, Israel, and Iraq has focused attention on nuclear arms control in Africa and the Middle East, it is Asia that has held onto its nuclear weapons, developed the capability to go nuclear with little additional effort, and refused to create any sort of regional or international arms control regime. The United States has announced its willingness to adhere to the South Pacific Nuclear Free Zone Treaty, provided its navy can still prowl the area with nuclear- powered ships that may or may not be armed with nuclear weapons. French nuclear testing at Mururoa Atoll in the area, not deployed nuclear forces, has dramatized the agreement, so it is probably symbolic, not compelling. It is unimportant whether nuclear weapons cause or only reflect international tension since either analysis still implies that nuclear weapons are worth controlling. As in so many other security considerations, the central issue is how the United States will influence the emerging competition of China and Japan as hegemonic regional powers and whether that competition will develop into an arms race.[20]

## Conclusion

The first requirement for a relevant, successful foreign policy for Asia and the Pacific nations is to recognize the region's importance to a world safe for American interests. Asian foreign policy cannot be a coda to policies that assume more importance for Europe and the Middle East. Regional crises should not determine global policy—nor should domestic political pressure. A second useful step would be to recognize that security concerns are not only legitimate—even with the end of the Cold War—but require strategies and forces developed for specific regional needs, not tied to global war plans of dated utility. Even if tainted by the odor of the Vietnam war, the Guam Doctrine for Asian military self-sufficiency (nuclear weapons excluded) is still applicable, but would require a greater investment in foreign military assistance than Congress is willing to approve (apparently preferring gold-plated American units to improved allied readiness). American planning need not revert to the "air and naval support only" doctrines of the 1940s to be effective. It only needs to consider various combinations of fly-in forces, stationary and mobile prepositioning, strategic air and maritime lift forces, and the forward deployment of headquarters and support elements, not just combat units. American planning should remember that speed of response is to regional crises what accuracy is to an air campaign. The armed forces themselves should establish an organizational culture that treats Asian service as something more than a great shopping opportunity. After more than a century of military engagement in Asia, the United States should be ready to deal with Asian security issues with the patience and seriousness they deserve.

Today, the cars, buses, and taxis crawl up and down the congested twelve lanes of Sejong-ro in downtown Seoul under the watchful eye of Admiral Yi Sun Sin, whose statue guards the land that he himself defended against the Japanese in the late 16th century. The intersection Admiral Yi guards is aptly named Kwanghwa-mun. Not far from Admiral Yi's memorial, the U.S. embassy fronts Sejong-ro. At the head of the boulevard is the "Capitol Building," originally built in 1926 as the center of Japanese colonial government in Korea. It was this building the American military government occupied in 1945, released to the regime of Syngman Rhee in 1948, and then liberated twice more in 1950 and 1951. The Koreans have started to tear down the building, which might have been built by the Germans in Strasbourg in the same Greco-Teutonic style and with about the same level of sensitivity. Its destruction will free the view of and from the sacred Kyongbok Palace, built in 1394. As of yet there are no similar plans for the U.S. Embassy, whose architectural style is Neo-Security, but the fate of the Japanese building should remind American policy makers down the boulevard that the wrecking ball of history may apply to them sometime in the future with equal force. If the inhabitants of the U.S. Embassy shape policies or have to execute decisions made in Washington that do not reflect the Asian reality of wealth and independence, the U.S. Embassy—in power if not in physical presence—will also disappear from central Seoul. The same phenomenon might apply in New Delhi, Kuala Lumpur, Jakarta, Canberra, and Taipei. In Saigon the vines and mildew have turned a similar building into an Ankor Wat of foreign policy errors.

# Chapter 6

# China[1]

## Arthur Waldron

1995 looks as if it may well be remembered as the year in which the world began to take seriously the possibility of a military threat from China. A series of Chinese actions—beginning in early spring—sharply focused Asia's attention on China's ability and willingness to use force. The seizure of a disputed reef in the South China Sea, the firing of ballistic missiles near Taiwan with the explicit intent to intimidate, and at least one close approach by Chinese aircraft to the Japanese Senakaku Islands—these actions and others elicited both public condemnation and even more private concern. Heightening the impact was a growing realization among China's neighbors that its military forces, although largely obsolescent and resistant to change, were nevertheless steadily modernizing. The Chinese have been importing new weapons systems, notably ex-Soviet anti-aircraft missiles, Su-27 jets, and quiet diesel Kilo-class submarines. At the same time, China's indigenous industrial capacities were improving. Asia's leaders have grasped that if China's rapid economic development continued to permit such arms purchases and technological upgrading, then at least a portion of the People's Liberation Army could prove a formidable foe in the not-too-distant future.

How to interpret these developments, however, is by no means clear. One school of thought, strongest in the United States, largely dismisses the idea of a Chinese threat. Its proponents argue that China's military capacity remains limited and, just as importantly, that conflict does not serve China's overriding national interest in development. The other interpretation, based on history and heard more in Asia, concedes these points, but claims that strong internal goals for economic development have not always prevented powers from undertaking military action in the past. In particular, these factors clearly did not prevent China from using its military force against her neighbors in 1995.

Resolving this problem of interpretation requires a recognition that Chinese ways of thinking about the use of military force are very different from their Western counterparts. In the recent past, Mao Zedong's highly unrealistic doctrines of "people's war" have predominated, and it will take the passage of time before such powerful concepts disappear from Chinese military consciousness.[2] In earlier periods, the Chinese have traditionally stressed the possibilities of using military threats and diplomacy together to "win without fighting" as Sun Zi puts it.[3] They have concentrated on speed, deception, and the careful construction of limited operations to avoid escalation. Traditional Chinese military thought is extremely sophisticated, and it is therefore not surprising that it still strongly influences much contemporary Chinese strategic and military thinking. Those traditional thought patterns help us to understand China's uses of force in 1995, for the Chinese circumscribed and controlled their actions in such a way as to permit them to use their limited military capabilities to real effect. But by the same token, this approach possesses glaring weaknesses, which China and the world may well face, if present trends continue.

China's newly-assertive military posture has three sources. First the Tiananmen massacre of 1989 discredited the military in the eyes of many Chinese, while at the same time bolstering the military's bargaining power within the government. Second, the Gulf War finally persuaded China's military leadership that its existing force structure, mostly Soviet systems of 1950s vintage and Chinese spin-offs, was obsolete. Third, and most fundamental, was a general crisis of legitimacy that confronted China's unelected communist government. At a time when world trends seem to be moving toward participatory politics and economic freedom, rapid domestic changes within China confront the regime with powerful demands for reform. These three factors are interacting to provide the basis of current Chinese politics, which at their heart represent an attempt to renew the regime's legitimacy—and hence its hold on power—by espousing a nationalist and irredentist program that only force can support. One can only understand China's recent military actions, and its ongoing program of force modernization, against this background.

## Military Modernization

Decisions regarding the replacement of the obsolete equipment of China's vast military reveals some of the critical differences between Western and Chinese approaches to military thinking. Westerners think in terms of complete and thoroughly integrated military systems, although this has not always been the case: the military with which Hitler launched his conquests more than fifty years ago had many serious weaknesses. The Chinese think more as Hitler did, in terms of tools for the mission. Like the Germans in the Second World War, they are willing to use force, even if their forces are not fully prepared, provided that the larger diplomatic and political context is favorable. Building a fully modern force is not the immediate goal of Chinese leaders, although continued economic development will make that revolution possible. But the task requires not only decades, but also major changes in existing structures, with reductions in personnel and weapons systems and increases in training of crucial importance.

Today, if measured simply by numbers, China's military represents an impressive force. It consists of nearly three million troops, equipped with more than 9,000 tanks, 4,000 fighter aircraft, fifty submarines, and approximately sixty major surface combatants. But nearly all of this equipment is outdated, while training levels and operational skills in the forces are generally low. Indeed, the most difficult challenge that the People's Liberation Army confronts today is the block obsolescence of many basic pieces in its inventory.

Nuclear and missile forces are the sole area where China is close to international standards. Chinese leaders understood the critical role of such forces for intimidation and deterrence as early as the 1950s and gave their development high priority. The Soviet Union initially supplied much of the technology, but the Sino-Soviet split in the late 1950s slowed development only temporarily. Indeed, if anything China's sudden vulnerability once the Soviet alliance dissolved persuaded policy makers of a serious need for their own nuclear deterrent.[4]

At present China possesses approximately twenty Dongfeng-5 intercontinental ballistic missiles, capable of reaching the continental United States, as well as more than sixty intermediate range ballistic missiles. In addition, the Chinese possess one ballistic missile nuclear submarine, as well as bomber forces. Although the Chinese have tested these systems, their nuclear capabilities provide no more than minimal deterrence and have numerous vulnerabilities. The bombers, for example, would have difficulty penetrating any modern air defenses, and it is not clear that China's nuclear missile submarine is truly operational.

Because of the importance of nuclear deterrence to China's strategic posture, however, research and development of nuclear weapons and delivery systems continues to receive high priority. Development of smaller and more efficient warheads moves forward at a pace that surprises some analysts. Nuclear testing also continues, although China has suggested that it will halt in 1996, once a global test-ban treaty is ratified. Missile technology is self-sufficient and relatively advanced, as regular commercial launches demonstrate. The Chinese are also reluctant to participate in the Missile Technology Control Regime, since they apparently have violated the regime by missile sales to Pakistan, despite pledges to the contrary.

China's nuclear arsenal looks small when compared to those of the United States or Russia, but the Asian context suggests a somewhat different assessment. China is the only East Asian country with such weaponry (although Japan could develop nuclear weapons easily, North Korea may be doing so, and South Korea and Taiwan have both abandoned nuclear weapons programs under outside pressure, although they retain the know-how and industrial base to move forward, if necessary). This means that in any conflict, China possesses ultimate deterrence—unless the United States steps in to back up an ally or friend. Washington's willingness to take such action is already limited and will further erode as Chinese programs, currently under way, come to fruition and enhance China's capacity to threaten the continental United States.

China clearly counts on fostering this ability, and using it to intimidate neighbors and restrain outside involvement in East Asia's security affairs. The "test-firings" of intermediate-range ballistic missiles into waters near Taiwan during summer 1995 suggest the uses China sees for such forces: the idea apparently was to terrify the Taiwanese and force the president, Lee Teng-hui, either to resign or to modify his policies. These goals were partially achieved: the Chinese created a sense of crisis and the Taipei stockmarket fell.

But longer-term reactions to this demonstration may prove less favorable to China. India, the only other major Asian nuclear power, continues to develop its nuclear force, which, although not as capable as those of China, nevertheless poses a threat. Non-nuclear powers in Asia, Japan most importantly, look likely to respond either by reemphasizing their solid alliance with the United States or by developing their own nuclear forces. Furthermore, while sufficient for intimidation, China's nuclear forces lack the numbers to be truly threatening.

One response to the Chinese missile program in general, and to the summer "tests" in particular, is that Japan, Korea, and Taiwan are considering the construction of theater missile defenses in cooperation with the United States. Such systems would, in effect, rob the small Chinese nuclear forces of their awesomeness, while confronting Beijing with the need either to alter its strategic approach, or to embark on an economically ruinous nuclear expansion program to counteract the effect of missile defenses. In other words, China's bid to seize military advantage in the nuclear area may well lead not to dominance, but to a costly and inconclusive nuclear stalemate in Asia like that which dominated the bipolar contest between the United States and the Soviet Union during the Cold War.

Other developments in Chinese force structure that are attracting concern in the Asian region and elsewhere could well have the same result. After nuclear deterrence, the most important item on the Chinese list of priorities is the ability to project force over areas claimed as sovereign territories—most importantly the islands of the South China Sea and Taiwan. Since such projection of power is above all a matter of air and naval forces, China has been devoting substantial efforts to modernizing those arms.

Since the 1970s, China's navy has grown rapidly: its conventional submarine force has increased from thirty-five to at least fifty (some estimates say 100); missile-carrying ships have increased from twenty to 200; and the Chinese have developed and deployed a variety of new craft. These developments have increasingly aimed at blue-water capability. Actual capacity remains limited: eighteen destroyers, of which only three are up-to-date and thirty-seven frigates, of which only three are modern types. The Luhu-class destroyer, which incorporates a variety of foreign components—French sonar and defense missiles, among others—is the most important new surface combatant, but reports suggest that this program and others have slowed for lack of funds.[5] Talk of an aircraft carrier has regularly surfaced, but so far nothing has actually happened. The most significant naval acquisition for the Chinese will undoubtedly be accession of Russian Kilo-class submarines (a quiet diesel), one of which has been delivered, with anything from three to twenty on the way, with possible technology-sharing agreements in the works.

Like China's nuclear program, its naval expansion program has probably served as much to alarm its neighbors and to elicit countermeasures as it has actually augmented China's military power. Japan, Korea, and Taiwan all possess more modern navies than China's, while the Southeast Asian states are all currently paying attention to naval development as well. Asian countries have ordered no less than two hundred modern warships for delivery within the next five years.[6] New Chinese capabilities, particularly the acquisition of quiet submarines, may pose security problems, but in the medium term will most probably not alter the actual naval balance in Asia—rather only lift the competition to new quantitative levels.

China's air force is encountering many of the same problems as the navy in modernizing its weapons systems. No easy solution exists to the problem posed by China's current inventory of thousands of obsolete Soviet-designed aircraft which, in combat, would be little better than deathtraps for their unfortunate pilots. China does not currently possess the ability to manufacture (or use) state-of-the-art aircraft, and even if it undertook a program today to develop such a capacity, even in cooperation with a power willing to share technology such as Russia, it would be years before new aircraft entered the active force in significant quantities.[7]

Acquiring hardware is, in any case, only one aspect of the larger problem of air modernization. At present China lags far behind in training: bomber pilots fly eighty hours and fighter pilots perhaps 100 hours per year, substantially lower than optimal training rates, and much of this training involves routine navigation, not practice for combat. Simulators are rarely available. Of the 10,000 pilots claimed by the People's Liberation Army Air Force, only 700 meet the top qualification as "special grade."[8] Manpower would, therefore, rapidly limit any sustained operation.

Rather than construct a genuinely modern air force by confronting the tasks of modernization in training, manufacturing, and logistics, however— what Western analysts tend to think of as true modernization—the Chinese appear to have adopted a different approach. Long-term research and development continues, but for the short-run, the Chinese air force is purchasing a limited number of modern aircraft—sufficient to stiffen the force—abroad. Most important is the Su-27, of which the Russians have already delivered twenty-six with twenty-four more on order. The Su-27 can serve either as an interceptor or for ground-attack and the Chinese evidently intend to use these aircraft to provide aircover over the South China Sea. In addition, Israel is developing an aircraft for China called the F-10, which involves substantial transfers of technology from the American F-16. The engines will be of Chinese manufacture: the Chinese expect prototypes within two years with full production in ten.[9] China's ability to support such advanced aircraft is limited—they must return the Su-27s to the factory in Komsomolsk for overhaul—but the aircraft's potential presence in Chinese inventories has already triggered reactions in neighboring countries. Vietnam, for example, is also acquiring Su-27s, while Taiwan is purchasing Mirage 2000s from France and F-16s from the United States.

Still, it is almost certainly true that, owing to the retirement of obsolete aircraft, the Chinese Air Force will be half its current size in ten years. "Even then," one report explains, "except for a small number of advanced fighters procured from Russia, the preponderance of China's force structure early in the next century will consist of fighters that *today* would be considered obsolescent."[10] But that is only half the story. Even such limited air and naval modernization has significance, provided the Chinese develop a coherent strategy and operational framework. It would be a serious mistake to dismiss Chinese efforts at modernization, as some Western analysts do, simply because they are incomplete and lack depth. China is currently looking for practical short-term answers to intractable long-term problems, and so far these acquisitions have worked rather well to give China what it needs. The resulting improvisations are easy to ridicule, but they nevertheless have the effect of augmenting China's usable military power.

## China's Strategic Framework

China looks weak by the standard of the advanced and integrated forces currently possessed by the United States—or even, qualitatively, against some of its neighbors' military forces. That assessment is misleading, however, when one places it within the context of Chinese strategic thinking. Since late 1994, Chinese military actions have perceptively changed in tone. At that moment, China began to display a new, more confrontational style in its dealings with the Asian region and with the United States. The most likely root of the change lay in the intensifying power struggle in Beijing. Deng Xiaoping, who had intentionally kept China's profile low and non-confrontational, was ill, and his would-be successors sought to prove their mettle by confronting foreigners. The United States encountered this new approach in October 1994. When the task force accompanying the carrier *Kitty Hawk* detected a Chinese submarine operating in the area, U.S. forces undertook standard defensive measures and launched aircraft and helicopters. These actions frightened and confused the Chinese. Reports suggest that their air force was unaware of their own submarine's operations and therefore could not understand why the U.S. task force had launched aircraft. Later, the Chinese maintained that the task force had violated China's territorial limits, and, after U.S. ships pursued the submarine back to its base, the Chinese warned Washington that next time their forces would "shoot to kill."

In February 1995 the Filipino government discovered secretly-constructed Chinese naval installations on Mischief Reef, part of the disputed Spratly archipelago, nearly a thousand miles from the Chinese coast. A group of concrete structures on stilts, with satellite dishes, antiaircraft artillery, and an anchorage frequented by Chinese frigates, lay within the Philippines' two-hundred mile territorial waters. The discovery sent shockwaves through the rest of Asia.

In July, China began a series of military exercises designed to intimidate Taiwan. The Chinese fired missiles into the sea less than a hundred miles from Taiwan, while Chinese aircraft and ships aggressively probed Taiwanese defenses. But perhaps the single most worrying incident came in August, when Japanese fighters scrambled to chase Chinese aircraft away from the disputed Senakaku islands (Diaoyutai in Chinese).

For China, these actions represented a strategic departure. Unlike previous exercises at intimidation (such as the brief war with Vietnam in 1979), the Chinese targeted states tightly linked to the international system and violated norms of peaceful behavior to which they had theoretically subscribed. Furthermore, they challenged, albeit indirectly, the United States, which, to some policy makers in Beijing, appears to be the greatest threat to China's future. Analysts remain divided about the origins of the new approach. Did it reflect, as seemed likely, factional infighting within the government? Or was it a fundamental change likely to endure?

Until the late 1980s, China's official rhetoric had stressed infrastructure and living-standards over armaments in the nation's economic priorities. But after the Tiananmen Square massacre military leverage increased. Now in the 1990s, China was willing to threaten and intimidate. The consequences of this trend were difficult to overstate. They could be as catastrophic for Asia as the uncannily similar policies followed by Wilhelmine Germany had been for Europe almost a century earlier.

The tension of the summer had decreased by the end of 1995, but had by no means dissipated. The South China Sea issues hung unresolved, while repression increased in Tibet, a sensitive point for India and its other South Asian neighbors. In Hong Kong, social and political tensions presaged a difficult transition to Chinese rule in 1997. As for Taiwan, when Assistant Secretary of Defense Joseph S. Nye visited China in November, the Chinese engaged in "'subtle exploration' of how the United States would respond in the event of a military crisis over Taiwan."[11]

The existence of so many clouds on the horizon was something new for post-Cold War East Asia. Neighbors accustomed to pacific dealings among themselves and with China on a "trading state" basis now faced complex strategic decisions. Would they acquiesce in Chinese military dominance as the price of continued prosperity, and if so, what exactly would that price include? Or would they seek to offset the Chinese threat by arming themselves and forming alliances? If so, with whom and on what terms? Would China's initial and unexpected success with its new policies—as in creating the *fait accompli* in the Spratlys, effectively unchallenged by anybody—simply lead to other and more consequential assertions? Where would Asians draw the line? Whatever the answers, it was clear to most Asian states that the patterns of international relations that had governed Asia since the 1970s were changing.

## The Hard Hand of History

Many of these nations might be even more perturbed were they to consider the influence of China's past. China today does not really understand the external world and therefore has difficulty in making realistic assessments of where its actions may lead. This dangerous situation is in part the product of the self-isolation of the People's Republic of China, a situation which has by no means ended today, despite astonishing openness compared to the situation in the 1950s or 1960s. But the Chinese disdain for the outside world has deeper roots. For millennia, China has paid little attention to its neighbors and regularly displayed a consequent inability to manage grand strategy. At the same time, however, traditional military classics have stressed not so much "warfighting" as understood in the contemporary West, but rather the methods by which the Chinese ancients believed they could win large-scale and decisive victories at low cost.

These approaches rest deeply in the Chinese past. Archaeologists increasingly agree that China's development as a unified civilization in the several millennia B.C. owed more to shared culture and ritual than to the conquest and institution-creation that, arguably, lay behind the emergence of the state elsewhere, particularly the west.[12] Certainly the texts that have defined Chinese civilization say almost nothing about conflict and warfare—except within a morally-defined framework that its outcome validates. In this they differ profoundly from the foundation sagas and epics of other civilizations, whether the *Iliad* or the *Old Testament* or *Beowulf*. As Mark Lewis notes, "The most commonly re-asserted view, deriving mainly from the Confucian but also from the Taoist and Legalist schools in the Warring States period and further developed in the Han, saw warfare as an undesirable expedient...to be avoided if possible, or at least to be carefully controlled."[13]

For much of pre-modern Chinese history, such a view of force made sense, or at least did not lead to disaster. The early wars chronicled in the *Zuozhuan* were among peoples culturally proto-Chinese and possessing comparable technologies. As for the barbarians—the *yi* and the *di* —they were peoples who lacked any decisive advantages over the Chinese, and who thus regularly proved willing to assimilate. Confucius's description of how education and exchange could gradually civilize the barbarous had a certain realism to it.

This cultural background today underpins China's long-term pattern of seeking to achieve maximum goals by using minimal means. Objectively speaking, however, the conditions that may once have made such an approach plausible had already disappeared by the fifth century B.C., when inner-Asian horse nomads appeared on the northern Chinese frontiers. These were the *hu* —a word that does not occur in the Chinese classics.[14] Able to defeat Chinese armies at will—a superiority that lasted throughout the Ming dynasty and culminated in the conquest of China by the Manchus—and furthermore not tempted by Chinese civilization, these nomads embodied a threat for which traditional Chinese approaches to strategy and statecraft had no answer. Indeed, such foreign conquest founded the final dynasty of imperial China, the Qing (1644-1912).

Dealing with the challenge would have required China to recast both its military forces and diplomatic policies. But this was never done. Instead of operating in an intellectual unity, Chinese security policy remained divided. Military specialists tended to understand the seriousness of the threat and seek to deal with it realistically through a mixture of force and diplomacy, but their influence was marginal in court debates and politics. Civilian figures, who had memorized the classics as children, believed in the unrealistic picture of war and diplomacy the classics presented and thus demanded maximal ends (subjection of the *hu*) with minimal means.

Ming dynasty policy toward the Mongols provides a good example of the problems such an approach created when the Chinese attempted to apply it where circumstances no longer fit.[15] The large and effective armies of the Mongols provided a solid military basis for ambitions of global conquest, and the first Ming emperors inherited much of their military system and techniques of operation. The result, until the middle of the fifteenth century, was an effective security strategy based on real force. Thereafter, though, a set of interlocking changes—in the cultural attitudes of the Ming, in the empire's economic wherewithal, and in its strategic priorities—cut real military power and provoked a search for ways to maintain status and dominance. The abiding monument of this search is the so-called "Great Wall of China," built by the Ming in the fifteenth and sixteenth centuries, an impressive but ultimately ineffective expedient. The court debates about strategy that accompanied its construction reveal the continuing influence of a baleful belief that minimal means could win maximal ends.

Even after the end of the dynasties in 1912, the same strategic *Weltanschauung* lingered on. Chinese politicians continued to define their state's power on a grand scale, far out of proportion to what armed force—or administration for that matter—could deliver. This grandiose vision has continued to form Chinese diplomacy, whose practitioners regularly assert objectives beyond China's actual grasp with, at times, serious consequences. Chinese policy has, thus, continued to focus so much on the impossible goal of gaining control of everything on the list of desiderata that it ignores practical steps toward achieving what is attainable. At the Washington Conference in 1921–22, the French representative, Aristide Briand, observed that "the principle of the territorial integrity of China, which France, on her part, fully accepted, had significance only if a definition of the boundaries of China were first determined upon." Wellington Koo, the Chinese delegate, responded that "the territories of the Chinese Republic were defined in its Constitution," a response followed by an inconclusive discussion that left the key question unresolved. This issue, when eventually applied to Manchuria, precipitated war with Japan.[16]

No one accepted Koo's answer then, nor would an analogous answer win assent today. China, by domestic law, claims territories around its entire circumference, from India to the Pacific, that other states claim as well. A rational policy analysis would suggest that, given the limitation of China's forces and the problems associated with multiple enemies and potentially multifront wars, Chinese leaders would abandon some of these claims, trade others off, and focus on the few that are of genuine importance. But the Chinese, whether strong or weak, have simply refused to modify such claims.

This unwillingness to accept the dictates of diplomatic logic has several explanations. One, China may expect the military balance to shift in its favor. If it is, indeed, the superpower some expect early in the next century, then it makes sense to establish claims now that can be redeemed later. A second explanation involves domestic imperial politics. The young Mao Zedong regretted "Japan's occupation of Korea and Formosa, the loss of suzerainty in Indo-China, Burma, and elsewhere."[17] He was neither the first nor the last Chinese irredentist. China's current pattern of territorial assertion resembles the European pattern ninety years ago: the claims of Germany, Greece, and Italy, among others, thoroughly disturbed Europe's peace with a none-too-happy ending, namely two World Wars.

But perhaps the most important reason China does not moderate its claims is that Chinese strategic thinking suggests caution is not necessary. Western theorists of war focus on physical destruction of the enemy's centers of gravity. The Chinese, by contrast, prize psychological dislocation and disarming the opponent. The object is to push an adversary from a state of order and intactness [*zhi*] to that of chaos [*luan*] in which the enemy's ability to resist collapses. The method is not so much the application of physical force [*li*] as it is of psychological pressure: operations aim to intimidate and deceive. The stress is on deception—*guiji*—and the impressiveness or awesomeness—the *wei*—of the dominating power.[18]

These operations occur most effectively in an environment of what might be called strategic dominance. This does not mean the possession of overwhelming force. Rather, it means having mastered the situation intellectually, exemplified in the legends of Zhuge Liang, the greatest strategist of ancient China. The adherents of the Han, Zhang Fei and Liu Bei, sought

Zhuge Liang out at a thatched hut in the mountains where he had taken refuge from the world. After much persuading, the great strategist pulled out a map and explained the dynasty's predicament and his suggestions, concluding: "First, take Jingzhou and make it your home base. Then move into the Riverlands and build your third of the triangle of power. Eventually the northern heartland will become your objective."[19]

The Han loyalists were desperate. The dynasty's rule was crumbling. In the Western tradition, one can imagine some warriors going out to solicit a great hero to join them, rather as the Greeks implored Achilles beneath the walls of Troy—seeking someone of bravery and great physical prowess. But in China it is a strategy that the heroes seek and which they value most. Interestingly, Zhuge Liang's counsel, in detail, involved making many trade-offs. He urged the Han to "come to terms with the Rong tribes on the west, placate the Yi and the Viets to the south, form a diplomatic alliance with Sun Quan, and conduct a program of reform in your own territory."[20] Victory in the end might be total, but the path to it required a good deal of adjustment.

When actual battle occurred, the Chinese placed great emphasis on the use of stratagems and on grasping fleeting operational advantages or *shi*. [21] The classical strategists urged the staking of much on a single throw. The idea being that, properly executed, a single operation can resolve a whole campaign. Achieving this is the theme of the vast semi-popular Chinese literature of stratagems: "lure the tiger down from the mountain," "beat the grass to startle the snake," and such like. These are operational maneuvers that produce victory at once conclusive militarily and decisive psychologically—single, brilliantly conceived applications of force that knock everything else into order.[22]

These visions of the limited use of force supporting vast objectives received considerable confirmation in the experience of early Chinese history, but the more recent past provides examples of its inadequacy and perils. China staked all on a single throw in Korea in 1950, where the surprise outflanking and envelopment of American forces was a dramatic success. But it did not lead to victory. Instead, it provoked in an attritional struggle in which hundreds of thousands of Chinese perished, and the United States, instead of being expelled, eventually involved itself more deeply and permanently in Asia. Attacks on Taiwan's outlying islands in the 1950s were less costly militarily to China, but like the Korean operation, their effect was opposite to that which the Chinese intended. Operationally, the war with India in 1962 was a dramatic Chinese success, but it poisoned a far more valuable diplomatic relationship with New Delhi, while initiating the process of modernization that has transformed India into a military power at least as formidable as China at the present time. The invasion of Vietnam in 1979 aimed to "teach a lesson." Instead, it revealed China's weakness while confirming Vietnamese enmity.

Such military vulnerabilities in the Chinese polity and the ways of dealing with them have passed down from the historical past and still have considerable influence over Chinese strategic thinking today. Certainly, the maximal ends/minimal means bind still applies. Weakness, not strength, is China's real position, but its rulers have a sense of entitlement and possibility that is quite out of proportion to what is feasible. A belief that China can achieve these goals through dexterous use of force also undermines real diplomacy: the business of alliance, reassurance, and threat that, over the long run, creates real power. So a series of cross-cutting tensions—between the givens of geography and resources, between the use of force and the use of diplomacy and compromise, and the wishes and imperatives of politics and rule—continue to frame China's strategic dilemmas today.

## The Changing Strategic Landscape

Diplomacy and domestic politics, as well as technology, have played important roles in fostering China's current approach to military issues. The most important development has been the disappearance of what was once a decisive constraint, the framework of the Cold-War stand off. During the Cold War and after the Sino-American reconciliation of the 1970s, the structure of international politics offered the Chinese the option of a relatively stable role in the world. Beijing's confrontation with the Soviet Union forced China to avoid conflicts with its other neighbors and placed great stress on its key security relationship with the United States. These limitations have vanished. Also, during the 1970s and 1980s China was domestically stable. Leaders from the "Long March" were still relatively vigorous (Deng Xiaoping was only 72 when Mao Zedong died), while the economic reforms that he and his colleagues introduced pleased ordinary Chinese. The passing of the older generation of Chinese leaders leaves newer, untried politicians in charge.

Without a Soviet threat to the North, China is now free to pursue issues previously subordinated, such as territorial claims in the South China Sea, the future of Taiwan, or disputes with the United States, without fear of facing the Soviet Union alone. Just as importantly, without a stable personal leadership to compensate for the lack of an institutional or legal structure, China faces the prospect of considerable political instability.

Most observers speak of China's current problems as a "succession struggle," which suggests that eventually a "successor"—a strongman like Mao Zedong or Deng Xiaoping—will emerge, and that politics will then continue, albeit with incremental changes, much as they have since 1949.[23] This is possible, but the magnitude of the forces unleashed since the 1970s—dizzying economic growth, vast demographic shifts, tides of new information and ideas—coupled with the political inflexibility of the present rulers, suggest that far greater transformations are in store. The recent past may not prove a reliable guide when China's political future is truly up for grabs. Possibilities for China include continued communist dictatorship, constitutionalism, political decentralization, factional struggle or civil war, and even general chaos.

Diplomatically, however, Chinese policy has tended to display a high degree of continuity. China has a long history of dealing with neighboring peoples. Many interpret this as a history of dominance. They see in it a "Chinese World Order" in which lesser states accept "tributary" status in relationship to a China superior in both cultural and military forces. There is some truth in such a picture.[24] This view still indirectly influences current expectations that the emergence of a new Chinese super-power dominating Asia would represent a return to traditional patterns. More realistic, however, is a second view. This sees China as understanding, quite early on, that it exists internationally in a world of equals, and behaving pragmatically to accommodate that fact.[25] Since the late nineteenth century that has been the official Chinese view, and finds its expression today in a punctilious attention to international law.[26]

Certainly China is vulnerable. By virtue of its geographical expanse, today's China is potentially involved on at least five distinct fronts. In Northeast Asia, China faces Japan, Korea, and a Russian Far East whose future is uncertain. In the northwest she shares borders with former Inner Asian states of the USSR, whose history and population overlap Chinese-held Xinjiang. In the southwest, it abuts the Indian sphere of influence, which includes Tibet, which China invaded and annexed in 1958. To the south lie Vietnam and its neighbors, and the areas of the South China Sea that China has steadily been annexing. Finally, to the south and east are Hong Kong and Taiwan, the most advanced and prosperous parts of the Chinese world, the first of which Beijing will receive in 1997, the second of which it insists it will eventually take.

Any state, no matter how strong, would be hard pressed to deal with all these contingencies, and the task is particularly difficult for China. Operationally, handling multiple fronts requires transport and logistics. Given the over-stretched rail network and the lack of roads, it is difficult for China to redeploy its forces. The land frontiers pose particular perils for China for they are porous and ill-defined. In many cases, peoples of the same ethnicities live on either side of the current international frontier. Trouble in Tibet or Muslim Xinjiang might originate as riots, then escalate toward terrorism and insurgency, and eventually draw in outside players, perhaps covertly at first. From Beijing's point of view, these represent the most worrying future scenarios, for they would be extremely difficult to handle and would inevitably draw forces away from the coast and the better-known issues.

Confronted with such multifaceted threats, states have normally responded by establishing priorities: by ameliorating conditions in occupied lands (such as Tibet), and internationally by making alliances and signing treaties with one set of neighbors, in order to concentrate against the most important threat. Even China, which has historically disliked such diplomacy, has made such trade-offs at least three times this century: when confronting Japan in the 1930s and 40s; when opposing the United States in the 1950s; and when offsetting the Soviet Union in the 1970s.[27] In each case, only an overwhelming threat forced China to conclude an alliance. But it also had the effect of reaffirming the legitimacy of the existing Chinese regime. Thus, resistance to Japan brought the Nationalists into the Grand Alliance with Britain, the United States, and the USSR, while greatly increasing China's international visibility and legitimacy. Chiang Kai-shek joined Churchill and Roosevelt at the Cairo Conference and his regime received international recognition as a democracy. Mao's decision to lean to the Soviet side in the late 1940s and during the Korean War had similar benefits. It elevated Mao Zedong to near parity with Stalin, and brought the mighty Soviet Union in as his patron and guarantor. Finally, Mao's decision in the 1970s to lean to the Americans brought him and his successors visits and tributes from Richard Nixon and succeeding American presidents as well as a decisive entry into the international community. Unlike the alliance with the Soviets (but like that of the 1930s and 1940s), the American connection of the 1970s also brought unwelcome pressure on China to liberalize, democratize, and pay attention to human rights.

The Soviet threat impelled the last of these three alliances. Its disappearance has led the Chinese to reassess its domestic costs. The war with the USSR which it once feared now appears inconceivable, while internal threats to the regime—seen most dramatically in 1989, not just at Tiananmen Square, but throughout China—are growing.[28] Because the current leadership has ruled out any sort of liberalization or democratization in response to popular demands, the highest priority both domestically and internationally has become to create and elicit acknowledgments of the regime's legitimacy.[29] The present leadership regards this legitimacy as indivisible: it extends around the whole Chinese periphery, and applies just as strongly to remote coral atolls in the South China Sea—where, objectively, Chinese claims are extremely weak—as to territory that has been Chinese for centuries. These claims are probably unsustainable, but they provide a potentially dangerous trigger for conflict in East Asia.

Chinese thinkers would seem to be aware that their *shi*—"advantages"— in the current environment are at best diminishing. Neighbors will match or exceed China's military power in the near future: Japan is already stronger; Taiwan will have a far more formidable air force within two years; even the Philippines have embarked on serious force modernization. In just two years Hong Kong's return to China will come. If, as seems likely, this reunion is botched, ill-will in the region will increase—and a domestic crisis could ensue in China as well. Therefore, strong pressures push Beijing to acquire as much as possible in the next two years, while the apparent window of opportunity remains open. China is more likely to lose territory in the years ahead than to gain it.

## The Implications of China's "Place in the Sun"

If China continues to pursue its territorial claims both by force and diplomacy, then the likely results are Chinese over-extension and the creation of an Asian anti-Chinese coalition. Despite those perils, such an approach appears to constitute the current national security policy of the People's Republic today. It creates serious risks for China and its neighbors.

China's current military policies aim not so much at creating large and completely modern military forces—although that remains a real, if distant, goal—but rather at developing a set of technological expedients that, combined with the appropriate strategy, could yield a harvest even in the present. A few modern aircraft, the ability to establish temporary local superiority, limited goals, a rapid operation carried out by surprise—this is the pattern China followed successfully in summer 1995 against the Philippines at Mischief Reef. It represents a pattern that must be recognized. Although China's force might still lag far behind that of the United States or even China's immediate neighbors, the *utility of that force* for China has proved substantial. But such a high-stakes game is dangerous. For one thing, it can lead to war: the Chinese cannot intimidate every adversary into settlement. For another, war will undermine politics at home. The high premium placed on not only operational success, but operational brilliance and decisiveness, means that failure will have devastating reverberations.

China's claims are so extensive and so absolute as to pose an insoluble security dilemma. Militarily, China is weak and would be hard-pressed to deal with a major military contingency in connection with any of its claims. Attempts to augment military power, moreover, will only fuel arms races that in the end could leave China worse off than before. But the Chinese have apparently ruled out prioritization of goals and trade-offs of one for another. Furthermore, attempts to secure advantages militarily work against China's simultaneous attempts to develop economically. Close to 80 percent of the foreign capital that fuels China's current economic modernization comes from two small, ethnically Chinese territories: Hong Kong and Taiwan. That flow of capital would dry up should any war occur that involves China. Likewise, China depends more and more on exports, above all to the United States, and conflict would instantly close those foreign markets. The use of military force, then, is not only unlikely to achieve the goals it sets; it will almost certainly precipitate a highly destructive economic crisis.

Why, then, do the Chinese refuse to readjust their policies? Of course they may—this author believes it highly likely that within five to ten years Chinese foreign policy will loosen appreciably, probably in connection with liberalization at home and that issues such as Taiwan and the South China Sea will then be resolved with relative ease. Recognition of real interests, both economic and political, could then lead to harmonization of Chinese policy with that of its neighbors.

But if that happens at all, it will occur in the future. Understanding the present situation requires recognizing that the Chinese continue to harbor illusions about the utility of military force, particularly when used in a limited fashion, in conjunction with diplomatic efforts, as described in the classics. That being the case, one cannot expect the Chinese to draw the same conclusions from their current military situation as the United States would, and instead of the caution the United States would expect, Americans may encounter risk-taking and boldness of a sort that could thoroughly destabilize Asia.

One can easily imagine a Chinese effort with limited force going awry, as happened in the Korean, Taiwan, and Vietnam cases already mentioned.[30] All were potentially dangerous, although none escalated (as was conceivable) into all-out war. In the first case, operational brilliance alone proved insufficient to achieve war aims; in the second, the USSR and the United States behaved in ways China had not anticipated; in the third, military resistance proved far fiercer than China had expected. The sorts of situations in which China may use force may well unfold similarly.

We have repeatedly mentioned the Chinese seizure of Mischief Reef in summer 1995. This was scarcely unprecedented: China has been steadily accumulating territories that it claims in the South China Sea at least since the seizure of the Paracels from South Vietnam in 1974. Nevertheless, the incident in 1995 marked something new. The Chinese move outraged the other claimants, because they believed China had earlier joined them in forswearing the use of force. Their reaction, although it fell short of force to remove the Chinese garrison, was nevertheless strong enough to shock Beijing. Not only did the ASEAN countries speak out together against China: even the United States joined in *sotto voce*. The specter that haunts Chinese strategic calculations—that of a great anti-Chinese entente—suddenly appeared uncomfortably close to reality. Hitherto China had counted on dividing the opposition by dealing bilaterally. But now as Jusuf Wanandi, the Indonesian strategist, has stated, the nations of Asia must work together, otherwise the Chinese "will clobber us one by one." The incident also spurred already substantial military buildups among China's neighbors. On the other side of the ledger, however, the crisis did not affect economic links.

What the next round holds is unclear. Beijing chose the Philippines as its target because it was weak militarily and diplomatically isolated, having unwisely forced its most important ally, the United States, out of Subic Bay. Moreover, the Chinese move caught Manila by surprise, and while the Filipino reaction was rather robust, it did not extend to actual force—even though the Philippines probably could have destroyed the installations, had it so chosen. As a result, however, the South China Sea issue came into diplomatic prominence, and the other claimants looked unlikely to remain divided. As for military options, everyone in the area increased patrolling and surveillance, making it unlikely that China will ever again find as favorable an opportunity as early 1995. Any future Chinese military operation would have to be larger and hence more visible. It would lack surprise, and it would most likely take place against protests and possibly resistance.

With the possible exception of Taiwan, which holds Itu Abu, the largest of the Spratly islands, the other claimants have allies who might well become involved. Vietnam, China's most important rival in the region, has recently joined ASEAN, established relations with the United States, and purchased some modern aircraft and ships. Consequently any operation against Vietnam would be fraught with danger. Even if successful, it would probably bring other Southeast Asian states into Vietnam's camp and thus undermine China's influence in the region. And it might fail: China confronts serious logistical problems in any potential conflict with Vietnam, while the Vietnamese are extremely tough and have long experience in confronting China. They do not require much to sink a Chinese flotilla—a few modern antiship missiles would probably do the job. And they certainly have proven that they possess the chutzpa to stand up to China. The domestic consequences of such a defeat for China might be catastrophic.

Reason would suggest that the Chinese and their neighbors resolve the dispute peacefully, as they might relatively easily, through the Law of the Sea. Doing that, however, would require some Chinese concessions over sovereignty—which are certainly possible. If the Chinese do not resolve the South China Sea issue, however, they will see their relations with their neighbors gradually poisoned and a polarization of the region.

## China and Taiwan

China claims the South China Sea as part of its national territory and makes the same claim with respect to Taiwan, where summer 1995 brought an unexpected increase in tension. The Chinese Qing dynasty ceded the island of Taiwan to the Japanese in 1895. Allied victory in 1945 saw the island returned to the Republic of China. In 1949 that government, having lost the civil war, took refuge on Taiwan. Since the 1970s, when the United States withdrew its diplomatic recognition, at Beijing's insistence, the Republic of China on Taiwan has been isolated diplomatically and its security relationships have been only vaguely defined (although the Taiwan Relations Act of 1979 requires the United States to assure that it possesses sufficient arms for self-defense). The People's Republic of China has always insisted on its right to Taiwan and has refused to renounce the use of force. Therefore it is not surprising that the issue of Taiwan's security continues to attract substantial attention.

The Chinese strategy against Taiwan employs force and diplomacy in the ways we have already discussed. Diplomatically, the Chinese have spared no effort to drive Taiwan from the international scene, to cut Taiwan's diplomatic and security relationships, and to give the Taiwanese only one choice: accepting the People's Republic of China's terms. Militarily, Chinese acquisitions of modern aircraft and submarines, as well as improved anti-aircraft capabilities, threaten to degrade Taiwan's security. Linked to this is an economic strategy as well: one that seeks to constrain Taiwan by building cross-straits trade to the point where it represents a substantial lever to influence Taipei.

Taiwan's military defense depends on two factors. First, its military forces have traditionally maintained a qualitative edge in equipment and training that nullifies much of the apparent numerical advantages enjoyed by the People's Republic. Second, Taiwan faces only one security threat, to which it can devote all its attention, while the People's Republic, as we have seen, confronts a long list of contingencies for which it must prepare. In recent years

Taiwan has renounced the use of offensive force against the mainland and concentrated instead on maintaining its ability to control the air over the Strait and keep the sea-lanes open: that is, on modern fighters and antisubmarine warfare.

For a while in the 1980s it looked as if People's Republic of China's attempts to isolate Taiwan would pay off. The United States refused repeatedly to supply more modern aircraft to re-equip Taiwan's aging air force. As a compromise, the United States agreed to share technology that would permit Taiwan to develop its own "Indigenous Defense Fighter," of which about forty are now in service. After the Dutch sold Taiwan two diesel submarines, China undertook an effective campaign of diplomatic threats which has so far prevented the continuation of further sales. In 1982, the United States agreed to limit military sales to Taiwan, provided tension in the area diminished. By the 1990s, however, the attempt to embargo arms to Taiwan was failing. Taipei's indigenous capacity to develop weapons was growing, fuelled by lavish funding and the employment of hundreds of first-rate Chinese engineers and scientists (as well as sharing of technology, not covered by accords). When China began to acquire genuinely threatening systems, the United States acted responsibly to maintain the military balance: thus, the U.S. government authorized the sale of 150 F-16s only after the Chinese had purchased Su-27s.

By the mid-1990s, Taiwan's military was in the midst of a major qualitative transformation. Numbers were drastically decreasing and the army in particular was being shrunk. Carefully focused expenditures on technology, however, were rising. By the late 1990s, the Republic of China's air force, totaling about five hundred aircraft, would consist of Mirage 2000s, F-16s, and IDFs, as well as indigenously developed AT-3 ground attack aircraft, and E-2T airborne control and warning—making it a formidable air force. The navy is also involved in extensive modernization, actively pursuing acquisition of submarines with the prospect of success at some point. It had procured LaFayette-class frigates from France and was producing versions of the U.S. Perry-class frigate indigenously. It was also procuring and integrating a variety of modern radars, missiles, and combat control systems in its ships. The upshot was that although Taiwan's military would remain far smaller than China's, its qualitative edge was increasing, and with that improvement so was the island's ability to say "No." The effect of international sanctions on Taiwan was proving not unlike those of attempted American sanctions against Israel several decades earlier: they unintentionally increased self-reliance, strength, and in the long run, Taiwan's independence of action.

So far China's strategists have proved incapable of dealing with this response from Taiwan. Their approach has mixed attempted intimidation with diplomatic suasion. They have focused on a closely-fought diplomatic chess game, in which the pieces are high-level visits and participation in international meetings. This absorbs a good deal of attention, but it is not decisive. Indeed, it is probably counter-productive, for its effect is to alienate and estrange the leadership and people of Taiwan. If China's goal is some sort of reunification with Taiwan, then the only realistic strategy is one that renounces the use of force and, for the moment at least, recognizes the status quo. The Chinese, however, refuse to take such an approach because they continue to believe in the maximal ends-minimal means approach, even to Taiwan. How minimal that minimal force will be, however, is an important question.

In summer 1995 some in Beijing seem to have expected that missile firings would cause chaos on Taiwan. In fact, the primary result was a 20 percent increase in Taiwan's military budget. Others speculate about economic sanctions or lightning-fast military operations that will force Taipei to yield without ever bringing on a full war. The real possibility exists that the next year or two will see some such attempt. The Chinese leaders are clearly worried that the 1995 legislative elections in Taiwan and 1996 presidential elections will bring to power an even more secure regime, one that would, as a democratically constituted authority, inevitably command increased international legitimacy. Moreover, additional deliveries of F-16 and Mirage 2000 aircraft, starting in 1996, will render Taiwan far less vulnerable to military blackmail. Finally, China is eager to bring Taiwan to heel before the return of Hong Kong explodes illusions about the feasibility of the "one country, two systems" model. Hence, there exists the real possibility of a crisis, which only serves to increase Beijing's doubts about American resolve, a result of sloppy U.S. diplomacy.

Taiwan's example points up both the peril for China and the dangers to the world of the maximal ends—minimal means approach. The great vulnerability of such an approach is that effective resistance shatters it. If the first throw fails, then the entire operation collapses. China cannot sustain a long-term fight, either logistically or politically, while other powers have time to think about intervention. The linkages between external and domestic politics in China means that a serious setback could lead to a major political crisis in Beijing.

Such scenarios are not difficult to envisage: Japan's superior fighter forces shoot down a dozen Chinese aircraft in the course of a challenge over the Senakaku islands; Taiwan's navy sinks major surface combatants during a confrontation in the straits; Vietnam effectively turns back a Chinese assault on one of its islands in the South China Sea. The repercussions within China are difficult to foresee. Would there be abrupt de-escalation and negotiation or an unexplained abandonment of the engagement, or a dramatic raising of the stakes?

Nor are these even the key questions. One can imagine a change of government—like that in Argentina following the ignominious failure in the Falklands. International involvement would be almost certain, and it could solidify an anti-Chinese entente in Asia. The economic consequences for China might be disastrous: nearly half its exports, after all, go to the United States; it is dependent on foreign petroleum and food grains, not to mention vast amounts of foreign capital for economic development. If China's currency becomes convertible soon, as seems likely, there could be a run on the *yuan* and an inevitable financial crisis. A general collapse into conflict in Asia could ensue from a single small, but miscalculated, Chinese use of force.

The possibility of such a conflict is a profoundly worrying prospect—one to which foreign policy makers should pay the utmost attention in coming years. Habit drives some commentators to use the concept of a "new Cold War" to look at Asia's future, but this is profoundly misguided.[31] The challenge is not global and ideological, like the Soviet threat, but rather local and involved with national interest—although it is still potentially very dangerous. Two classic cases in balance of power politics offer the most informative historical parallels: first, the problems created for Europe and eventually the United States by the rise of Imperial Germany in the years leading up to the First World War; and second, by the responses of Japan to Chinese assertiveness in the 1920s and 1930s, which led directly to the outbreak of the Second World War in Asia, and likewise involved the United States.

In neither case were the stakes anywhere near as high as those ostensibly at issue during the Cold War, but in both cases the outcomes were disastrous. The policies of the Kaiser, Grand Admiral Tirpitz, and others strongly resemble those of China today. Imperial Germany's leaders envisioned not so much war as the achievement of goals without war. The Kaiser intended his fleet not to fight, but to frighten Britain; Berlin's diplomacy sought to use momentary pressure and advantage to secure interests without precipitating conflict. Indeed, the whole German understanding of the military future was delusory: the Schieffen plan led Berlin to expect a victory over France by Sedan Day, in early September 1914. Something similar is occurring in the strategic thinking of China today—an approach that imagines that with bold and assertive, armed diplomacy a few dozen advanced aircraft, ships, and missiles can transform the Asian balance of power.

China, after all, has attempted such assertion before—when it launched an assault on the "unequal treaties" in the 1920s. The Chinese calculation was that militancy and hard-line diplomacy would win concessions from the powers—and indeed it did, for World War I had exhausted the European states and the United States was turning inward. The calculation failed cat-astrophically, however, when it came to Japan. The Chinese seem to have thought that Tokyo would yield as easily as Brussels or even London, but Japan, sensing vital interests at stake and alienated by the Western failure to take its concerns seriously, turned to a unilateral policy in Asia, with results that are well-known.[32]

Both situations cast light on the East Asian present and future. Wil-helmine Germany blundered into the First World War not least for reasons of domestic politics. Its autocratic leaders turned aside the counsel of those—like Bismarck—who understood the real risks and adopted a high-profile pol-icy in pursuit of a "place in the sun" in sublime confidence that they alone understood the future and that their risky schemes would yield large gains at little cost. China's position today is similar. A government that is repressive at home is likely to have the same instincts abroad. Those in Beijing who understand both the needs for domestic liberalization and foreign policy mod-eration have evidently been sidelined. Reports suggest that Deng Xiaoping had to intervene, from his sickbed, to restrain provocations toward Taiwan. At the same time, external responses to China's actions make the situation more risky for Beijing. Logically China should be reassuring its neighbors and smoothing the way for its own emergence—which is scarcely in doubt—as a powerful state. Instead of doing this, however, China has behaved in ways that increase the vigilance and hostility of its neighbors.

This is perhaps fortunate. In the German case, the coalition against Berlin solidified only after the First World War began. In the current Asian case, however, the coalition is forming at least as fast as the Chinese threat is developing, which opens the possibility that it will effectively deter that threat. For there is another possibility, which is even more worrying. Suppose China were to learn the lessons of Germany's premature entry into conflict and plan and calculate correctly, reassuring and dividing its neighbors, and thus avoiding upsetting the international system until it possessed the where-withal to enforce its wishes? What would be the reaction of the world then? Suppose, furthermore, that China were to reconcile successfully with Hong Kong and Taiwan, and thereby acquire both strategic territory and substantial economic and intellectual resources. Were such a China to play diplomacy effectively, it could quite likely make itself the chief power in Asia. Were such a state also able effectively to organize the Inner Asian frontiers—Mongolia, the Russian Far East, and the Turkic territories beyond Xinjiang—it would also become the dominant player on the Eurasian landmass. But for the pre-sent such possibilities appear remote, given China's unwillingness to think in realistic terms.

## Conclusion

We should note two enduring constraints on Chinese behavior, and thus on the realization of such dramatic possibilities. One is Chinese politics. The present regime is brittle and would not likely survive any serious defeat. It appears unequal to administering the territories it already controls, not to mention reorganizing continental Eurasia beyond its frontiers. Any successor regime, whether authoritarian or democratic, would have to be chastened by the collapse of its predecessor, and thus, likely to adopt cautious foreign policies. A democratic regime, moreover, would possess the legitimacy to settle many of the current disputes without weakening its own hold on power. The other is the risk of overextension. Any single, serious military contingency, no matter where, will absorb China's full resources and thus leave nothing to deal with others. Thus, a Taiwan crisis would leave the South China Sea wide open; a problem with India would weaken the coast; unrest on the Inner Asian frontier would shift resources far inland. The dilemma of choosing between land frontier defense (*sai fang*) and coastal defense (*hai fang*) was recognized at least in the Qing dynasty, but it has not disappeared today.

To these internal constraints on China one must add the imponderable of international action. If China's neighbors and the United States behave prudently—which means resolute application of deterrence when Beijing seeks to use military power, coupled with diplomacy and engagement designed to foster peaceful development—then the U.S. and its allies can keep the possibility of conflict low. Even a small amount of deterrence—for example, an American ship or two "observing" in the target zone if China fires missiles again—will be taken seriously by Beijing and most likely result in a modification in its behavior.[33] The danger is that the U.S. will not take such small and prudent steps, because, as has often happened in the past, they are thought risky or provocative. Under those conditions, China's behavior, like that of Wilhelmine Germany, will not be self-limiting. Policy makers in both Asia and the West should understand that Beijing will then most likely continue to probe until, as is inevitable, it encounters resistance. The results could well be disastrous for all involved.

Chapter 7

# America and India: A New Approach

*Stephen P. Cohen*

I ndia has always puzzled American policy makers. Its size, its political
weight, its claims to moral authority, and its economic and military
potential have frequently demanded high-level American attention. Yet,
India has always appeared to be an "emerging" or "rising" power—but one that
never quite arrives.[1] A number of U.S. administrations have launched initiatives in New Delhi's direction or, more recently, responded to overtures from
India for closer relations. None of these efforts has resulted in a sustained relationship. Each time, American policy makers have lost interest or turned
away—perplexed over New Delhi's obsession with Pakistan and unwilling to
choose sides between two regional antagonists—both of which Americans
usually regard as friends. Thus, India has never quite figured as an ally—nor
has it been seen as an enemy. It just does not fit into any of the major categories that have dominated U.S. strategic thinking for more than fifty years
and which continue to do so.[2]

During the Cold War this did not matter much. American policy toward
India was on auto-pilot. The criteria of the Cold War determined all critical
decisions regarding New Delhi and Islamabad, including the formation of
regional alliances. The first such alliance was with Pakistan (in 1951); a close
relationship with India followed soon thereafter (after the India-China war
of 1962); however, as the Soviet and Chinese threat to the region receded,
and as both India and Pakistan used American-supplied weapons in their 1965
war, Washington virtually withdrew from South Asia. The Nixon-Kissinger

"opening" to China via Pakistan led to a brief revival of U.S.-Pakistan relations in 1970-1971 but only the Soviet invasion of Afghanistan in late 1979 drew Washington once more into the region as a major aid and arms supplier (again to Pakistan). That program has ended, although in October 1995 Congress modified the Foreign Assistance Act to permit resumption of economic aid and military sales to Pakistan, despite evidence of the latter's covert nuclear weapons program.

However, American policy makers never completely ignored purely regional power politics. During the first and the last alliances with Pakistan, Washington offered compensatory military and economic aid to New Delhi (albeit, partly to protect the investment in Islamabad). By the end of the Cold War India had received considerably more overall aid than Pakistan. Today, the United States has good economic, political, and even bilateral military relations with both India and Pakistan. But these do not add up to a coherent regional policy.

The *particulars* of America's engagement with South Asia's largest power, India, and the one regional state that has sought to balance Pakistan, are not that different now than thirty years ago. Then, as now, India bitterly opposed U.S. military aid for Pakistan; New Delhi and Islamabad could not bring to fruition U.S.-encouraged talks on Kashmir; and there was a major debate raging in India over "going nuclear." However, the strategic context for Washington, Islamabad, and Delhi has altered radically since the end of the Cold War. There is no Soviet Union and thus for Americans there is no longer the central antagonist that helps shape a coherent, if flawed policy towards both India and Pakistan. For Indians there is no longer a quasi-friendship which gave Delhi enormous international freedom of movement for four decades, while for Pakistan there is no pretext for an alliance with the United States, which in turn provided the wherewithal to challenge India militarily.

America—a country that acquired the habit of working closely with allies of all political stripes—now finds itself without an adversary who poses a threat of such immediacy and magnitude to justify the search for allies. Instead, American strategy revolves around the speculation as to which states might emerge as such a threat and thus which states the United States might (eventually) court as allies. India, which had acquired the habit of playing off the superpowers and even exploiting them (towards the end of the Cold War, it benefitted enormously from its relationship with the Soviets) refuses to contemplate an alliance with the sole superpower (even if one were possible). Nor, however, can India's strategic elite imagine themselves joining with China, Iraq, Iran, North Korea, or other anti-status quo powers to *challenge* the United States.

This essay will discuss not only the specifics of America's convoluted relations with the major South Asian states but why the changed strategic context demands—but has not yet received—a fundamental rethinking of the content of American and Indian policies. The prognosis is not good: six years after the Cold War India and the United States (although not Pakistan) have yet to come to grips with the altered strategic and regional environment of South Asia. Pakistan understands these changes (indeed, it anticipated them a number of years ago), but Islamabad has demonstrated a near-fatal ineptness in matching objectives to capabilities. The result is that it is one of the most dangerously overextended states in the world.

We will first offer a new explanation of the central India-Pakistan conflict. This conflict inhibits the United States and other outside powers in working with India or Pakistan toward larger strategic objectives. In addition, it has drawn outsiders into the region as conflict managers, especially after 1990, when the contestants probably issued explicit nuclear threats. We will then address a number of other key regional issues, including the role of China in South Asia and the prospects for nuclear proliferation. Finally, we will turn to the central quandary the United States faces in the region: developing a policy for an area where the United States has several important interests, but where none seem vital.

## The Core Conflict

Until August, 1947, when the British abandoned their imperial responsibilities, South Asia was a single strategic entity. The partition of the Raj created two major states, each with its own panoply of armed forces, each with its own—but divergent—strategic vision. These visions proved to be both wrong and incompatible. Mohammed Ali Jinnah, creator of Pakistan, assumed that India and Pakistan would cooperate on larger strategic issues but that the minority "hostage" Hindu and Muslim populations in each state would ensure proper behavior towards each other. The Indian leadership expected Pakistan to collapse and saw any India-Pakistan cooperation as both unnecessary and, indeed, a delaying of the inevitable.

The clash of expectations turned the British Indian Raj upon itself. Before 1947 the British had drawn upon Indian manpower to stabilize (or intervene in) the Middle East, North Africa, Southeast Asia, Central Asia, and Europe. By the end of World War II India was the world's third largest producer of military equipment, and ranked ninth among the world's largest industrial powers.[3] Had partition not occurred, or if the states had entered into a strategic alliance, or even if they had only demilitarized their border, India—not China or Japan—would be Asia's greatest military power. Instead, South Asia is a house divided, as India and Pakistan spend most of their time and energy trying to weaken each other. A flawed imperial retreat allowed outsiders to meddle, for benign or malign reasons, and Britain, France, the Soviet Union, and the United States have each supported India or Pakistan (or sometimes both) at various times, usually for extra-regional purposes. The most recent entries into the list of regional peacemaker have been Iran and China, each of which has pursued a "balancing" strategy between New Delhi and Islamabad.

No consensus exists on the reason for the India-Pakistan conflict.[4] The Indians view the conflict as systemic and believe that larger, greater India finds it difficult to deal with smaller states, such as Pakistan, that are irredentist in their regional objectives. Compromise will not work because Pakistan aims to continue the fragmentation of secular, multiethnic India. The Indian response is to wait out the Pakistanis until they realize that accommodation is inevitable. However, if the opportunity arises, as in 1970, many Indians would not be adverse to giving Pakistan a push into extinction. The Pakistani position, especially that of the military, is that the conflict is inherent in the nature of India's leadership: expansionist, intolerant, and bent on reversing past humiliations. Finally, most Americans seem comfortable with the argument that the India-Pakistan conflict rests in deep ethnic, religious, differences that not only threaten to explode into war (three in the past forty-eight years), but detract from the more urgent task of economic development and nation building.

## Paired Minority Conflicts

In a sense these views all reveal part of the truth. But a more comprehensive explanation of the persistent conflict between India and Pakistan, and especially its worsening after the first fifteen years of independence, is that the two states share certain features with other long-lasting, and apparently intractable conflicts.[5] As in the case of the Arab-Israel dispute, the conflict between Tamils and Sinhalese in Sri Lanka, or the strife between Catholics and Protestants in Northern Ireland, the most enduring cause of conflict in South Asia is the existence of *paired* perceptions that ones's own state, nation or ethnic group or sub-national entity is vulnerable and under assault from the outside. Each side sees itself as a minority, or as a weaker state, facing a more powerful entity. In these "paired minority conflicts" it is difficult for one side to offer concessions, or to compromise on even the most trivial issues. To do so appears to confirm others' perceptions of one's own weakness and to invite further demands. Such toxic conflicts draw on an inexhaustible supply of hatred towards the other side as well as distrust of those who advocate dialogue or compromise. When either side feels at a disadvantage, it will refuse to compromise for fear of being driven further down the road of concession. But the same leadership, when it holds the advantage, also refuses to compromise on the grounds that the stronger power can bend the weaker to its will. As if they were on a teeter-totter, the two sides take turns moving up and down, momentarily reaching a state of equality, but always, in fact, in a state of dynamic imbalance that inhibits prospects for long-term negotiations.

These conflicts also have a moral dimension. Aristotle argued that men use politics to seek justice. In South Asia, a sense of injustice legitimizes conflict because it seems to offer the only way to protect a threatened group, and that group is threatened precisely because of its moral or material superiority. Thus, past Indian or Pakistani defeats and current weaknesses are "explained" by Indian and Pakistani virtues.

Perhaps the best-studied case of a paired minority psychology exists in the Middle East. There, Israelis point to the numerical superiority of the Arab (or Islamic) world and make a persuasive case that Israel stands isolated, surrounded, and threatened—David facing Goliath. Yet Arabs see themselves as a threatened minority. While they may outnumber Israelis, they see Israel as an extension of Europe, and the Arab (or Islamic) world remains in a position of political, military, and even numerical inferiority to this larger alliance.

Another acute case of a paired minority conflict exists in South Asia on the island state of Sri Lanka.[6] Here, a minority Tamil population feels itself under political, economic, military, and cultural threat from the dominant Sinhala community. Yet, the Sinhalas, incited by intellectuals, politicians, and a militant Buddhist clergy that sees itself as defending the faith (against Hinduism, represented on the island by the predominately Hindu Tamils) believes *itself* to be the threatened minority. Sinhalese Buddhists may hold the majority on Sri Lanka, but some sixty million Hindu Tamils live just across the water in India. The Indian Tamils represent the sharp edge of this threatening and apparently militant enemy. Thus, both Sri Lankan Tamils and Sinhalese, like Arabs and Israelis, see themselves as threatened and vulnerable.

History plays a key role in perpetuating such dual-minority psychology. Arabs, Israelis, Sinhalese, and Tamils all draw sustenance from the way in which they posit the present and future in the context of the past. Each recalls an era of majority status, great power, and expansion. While now a threatened minority, they believe that their culture and society was once especially notable. Thus, their present minority status appears incongruent with the past, while there are significant chauvinist elements in each community to exacerbate the sense of threat.

Although the India-China relationship influences South Asia's central regional paired-minority conflict, between India and Pakistan, the former relationship is structurally different and does not demonstrate the same degree of pathology. While many Indian strategists still seek revenge for the humiliating Chinese victory over India in the 1962 border clash and regard Beijing as a fundamental threat, their fear is not reciprocated. The Chinese have tended to dismiss India as a client of America or the Soviet Union. Beijing remains unyielding in its attitude towards the contested border, although it has engaged in confidence-building measures and mutual force-reduction along the most sensitive portions of the frontier. These "positive" changes in the India-China relationship result from new Indian vulnerabilities (the loss of the Soviet patron) and a more opportunistic Indian foreign policy (moving closer to the United States by improving its relationship with China), not any basic change in Chinese policies. It is hard to tell whether Chinese "reasonableness" or Chinese bellicosity offers a greater insult to those Indian strategists obsessed with the humiliation of 1962.[7] There is widespread belief among Indian politicians and strategists that their state is under threat from one or another combination of Islamic, Western, Chinese, and small regional powers. This strategic community has what the Indian journalist, Shekhar Gupta, refers to as the "paradox of a majority's minority complex."[8]

Some Indians see their country as surrounded by a sea of extremists Muslims, who already have infiltrated the Indian Muslim minority. Others see India as threatened by an *alliance* of extremist Muslims with the West—as represented by U.S.-Pakistan alliance. Until quite recently China appeared as a threat—in a triple alliance with Islam and the West.[9] Indian perceptions "of the threat" have rotated among these, singly or in groups.

Why then is India threatened by some combination of Pakistan, Islam, China, and the West (led, in Indian eyes, by the United States)? It is because outsiders are jealous of India and try to cut it down to size. This Indian sense of weakness and vulnerability contrasts with India's "proper" status as a great power, stemming from its unique civilization and history. Yet, the day-to-day reality is of an India divided between north and south, east and west, with rebellious and ungrateful minorities (especially Sikhs and Muslims). For many Indian leaders these threats add up to a vulnerable state, beseiged by internal and external enemies.

Among Pakistanis, the central explanation of peace and war is that from the first day of independence India has attempted to crush Pakistan. They see themselves in danger of being overpowered by an increasingly Hindu, extremist, and militant India—a state that seeks to extend its influence to the furthest reaches of South Asia and neighboring areas. Pakistan's self-image bears an eerie resemblance to that of Israel. Both states were formed by a people who were persecuted when living as a minority, and now, even though they possess their own state (which is, coincidentally, based on religion), they remain threatened by powerful enemies.

## Origins: From Majority to Minority

How are psychological minorities created out of physical majorities, or pluralities? India is the most important case since it is larger than any of its neighbors, except China. There are three processes at work: 1) the influence of South Asia's own many-layered history; 2) the lessons learned by politicians and strategists from their own societies; and 3) generational differences among and within the Indian and Pakistani strategic communities.

### Tradition and Strategy

Both Hindu and Islamic traditions contain the idea of a war-crowd, of inherently hostile rivals.[10] The ancient Indian tradition of statecraft *defines* antagonists in terms of proximity to oneself. Any kingdom that touches your border is either a potential threat or a potential victim of one's own expansion.[11] For Kautilya, all statecraft revolved around the manipulation of concentric rings of allies and enemies—ancient Indian strategists quite literally invented the phrase "my enemy's enemy is my friend." The Indian statesman received the lesson that force, war, diplomacy, deceit, and moral authority were all instruments of statecraft, applied when and where the appropriate situation occurred.

The *Arthashastra* offers no instruction on the maintenance of an empire, only on the conquest of others and their absorption into the state itself. For Kautilya "waging peace" was a strategy pursued only when the king "finds himself in relative decline compared to his enemy." Otherwise he could "remain quiet," wage war, prepare for war, build alliances with others, or wage peace in one direction, and war in another. In all of this, the goal of the king is "progress," defined solely in terms of the security and welfare of one's own state.[12]

The *Arthashastra* 's labyrinthine permutations of peace, war, alliance, deception, strong, weak, near, and far yields up an astonishing variety of policies—very much in the Hindu tradition of exhaustive analysis of every position and possibility. It is the *Kamasutra* of statecraft. But its underlying assumptions have not changed over time. There is a powerful image of a state surrounded by threats, not opportunities, of a dog-eat-dog world, in which the welfare of one's own state (and in the *Arthashastra* the king's welfare is the same as the state's) always comes first.

As for Islam, *some* of its teachings portray a world divided between believers and unbelievers, and set forth the obligation of the former to convert the latter. For South Asians this is not a theological or theoretical injunction—great waves of Islamic invasion from both Central Asia and the Arabian peninsula that began in the eighth century transformed the region. These invasions displaced or destroyed dominant Hindu castes throughout north India, while Hindu castes had to enter into alliance with Muslim rulers. From the perspective of most Pakistanis this invasion purged and reformed India, a matter of pride and progress. For Pakistani extremists, the process of purging a corrupt Hindu-dominated India has only begun; and they await the breakup of India with some relish.

More recent Indian history, read and written differently by Indians and Pakistanis, reinforces the notion of threat. The nineteenth century Hindu revivalist and modernization movements acknowledged India's material vulnerability vis à vis the West, but asserted its spiritual superiority. India might appear as temporarily weaker, but morally greater. India's riches and treasures attracted outsiders in the past. In the future, a strong India should keep outsiders at bay.

This historical experience of conquest, domination, and absorption strongly dominates the Indian view of regional conflict, especially its relationship with Pakistan. For most elite Indians the existence of Pakistan, and the period of British rule over India, is *de facto* evidence of a betrayal of India by Muslims to other Muslims, and then to the West. In Islamic-Christian relations, Hindus are the odd-men out.

While India's past greatness has not been quite so evident in the twentieth century, it has, in the minds of most intellectuals and political leaders, the potential of "emerging" once again. Alarmed by its greater moral and spiritual authority, the decadent states of the West, in particular, feared competition from India. Hence, they kept India backward, even as they professed friendship. This view, drawn from a special view of history, is shared by liberal and conservative Indians alike: *someone* is trying to prevent India from again assuming its great role in regional and world affairs. And that "someone" or "other" often enters into a conspiracy with local enemies, since Bangladesh, Nepal, Sri Lanka, or even Pakistan are not credible threats in their own right. New Delhi wags have give a name to this fear of outsiders: the "East India Company Syndrome." Sandy Gordon has identified this quality as part of India's "strong-weak" strategic character.[13]

## Internal Sources

An Indian general once characterized India-Pakistan wars as "communal riots with armor." I have frequently used the phrase to describe relations between the two states because it suggest a deeper truth about their conflict and the ways in which it is conducted.[14] The communal riot is a set-piece in South Asian administrative history. A conflict between two ethnic, religious, or linguistic groups erupts because of both proximate and long-term considerations. In almost every case the leaders of both sides tell their followers that they are vulnerable and threatened and must strike first because waiting would put their side at a disadvantage. This is easy to do in India, since it is a country that does not possess a domestic majority community. In South Asia, communal riots do *not* usually involve what is now termed "ethnic cleansing" (an attempt to rid a city or region of a minority community).[15] More often, both sides see the riot as one of a series, each followed by a temporary truce, but sooner or later to break out again when required. In the typical communal riot both sides not only battle each other, but keep an eye on outside forces (the police, the civil administration, and politicians) who may or may not play favorites, and who may or may not speedily act to end the conflict.

In many ways, the wars between India and Pakistan of 1947-1948, 1965, and 1971, and the near wars in 1955, 1987 and 1990, follow a pattern resembling a South Asian communal riot: while both states have conflicting relations with other neighbors and other states, they return again and again to each other. As in the riot, the causes of conflict run deep, and wars are as predictable as riots stemming from religious, linguistic, or caste hatreds. In mitigation, however, one should note that most communal riots in South Asia, like the wars between regional states, are not total wars in the Western sense—although with the advent of nuclear weapons India and Pakistan now have the means to conduct such a war.

This element of inevitability is the most destabilizing element of the "communal riot with armor" model. In the end, it leads one to ask not whether one can trust Indians or Pakistanis to fulfill their obligations in negotiated agreements that lacked incentives for compliance, but whether, under the influence of communal images of their destiny, they can be trusted in cases even where it is in their self-interest to comply.

## Generation and War

Finally, the current pathological phase of the India-Pakistan conflict also results from generational circumstances: certain age groups in both countries gained a strong sense of fear and insecurity at an early age, and such fears shape foreign and strategic policy. The diplomats, generals, politicians, academics, and journalists who constitute the foreign policy elite number no more than a few thousand in Pakistan, and perhaps five times that in India. One can moreover divide them into three generations.

The first generation, the founding fathers—Mahatma Gandhi, Sardar Patel, Mohammed Ali Jinnah, and Jawaharlal Nehru—devoted their lives to two goals: achieving independence and building new states and nations. With the exception of Gandhi, they did not believe that partition would lead to conflict between India and Pakistan. On the Indian side there were those who expected Pakistan to collapse inevitably, but who did not see the need to precipitate that collapse by war. In Pakistan Jinnah assumed that good relations would exist between the two countries; his expectation was that of a multi-religious Pakistan, counterpoised against a predominately Hindu India, with both possessing significant minorities whose presence would serve as hostages to good relations.

The second generation of Indian and Pakistani leaders was not prepared to solve the problems left by partition. Nothing in their experience led them to develop a strategy of regional reconciliation. They reached a number of agreements which cleaned up the division's debris, and they installed trade and transit treaties, hotlines, other confidence-building measures as early as the 1950's. Indeed, at the rate they were moving, India and Pakistan seemed headed toward detente. But the second generation, especially in Pakistan, turned to foreign policy as a means to shore up their weak domestic position, and everyone (except Nehru) found themselves infected with the Manichean bipolarity of the Cold War.[16] In any case, both sides still believed that *time* was on their side—if they waited long enough, the other side would falter, collapse, or yield.

However, the second generation encountered two great post-partition traumas. For Indians, this was the defeat at the hands of the Chinese in 1962; for Pakistanis, the division of their country at Indian hands in 1972. The ten-year difference is important: Indians have moved further towards reconsidering their great humiliation than Pakistanis, and have begun to think of a normal relationship with China; Pakistanis find it harder to imagine detente with India.

These two events shaped the *Weltanschauung* of successor generations in both countries. There were a number of similarities:

- In each case, the other side dismisses the seriousness of the event. The President of Pakistan, Ayub Khan, did not, in 1962, believe that there was a real India-China conflict, and even today Pakistanis belittle Indian obsessions with Beijing. Indians blithely assume that Pakistanis have more or less forgotten the events of 1972, and cannot understand why Pakistan's leaders are suspicious when New Delhi professes good intentions.

- In each case, an external conflict had profound domestic political consequences, not a small matter in a democracy. No Indian politician has ever admitted publicly that the Indian case has flaws, or suggests that India and China exchange territory, lest he or she be attacked for betraying the motherland. No Pakistani can publicly talk about a settlement of Kashmir short of accession to Islamabad lest they be attacked for being pro-Indian and anti-Islamic. Fortunately, there are some in both countries eager for dialogue and a possible resolution of the conflicts that divide the two nations.[17]

- Each trauma led directly to consideration of nuclear weapons and the further militarization of the respective countries. In India's case the lesson of 1962 was that only military power counts and that Nehru's faith in diplomacy without firepower was disastrously naive. Indians have, like Pakistan, spent too much on defense ever since. With the Chinese test of a nuclear weapon in 1964, the Indian strategic community began a thirty-year debate over the nuclear "option." The linkage between the trauma of 1972 and a nuclear program is even closer in Pakistan—and for Zulfiqar Ali Bhutto a nuclear weapon possessed the added attraction of enabling him to reduce the army's power. What an irony that Pakistan has wound up with both a nuclear program and a powerful, if bloated army!

- Finally, each crisis generated hostile attitudes toward the United States. While America initially supported India against China, and still, technically, endorses India's position on the McMahon line, Washington retreated from its major military assistance program and withdrew from the region entirely after 1965. For Indians of this generation disappointment in America turned to fury when they learned of the U.S.–China rapprochement. This, more than anything else, drove New Delhi into Soviet arms. For Pakistanis, of course, U.S. support in 1971 was inconsequential, and from that moment the Pakistani leadership, civilian as well as military, acquired a deep distrust of the United States. When Pakistan and the United States did cooperate on Afghanistan, Islamabad extracted a high price indeed.

The second generation, still in power, rehearses history and their own lives and careers as a record of the increasing hostility of the other side. They conclude regional failings are entirely the responsibility of someone else. They offer a litany of grievances against outsiders, especially America, for failing to see the region realistically and accurately. They also resent the perceived apathy and ignorance of the West, because it implies that their own careers and countries are unimportant.

Thus, Indians acquired a sense of persecution after Nehru's death. Along with Gandhi, and other members of his generation, Nehru had a vision of India as *such* a great country that others could not easily threaten it. They saw Indian history as so magnificent that India could stand up to all external threats without much outside help and without concern that it might fail. For them, India could be patient; Gandhi's assassination was linked to his acceptance of Pakistan, and his sending the agreed-upon share of undivided India's economic and military assets. The generation that witnessed the traumatic 1962 loss to China lacked such confidence. Their insecurity led to alliance with Washington, then with the Soviet Union, then to anti-American hysteria, then to an arms-buying spree, and finally to the forcible division of Pakistan—but not to an honest appraisal of the past, including the 1962 defeat. The encircling ring of states around India provides a ready-made image of threat from every direction. India sees threats from the north, the east, the west, and even over the horizon. Indian naval propagandists eagerly point out the threat from the sea, from whence both the Arabs and the Europeans came, and—twenty-five years ago—the USS *Enterprise* .[18]

Similar images of encirclement grip Pakistan. In this case, after the Soviet invasion of Afghanistan, such threats were visible just across *both* borders. The refusal (amounting to a betrayal) of Pakistan's Islamic allies and China, let alone the fickle United States, to provide effective assistance to Islamabad when it was under attack in 1971 magnified the threat as well the sense of betrayal. The *Enterprise*, recalled by Indians of the second generation as a threat, represents the cynical gesture of a false friend to their Pakistani counterparts.

## Kashmir

Kashmir is an especially important component in the India-Pakistan relationship, because it forms much of both self-images. While it is of economic, strategic, and military importance to both sides, and because it was of personal importance to a number of South Asian leaders (the Nehru family originally came from Kashmir, and the contemporary Pakistani politician, Nawaz Sharif, is of Kashmiri origin), Kashmir's entanglement with competing national identities sets it apart from other issues. From the beginning, Kashmir had the quality of being both a problem and a solution—it is hard for Indians or Pakistanis to talk objectively about Kashmir since it is, for each, now intimately connected to their respective national identities.

Both sides see Kashmir not only as lost territory, but also as *hostage* territory—a piece of the political order that some larger objectives threaten. These objectives are somewhat different for Indians and Pakistanis. For many Indians, led by Nehru, Kashmir was essential to maintenance of a secular state: if Kashmiri Muslims achieved separation from the rest of India, what could prevent the remainder of India's vast Muslim population from making special, even territorial, claims on the Indian state? Directed by Pakistan, such a movement would result in the further breakup of India.[19] For Pakistanis, Kashmir also represents a hostage: only in this case less a threat to the physical existence of Pakistan than as a threat to the *identity* of Pakistan, a nation created to preserve and protect Muslims in South Asia. As long as Muslims remain under Hindu dominance (Kashmir is the only Muslim-majority state in Hindu-majority India) then Pakistan's original purpose remains unfulfilled.

The emergence of a separatist Kashmiri movement, with its assertion of a distinct national identity (however imperfectly defined) comes as a challenge to both Delhi and Islamabad, and may, ironically, make a resolution of the Kashmir problem, possibly by creating a situation of "nested" minorities. Kashmiris are a minority in both India and Pakistan; Indians and Pakistanis are afraid that the wrong solution to Kashmir will further exacerbate their own internal stresses; within Kashmir, Hindus and Buddhists live as minorities among a Muslim population; the Valley Kashmiris, Hindus, and Muslims, are a minority in the larger state of Jammu and Kashmir (as are other Kashmiri communities: Mirpuris, Jammu Hindus, and Ismaili Muslims who live in the Northern territories, and so forth).

Since the parties to the dispute view themselves as threatened, or as a minority, in one sense or another, a resolution of the dispute must rest on principles that reassure minorities, or putative minorities, or "nested" minorities. Two of these principles suggest themselves now that India and Pakistan are both democracies, and because most Kashmiri separatist or militant groups accept democracy. One is some variety of self-determination—if not a "plebiscite," as originally agreed to by India, then some variation on the theme associating Kashmiris of various religions and ethnic identity with the process. The second is the protection of minority rights (embedded in the Indian and Pakistani constitutions.)[20]

❦

# China and South Asia

China has been influential in South Asia for many years, although Chinese strategists do not like to see their state described as a South Asian power. They also resist the suggestion that they might eventually emerge as a regional peace maker. Beijing's earliest dealings with South Asia saw it attempt to consolidate its porous and ill-defined frontiers. Chinese communist leaders were wary of Jawaharla Nehru, even though he abandoned the special position in Tibet that India inherited from the British Raj. Chinese concern with India intensified in 1959 after New Delhi provided sanctuary for the Dalai Lama when he fled Tibet after a Chinese crackdown. To the Chinese this Indian action belied professions of goodwill. Some informed Indian observers of India-China relations argue that Chinese anxiety over Indian intentions toward Tibet, rather than the dispute over the India-China border, was the real cause of the 1962 war.

For the past twenty years China's chief interest *in* South Asia has been to build up Islamabad as a counterweight to Soviet power. China even provided Pakistan with nuclear technology and enriched uranium, with plentiful (but obsolete) armor and fighter aircraft, and diplomatic support. Having achieved this, the Chinese reaped a strategic bonus in the positioning of Islamabad as a balance to India. Beijing's support for Pakistan slackened after the collapse of the Soviet Union, although it still provides significant military equipment, including medium-range missiles, to Islamabad. With the breakup of the Soviet Union, Beijing moved to normalize relationships with India, and the two have stabilized their contested border with a series of troop pull-backs and high-level discussions. China's position on Kashmir, on the India-Pakistan dispute, and other regional issues has moved to a point not very different from that of the United States and other outside powers. However, it is unlikely that Beijing would soon contemplate the role of regional peacemaker. For both India and Pakistan, China is intimately linked to relations with the United States. With the Russians no longer a key player in South Asia, the regional strategic structure has resolved itself into a lopsided U.S.-China-India-Pakistan rectangle.

China's impact on India has been more important than India's on China—a fact that still galls some Indian strategists. When India's foreign policy community looks at China it recalls a series of humiliations and betrayals. After a period of pseudo-friendship (the "Hindu-China Bhai Bhai!" or "India and China are brothers!" era), the 1962 war represented a massive Chinese betrayal to many Indians that contributed to Nehru's physical and personal decline and indirectly forced India to negotiate with Pakistan on Kashmir (one of the terms of Anglo-American military aid that briefly flowed into India after 1962). The 1964 Chinese nuclear test and explicit Chinese threats against India during the 1965 India-Pakistan war immediately followed the 1962 war. The final China-related humiliation for the Indian strategic community involved the United States: after ten years of hearing American exhortations that India had to resist Chinese aggression, Indians saw the United States secretly (and through the good offices of Pakistan) bring about in 1970 its own detente with China. This double betrayal, more than anything else, pushed India into the arms of the Soviet Union and contributed to deep distrust of America.

Indians have debated four different strategies toward China—three of them publicly, one more privately. From 1962, India pursued a strategy of containment toward China, first an alliance with the Soviet Union and the United States, and then, after 1971, with the Soviets alone. With the Soviet Union's demise, the "containers" (who seek to regain control over Indian-claimed territory occupied by China from at least 1959) have tried to persuade the United States and other powers that China still represents a threat to all Asia and that a military/political barrier must be erected to dissuade China from further adventures.

After the Soviet Union's collapse, a segment of the Indian strategic community has advocated a second view—joining with China to contain the sole superpower, the United States. This group has revived the notion of "Asian solidarity" and appealed to Chinese fears of Washington and of U.S.-Moscow entente. Their hidden agenda may be the return of Chinese-held territory claimed by New Delhi.

A third Indian position, the "normalizers," has been invisible for many years, but does have its advocates and seems to be the position held by India's former prime minister, P. V. Narasimha Rao. This group stresses improvement of bilateral Sino-Indian ties, leading to the eventual return of some Indian territory and the "normalization" of Indian-Chinese relations. It tacitly admits that the Indian position on the border question had flaws. Strategically, this policy has important implications. A closer relationship between India and China leaves open the option of joining with China against the United States on selected issues. More importantly, in view of the bitterness of India-Pakistan relations, and Pakistan's continued encouragement of separatist and terrorist groups in Kashmir and elsewhere, such an approach may also represent a strategy to detach Pakistan from China. If another India-Pakistan crisis should develop Delhi wants to ensure that Beijing remains neutral.

Finally, a fourth view is sometimes heard within the Indian strategic community, occasionally by the "containers," and even among those who would, for the moment, join with China against Washington. They understand that

New Delhi holds a powerful card in its relationship with Beijing: the dispo-sition of the Tibetan exile community. The Indians could play this card as part of a normalization process with Beijing, but they could also activate it during a period of internal distress in China, or in retaliation should China renew support for separatist groups in India. The Indians have the options of evicting the Dalai Lama, or of allowing the Tibetans to articulate their demands for independence or greater autonomy within China more publicly, or of supporting once again the Tibetans militarily. If Chinese concern is any measure of the importance of the Tibetan issue, then New Delhi still holds powerful cards, and there are a number of Indian strategists who believe that Nehru was foolish to have earlier yielded Tibet to China without a *quid pro quo*. India's public preoccupation with China represents both a legitimate security concern and a rationalization for its own nuclear research and devel-opment programs.

## Toward a Balance of Terror

Several American administrations have declared nuclear proliferation to be the most important issue in American relations with India and Pakistan. President Jimmy Carter first articulated this—a view he quickly retreated from when the Soviets invaded Afghanistan. The Bush Administration found itself drawn into the region when it tried to manage an impending nuclear crisis in 1990. Soon afterward, American officials declared South Asia to be the most likely place to witness the first nuclear exchange since 1945.[21] Sub-sequently, Pakistan and India briefly found themselves included as objects in the search for "rogue" powers, as Washington agencies sought new threats.[22] But both remained at the forefront of American proliferation concerns through 1994-1995, because neither power had signed the Non-Proliferation Treaty, then up for permanent extension. But American policy makers lost sight of the reasons why India and Pakistan had moved to positions just short of declared nuclear-weapons status. Each arrived at this point because of important strategic and political reasons, not because they were "rogue" or irresponsible powers.

Indian interest in nuclear weapons goes back to the Chinese test of 1964, although there was an earlier pro-weapons faction, led by Dr. Homi Bhabha, in the Indian scientific community. The Chinese test came two years after India's devastating loss in the 1962 war, after Nehru's death, and at the time when the new American-Indian alliance was fraying. In the 1960s, and today, according to recent authoritative public opinion polls, Indians: 1) believe strongly in global nuclear disarmament; 2) do not want to be perceived as a nuclear-armed bully; 3) will build and deploy nuclear weapons, if they feel it is in their vital security interests (with likely threats coming from both China and Pakistan); and 4) have learned from the United States, and other countries, that the possession of nuclear weapons is a mark of national greatness. These are, obviously contradictory views; this is one reason why India has yet to build and deploy a nuclear weapon, while at the same time has maintained a nuclear option. Even today the vast majority of Indians do not want to go nuclear unless conditions three and four overbalance conditions one and two.

As for Pakistanis, the view there is that: 1) they would prefer to defend their country by conventional means—this proved impossible in 1971; 2) the Brasstacks crisis of 1987 was evidence that India still harbors hostile intentions toward their country; 3) nuclear weapons ensure that India will not again attempt the destruction of Pakistan, either by conventional or nuclear means; and 4) the overt deployment of nuclear weapons, or admission that Pakistan possesses one, would be politically costly, and thus should be deferred.

These views are also contradictory. Pakistan, like India, sees an advantage in possessing nuclear weapons, but recognizes the downside. Indeed, Pakistani and Indian scientists have pointed out the risks of accidental nuclear detonation, while one study has demonstrated that there are only a few months during the year when either side can "safely" use nuclear weapons without suffering massive fallout on its own territory.[23] When one adds to this the possibility that aid might be cut, that outsiders might refuse to invest in a nuclear-armed region, and that possession of nuclear weapons will do little to address deeper economic and political problems in South Asia, one comes up with a solid list of reasons for moving slowly.

Whether "de facto," "threshold," "undeclared" or "emergent," there is no question that India and Pakistan have the capacity to become nuclear states, even if they have not yet acquired a nuclear capability—indeed, even if they never acquire or deploy nuclear weapons.[24] There is a consensus that large-scale war will result not only in stalemate but that a stalemate will lead one—and then both—states to reconsider their declarations of non-nuclear status. This, in turn, raises the terrifying possibility of the actual use of nuclear weapons.

South Asia has arrived at a situation that George Perkovich describes as "nonweaponized deterrence."[25] Both countries have the capability of developing nuclear weapons, and this capability has created a state of mutual nuclear deterrence—if one side were to threaten, or to actually use, nuclear weapons, the other could respond in kind.[26] It also makes it less likely that India and Pakistan will engage in full-scale conventional war for fear of escalation. Indeed, there has been no large-scale war since 1971, and even that conflict remained limited, since India did not extend the war to the western frontier with Pakistan, although it did divide Pakistan in half.

Thus, there is now a South Asian "half-way house" between weaponization and abstinence. The Indian and Pakistani armies shoot at each other regularly on the Siachin Glacier, just north of the Vale of Kashmir. Both countries have harassed each other's diplomats; and there is strong evidence that each supports dissident groups in the other state. Nonetheless, both states have carefully avoided escalation. It is a situation that resembles the Cold War, even down to the extension of conflict to third states. This state of affairs in the region has received criticism from two directions. First, nuclear hawks in both countries—and some American experts—argue that deterrence must rest on real weapons and a credible threat that they will be used. This view argues that nonweaponized deterrence is inherently unstable. This group would actually prefer both India and Pakistan to go nuclear.

On the other side, some in the Clinton Administration and in Congress obsessively focus on the global Non-Proliferation Treaty. They believe that nonweaponzied deterrence, or any other half-way house between weaponization and a capability, implies approval of nuclear weapons. They also fear that tolerating an ambiguous nuclear regime endangers a permanent extension of the Non-Proliferation Treaty (although they were willing to make significant adjustments in the case of at least one state, North Korea, that had signed, and then violated, the treaty, while neither India nor Pakistan are treaty signatories).

Neither view is correct. Nonweaponized deterrence is probably unwise in the long run but it has existed in South Asia for six years. Nonweaponized deterrence is a place on the proliferation ladder where both countries can pause and reflect before moving upward. American policy should aim to stabilize the present situation, while working with the two nations to see if they might move back *down* the proliferation ladder. The one contingency that might suggest another strategy would be China's emergence as a hostile, aggressive force in Asia, and thus the need to balance China with another regional nuclear power—presumably India.

As quasi-nuclear powers India and Pakistan face two tasks. The first pertains to the maintenance of the incipient balance of terror and avoidance of nuclear accidents. This is not merely a problem of permissive action links, insensitive high explosives, acquiring secure second strike forces, and overcoming other technical challenges associated with being (or almost being) a nuclear state. It also pertains to the linkage between nuclear weapons and other weapons.

Iraq used its chemical program to protect its weaker nuclear program. Baghdad assumed that the threat of chemical war could deter Israel and the

West from attacking Iraq's more serious nuclear infrastructure. The problem is somewhat different for the two South Asian states: they have accomplished nuclear programs but weak chemical and biological programs. But their armies are more professional than Iraq's. In their case, they must develop a strategic doctrine which somehow links weapons of mass destruction to conventional arms in a way that the armed forces themselves accept a more limited role. This is particularly difficult in Pakistan, which is why nuclear weapons were so attractive in 1972 to Zulfiqar Ali Bhutto, when he was looking for ways to reduce the army's influence. Would the military allow nuclear targeting to remain exclusively in civilian hands? Probably yes, in India, but certainly not in Pakistan. President Zia was asked, just before his death, who in the military would control the use of nuclear weapons, especially if he were to leave office. The air force, which might be expected to deliver them, or a politically more trustworthy army, or a combination—with what consequences for tactical flexibility and site security? He evaded reply, only muttering that "it could be a problem," but he was aware that nuclearization—or near-nuclear status—raised a host of strategic, doctrinal, technical, and political problems.

However, it is also true that quite apart from the need to balance each other's programs, regional nuclear hawks argue that nuclearization provides the opportunity for Indian and Pakistani policy makers to advance important interests and to demand admission to the ranks of the regional great powers. A nuclear India would also feel more confident in addressing the United States and China as near-equals, and even in demanding a subsequent general reduction in nuclear arms. The nuclear lobby does not mind Pakistan achieving nominal equality with New Delhi, as long as New Delhi can claim a rough form of equality with Beijing and a declining Moscow and Washington. Nevertheless, India (and Pakistan) must calculate the cost to their present economic reform programs should the Western powers and Japan punish them for flaunting the global movement toward denuclearization.

Support for the present nonweaponized deterrence regime neither concedes the inevitability of an overt deployment of nuclear weapons nor fails to address it, should it occur. For now, the United States should concentrate on efforts to contain these programs in anticipation of the day when regional leaders agree that eliminating them is in their own interest. Doing so requires developing a broad band of strategic, economic, and technological policies, some of which require modification in the Pressler Amendment (that is a Pakistan-specific amendment to the Foreign Assistance Act) and the Nuclear Non-Proliferation Act, which prevents provision of even fully-safeguarded civilian reactors to India or Pakistan unless they sign the Non-Proliferation Treaty.

The U.S. Congress has recently debated these issues, with mixed results. A bipartisan coalition backed the president's request to modify the Pressler Amendment to allow transfer of economic and humanitarian aid as well as over $300 million in military sales. Pakistan's request for the delivery of sixty F-16 aircraft was denied, although an attempt will be made to return monies already paid to the manufacturer. But the package (known as the Brown Amendment, for its sponsor, Republican Senator Hank Brown) did not address the deeper regional conflict between the two states, nor did it consider the context of America's larger strategic and regional interests. Prompted by Benazir Bhutto's personal diplomacy, and a combination of a dislike for India and sympathy for Pakistan, the legislative process generated considerable heat but little light. Presented with no good options, several senators publicly stated their frustration with the administration and the apparent lack of coherent regional policy.

The inept handling of the issue by the administration, and the laments of confused senators and congressmen (who were, in the words of one expert witness, Michael Krepon, presented with "no good choices"), suggests a troubling question. Is this the best one can hope for in terms of America's policy toward South Asia, and the Indian-Pakistani conflict? Is it impossible to place such an important act (selling arms to one friendly state, Pakistan, knowing that the act would threaten another friendly state, India) within a larger strategic approach to South Asia, an approach that encompasses both nonproliferation and other important American interests? It is this question—whether or not the United States should be satisfied with an admittedly weak policy because the region itself does not provide the material for a more coherent approach—to which we now turn.

## America and South Asia

There is reason to be pessimistic about South Asia. The region has witnessed an unprecedented series of conflicts, often fanned by neighbors. Political corruption has increased dramatically. Guns and bombs are now regularly used to eliminate politicians; moderates are under pressure, especially in Pakistan. Tragically, the arrival of democracy in that country seems to have set back Islamabad's willingness to negotiate with New Delhi—even if the latter wanted to negotiate—over Kashmir and other problems. Furthermore, the end of the Cold War has exacerbated regional insecurities by removing the chief outside supporters of India and Pakistan. This happened just as both countries confronted each other in 1990 with nuclear threats, implied and explicit. Finally, a series of violent deaths of senior political leaders (especially

Zia in Pakistan and Rajiv Gandhi in India) and the coming to power of weak or unstable governments has heightened the sense of insecurity in both nations.

There is a general American belief that the India-Pakistan dispute rests on an "age-old" conflict between Hindus and Muslims, and is intractable. The recent flare-up over Kashmir suggests to many Americans that the dispute is beyond resolution. Finally, the existence of nuclear weapons on the subcontinent suggests to some that the U.S. would best be advised to keep its distance—a regional nuclear war would not directly affect the United States or its allies, nor is there much possibility now (with the Cold War's ending) that it might catalyze a larger nuclear war between major nuclear powers. In sum, it is possible to make a plausible case for a hands-off policy. The United States has too few resources, too little regional expertise, and no vital interest in South Asia—better leave the region to itself until a more opportune time.

Three important facts undercut the case for a hands-off policy. First, the characterization of the India-Pakistan dispute, and even the conflict over Kashmir, as "intractable" at best represents a partial truth. The intractablility of India-Pakistan relations, of the Kashmir conflict, and of other regional disputes has waxed and waned over the years with a number of insignificant agreements between the two states reached in the first two decades of independence. Furthermore, there has been no war between the two states for twenty-five years. Second, the remarkable accomplishments of American diplomacy over the past five years strengthens the case for a more activist policy. The Middle East peace process has borne fruit, the Cambodia conflict is near resolution, South Africa has been transformed, and an activist American diplomacy in Northern Ireland and (perhaps) the former Yugoslavia demonstrates the power of both the idea of reconciliation and the effectiveness of American diplomacy. Third, the nuclear issue will not go away. India and Pakistan have behaved responsibly as near-nuclear weapons states: there is no evidence that either has exported nuclear materials or expertise to other states, they have not hypocritically signed and then violated the Non-Proliferation Treaty (as Iraq and North Korea did), and there are powerful reasons why neither will want to move ahead to become full-fledged, overt nuclear weapons states. Nevertheless, deeper anxieties and insecurities drive their nuclear programs and unless these are addressed, the nuclear programs may move in unpredictable and dangerous ways. The CIA's estimate that South Asia is the most likely place in the world for a nuclear war to start is probably correct.

There are also deeper forces that could move the two states toward greater cooperation, if not detente.[27] Five such trends are of special importance: the increases in non-official interaction on strategic and arms control issues, the growth of trade between the two states, the fact that both are now democracies, the restraint imposed on regional military ambitions by the presence of nuclear weapons and the emergence of a new generation of leaders (especially in India), a generation less interested in confrontation and the past.

In this context, an American role that supplemented regional trends toward dialogue and detente could prove decisive. Given such an American role, it is possible to be optimistic about South Asia's future, even acknowledging the fundamental differences between India and Pakistan. Some of these differences are ideological, while others pertain to the very national identities of two states. These differences will not soon disappear but on balance an outside "helping hand" would make a considerable difference.

## A Regional Peace Process

In the past five years the United States has let slip a unique opportunity to construct a new policy toward India and South Asia. When the Cold War ended, American influence in the region was at its height. Pakistan (where a new democratic government owed its existence to American intervention) was still dependent on the United States, while India's patron, the Soviet Union, had vanished. The Bush administration, which had played an important conflict-resolution role during the spring 1990 nuclear crisis that arose over Kashmir, had decided to make South Asia a high priority in its second term. In the U.S. bureaucracy, there were also plans for a comprehensive regional American strategy. Bush's defeat in November 1992 halted all developments and, three years into the Clinton administration, U.S. policy remains in disarray.

The Bush administration's assumptions (and those of the Reagan administration, when some planning was done toward a post-Cold War world) was that America would have diverse and continuing interests in South Asia (democracy, non-proliferation, economic liberalization, and so forth) and should attempt to work with India and Pakistan to pursue common strategic objectives. American statements identified these objectives as early as 1987, as peace keeping in and outside the region and possibly containment of China. The United States has no *vital* interests in South Asia (defined as something worth going to war over). The region ranked somewhere below the middle in terms of overall American priorities, but not at the bottom. The fate of a quarter of the world, which possesses a potential for nuclear war, demands some level of attention.

The first requirement for American policy is a broad strategy to replace the Cold War framework; the second is the application of assets to carry out that strategy. What kind of strategy is appropriate? In the days of the former Soviet Union, the United States pursued containment and then accommodation. In the case of China there was, at first, a policy of containment, but this yielded to an alliance against the Soviets. In the case now of Russia and China, the United States is debating the merits of a new balance of power strategy versus some form of cooperative diplomacy. None of these models quite fit South Asia. India is not likely to become a close ally of the United States, nor will the United States need to contain it. The United States might work closely with India on one project or another, but this is also true of Pakistan.

The models that are appropriate for the India-Pakistan conflict are the Middle East peace processes and other regions where the United States has made low-key but sustained efforts to resolve regional or national disputes that, like the India-Pakistan conflict, were also once seen as intractable. Successful efforts in South Africa and Cambodia come to mind. South Asia needs a matrix or a template that can shape the components of American policy to support a central objective of normalizing India-Pakistan relations. Most importantly, America can only reach its wider regional goals, if it works toward achieving that normalization. The one exception is the enhanced economic liberalization of India, already well-underway, which is of direct benefit to the United States, the largest investor in India. However, this liberalization has barely touched Pakistan, and without further movement in the bilateral conflict between India and Pakistan, American investment in the region remains at risk.

A South Asian regional initiative would provide a framework that allows the United States to help the region move toward greater cooperation, reduced arms spending, and containment of the Indian and Pakistani nuclear programs. It will also address the critical problem of communal conflict within India, a problem which is coming to dominate India's relations with both Bangladesh and Pakistan. Such a regional initiative might be similar to the Middle East peace process, but it should not require vast financial resources or a military commitment. It requires only one significant (but scarce) new American asset: time—the undivided attention of a handful of policy makers over a four-to-five year period.

Policy makers in the Bush administration admitted that the idea of a regional peace initiative made strategic sense, but they lacked the time to devote to the region—the same people were also deeply involved in the Middle East peace process, and then the management of the Gulf conflict. At that time, some argued that the moment was not yet right for American involvement in a regional process.[28] They were wrong. That was the time to begin such an initiative, and the Clinton administration's failure to develop a comprehensive regional policy only compounded the mistake.

The main components of a new regional policy for South Asia might consist of:

1. A presidential declaration, preferably during a visit to South Asia, of the importance of the region to the United States in a number of dimensions: the maintenance of democratic political systems, human rights, economic growth and investment, non-proliferation, and strategic cooperation with regional states. There has not been a presidential visit to South Asia for over seventeen years and such a visit would symbolize a fresh approach to the area.

2. Co-sponsorship of a long-term regional peace plan by the United States and Japan, and probably Russia, Germany, and Great Britain. Japan is crucial, since Tokyo carries considerable moral weight in the region on nuclear matters and its investments and aid programs in the region exceed those of the United States. Smaller regional states might be invited to join, but the process should not shoulder aside such regional mechanisms as the South Asian Association for Regional Cooperation (SAARC). A difficult question is whether two would-be regional peace makers, Iran and China, should participate.

3. Led by the United States, there could be a "framing" United Nations' resolution that would place earlier UN resolutions on regional peace in a contemporary context and incorporate some of the principles of the 1972 India-Pakistan Simla agreement (which suggests bilateralism, but does not exclude a larger dialogue). These UN resolutions would be South Asia's "242."

4. As in the Middle East, a regional peace process should incorporate a number of substantive committees, dealing with various components of India-Pakistan relations. These include nuclear proliferation, the conventional arms balance, the status of Kashmir, trade, environment and ecological issues, and the free flow of people and ideas.

5. Support for "Track II" diplomacy should be maintained. There are now forty different India-Pakistan or regional dialogues, many funded by the U.S. Information Service, or by private American, German, Japanese, and European foundations.[29] These are having an impact on public and elite opinion, especially on younger scholars and strategists as well as business communities in India and Pakistan. While it is true that the political leadership in these two states might not now be capable of reaching a larger agreement, this is the time to prepare the ground for future leaders who will.

6. The process will have to be a long-haul effort to change regional strategic policies and perceptions. As in the Middle East, there will be no quick
solutions. For example, India (and Pakistan) will not, for the foreseeable
future, sign the Non-Proliferation Treaty. The peace process should look
further down the road to a time when India and Pakistan will have no
reason not to sign the Non-Proliferation Treaty, or a variation, just as
Israel will be able to de-weaponize itself if, at the end of the Middle East
process, it finds itself surrounded by reasonably friendly states.

7. A key part of a regional peace process tailored to fit South Asia would be
a package of incentives and disincentives. Some of these may require
changes in American laws (MTCR restrictions on India, and prohibition
on civilian nuclear assistance to both India and Pakistan). But Congress
has written laws which allow for such packages for Israel and supportive
Arab states and there have also been large-scale adjustments in American
policy in order to deal with North Korea. Most relevant American legislation dealing with South Asia is *preventive* and sanction-oriented, as it
punishes states for violations of American norms on proliferation, human
rights, and so forth; it provides no *incentive* for cooperation and may have
driven both Indian and Pakistani nuclear programs deeper underground.
Indeed, continued pressure on these programs, without a concomitant
indication of how the security of both states might be enhanced by yield-
ing to such pressure, is counter-productive. Incentives and disincentives
should be *proportionate* to the actions of India and Pakistan. Otherwise
they lose their credibility.

8. A Camp David setting would be appropriate at some time after the
process begins. With recalcitrant and weak political leaders such as
Benazir Bhutto and Narasimha Rao, it would be unwise to begin at the
top until there is wider bureaucratic and political support within the leadership of the two powers for a regional process. But there may come a
time, as in the Middle East, where only direct presidential intervention
will ensure that the process continues. For the moment, a special presidential emissary based in the White House is a basic requirement. Sustained attention at this level could develop a strategy coordinated with
allies and friends, and presented to Delhi and Islamabad with a suitably
attractive package of incentives—and a suitably fearsome package of
sanctions.

❦

## The Politics of the Process

Islamabad would support *any* international initiative to promote a dialogue with India for two reasons. First, Pakistanis are certain that India will reject such proposals, and there is something to be gained by appearing to be reasonable. Second, nothing will be lost on Kashmir. India, initially, is not likely to support a regional peace process and has resisted more modest proposals in the past. Indians believe that by moving closer to Washington, but avoiding dialogue with Pakistan, they can force Islamabad into declaring its nuclear status, expose Pakistan's hand in Kashmir, and may even get Pakistan labeled as a terrorist-supporting state (thus deflecting criticism from their own deteriorating human rights situation.)

These are initial positions, but in the long run they might change. India, as the most powerful state in the region, has less to lose by entering into a long-term dialogue with Pakistan and has something to gain in terms of relations with aid donors, investors, major strategic powers, and the smaller states of South Asia. Pakistan, however, cannot afford to make a mistake. It has reverted to the multi-polar diplomacy of Zulfiqar Ali Bhutto. With China, Saudi Arabia, and even Iran as friends, who needs Washington? With a bomb in the basement, who needs American weapons? With India in the throes of internal chaos, who needs Delhi?

At some point, an American-sponsored regional peace initiative will need coordination with Congress. Old laws have to be modified, and new agreements or treaties passed. But such an initiative would be helpful to a Congress that is besieged by a variety of South Asian special interests. A proposal that advanced *American* goals in a coherent fashion might just be welcomed by congressmen and senators besieged by Indian and Pakistani lobbyists, pursuing the South Asian cold war in Washington. As in the case of the Middle East peace process, a South Asian peace process would allow Congress to play a cooperative, rather than an adversarial, role with the executive branch.

## If It Works

We are heading toward a world of regions. There will be no great ideological battles in the future, although there will always be the need to contain one or another expansionist power. No South Asian state is a likely candidate for containment. This leaves the United States with the choice among policies of apathy (steered intermittently by such extra-regional concerns as non-proliferation and human rights), alliance (against some other region or power), balancing powers *within* the region, or appeasement of India. This later course might make things worse, since India's insecurity does not stem from frustrated ambitions, but from its own history and self-image. The optimum strategy would be one of *mutual cooption* between India and the United States—cooption falling somewhat short of alliance and somewhat more than cooperation. Through cooption the United States can influence India's nuclear decision, and manage a degree of military cooperations in such places as Somalia and Cambodia, and even engage in quiet discussions about the possible need to contain a more militant and aggressive China.

Some of these considerations also apply to Pakistan. Pakistan is not as important a state as India, but it is important enough—and any strategic, political, or military relationship with either state demands an accommodation of the other, since they share in the defense of the subcontinent. This inescapable fact compels an American effort to reconcile the two, if it wants to work with either. This effort can effectively be joined by Japan and other countries interested in the stability of the region (to put it in positive terms) or worried about the nuclear and military byproducts of regional instability (to put it in negative terms).

What would the United States gain? First, the prospect of greater strategic cooperation with India in and out of South Asia; second, continued cooperation with Pakistan; third, the deferral of their nuclear arms race, and possibly its termination at some future date; fourth, greater assurance that the two states will not precipitate a major crisis and might even begin to discuss the modalities of a settlement of the Kashmir conflict (which is both a cause and the consequence of their hostility); fifth, the United States will have made a significant contribution to stabilizing the environment in which a fragile Pakistani democracy is growing and a troubled Indian democracy is struggling.

South Asia is not yet in deep crisis, but it is drifting. The strategic initiative outlined might just prevent the region from sliding into a conflict that would dwarf the ethnic cleansing of Yugoslavia or that might again lead to a possible use of nuclear weapons. It would be tragic if the United States, at the peak of its influence in South Asia, failed to attempt what it has done elsewhere: an exercise in preventive diplomacy. The United States need not conduct such an exercise alone—other major powers, especially Japan, would have a role to play. Such an exercise would not be costly, either in terms of material or military resources. It would advance important American interests as well as the interests of the one-fifth of the world that lives in South Asia.

# Chapter 8

# Korean Security in a Post–Cold War Northeast Asia

*Taeho Kim*

T he Asia-Pacific region is so vital to U.S strategic and economic interests that the United States must revise its current security policy to cope with fundamental and rapid change in the area. The key question for American policy makers must be how they will deal with a shifting balance among key states in Asia and the Pacific rim, while safeguarding American stature and interests as a Pacific power. During the Cold War, U.S. policy consistently pursued global containment but a new strategic environment requires more flexibility in American policies and vision. But such a change will remain an elusive goal if the United States allows domestic political and financial constraints to combine with a Eurocentric mind-set and policy process.

The gap between America's objectives and its ambiguous policies towards the region is increasingly apparent in its strained relations with key Asian states. These difficulties include roller-coaster nuclear negotiations with North Korea, new disagreements with China, and arguments with Indonesia and several other nations in the region. Moreover, many Asian nations now believe that the recent cuts in defense budgets render the United States ill-prepared to meet major contingencies in even such a crucial area as Northeast Asia. The 1990–1992 reduction of over 30,000 U.S. troops in Asia has considerably aggravated this perception.

The United States has a considerable stake in the region's prosperity and stability. The Asia-Pacific region has registered the world's fastest economic growth for the last three decades. By 1991, the region's total GDP equalled roughly that of the United States and will reach one-third of the world's total GDP over the next decade, growth the World Bank has called the "East Asian Miracle." By 1993, U.S. trade with the Asia-Pacific region ($384 billion) was over 70 per cent greater than U.S. trade with the European Union.[1] During the first decade of the twenty-first century, trade across the Pacific could double that across the Atlantic. As Winston Lord, Assistant Secretary of State for East Asian and Pacific Affairs, noted, "today no region in the world is more important for the United States than Asia and the Pacific. Tomorrow, in the twenty-first century, no region will be as important."[2]

This chapter will examine the implications of recent security developments in Northeast Asia, a crucial sub-region of Asia-Pacific, with an emphasis on Korean security problems. It will first identify the defining characteristics of, and regional perceptions on, the shifting Northeast Asian security environment. It will then focus on Korean security issues, including the current state of inter-Korean rivalry, North Korea's conventional and nuclear capability, and the U.S. role and capability in peninsular and regional security. Finally, we shall explore the prospects and problems of establishing a multilateral cooperative security mechanism in Northeast Asia.

## The Changing Northeast Asian Security Environment

Asia is notable for its population and size as well as its political, cultural, and topographical diversity. Economically, Japan and China represent the world's second and probably third largest economies respectively. South Korea (the Republic of Korea) and Taiwan (the Republic of China) are also economic powerhouses, ranking in GDP among the world's top fifteen nations. Only North Korea (the Democratic People's Republic of Korea) remains an economic basketcase. On the other hand, Northeast Asia is probably the world's most heavily militarized area. The armed forces of the major players (China, Japan, the Koreas and Taiwan) total a staggering 5.4 million troops, while their combined defense budgets in 1994 reached nearly $76 billion.[3]

Unlike those in Europe, Asia's security arrangements have been predominantly bilateral. Multilateral security regimes are of recent origin, and there exist no significant formal arms control agreements among the Asian countries comparable to those in Europe. Moreover, post–Cold War Asia has the potential for even more dangerous confrontations than the present conflict-ridden Europe. Northeast Asia is conspicuous for the uncertain future confronting its two communist nations—China and North Korea. Both countries are in the middle of substantial leadership transitions. The persistence of nationalist ambitions and territorial disputes among virtually every Asian state promises a fast-moving, uncharted future. While the conflicts now occurring in Europe have not involved the major powers, any future conflicts in Asia might well draw in the richest and most powerful regional actors.[4] These strategic uncertainties make any analysis of the Northeast Asian security environment all the more complicated.

Asia is now more peaceful that at any other point in this century. A principal contributing factor in the region's economic success has been the relatively stable environment, in which the United States played a crucial balancing role. It is thus ironic that in the early 1990s defense expenditures have grown faster in most of East Asia than ever before.[5] More important, despite the end of Cold-War superpower rivalry and the decline of global arms markets, East Asia almost doubled its share of the total world arms imports and licensed production in the period 1984-1993, from 12.4 percent in 1984 to 21.1 percent in 1993.[6] The lack of security and confidence-building measures, let alone any formal arms control regime, adds urgency in assessing the risk of arms proliferation in Asia.

Recent developments in East Asia have far-reaching implications for regional security and stability; at least four stand out. First is the decline in U.S. military presence and role in the Asia-Pacific region. Although global detente and the snowballing U.S. budget and trade deficits put U.S. force reductions in the cards in the late 1980s, the July 1989 Nunn-Warner Amendment, requiring a comprehensive review of U.S. security commitments to Asia, began the drawdown. Confronting an unyielding Congress in April 1990, the Bush administration introduced the East Asia Strategic Initiative (EASI I, later updated in July 1992 as EASI II)[7]. This initiative set a specific timetable for the phased withdrawal of U.S. troops, including those in South Korea, from Asia and called for Asian allies to assume a greater burden sharing in defense. The reduction called for withdrawal of over 30,000 U.S. troops from Asia in 1990-1992, including 7,000 from South Korea, 5,000 from Japan, and all from the Philippines.

To cope with regional concerns and buttress U.S. national interests, the Clinton administration has recently announced a reassessment of troop reduction plans. In contrast to the two previous East Asia Initiative reports, the February 1995 Department of Defense (DOD) report, entitled *United States Security Strategy for the East Asia-Pacific Region*, "reaffirms our [U.S.] commitment to maintain a stable forward presence in the region, at the existing level of about 100,000 troops, for the foreseeable future."[8]

The reduction of American forces in Asia could result in substantial changes in the security climate there. The U.S. presence has not only prevented the rise of a regional hegemon, but has also retarded development of independent, regional military powers. Regional perceptions regarding a continued U.S. commitment will remain the most critical factor in determining how individual Asian states calculate their security requirements as well as the overall balance of power.

The second strategic development in Asia has been the resurgence of military ties between China and Russia. Since Gorbachev's visit to Beijing in May 1989, Beijing and Moscow have increased the pace, scope and level of military cooperation—a cooperation which now includes the sale of advanced aircraft and submarines, the transfer of technology and scientific personnel, and close defense-industrial ties.[9] The current level of military cooperation between China and Russia could well develop into an even closer relationship, a fact underlined by the flurry of mutual high-ranking visits, their close military-industrial collaboration, and Russia's willingness to sell China "the most sophisticated weapons and armaments."[10]

The expansion of Sino-Russian military cooperation, especially the sale of advanced weapons systems and technologies, has far-reaching implications for the balance of power. Not only has the Chinese People's Liberation Army (PLA) capitalized on Russia's financial pinch to acquire top-of-the-line weapons and spare parts, but it also has tried to improve its technological position substantially through offset and coproduction arrangements for advanced Russian weapons systems. It is reasonable to expect that China will acquire more weapons and weapons' technologies from Russia over the coming years. Barring an unforeseen disruption in relations, Russia's financial crises and China's ability to finance requirements for defense modernization from its rapidly expanding economy will shape the future course of their military transactions.

The third major security trend has been the relative rise in the influence of China and Japan in post–Cold War regional affairs. Japan is the world's largest creditor nation and has the world's second largest economy after the United States. Not only is Japan the largest donor of official development aid in East Asia and in the world, but it also maintains the world's second largest defense expenditure with $48 billion in fiscal year 1995 devoted to defense.[11] From this perspective, Japan is already a *potential* major military power of great significance in any regional strategic equation.

During the Cold War, deterrence of the Soviet Union furnished the raison d'être for the U.S.-Japanese alliance. Now the alliance no longer has a particular enemy state on which to focus, unlike the U.S.-Korean alliance against North Korea. The increasingly discordant trade relations between the U.S. and Japan and Japan's role in the Gulf War may also prompt Japanese leaders to redefine their security relationship with the United States and their regional and international security role. In addition, major changes in Japan's approach to its security may be on the way. Even though Japan failed to send troops to the Gulf War and only deployed minesweepers after the fight, the Diet passed a Japanese peace-keeping operations bill in June 1992. That move allowed the dispatch of 700 Japanese soldiers to support UN peace keeping in Cambodia three months later. Thus Japanese ground troops went overseas for the first time since 1945. Moreover, the Japanese have undertaken a series of moves to occupy a permanent seat on the UN Security Council, partly in response to U.S. and UN calls for a greater Japanese "contribution" for regional defense and UN peace-keeping operations. The electoral debacle of the Liberal Democratic Party (LDP) in July 1993, however, suggests just how unstable the Japanese polity might become. Caused primarily by financial scandals and the failure of electoral reforms, the collapse of the LDP's 38-year dominance casts a long shadow over the future of U.S.-Japanese security relations.

Compared with China, Japan has primarily adopted a defensive military posture. Not only does it lack offensive capabilities such as strategic missiles, long-range bombers, and significant amphibious capabilities, but it is still heavily dependent upon the United States for its own defense. Moreover, Japan's non-nuclear and no-arms-export policies reinforce its defensive military posture. The immediate concern of its neighbors will remain Japan's economic expansion, based on its vastly superior managerial, technological, and financial prowess. Thus, Japan remains predominantly an economic power but one with vast military potential.

In contrast, China has become an independent military power with growing economic capability. China is the only Asian nation with strategic nuclear forces, and it finances the world's largest military of three million soldiers and thus maintains a position that might precipitate major changes in Asia's strategic environment. Even if China poses no direct security threat to the United States or Russia, it still wields enormous influence on nearly every country in Asia. Moreover, a series of recent external and domestic developments, including the U.S. drawdown, a dissipation of the Soviet threat, China's own growing influence in the region, and its high economic growth, have presented an unprecedented opportunity to modernize Chinese forces extensively, an option not available since the founding of the People's Republic of China in 1949. At a minimum, the substantial reduction of forces along the 4,300 kilometer Sino-Russia border has allowed China to divert the surplus manpower elsewhere, while freeing up resources to modernize obsolescent military equipment.

China also carries the historical baggage of territorial claims against most of its neighbors.[12] China, Taiwan and Vietnam all claim the Paracel Island group. All these states, as well as Malaysia, the Philippines, and Brunei, claim the Spratlys. In Northeast Asia, China has involved itself in territorial disputes with Taiwan and Japan over the Diaoyudao (Diaoyutai)/Senkaku Islands, and with South Korea over the dividing line of the continental shelf in the Yellow Sea. In the light of its past record of limited offensive military actions against its neighbors, China's ongoing military buildup has become a source of increasing concern for most Asian policy makers. Just as disturbing to the status quo is China's reemergence as North Korea's closest ally. The Chinese have already provided weapons, military technology, and direct assistance to other Asian nations, such as Pakistan, Thailand, and Burma (Myanmar). Despite its repeated public denials to the contrary, China appears to be a major contributor to the proliferation of military technologies and weapons to a host of Third World countries in the Middle East, East Asia, and Africa, including potential nuclear and missile capabilities.[13]

China's search for great-power status, its double-digit official defense budget increases, its territorial claims, Japan's future "unilateralism", naval modernization, political uncertainty, and economic power fuel the age-old Asian debate over whether China, or Japan, or both, will eventually pose a threat to Asian stability. The door to Japan's rearmament hinges upon two major factors: the future of U.S.-Japanese security relations—the present "linchpin" of Asian stability—and the depth of Japanese consensus for a pacifist domestic and foreign policy. For the immediate future, Japan's most pressing security policy issue is the need to meet the U.S. demands for increased Japanese political and military participation in the region without raising the specter of a remilitarized Japan in the minds of Asian leaders and people.

On the other hand, judging from China's willingness to use force outside its borders and the extent of its involvement in Asia's major sources of tension, from territorial disputes to arms buildup and from the Korean peninsula to the South China Seas, China could well represent a long-term rival for the United States and a potential threat to Asian stability. The prospects for such developments remain clouded at the present by China's political uncertainty, its lack of military "transparency", and frosty relations with the United States.

An equally important question is whether a prosperous but economically independent China would have a stabilizing effect on Asian security. Simply put, students of economic liberalism tend to believe that prosperity and interdependence will be conducive to the development of social and political liberalization in China. The proposition appears untenable for three major reasons. Economic interdependence could heighten rather than defuse political tensions; Western countries may well not be able to capitalize on the deterrent value of interdependence, and a weaker China is vulnerable to interdependence whereas a stronger China will not be.[14] In contrast to the liberal-capitalist argument, a realist would argue that China's growth from a weak and poor state to a powerful and rich one is likely to produce an assertive, chauvinistic foreign policy. Realists have long argued that the transition during which a major power with high growth rates catches up to a declining dominant power represents a highly dangerous period and could result in "hegemonic war."[15]

The fourth—but not the least important—strategic development in the region is the increase in sophisticated military capabilities of mid-level nations which has caused a new round of regional arms buildup. Despite relaxation of superpower rivalry, nearly every Asian state is spending more on national defence, and most have launched force-improvement measures, especially in naval and air capabilities.[16] One should also see North Korea's nuclear weapons program as part of security enhancement efforts in the midst of declining outside support and recent economic difficulties.

With the notable exception of North Korea's nuclear program, the interplay of economic vitality and insecurity has driven the current trend of a regional arms buildup throughout Asia. This sense of insecurity is not necessarily a result of any immediate fears, but rather of strategic uncertainty regarding the future American role and presence and the growing influence of China and Japan in regional economic affairs. Current economic vitality and growing democratization notwithstanding, Asia's potential sources of tension are extensive and complicated. For the foreseeable future, Asian nations will have to cope with a shifting security environment in which a "reluctant America," an "impotent Russia," an "uncertain Japan," and a "resurgent China" coexist. It is in this uncertain context that one must assess the security of the Korean peninsula.

## The Korean Peninsula: The Cold War's Last Front

The crux of the Korean security problem remains remarkably unchanged: a land-based military threat from North Korea. Situated at a geostrategic and economic crossroads, the Korean peninsula continues to represent a major flashpoint plagued with tensions and uncertainties. In particular, North Korea's nuclear mania and Kim Il Sung's death have further clouded the future of the peninsula. Except for a brief thaw in the early 1970s, inter-Korean relations during the Cold War evoked unbridled hostility and antagonism. North Korea is a closed and militarized society with a standing army of one million men out of a total population of 22 million. Since its founding in 1948, it has followed an inward-directed, autarkic economy with an emphasis on heavy industry. As evidenced by the collapsed Soviet empire, Stalinist controls of the economy are too inefficient to provide a diversified and flexible economic structure.

On the other hand, South Korea's population tops 44 million people, while its armed forces number 655,000 active-duty personnel. Since the early 1960s, it has adopted an export-oriented economy with resounding success, and during the past two decades, its economy has achieved the world's fastest growth—its average annual GDP growth from 1980-1991 was 9.4 per cent. According to Bank of Korea estimates, the South Korean economy was eighteen times larger than that of North Korea in 1994 with the gap continuing to widen.

During the Cold War, North Korea held a prominent geostrategic and ideological position for both China and the Soviet Union in their competition against each other and their confrontation with the United States and its allies. Kim Il Sung could skillfully play off Beijing and Moscow to extract military, economic, and political support. In the early 1990s, however, developments on the peninsula and in the external world adversely affected North Korea. The disintegration of the Soviet Union and South Korea's normalization of relations with Russia (beginning in September 1990) and China (August 1992) have further isolated Pyongyang, while also resulting in the drastic reduction of outside military and economic assistance. Domestically, the North Korean economy has shrunk by an average of 4.5 percent per year since 1990.[17] Food shortages remain pervasive and severe, especially in rural areas. Lack of electrical power has already dropped the industrial utilization rate below 40 percent of capacity. For North Korea, the solution to such problems demands greater internal autonomy for technocrats, factory managers, and workers and a willingness to tap technology and capital from the outside world. But in 1948 Kim Il Sung, the "Great Leader," closed all doors to the outside world to maintain his absolute control over North Korean society. The doors have remained largely closed since his death.

Despite South Korea's present confidence on the economic, diplomatic, and ideological fronts, the military prospects, should a conflict between north and south occur, are less sanguine. Even without a nuclear capability, North Korea's conventional military capabilities as well as the size, deployment, and equipment of its army pose a significant threat to South Korea. Not only is the North Korean Army numerically superior and highly mechanized, but the North Koreans have concentrated 65 percent of their offensive elements within sixty miles of the demilitarized zone. Since Seoul, the South Korean capital with its population of 12 million people, is just thirty miles south of the Demilitarized Zone, South Korean forces possess little strategic depth. While the South Koreans, backed by U.S. forces and their own industrial infrastructure, have captured a substantial technological edge, North Korea's quantitative and geographical advantages could well cause unacceptable damage to the South, especially upon Seoul, in case of war.

Moreover, North Korea's nuclear weapons program represents a major military threat. Even though Pyongyang signed the December 1991 Joint Declaration of the Denuclearization of the Korean Peninsula, the January 1992 International Atomic Energy Agency Safeguards Agreement, and the October 1994 Agreed Framework between North Korea and the United States, its nuclear program remains a serious concern for both peninsular and regional security. It is difficult to calculate why North Korea clings so tenaciously to its nuclear weapons, given the secrecy of North Korean society. But its aims probably include the utility of nuclear weapons as a "strategic equalizer," as a bargaining chip, as an effective deterrent, and as a political instrument against a hostile world.[18]

For the past three years North Korea has indeed behaved like a state hiding a nuclear program. It has neither completely withdrawn from nor returned to the Non-Proliferation Treaty. Moreover, the North Koreans have adroitly tied the survival of their regime to regional stability (i.e. sink or swim together) and the future of the nuclear nonproliferation regime, Seen from this perspective, Pyongyang may well use the nuclear gambit as its last and only instrument for the survival of the regime.

In signing the October 1994 Agreed Framework,[19] North Korea agreed to freeze and later eliminate its nuclear program in return for two 1,000-mw water reactors—to be supplied by a U.S.-led international consortium. Additionally, the U.S. agreed to deliver an annual supply of 500,000 tons of heavy oil, to lower barriers to trade and investment to North Korea, and to take steps towards the exchange of liaison officers. In short, by agreeing to fulfill its previous obligations to the International Atomic Energy Agency, the North Koreans achieved a comprehensive deal consisting of energy support, economic benefits, and diplomatic contacts. As one commentator has observed, North Korea achieved "a remarkable demonstration of the power of the weak and a telling example of the new realities in the...post–Cold War world."[20]

The North Koreans have recently accelerated development of missile systems and appear to have stockpiled chemical and other weapons of mass destruction. In May 1993, they successfully test-fired an improved version of the Scud-C (Rodong-1) missile with a range of over 500 miles over the East Sea (Sea of Japan) and, again in June 1994, two sixty-mile range anti-ship missiles.[21] They are also in the process of developing Teapo Dong-1 and Taepo Dong-2 IRBMs. In addition, North Korea, which is not a signatory to the Chemical Weapons Convention, operates six factories producing various chemical agents and has set up chemical warfare platoons even at the regiment level.[22] Taken together, its actual and perceived nuclear and missile capability, coupled with its forward-deployed offensive forces near the Demilitarized Zone remain the most worrying to South Koreans and U.S. defense planners. The sudden death of Kim Il Sung on July 8 1994 and the ensuing political uncertainty in North Korea have further complicated the future of the peninsula.[23] While Kim Jong Il became the supreme commander of the North Korean Army in December 1991, he has yet to assume two important positions left vacant by his father's death, the presidency and the general secretaryship of the party. The tyranny of Kim Il Sung was so thorough and lengthy that the longer it takes to fill the power vacuum, the riskier Kim Jong Il's political future will be. An array of domestic and international factors, including his governing skills, international recognition of his leadership, and the state of the North Korean economy will determine his position. For the moment, the leitmotif of continuing Kim Il Sung's "revolutionary tradition" represents the most valuable source of Kim Jong Il's power and legitimacy. But it is questionable how long the revolutionary tradition can persist amidst a deteriorating economic situation and mounting international pressure to halt the nuclear program.

In the years ahead, South Korean and international attention will remain focused on North Korea's nuclear program. But South Korea will soon have to confront the dual tasks of maintaining a credible deterrence against a North Korean surprise attack, while charting out the role of unified Korean armed forces in peninsular and regional security in the future. Preparing for the contingencies that might arise out of North Korea's current dilemma are not just security concerns for the present South Korean government. They will also constitute the most pressing challenge for eventual reunification. Just how and when North Korea terminates (e.g., implosion, explosion or peaceful integration) is an issue of first order for the future status of a unified Korea.

As long as the present tensions persist, as a result of North Korea's military posture, the combined South Korean-American defense against the land-based threat must represent the backbone of diplomatic and economic policies towards North Korea. Over the longer term, however, South Korea needs to consider the security issues that might confront a future unified Korea, including the size, deployment, and role of the armed forces. Such thinking will not only represent a critical confidence-building measure necessary to calm the potential misgivings of neighboring states on the ramifications of a unified Korea, but will greatly reduce the costs of unification and the risk of social dislocation thereafter. Korea cannot afford an unprepared and precipitous German-style reunification. Of particular importance is the linkage between North Korea's nuclear weapons program and the nuclear stance of a unified Korea. At present, South Korea envisions a *nuclear-free* unified country and has repeatedly made that position clear. On the other hand, several noted international security scholars have speculated on the possibility of South Korea inheriting North Korea's nuclear weapons program.[24] Their speculations err, however, on at least two major grounds: 1) South Korea's possession of nuclear weapons, now or when unified, would immediately jeopardize a Korean-American alliance; and 2) nuclear weapons would not enhance stability on the peninsula, particularly given the vast difference in potential between the peninsula and the surrounding major powers. On the contrary, nuclear weapons would be more likely to invite instability.

Finally, South Korea's security challenges require a continued American commitment and capability to deter and, if deterrence fails, to fight the aggressor effectively in terms of lives, cost, and rapid war termination. Ideally, for the South Koreans, the U.S. must be able to allocate an adequate force for contingencies in the peninsula according to their respective levels of priority. However, political, financial and conceptual confusion among American policy makers has recently raised questions over this simple reality.

## The American Role in Peninsular Security

Reflecting Northeast Asia's high priority in American strategic planning, the United States has traditionally deployed considerable forces in Japan and South Korea along with elaborate base and defense arrangements. In Southeast Asia and South Asia, the U.S. presence thins out to such places as Guam, Diego Garcia, and Singapore with an emphasis on access and joint-exercise agreements.

Global change has also hit the U.S. military hard. The most visible and immediate result has been a sharp reduction in the U.S. force structure. The Bush administration's "Base Force" strategy represented the first in a series of force reduction plans,[25] replacing a commitment to fixed bases with an emphasis on increasing access to friendly, but not necessarily allied, installations. By 1994 the strategy had reduced forward presence in the Asia-Pacific region to about 100,000 personnel and that in Europe to 166,000. While the size of the former drawdown was not as dramatic in numerical terms as the latter, the maritime nature of the Pacific theater guarantees that the U.S. forward deployment is more thinly spread and will have to rely more on air and sea-lift capacity over long distances, as well as on local support in the case of regional contingencies.

President Clinton's administration cut U.S. force levels further, a reflection of Clinton's promise to revitalize the American economy. In addition, the Clinton presidency has brought to the fore such diverse foreign and domestic policy objectives as welfare, democracy, human rights, issues previously subordinated to security considerations during the Cold War. Shifting resources from defense to domestic programs seemed not only necessary but also inevitable.

Departing from the previous administration's defense posture, Clinton's first Secretary of Defense, Les Aspin, broached in June 1993 a new military doctrine called "Win-Hold-Win."[26] This doctrine called for the U.S. to maintain a force level large enough to win one regional conflict while "holding" the other until the forces from the first regional theater became available. The new strategy immediately drew critical attention from Korean and Japanese officials, who correctly discerned that the approach would result in the delay of U.S. reinforcements in case of a conflict on the Korean peninsula, should the United States have also become embroiled in the Middle East. Strong criticism, even from within his own administration, eventually forced Clinton to drop the "Win-Hold-Win" strategy and reaffirm U.S. commitment and military presence during a widely publicized trip to Tokyo and Seoul in July 1993. As a result, the abortive "Win-Hold-Win" strategy gave way to the "Win-Win" strategy of fighting two major regional contingencies "nearly simultaneously," a bold statement of intent, if short on strategic realism.

The September 1993 Bottom-Up Review summarized the requirements of the latter strategy. The review envisioned a force structure consisting by 1999 of fifteen active and reserve army divisions, twenty air force wings with 184 bombers, 346 navy ships with twelve aircraft carriers (including one in reserve), and an active duty marine corps of 174,000.[27] It enshrined the prevailing strategic trend of projecting army units from bases within the continental United States, relying on offshore naval and air-strike capability, and emphasizing "places, not bases" for the forward deployment of U.S. troops in Asia and the Pacific. Thus, Allied countries, in addition to greater defense burden sharing, will have to bear a greater burden during the initial phases of a major conflict. Renewed American assurances notwithstanding, the question of how the U.S. will finance such force requirements amid ongoing defense budget cuts remains unanswered.[28]

Even at current funding levels, the U.S. military would be hard pressed to meet its missions.[29] Two or three of the army's fifteen or sixteen divisions will remain committed to NATO and peace-keeping operations. A maximum of thirteen or fourteen army divisions will then be available for major regional contingencies. As few as four divisions could be available in the initial phases of a conflict in Korea. This figure is, however, a far cry from the estimates of General Gary Luck, commander of the Combined Forces Command in Korea, who believes that he will need as many as 400,000 reinforcements in addition to the 26,000 soldiers already in place.[30]

Air force projected levels of twenty wings and 184 heavy bombers also fall short of mission requirements for two major regional conflicts. With two or three wings committed to NATO and peace-keeping operations and three or four more needed for home defense and training, only thirteen to fifteen tactical fighter wings could be available for contingencies. By comparison, the equivalent to ten fighter wings deployed to the Gulf during the war against Saddam Hussein. As former chief of staff Merrill McPeak has noted: "I have a tough time thinking we could fight two Koreas or two Vietnams in the middle of this decade."[31] Similarly, the air force plans to reduce its heavy bomber force to only 107 aircraft, while an increased airlift capability depends entirely on the troubled C-17 project.[32]

The navy's future capabilities are no more reassuring. The Bottom-Up Review's active carrier force of eleven will have to cover the Mediterranean, the Persian Gulf, and the Western Pacific. With one carrier committed to NATO, the remaining ten would cover regional contingencies. Given the navy's practice of maintaining three carrier battle groups for each one fully operational in a distant theater, the navy will have only three and sometimes only two carriers available early in a crisis. The distances to the theaters, the lengthened overseas assignment of naval personnel, and the lack of overhaul facilities suggest such "carrier presence gaps" would soon become a reality. That poses awkward questions of security for Korea where the type of warfare most likely to occur would require an offshore strike capability, which depends on carrier forces.

The above analysis of the Bottom-Up Review's projected force levels in 1999 suggests that overall U.S. military readiness will be far lower in the future than now, *and* that the ability of the U.S. military to respond to a crisis in Korea might well be jeopardized. Any U.S. military commander, called upon to fight a Korean War, would know full well that North Korea's armed forces—their size, equipment, and morale—are considerably stronger than the Iraqi Republican Guard and that a swift, resounding victory like that achieved in Desert Storm would be virtually impossible.

If Korea, one of two overseas areas with the highest priority in U.S. strategic planning, remains unsure of U.S. capabilities, the rest of Asia has good reason to feel vulnerable to shifts in the regional balance of power. Aware of the looming U.S. strategic decline, both the United States and Asian nations have begun to explore the possibility of establishing regional mechanisms to supplement American security commitments.

## A Multilateral Security Mechanism in Northeast Asia?

In the last few years the number and diversity of proposals for multilateral dialogue or mechanisms in Asia has grown remarkably.[33] Until now, however, progress has been confined to the economic, not the security, front. Multilateral economic regimes such as the Asia-Pacific Economic Cooperation and the Pacific Economic Cooperation Council have been thriving, but there have been few corresponding achievements in the security arena. The reason for the success in regional economic cooperation has been straightforward: all the states in the region want to improve their economic profile through beneficial trade arrangements.

Understandably, the United States has supported multilateral arrangements in Asia. The successful convention of the first Asia-Pacific Economic Cooperation meeting in Seattle in November 1993 also shored up the stature of the United States as a leading economic power in the Pacific, even if its share in the Asian market has declined steadily in relative terms. On the other hand, from the beginning its Asian allies and friends have been suspicious of American sponsorship of multilateral security dialogues in the region. To begin with, during the Cold War the United States long opposed any Asian multilateral security regimes which might have eroded the coherence and effectiveness of America's bilateral alliances throughout Asia. For example, the U.S. flatly rejected Soviet naval arms control proposals, because if instituted, they would have penalized the United States, an interoceanic power, more than the Soviet Union, a continental power. Secondly, the context and timing in which multilateral ideas appeared raised doubts. Even though U.S. force reductions began during his administration, Bush and ranking officials in his administration largely remained convinced of the enduring value of bilateral security alliances. They clearly believed that a multilateral security approach would be more useful in addressing particular problems such as the Cambodian peace settlement and the resolution of the North Korean nuclear problem. In contrast, Clinton's open support of Asian security multilateralism coincided with his desire to cut the defense budget. He thus raised the suspicion in Asia that the U.S. had designed the multilateral approach to compensate for the reduction in U.S. presence.

Not surprisingly, South Korea and Japan foresaw the new administration's approach as setting the context for further reductions of U.S. forces in Asia. After all, multilateral security is reminiscent of America's NATO policy. Despite its repeated appreciation that "Asia is not Europe," the Clinton administration has pursued a policy towards Asia of limited applicability, European orientation, and "indiscriminate internationalism."

As noted earlier, Asia's political and geographical diversity is such that its subregions confront generally different security problems. Land-based inter-Korean confrontation, for example, requires an approach quite different from disputes in the South China Sea, which are maritime and multilateral in nature. This also partially explains why far more programs in multilateral security dialogue have occurred in Southeast Asia than in Northeast Asia. In Northeast Asia there have been no significant multilateral dialogues, let alone institutions, comparable to the limited progress in Southeast Asia. Such notable efforts in the early 1990s as Australia's Conference on Security and Cooperation in Asia and Canada's North Pacific Cooperative Security Dialogue died for a variety of reasons, including the putative Soviet advantage, regional state indifference, and lack of concrete proposals. Even if Russia's retreat from regional hegemony has brought considerable change in the trends and characteristics of the post–Cold War climate, the difficulties in Northeast Asia's security agenda still persist and indeed predate the end of the Cold War.

The single most important reason is that the major regional security problems remain predominantly bilateral: North and South Korea; China and Taiwan; China and Russia; and Russia and Japan. Underlying these bilateral security issues are persistent territorial and border problems. Most claimants, especially those in a stronger position, are wary of outside involvement in disputes. Moreover, the disputants largely agree that the two principals should discuss and negotiate their bilateral security problems first before broadening the scope on negotiations into multilateral participation.

Second, compared with relations among Southeast Asian nations, the contacts and conflicts among Northeast Asian nations have been far more hostile. In particular, Northeast Asia as a region possesses a far higher state of militarization than other areas of Asia, in part a result of the intensity of historical hostilities and lingering disputes over sovereignty. The Korean peninsula, the Taiwan Straits, and the "Northern Islands" lying between Japan and Russia are prime examples.

Third, China and North Korea have long opposed multilateral approaches to international security. China has traditionally resisted joining international security arrangements. With the exception of the UN Security Council, in which it maintains the prerogatives of a permanent member, China has guarded a deep-seated suspicion over security arrangements with a multilateral tint and has rarely participated in multilateral security talks.[34] It has preferred limited, bilateral negotiations, such as the Sino-Russian border troop reduction talks. In particular, bilateral negotiations with smaller states provide China with a significant advantage and allow Beijing to define what

and how to discuss with whom. North Korea also follows the Chinese practice of "divide and rule" in its relations with South Korea and the United
States. In this context, North Korea has long attempted to convert the multi-
dimensional nuclear issue into an American-North Korean bilateral agenda,
one that eventually resulted in the October 1994 agreement. This Chinese
and North Korean opposition to multilateral agreements means that no such
schemes can cover the two most likely sources of conflict in Northeast Asia—
the Korean Peninsula and the Taiwan Straits. Moreover, Chinese and North
Korean secrecy over their own defense data creates a major barrier to multilateral cooperation.

Fourth and finally, the remaining defense relationships among key
regional states are bilateral. They include formal U.S. alliances with Japan
and South Korea, U.S. unofficial, but friendly, ties with Taiwan, and China's
formal security relationship with North Korea. While such ties remain a
legacy of the Cold War, any alterations in the existing network of bilateral
security alliances will result in considerable instabilities. Therefore, Northeast Asian countries often see proposals for dialogues on multilateral security
as encroaching upon existing bilateral security arrangements or as being
insensitive to the root cause of the security problems in the region.

Thus, in stark contrast to the viability of the multilateral economic connections throughout the region, there have been no comparable achievements in multilateral security efforts. In Southeast Asia limited progress has
occurred in multilateral security dialogues, but their long-term success
requires a viable security agenda, China's cooperative behavior, and a more
inclusive membership. Failures in a multilateral approach to Northeast Asian
security, on the other hand, largely stem from the bilateral nature of conflicts,
a high level of hostility and militarization, Chinese and North Korean opposition, and the lingering impact of bilateral security arrangements. America's
ill-timed and ill-conceived support for Asian security multilateralism has thus
inspired little confidence among its Northeast Asian allies who have felt that,
in tandem with its reduced presence, the United States is pursuing new policies, insensitive and even irrelevant to their pressing security problems in the
region.

## Future Prospects and Policy Recommendations

In considering a long historical epoch, strategic disturbances in contemporary Asia may well only demarcate one era from another. As both the
United States and the Asian-Pacific countries search for new organizing principles, their relative power and positions are bound to change. What has

remained remarkably consistent throughout history, however, has been the dire but unforeseen consequences of major changes in the status quo—as in the case of Imperial Japan's appearance on the world stage or the Chinese Revolution.

Fortunately the strategic shifts now occurring on both sides of the Pacific are not yet of such vast proportions. But statesmen must address the underlying causes of existing problems immediately and resolutely or they risk frightening consequences in the future. The following issues should be of immediate interest to policy makers:

a. *Balanced and Region-Specific Strategies*. Of paramount importance is a recognition of the generic difference in the security problems of the Asia-Pacific region, of Europe, and among the subregions of Asia itself. The land-based threats on the Korean peninsula require different solutions from the maritime disputes in the South China Sea.

b. *Credible Military Requirements and Presence*. Military power is seldom a goal, but rather a means to an end. It is equally true, however, that military power directly influences the achievement of political goals. The Bottom-Up Review's reductions have lowered morale, readiness, and confidence and may in the long-run affect the interests of the United States. Credible military capabilities represent the backbone of American foreign policy and its relations with its allies.

c. *The Korean Peninsula*. Early breakthroughs in inter-Korean relations are unlikely. Thus, U.S. and South Korean defense planners must fully prepare their forces to meet North Korea's conventional military capabilities and an uncertain future. In the meantime, the United States must pursue a resolution of the nuclear issue in accordance with the Agreed Framework negotiated in 1994. China's role during the North Korean nuclear odyssey is dubious and, at most, limited. In fact, not only has China consistently supported North Korea's negotiating position, but it is a direct beneficiary of the North Korean nuclear problem.

## Conclusion

Northeast Asia's high level of militarization and the problem of divided nations—China and Korea—are legacies of the Cold War but they are still capable of precipitating major conflicts in post–Cold War Northeast Asia. Confidence-building measures and arms-control measures are highly desirable but multilateral agreements, at least given the current state of relations in the region, could well produce effects opposite from that intended—more suspicion and greater arms buildups. The United States needs to strengthen the existing network of bilateral security ties with credible military force. With the exception of North Korea, all the other Northeast Asian states, including China, support or understand the continuing importance of America's pre-eminent role in the region.

The future of Northeast Asian stability and security will be increasingly dependent on China and Japan and America's relations with both countries. A continued U.S.-Japan security relationship is vital to American interests and to Asian security. But how long the current security ties will remain acceptable to their respective publics remains uncertain. While popular anti-militarism is now strong in Japan, historic Japanese extremism in foreign and security issues since the mid-nineteenth century does not reassure.[35] To address these policy problems, active U.S. engagement in Asian security and greater defense burden sharing by its allies are necessary, but not sufficient. Both American and Asian governments need to expand the scope of dialogue and communication with each other's public and legislatures to strengthen the mutual bonds. Careful handling of political and economic issues and firmer security ties must guide the maturing U.S.-Asian relationship into the twenty-first century.

# Chapter 9

# Security Issues in Southeast Asia

*Jeffrey Grey*

For several decades during the Cold War Southeast Asia formed a vicarious battleground between East and West, exemplified by the United States' drawn-out and ultimately unsuccessful commitment in Vietnam. In the post-Cold War era, security issues in Asia and the Pacific have become more complex and intractable. Southeast Asian governments now operate in a volatile environment in which strategic concerns of emerging regional powers have replaced the familiar strategic considerations of superpower competition. China's future role in Southeast Asia, the consequences of America's withdrawal from the region, and the evolving relationships among the Association of Southeast Asian Nations (ASEAN—whose members are Indonesia, Malaysia, the Philippines, Singapore, Thailand, and Brunei) are critical questions in the analysis of the current and future security policies within, and toward, Southeast Asia.

## The Strategic Context

National and regional security issues have always represented the raison d'être for ASEAN, although the organization handles important economic, diplomatic, and cultural functions as well.[1] The Bangkok Declaration of 1967 prompted ASEAN's foundation and the regional political problems at that time have shaped the organization's approach to national and regional security. On one hand, member states saw economic and social development as a key element in reducing the appeal of communist revolutionary movements. Thus, they conceived of national security in broad social, rather than narrow military, terms. This approach remains a central element in ASEAN security thinking. Internally, the member states emphasized a commonality of purpose as a mechanism to overcome a history of territorial and ideological disputes among them—for example, Indonesia's "Confrontation" with Malaysia between 1962–1966—and to deal with the Communist states in Indochina. The admission of Vietnam to membership in ASEAN in August 1995 marks the culmination of a long process whose genesis extends back more than twenty years.

ASEAN's final security function related to the presence of powers external to the region, principally the United States and United Kingdom. Although most members regarded the presence of these powers as temporary, ASEAN's position was complicated by the fact that the British and American forces had proved important instruments of stability in, for example, the defense of Malaysia against internal subversion and external threats or in a deterrent capacity in Thailand during the Laotian crisis. For a long time, agreement on how to deal with foreign military presence eluded member governments. As a result, the Declaration of Southeast Asia as a proposed Zone of Peace, Freedom, and Neutrality, signed in Kuala Lumpur in November 1971, resolved little. Moreover, these difficulties were exacerbated by formal treaty ties which existed among many Southeast Asian states and their external power protectors; a long-standing relationship between the United States and the Philippines, the South East Asia Treaty Organization (SEATO), the Anglo-Malay Defense Agreement (AMDA), and the Five Power Defense Arrangements (FPDA). Only Indonesia has remained free of formal ties of this sort.

Until the 1980s, the force structures and doctrinal assumptions of ASEAN's armed forces reflected the period of anticolonial struggle and counterinsurgency which most members had undergone between the late 1940s and the mid-1960s. For the Malaysians, this experience was the "emergency" between 1948-1960 and the *Confrontasi* with Indonesia from 1962-1966; for Indonesia, the secessionist struggles in Aceh and the South Moluccas and the fight against the Darul Islam in West Java; for the Philippines, the suppression of the Hukbalahap; in Thailand, apprehension over the intentions of the Communist Party in Thailand with its close ties to the Chinese, as well as the instabilities which threatened to spill over from the Vietnam war; and for Brunei, the short-lived rebellion of December 1962.

In practical terms this meant a number of things. As most of the conflicts in which ASEAN armed forces engaged were insurgencies or counterinsurgencies, they have, for the most part, developed no clearly formed doctrines for waging conventional war.[2] On the rare occasions when ASEAN armed forces have confronted a conventional military opponent—as the Indonesians did with the Dutch over the future of West New Guinea in 1961–1962—their inability to operate at such a level was soon made abundantly clear by the military results.[3] Only Singapore, with its markedly different strategic circumstances and concerns about certain of its immediate neighbors, has structured its armed forces on the basis of a conventional emphasis.

This emphasis on counterinsurgency transformed the army in ASEAN states into usually the largest and most influential of the three services. The air force has customarily occupied second place, while the navy, with no more than brown-water capabilities, has ranked third. In some ASEAN states, such as Indonesia, the police have formed a fourth, paramilitary arm of the security forces, just as they did in Malaya, combatting insurgents during the emergency in the 1950s. But the broader sense in which ASEAN states have defined security means that their armed forces have often had nonmilitary functions within society that are almost as important as overt military roles. Again, Indonesia provides the best example with the doctrine of *dwifungsi*, or dual function, but all ASEAN states subscribe to general notions of comprehensive security that go well beyond formal notions of military power. The Malaysian prime minister, Dr. Mahathir, has expressed this clearly; "Security is not just a matter of military capability. National security is inseparable from political stability, economic success, and social harmony."[4]

In general, ASEAN governments do not issue public reviews of their defense policy or capabilities (although this is changing). For the most part, these countries are not open societies in the Western sense. Public statements made on defense issues are usually general, a point which one needs to bear in mind when assessing security concerns in the region. In many cases, the military exercises the predominant role in formulation of defense policy, with the concomitant result that the governments release little detailed information on security policy or on the process of debate and policy formulation within the bureaucracy.

Security postures within the ASEAN countries began changing in the 1970s as a consequence of the communist victory in Indochina. The U.S. presence in Indochina, together with British, New Zealand, and Australian troop commitments in Malaysia and Singapore, had permitted the ASEAN states to concentrate on internal affairs. The withdrawal of U.S. forces from Vietnam (though not, at that stage, from Southeast Asia), the departure of the British from "east of Suez," and the heightened Soviet presence concomitant upon communist victory in Vietnam in 1975 had the potential to alter substantially this situation. The Bali Summit of February 1976 reflected this changing period. Hostilities among China, Vietnam, and Kampuchea underlined concerns about the internal situation still further. Change was not dramatic, at least immediately. The continuing presence of the U.S. Seventh Fleet in the Philippines balanced the Soviet presence at Cam Ranh Bay, while changes in Chinese policy in the post-Mao era led to the defeat of the remaining communist insurgencies, notably that waged by the Malaysian Communist Party from its cross-border bases in southern Thailand. The debate from the mid-1970s to the mid-1980s took place in a period of sustained economic growth in the ASEAN region, which permitted a buildup in the conventional armed forces throughout the area. The major beneficiaries of conventional weapons acquisition programs were the armies and air forces, rather than the navies—an indication that ground forces and their support continued to dominate defense decision making as well as the fact that regional maritime threats had not yet developed, the Soviet naval presence in Indochinese waters not withstanding.

One needs to make two important points about recent weapons acquisition programs among ASEAN states. They have remained for the most part limited in size, scope, and cost, certainly in comparison to equivalent processes elsewhere. Moreover, they do not in any way constitute an arms race within ASEAN itself. The ASEAN states are not rivals in this sense and, past history notwithstanding, have no intention of using expanded conventional capabilities against each other. In addition, the desire to maintain stable national economies has further limited weapons acquisition. Competition among the armed forces of the region therefore remains limited and balanced by other considerations.[5] The formation of the ASEAN Forum, announced in July 1993, underlines further the cooperative nature of ASEAN deliberations. The Forum consists of the six member states and seven dialogue partners (Australia, Canada, the European Community, Japan, New Zealand, South Korea, and the United States) with the invited participation of five other regional states (China, Laos, Papua New Guinea, Russia, and Vietnam). The express purpose of the Forum, which met first in 1994, is to discuss regional political and security issues.

A more optimistic reassessment by ASEAN countries of Vietnamese capabilities and intentions combined with an economic downturn in the mid-1980s to cause a partial decrease in equipment acquisitions, but this proved short-lived in light of growing concerns over Chinese ambitions. A renewed burst of acquisition and modernization, with a new emphasis on maritime capabilities, has resulted from an equivalent change and development within China's military forces. As one analyst has noted, "the Chinese Navy is at the forefront of the vigorous modernization drive" mounted by China since 1985, while its strategic assumptions have moved away from the long apprehended war with the Soviet Union to encompass "small-scale and potentially intense limited war."[6]

These developments represent a fundamental shift in Chinese military power away from the defensive doctrine of people's war associated with Mao towards a capacity for power projection and in certain circumstances "first strike." Previous Chinese operational concepts confined the navy to a coastal defense role. The consequences of the resulting neglect of naval power showed clearly during the brief fighting with Vietnamese naval forces over control of the Paracels in January 1974. A naval doctrine of "offshore deterrence" has accompanied the large-scale acquisition and modernization program of the Chinese Navy, while Chinese naval units have regularly engaged in long-range fleet exercises in the Pacific, the Indian Ocean, and the South China Sea since 1986. This transformation in Chinese strategy or, perhaps more accurately, the revival of Chinese maritime traditions, is a product of the economic pressure exerted by China's burgeoning population and dwindling resources. This situation has prompted a revitalization of territorial claims to the presumed resource-rich South China Sea, centering on the Spratly Islands.

The "Law on Territorial Waters and Adjacent Areas," promulgated in February 1992, lists those territories in the South China Sea whose sovereignty remains in dispute: principally the Spratly, Paracel, and Pratas Island groups, and the Scarborough Shoals. Access to, and control of, resources is one issue, as is a belief that control of the island groups provides defense in depth. At the moment the Chinese are disputing ownership with Taiwan, the Philippines, Malaysia, Indonesia, and Brunei, but principally with Vietnam, while the outcome of successive Law of the Sea regimes pursued in international fora since the 1970s has intensified the whole issue of sovereignty and access to off-shore resources.

On the one hand, despite China's heightened maritime posture, the Chinese are as yet incapable of enforcing the claims they have asserted in the South China Sea. While they have moved recently to boost their aero-maritime capability by purchasing a surplus Soviet aircraft carrier from the Ukraine (an acquisition which has stalled but which may yet reach fruition), it will be a decade before China can deploy a carrier at any level of effectiveness. Given the growth in the economy, the capacity and skills of their industry, and the eagerness with which China is pursuing high technology, Chinese ability not only to maintain but indeed to construct carriers cannot be far off.

On the other hand, ASEAN navies recognize that they cannot hope to match the Chinese Navy even as a combined force. The trend toward small, missile-armed attack craft in ASEAN navies has given way to the purchase of frigates, maritime aircraft equipped with antishipping missiles, and submarines, although as yet the latter are present only in small numbers. But any form of naval arms race with the Chinese would be destabilizing both economically and in terms of ASEAN's external relations. For these reasons, the ASEAN states are keen to keep an American presence in the region as a counterweight to Chinese ambitions, while seeking the neutralization of the Spratlys as a means of containing China—"to use the semi-enclosed sea as a buffer against China."[7] The Chinese have signalled a willingness to put aside the dispute over sovereignty in favor of cooperative exploitation of the area's resources, but have unyieldingly maintained their assertion of sovereignty over the area.[8]

The movement in the ASEAN force modernization toward heightened aerial and maritime capabilities is to a large extent explained by Chinese assertiveness, together with a lessening of perceived internal threats to stability. Nevertheless ASEAN countries have not discounted such internal threats entirely. In both the Philippines and, to a lesser extent, Indonesia, internal subversion in Mindanao and separatist sentiment in Timor, respectively, continue to occupy military attention and resources.

## National Security Policies within ASEAN

Although mutual security remains a fundamental tenet of ASEAN, security relations among the member states have continued on an individual basis and have usually remained bilateral within the organization and among those external to the region. The admission of socialist Vietnam will further complicate this picture. As a consequence of such complex arrangements, this section will examine the defense postures of the member states on an individual basis.

Indonesia's military forces are relatively modest compared to its size, with the army dominant in both civil and military spheres of national life. Indonesia musters some 270,000 personnel in its military forces, of whom slightly over 200,000 are in the army. The armed forces are also lightly equipped, with all three services deploying a polyglot collection of arms and equipment that reflect the various historical phases of their development: older and generally obsolete Soviet-supplied aircraft and naval vessels, second-hand French armored vehicles, and a mix of advanced platforms (twelve U.S. F-16 fighters and small numbers of Dutch and German surface and sub-surface vessels). The Indonesians have purchased expensive hardware in small batches to maintain a capability to support possible future expansion, while most other acquisitions are driven almost entirely by cost considerations. The Indonesian Navy is in the process of acquiring most of what is left of the former East

German naval forces, some twenty-nine vessels in all, a purchase which caused considerable internal disagreement between the armed forces and the powerful minister for Research and Technology, Dr. B.J. Habibie. The dispute may reflect the armed forces preference for "value for money" purchases, but which Habibie pushed as a vehicle for the modernization of the country's shipbuilding industry.[9] Internally, the armed forces continue to confront complex and difficult internal security tasks in East Timor, a region which also poses significant problems for Indonesia more in the diplomatic than the military sphere. In conventional terms, Indonesian defense efforts are likely to concentrate on the protection of offshore assets and the control of sea lines of communications.[10] While modernization of the armed forces is likely to continue, it will do so in an undramatic fashion.

The development of Malaysian defense policy is an excellent illustration of the general trend of ASEAN as a whole. At its independence in 1957 Malaysia confronted the final stages of a communist insurgency that had at one stage fully taxed the Far Eastern resources of the diminished British Empire. Malaya/Malaysia's external and conventional defense was for a time assured by the British through the agency of the Anglo-Malay Defense Agreement (AMDA), signed in 1957 and modified in 1963.[11] British and other Commonwealth forces based in west Malaysia bore the brunt of the effort against Indonesia during the period of "Confrontation" between 1962 and 1966. Although the Malaysian armed forces expanded considerably in the 1960s, their functions remained overwhelmingly counterinsurgency and internal security, further emphasized by the inter-communal violence that erupted in 1969. The Five Power Defense Agreements created in 1971 following the withdrawal of British forces and the ending of the Anglo-Malay Defense Agreement extended this process. A significant proportion of Malaysia's air defense under the integrated Air Defense System, for example, rested on Australian squadrons based at Butterworth. But Britain's withdrawal, the revival of territorial claims to the Malaysian state of Sabah by the Philippines in 1968, and the defeat of the United States in Vietnam convinced Malaysian authorities of the need to build up their own conventional capabilities, especially in the air and maritime arenas. The structure of the Five Power Defense Arrangements remains important to Malaysia, however, not least for the opportunities for joint training and exercises that it continues to provide, the most recent air and naval exercise being that conducted in September 1995 with units of the Royal Australian Navy.

As elsewhere in ASEAN, the Malaysian Army has dominated the armed forces (with some 90,000 men out of 115,000). The threats posed to national security by the Malaysian Communist Party and the North Kalimantan Communist Party in the Borneo states—only resolved through negotiated agreements in 1989 and 1990 respectively—furthered the focus on ground forces. At the same time, however, the importance and capabilities of the Malaysian Navy have grown, and the navy and air force have been the prime beneficiaries of the Anglo-Malaysian Memorandum of Understanding signed in September 1988. That agreement represented not only Malaysia's largest defense contract, but at a value of $1.6 billion, "the largest single arms deal in the region except for the U.S. and Soviet shipments to Vietnam."[12] The navy discharges two critical functions: the control and protection of offshore assets (over which Malaysia is in low-key dispute with every other regional power) as well as maintenance of the sea lines of communications between east and west Malaysia. The army has created new and conventionally-oriented roles for itself through involvement in UN-sponsored peace-keeping efforts in Cambodia and, more recently, Bosnia, while the Malaysian armed forces as a whole remain prepared to deploy to east Malaysia to deal with potential secessionist movements.

Singapore's defense problems are unique. The Singapore armed forces have always maintained a greater conventional orientation than those of their neighbors, not least because since independence in 1965, Singapore has not confronted the challenges to internal security or insurgency that have confronted its enemies. Singapore maintains a substantial qualitative edge over the other armed forces in the region and in a crisis could dispose of some 55,000 active duty personnel, supported by reserves that number a quarter of a million. Singapore's "total defense" concept (military force allied to diplomacy backed by internal stability) is the island state's response to its fundamental military problem, a lack of strategic depth in a territory of only 630 square kilometers. Singapore has heavily armed and regularly modernized its regular forces, as well as significant reserves—a reflection, as in all other aspects of national life, of the dynamism and technological emphasis of the national economy. Singapore has also regularly demonstrated a willingness to spend money to maintain its qualitative edge over its Southeast Asian neighbors. In 1983 the air force acquired four E-2C airborne early warning aircraft at a cost of $600 million, at a time when Australia deemed such a purchase beyond the means of its defense forces. An active participant in the Five Power Defense Arrangements, for psychological as well as practical military reasons, Singapore maintains an extensive training regime for its forces. These frequently occur off-shore due to the lack of appropriate facilities in its own territory. The agreement negotiated with Australia in 1994 to conduct advanced flying training in northern Australia typifies such arrangements.

On the other hand, experts remain divided on the impact Singapore's aggressive defense posture has had on its neighbors. One commentator has concluded that Singapore's policy comprises "a system of security that other

Southeast Asian countries still strive to equal."[13] But others have pointed to the warnings sounded by senior Singaporean figures such as first deputy prime minister Goh Keng Swee in 1984: "We are not Israel and southeast Asia is not the Middle East."[14] The extent to which Singaporeans feel beleaguered, a Chinese enclave in a sea of Muslim Malays, is reflected in their approach to defense planning and has proven a source of discomfort and concern to both Indonesia and Malaya. Equally, Kuwait's example has probably not been lost on the Singaporean high command.

The fourth major player in ASEAN is Thailand. Its army has dominated the country since the 1930s. During the 1960s a sizeable U.S. military presence on Thai soil, together with the guarantees provided through SEATO underwrote the nation's security from external threat. As a result, the Thais tailored their armed forces for the counterinsurgency role. At the same time, the Thai Army has developed under American influence since the early 1960s with a considerable mechanized capability, built originally around some 600 light tanks and armored personnel carriers of American provenance. This capability was reinforced in the 1970s when, under a succession of military governments, the army acquired several hundred medium tanks, self-propelled and towed artillery, and a further 200 armored personnel carriers from the Americans, as well as additional light tanks from Britain.

In the 1980s the Thais reinforced their armored forces again through purchases of armored vehicles at highly favorable rates from the Chinese (intended by the latter as a counterbalance to Soviet aid to Vietnam) and additional equipment from the United States. The emphasis upon armor and mechanization was of little benefit in Thai efforts to defeat their indigenous Communist insurgency, but was significant in two other contexts. The purchase of Chinese equipment signalled Thailand's position clearly to the Vietnamese following the latter's invasion of Cambodia. In addition, the maintenance of sizeable conventional ground forces conferred on the Thai military the capability to resist a conventional (i.e., Vietnamese) invasion in order to buy time for Thailand's friends (i.e., the United States) to come to their assistance.[15] The effectiveness of these forces is another matter. Thai military capability has generally remained low, as a series of not very successful skirmishes in 1987–1988 along the Thai-Loatian border clearly demonstrated. Moreover, observers of Thai forces in Vietnam during the 1960s regarded them as generally poor, then as now, a consequence of the high degree of politicization within the Thai officer corps.

More recently, Thai priorities in acquisition and modernization have shifted to the navy, although Thailand itself faces no identifiable maritime threat. An ambitious program of expansion and modernization which extends to the commissioning of new Chinese-supplied frigates and the projected acquisition of one or two helicopter carriers, has occurred partly as a result of institutional dynamics within the Thai armed forces—particularly its heavy involvement in politics—and partly through concern that Thailand's dominant position on the mainland of Southeast Asia might be eclipsed (although by whom is not clear). As elsewhere in the region, ambitions, intentions, and capabilities intermix independently and it is unlikely at present that Thailand, having returned again to civilian government in 1992, will launch a major arms buildup with its potential to destabilize the economy and Thailand's relations throughout the region.

The lesser military partners in ASEAN are the Philippines and Brunei Darusalam. The latter, a small, oil-rich state in northern Borneo, has a small standing army of three battalions, one of which is provided by British-officered Gurkhas, with the whole under the personal command of the Sultan. Although there are no obvious external threats to Brunei's sovereignty or integrity, attacks on oil facilities and the possibility of internal dissent—perhaps driven by Islamic fundamentalism—remain of considerable concern to the Sultan. In October 1989, he upgraded his forces' capabilities through a $400 million arms purchase from Britain. Brunei joined ASEAN in 1984, and although its relations with regional partners have been generally good, its defense policy remains motivated by traditional concerns over the attitudes and ambitions of its larger neighbors. The British have guaranteed Brunei's security for decades, but the withdrawal from Hong Kong in 1997 and the departure of the Brigade of Gurkhas from the Far East will leave a gap which Brunei will find it difficult to fill from its own manpower resources. (The country's total population is only 280,000). Rich and strategically vulnerable, Brunei, not surprisingly, has forged strong defense links with Singapore.

Like Thailand and Malaysia, the Philippines left the question of defense against external threats to a protecting power, in its case the United States. That state of affairs continued until 1991 when Filipino demands for more money and the devastation of Clark AFB by the eruption of Mount Pinatubo decided the Americans against the renewal of the basing agreements. Like most of its ASEAN counterparts, the armed forces of the Philippines confronted a range of counterinsurgency and internal security tasks in the years after independence in 1936. Unlike its neighbors, however, the Filipino government has continued to face these threats. The insurgencies conducted by the Communist New People's Army and the Muslim Moro Army and its various splinter groups have proven manageable but not soluble. The Moro insurrection, in particular, is not susceptible to the solutions which offered themselves to the governments of Malaysia and Thailand, i.e., the collapse of the Communist bloc and a new accommodation with China. During the Marcos and Aquino administrations the Filipino Army, or elements of it, was also used in a praetorian and regime-supporting role in major population centers as well as in the countryside. But this role has diminished considerably under President Fidel Ramos, former chief of staff of the armed forces.

The U.S. withdrawal placed considerable pressure on the government to restructure and modernize the armed forces of the Philippines along conventional lines, but the serious economic difficulties and a general antimilitary atmosphere meant that resources are not available even for a military which is small relative to the population—106,000 out of 65,000,000. The Philippines remains in dispute with the Chinese over the Spratlys, while at present the country is incapable of enforcing its rights within the 200-mile exclusive economic zone. The United States has made it clear that its Mutual Defense Treaty with the Philippines does not extend to disputes over external territories (specifically the Spratlys), while the armed forces of the Philippines now face block obsolescence in their military equipment. Any effort at expansion and modernization will have to be a total, and hence expensive, replacement of equipment. A minuscule budget allocation of $1.6 billion to modernize the military forces—announced in 1993—will last over the next fifteen years—in effect resulting in no substantive improvement. The unfortunate state of the armed forces, however, merely reflects the decline of the Philippines generally.

Vietnam's admission to membership in ASEAN in July 1995 has the potential to alter relations within and outside the organization. In the 1980s, ASEAN (and others) viewed the Soviet presence in Vietnam and Vietnam's own policies towards its neighbors as legitimate grounds for concern, although as the decade wore on these clearly became less threatening. Although Vietnam maintains the largest army in Southeast Asia with a total military establishment of 850,000, the capabilities of these forces remain firmly fixed in the 1970s, while the withdrawal of Soviet support has degraded capabilities still further. Economic pressures have led to wholesale reductions in the standing forces, and these will probably continue as Vietnam devotes more attention to economic development and modernization. Even so, in 1994 the People's Army of Vietnam still disposed of more than sixty divisions. Yet, despite its mechanized assets and considerable artillery and air defense assets, the Vietnamese military has become a "poor man's army."[16] A struggling industrial base, the disappearance of Soviet support facilities, and a weak logistics system mean that while Vietnam can dominate its less powerful Indochinese neighbors, Laos and Cambodia, should it choose to do so, it lacks the ability to intervene elsewhere in the region. Its navy is essentially a brown-water force—no match for China's growing naval might. The air force and the air defense system, developed in response to the threat of U.S. air attacks in the 1960s and 1970s, have few really modern capabilities—neither AWACS nor airborne refueling capabilities. Critical shortages of spare parts and inadequate maintenance cycles affect all three services.

Clearly Vietnam regards its membership in ASEAN as a means to boost its domestic economic development. As the Chinese have found, domestic political reform and even unrest will likely accompany this process. In common with other regional powers, Vietnamese authorities view internal stability as critical and anything that undermines that stability as a primary threat to national security. Externally, Chinese activity in the South China Sea and conflict over the Spratlys pose further threats to Vietnamese interests, threats they are ill-equipped to face at present. Membership in ASEAN does not necessarily improve Vietnam's position, since there is now a potential for Vietnam to become ASEAN's "front-line" state in the groups's relations with China.[17] Internally, Vietnam's membership in ASEAN may impose strains on the consensual approach that has characterized ASEAN fora. In the defense arena, however, Vietnam has already indicated its likely path in developing and maintaining its national security policy through the opening of defense ties, as yet low-level, with five of its ASEAN partners (Brunei excepted), as well as with India.

The absence of multilateral defense cooperation complicates ASEAN's response to post-Cold War security issues in the region. Much of the activity, such as exercises and competition, manifested in an "arms dynamic" which sees individual states match each other's recent acquisitions, occurs on a bilateral basis.[18] It seems now that the key to reducing tensions in Southeast Asia may lie in a new security system which incorporates ASEAN and the wider Asia-Pacific region.[19] Thus, it is to the roles and perspectives of external powers and the influence of other forces that we now turn.

## Other Actors, Other Factors

ASEAN states are not the only ones with interests in Southeast Asian security issues, and their actions and deliberations often reflect the actions of external actors (hence the ASEAN Forum). Chinese policy and aspirations are critical, but the impact and influence of four other out-of-area powers— the United States, Japan, India and Australia—are also important for any analysis of Southeast Asian security. Related to this is the thorny issue of nuclear proliferation, already a factor in South and Northeast Asia and one on which ASEAN and other regional players hold decided views.

The United States has played a central role in Southeast Asia for decades, but the end of the Cold war has imposed additional complications on its role in the area. The fact that ASEAN is not a formal security organization, in which member states still do not trust each other sufficiently to broker multilateral security arrangements, means that the United States, as the remaining global power, confronts potentially overlapping, even conflicting, tasks and responsibilities at a time when Congress wishes to wind down overseas U.S. military commitments, particularly where policy makers in Washington cannot point to any direct threat to American interests. To make matters more complex, the United States must decide the balance of advantage in fostering the continuing economic stability of a dynamic region in the world economy, while also maintaining good relations with powers such as China, whose aims in Southeast Asia conflict with those of ASEAN. The United States also wants to develop clear and consistent positions on issues such as human rights and labor relations with countries in and out of the region, whose views on these issues are directly divergent, and who will resent what they perceive as Western interference in their internal affairs.

American force restructuring and down-sizing has had less immediate impact in Asia and the Pacific than in Europe, but a continuing preoccupation with budget slashing in Congress and the withdrawal of forces from Asia (even where, as in the Philippines, this has been done under local pressure) raises doubts about U.S. commitment in the region. This is especially true for regional allies who receive less priority in U.S. strategic planning. In its recent Defense White Paper, however, the Indonesian government noted that declining U.S. defense expenditures "only change the method of maintaining military capabilities in the Asia-Pacific region and do not lessen U.S. interest in controlling the situation in the region."[20] The fact that the member states do not agree on the desirability of U.S. involvement in regional security affairs complicates the picture. Indonesia and Malaysia are traditional proponents of the non-aligned movement and strong supporters of the Zone of Peace, Freedom, and Neutrality. Smaller states, such as Singapore and Brunei, suspicious of their larger neighbors, are more favorably disposed to American presence as a guarantor of stability and a check on others. The Filipinos, by their actions, have probably rendered themselves irrelevant to American strategic planning. In recent months Vietnam has even floated the idea that the U.S. Seventh Fleet might resume basing rights at Cam Rahn Bay, which probably has more to do with considerations of the benefits to the Vietnamese economy than anything else. As part of the shift from basing rights to access agreements for U.S. forces, the ASEAN partners have sought to step up the levels of bilateral military contacts through visitation rights and exercises.

But the fact remains that for the present the United States regards Northeast Asia (basically Japan and South Korea) as a higher priority than Southeast Asia, and as long as the security relationships in the latter region remain benign, that posture will likely continue.[21] The United States has made it clear in the 1990s, as it did under ANZUS in the 1960s, that conflict over external territories will not result in the invocation of mutual defense arrangements. Multilateral consultive arrangements among ASEAN, the United States, and other interested partners offer some potential for stability within the region. The willingness of ASEAN states to engage in such processes, however, will to a certain extent depend on America's record on issues such as democratization and human rights, which Southeast Asian governments do not divorce from the broader security concerns with quite the same ease as do governments in the West. Several nasty, though essentially minor, disputes between Singapore and the United States over the exercise of Singaporean law against American nationals, and rather more serious attempts by the Malaysian prime minister, Dr. Mahathir, to exclude "non-Asian" nations from a new Asia-Pacific economic grouping, the East Asia Economic Caucus, suggest the dangers here.

The ASEAN countries regard neither Japan nor India as serious factors in their security calculations, although for slightly different reasons. The sensitivities throughout Asia towards Japanese military presence outside the Home Islands remain intense, and even the limited role of Japan's Self-Defense Force personnel in the UN peace-keeping mission in Cambodia exercised the capitals of Southeast Asia.[22] In general, Japanese security concerns remain focused on a continuing American presence in Northeast Asia, a fear of nuclear proliferation in North Korea, possible further hostilities on the Korean peninsula, and the generation of economic growth. However, Southeast Asia provides major sources of raw materials, valuable markets, and investment opportunities for Japan, while the sea lines of communications which pass through Lombok and Sunda Straits are vital to the prosperity of the nation. A Japanese "breakout" from international and domestic constraints, which currently bind its national security policy, is unlikely at this point, short of a radical deterioration in the international order in the Asia-Pacific region.

India's alignment with the Soviet Union and its long-standing security concerns with China and Pakistan have meant that for much of the postwar period India has taken little interest in, and enjoyed limited interaction with, Southeast Asia and the Western Pacific. Economic considerations in the face of the creation of strong trading blocks in Europe, North America, and the Asia-Pacific region itself—from all of which India has been in danger of exclusion—have driven India's revived interest in ASEAN and the Asia-Pacific region more generally. Strategically, the Indians remain concerned about Chinese intentions, not only along their common frontier, but deep into the China Sea, and about the future orientation of Burma, which occupies a strategic position on India's eastern border and which the Indians would prefer to see neutralized through eventual membership in ASEAN. India's remaining security concerns with the subcontinent, relations with Pakistan, and the declining national security situation in Sri Lanka, are essentially concerns of India alone.[23] The Indian government has toned down the aggressive foreign policy of the 1980s that characterized the Ghandis; it is unlikely to assert itself too vigorously in Southeast Asia as it develops economic and strategic relationships throughout the region.

A growing competition between China and India, both nuclear capable powers, is likely to strengthen the move for the declaration of a nuclear-free zone in Southeast Asia, to which end a draft treaty already exists. ASEAN has given the United States undertakings that the declaration of any such zone would not affect the rights of passage for nuclear-powered or nuclear-equipped ships and aircraft, the cause of the suspension of ANZUS and the decline in American relations with New Zealand in the 1980s.[24] While the Americans have objected to such a zone, as they now have to the South Pacific Nuclear Free Zone, it is unlikely that a similar declaration in Southeast Asia will proceed further in the near future. However, the reaction in Southeast Asia and the South Pacific to the resumption of nuclear testing by the French in late 1995 emphasizes the importance which the region attaches to the issue, and the United States would be unwise to ignore or downplay the depth of feelings.

Engagement with security issues, trust and confidence-building measures, and enhanced contacts with regional military forces are part of Australia's wider engagement within the region. Australia enjoys a number of significant advantages in its relations with ASEAN states and with some of the external players. Although small, the Australian Defense Force remains the most capable in the region. Australia enjoys good relations through membership in the Five Power Defense Arrangements with Singapore and Malaysia, while military relations with Indonesia have become appreciably closer in recent years. The level and scope of joint exercising has increased to the extent that Australia invited Indonesia to participate in the Kangaroo joint exercise in northern Australia in June 1995, the large biennial training exercise conducted by the Australian Defense Force jointly with forces from its alliance partners and regional armies. In addition, Australia continues to enjoy a strong connection with the United States and enjoys a level of access out of proportion to its actual role in American strategic considerations. On the other hand, Southeast Asia, which is of primary strategic concern to Australia, is of declining importance to the United States, and neither sentiment nor history will be sufficient in themselves to maintain the alliance at its Cold War levels.

A number of military developments within the Asia-Pacific region itself are or will become of concern to Australian policy makers. Acquisition of advanced conventional weapons systems by powers in the region has the potential to erode the qualitative edge which Australia currently enjoys. Although at present only Singapore can match Australia's technological capabilities, technology transfers into the next century will likely alter this situation. Of greater concern is the potential for the proliferation of weapons of mass destruction, especially chemical weapons, of which the Vietnamese possess a number. Australia has taken the lead in regional and arms limitation conferences and will continue to do so, with the support of its regional partners. The increasing cost of advanced weapons systems, and the absence of an identifiable threat to Australia itself, will constrain the Australian government's ability to maintain, modernize, and enhance its military capabilities in a climate where budget allocations to defense are increasingly under attack. In this context, a number of Australian defense commentators, particularly Paul Dibb, have called for a greater emphasis on Australia's defense self-reliance, coupled at the same time with a closer involvement for Australian defense industry in the Asian Pacific marketplace.[25]

## Fault Lines

There are three fundamental security issues which pose potential threats to South Asia's stability: a modern and dynamic China which acquires status as a global power early in the next century; the potential for conflict within ASEAN itself; and external factors such as the potential disintegration of Papua New Guinea.

China's rapid economic growth and the development and acquisition of modern military capabilities mean that in the twenty-first century China's predominance in the region will become a fact rather than a fear. While it is certainly possible that China would seek a hegemonic role in Southeast Asia, China's recent international behavior complicates the picture. Chinese internal policies (human rights abuses and crackdowns on dissidents) are not necessarily a guide to China's attitude to issues on the world stage, as its signing of the Non-Proliferation Treaty in 1992 and its role in helping to broker a solution to the Cambodian crisis suggests. China has established diplomatic relations with Singapore and Indonesia and has thus lessened the suspicion and hostility that has characterized its relations with those two nations for several decades. But ASEAN capitals do perceive China's assertive strategic and military policies as threatening.[26] Regional investment in the Chinese economy may help to lay the conditions for further modernization of Chinese military capabilities, while increasingly close economic engagement in China may complicate relations with Beijing still further, especially in a crisis.[27]

Dealing effectively with the challenge posed by China will require all of ASEAN's collective will and resources. The indications are that, short of a catastrophic shift in relations within the region of a kind which one cannot predict, ASEAN will move towards greater cooperation and development of confidence-building measures, aimed ultimately at developing multilateral security cooperation within the region.[28] The widening of ASEAN membership to include Vietnam is one such mechanism. Growing economic interdependence within ASEAN and the genuine importance ascribed to internal stability makes armed conflict between ASEAN partners unlikely. This is not to say that tensions will not continue. But military efforts by member states are likely to be directed outward to deal with external challenges to the region, or inward, within the territory of individual countries. In this last respect, the continuing insurgency in Timor will pose further problems for Jakarta in its relations with Australia, the United States, and possibly the European Community.

The third area of concern is Papua New Guinea. After twenty years of independence from Australian supervision, the country is in danger of disintegration, exemplified by the secessionist struggle on Bougainville and an increasingly serious internal law-and-order problem both in the cities and in the countryside. Despite generous budgetary support from Australia since 1975, the Papua New Guinea economy is in serious difficulty and, in 1995, the World Bank took preliminary steps towards regulating the country's financial affairs from without, a move resented in Port Moresby. Australia would view the collapse of Papua New Guinea seriously, a reflection of the formal defense relationship between the countries. Jakarta would view such a collapse even more seriously. Indonesian sensitivities over the operation of the Organisasi Papua Merdeka (or Free Papua movement) in the Indonesian territory of Irian Barat, bordering Papua New Guinea, would greatly increase in such circumstances. In this eventuality, Australia would find it difficult to intervene directly on the grounds that such action would be viewed as "neocolonialist." The Indonesians would not be so inhibited and, in the event of an Australian failure to restore order directly, would probably do so themselves, thus replaying to some extent the sequence of events surrounding the occupation of East Timor in 1975. The impact on Australian-Indonesian relations in such circumstances would be severe, with considerable collateral effects within the rest of ASEAN.

# Conclusion

Security policy in Southeast Asia is at a turning point. The maturing ASEAN states hope to promote and safeguard common interests, but commonality of interest eludes them in several areas. All share a general concern over the growth and expansion of Chinese military power, both generally and in its practical application over disputed territories in the South China Sea. Most view continued American military presence in the region as a force for stability, but the United States itself regards its interests in the area as of less importance that those in North Asia, centered on Japan and Korea. India and Japan are engaged in a process of cautious engagement with Southeast Asia and the Pacific, the latter constrained by its history, the former by enduring security concerns to its west and a sluggish economic performance. Australia, for so long in but not of the region, is rapidly coming to terms with its geography and fashioning its policy accordingly. But Australia is not in a position to direct, much less dictate, the future direction of security policy, while for historic reasons some of the principal players remain suspicious of Australian motives. Currently, there is no arms race in Southeast Asia, but the potential for one exists. In Asia and the Pacific, as in Europe, the end of the Cold War has brought with it an end to the certainties and comfortable assumptions of earlier and simpler periods.

Chapter 10

# Japan's Emerging International Security Policy

*John E. Endicott*

1 995 represented a watershed in Japan's history—a watershed in terms of natural and man-made events, each significant in isolation, but collectively representing the possibility of fundamental change in the way Japan thinks about its security policy. On 17 January the Hanshin earthquake took a devastating toll in human lives and property in and around Kobe. The sarin gas attacks in early spring resulted in exposure of a bizarre religious cult, the Aum Shinrikyo. The April mayoralty elections in Tokyo and Osaka saw the rejection of major, established political parties by the electorate. The Social Democratic Party faced defeat in elections for the Diet's Upper House on 23 July. The culmination of the auto import dispute with the United States served only to enhance the political fortunes of the principal Japanese negotiator, Ryutaro Hashimoto, minister of international trade and industry. The Lower House marked the fiftieth anniversary of the end of World War II by passing a resolution expressing "sincere remorse" for the role played by Imperial Japan. Finally, the alleged rape of a twelve-year-old girl in Okinawa by two marines and a sailor became the catalyst of an explosion of Okinawan resentment at the continued presence of U.S. forces in Japan.

In all states, the interaction of domestic determinants as well as the external environment mold national security. In Japan policy is sometimes the result of inside pressure (*naiatsu*), and sometimes of outside pressure (*gaiatsu*). Domestically, this past year, Japan experienced a number of internal problems that ultimately influenced security policy. First and foremost, Japan lingered in one of its longest post-war economic recessions, a slowdown that began in 1990 and which tenaciously continues. Not only has the real estate bubble burst, reducing the paper assets of financial institutions by one-third, but unemployment has increased to levels unseen since 1953. An extremely strong yen created negative investment patterns as Japanese manufacturers relocated many of their manufacturing functions off shore and thus hollowed out Japanese industry. New and intense techno-competition from Taiwan, Korea, North America, and even China in such areas as computer chips and flat panel displays also took its toll on Japan's economic position. The recession and concurrent industrial restructuring have continued attacks on the concept of permanent employment. These trends have reduced the confidence of both Japanese entrepreneurs and the Japanese generally in the ability of their economy and nation to sustain its status as an economic superpower.

The Hanshin earthquake, coming at a time of increasing turmoil in Japan, cast unusual shadows on the country's internal situation and affected security issues in an unusual way. The polity's faith in scientists and technologists was severely shaken not only by their inability to forecast the disaster, but, more importantly, by the damage it caused. Moreover, the extraordinary slowness of the Japanese bureaucracy's response to this disaster had a devastating impact on confidence in government. Self defense force relief personnel waiting in vain for local civil authority to "activate" their assistance did not sit well in Kobe, or the rest of Japan. Furthermore, local bureaucrats refused U.S. offers of assistance, including naval vessels with space for 2,000 homeless. These actions had a strange—almost perverse—nationalist tone. Finally, commentary on national television castigating inept Tokyo bureaucrats for inaction, or worse, captured the notion that Japan needed dramatic relief from nonresponsive bureaucratic structures on the one hand and inept political leadership on the other. So intense was the resulting public censure that when the sarin gas attack hit the Tokyo subway system, public security forces reacted with positive determination, including mobilization of self defense forces before requests from civil authorities. The public supported a swift and comprehensive reaction that eventually resulted in the arrest of the leader of this religious terrorist group and most of his senior advisors. Japanese applauded termination of Aum Shinrikgo's status as a religious organization by Tokyo's newly elected mayor.

Six months after the Kobe earthquake (on 18 July 1995), the government approved a new national disaster plan requiring local authorities to increase their level of cooperation with self defense forces, to permit civil surveillance of disaster areas by self defense forces (SDF) without local requests, and in the event of communication breakdown, to allow the self defense forces to initiate rescue operations.[1] This rapid reaction to demands for reform of the thirty-two year old natural disaster regulations received an additional spur from the unprecedented terrorist action of Aum Shinrikyo, an assault on civil order that left most Japanese stunned. Most professional security personnel knew that Japan needed significant antiterrorism reform. This commitment to increase the ability of domestic security forces to respond to the new and threatening environment received additional public support, when terrorists—likely from the Aum Shinrikyo—gunned down the police bureaucrat personally coordinating the efforts of police and self defense forces in the sarin attack investigation. These events greatly altered public attitudes, which until then had questioned the legitimacy of military force even for self defense. In fact, the Social Democratic Party maintained that such a role was unconstitutional until the Murayama government, with a socialist prime minister, came to power in 1994. The acceptance of the armed forces' constitutionality, a major shift in public perception, and acceptance of a national security mission came within a year. Most Japanese now view the self defense forces not only as constitutional, but as necessary.[2]

General dissatisfaction with the economy, the pace of reform in politics, and exasperation from the major disasters had a considerable impact on local elections in April. Stunning the political establishment, two unaffiliated candidates for governor in Tokyo and Osaka won over established party candidates. The victor in Tokyo, Yukio Aoshima, ran on a platform that he would not spend "one sen" (one hundredth of a yen) to save several savings banks that the outgoing mayor had promised would receive as much as $360 million in a plan to save their scandal-ridden institutions.[3] In addition, Aoshima pledged to halt Tokyo's assistance to a multi-billion dollar "city Expo." Having won the election, after a short period of review, he honored his pledges with the strong support of the electorate.

On 23 July, the restructuring of the political system from the ballot box continued in elections for the upper house. Japanese voters had waited for top-down reform from the election of Hosokawas and the break-up of the Liberal Democratic Party's monopoly in 1993. Reform, of sorts, had occurred in the security arena with the creation of the Murayama Liberal Democratic Party-Socialist Party-Sekigake Party coalition. The socialists recognized the constitutionality of the self defense forces, the legality of the U.S.–Japan Security Treaty, and even the potential use of the Japanese military in limited peace-keeping activities. This recognition by the Socialists had largely removed these issues from political contention.

Rather than acclaim as heroes of reform, the socialists and liberal democrats heard charges of gross opportunism. While they removed historic impediments to political cooperation and made great progress toward the realization of a national security consensus, reforming political leaders received only censure from the public. The public saw the politicians' objective not as creation of a new security policy consensus, but only as an expedient to remain in power. The socialists—the party that had significantly altered its forty-year security policy—paid dearly for what its followers considered an unprincipled compromise. In the Upper House elections, the party dropped from sixty-three to thirty-eight senators, a loss of twenty-five seats. The Shinshinto, now seen as the prime "reformist" party, gained twenty-one seats in this election and now has fifty-six seats in the Upper House.[4]

The liberals fared better than their socialist allies, but were still surprised at the strength of the reform elements—organized and unorganized. One of the liberal democratic leaders, Ryutro Hashimoto, Minister of Trade and Industry, tempered the negative re-election results by his vigorous actions in the showdown over trade policy with the Clinton administration. The United States continued the efforts of past administrations to increase market access in Japan, especially for automobiles and auto parts. The policy was not new, but its implementation was. Using Micky Kantor, his campaign manager and an expert in international trade, Clinton set out to right the perceived inequities in the auto trade. This high pressure policy to change Japanese bureaucratic behavior was ultimately successful. But in the wider security context it was an expensive victory. A campaign of intensive media manipulation, bombast, and courtroom confrontations seemed inappropriate in dealing with an ally who, in security terms, the United States calls the keystone of its Pacific policy and the linchpin of its Asian presence. Although a compromise avoided an eleventh-hour imposition of sanctions, a real reassessment of the U.S.-Japanese security relationship already underway accelerated. U.S.-Japanese talks took a new and increasingly angry tone in Japan. Assurances from the State Department and its representatives that bitter exchanges between Hashimoto and Kantor would not affect its security relationship may have only revealed *tatemae* or surface feelings.

The Japanese—for whom the basic article of faith has been the U.S. promise to provide a reasonable defense of Japan based on a credible nuclear umbrella—did not find 1995's events reassuring. Those in the United States who see long-term utility in security cooperation and the mutual security interests of both countries, such as Assistance Secretary of Defense for International Security Affairs Joseph Nye, have attempted to demonstrate the rationality of such cooperation. But Japanese observers must place the actions of only one actor in the Executive Branch in the larger context. As Japan examines its security policy for the next decade, it will regard 1995 as a key year in creating new domestic pressures on security questions. Japan will also see this year as one where bilateral relations with its most important ally became measured by more than friendship.

# The Regional Setting

Other external actors, for example the Peoples' Republic of China, Russia, the two Koreas and Taiwan, complicate the immediate Asian security environment for Japan. China represents past memories, current opportunities, and future challenges. The Japanese have genuine security worries about the colossus to their west. China tested nuclear weapons only days after the May Non-Proliferation Treaty Review Conference endorsed indefinite extension of the treaty, tested again in August 1995, and refused to join in the Korean Energy Development Organization. While China sees an almost unlimited threat from Japan, including nuclear arms,[5] Japan sees, in China, real defense budget growth rates. Increasing naval capabilities and the 1992 Naval Territories Law that codified China's claims to the Spratlys and Paracels have provoked considerable alarm. Japan worries about Chinese nuclear and missile proliferation, as well as plans for modernizing the People's Liberation Army and Navy.[6] Furthermore, the transition to a post-Deng Xiao-Ping China is unsettling. Politically, looking at China from an historic perspective, the Japanese understand that the collapse of the previous Chinese empires followed on the heels of popular uprisings, internal divisions, or a failure to meet minimal societal needs. Japan sees a potential series of destabilizing factors within China, any one of which could undermine the present regime. Excess population, the potential for runaway inflation, insufficient oil to meet the needs of a rapidly expanding economy, corruption, economic imbalances between coast and hinterlands, human rights abuses, failure to respect international contract obligations, a major military buildup, and significant cleavages and competition within competing elites, all provide major worries.[7]

Russia poses very difficult problems, not increasing strength but increasing weakness. A comment that Russia no longer maintains operational nuclear ballistic submarines in its Pacific Fleet has two meanings.[8] One meaning is positive. Japan would welcome the decrease in the nuclear threat. The other meaning is the growing awareness in Japan that nuclear pollution from inadequate Russian storage methods poses a major threat to safety in the Pacific. The impotence of its northern neighbor increases the likelihood that Japan's outstanding territorial issue with Russia, the southern Kuriles, will remain unsettled and a considerable irritant. A stronger, more dynamic Russia might come to a territorial accommodation with Japan, but a weak Russian leadership would confront vociferous cries from nationalist extremists.

The two Koreas each present special security problems as well as opportunities for Japan. Divided, they represent a threat with millions of troops confronting each other at the highest levels of alert. United, the Korean peninsula would represent a new and potentially favorable, but troublesome, regional power capable of playing a key security balancing role in Northeast Asia. As North Korea struggles to maintain its position in the region, especially vis-à-vis South Korea, Japan views both possibilities with increasing concern. In addition, the North Koreans are increasingly unable to sustain the economic cost of their armed forces. Taking the "cheap way out," they have turned to a nuclear weapons program that has, from their standpoint, been successful in capturing regional attention as well as world-wide response.

Most recently, the Japanese have considered whether they can justify defense expenditures to counter possible North Korean special forces attacks on the Home Islands. Recognizing that significant North Korean special forces capabilities aimed at South Korea could attack Japan with little adjustment, the Japanese defense establishment has made developing a force capable of dealing with such incursions one of its highest priorities.[9]

The North Korea's instability further concerns the Japanese. North Korea appears to prefer the policy of continued *Chuche* or self-reliance rather than a more positive interaction with the international community.[10] Thus, Japan's policy of normalizing diplomatic relations with North Korea progresses at a snail's pace, constrained by regard for South Korean sensitivities on one hand, and the pace of improvement in U.S.-North Korean relations on the other. Still unconvinced that a united Korean peninsula is in Japan's interest, Japanese security and business communities have focused on American confidence in new enterprises in North Korea. Moreover, North Korea's long outstanding demands for major reparations from World War II assure that normalization of relations will not take place any time soon. Negotiations restarted and made some headway during talks to supply North Korea with several hundred thousand tons of rice, some as aid and some at subsidized prices. Once the Japanese finished the transaction—after astonishing demands from North Korea—bilateral talks slowed to a crawl. Any precipitous haste in settling long-standing problems would suggest a desperate attempt within North Korea to save the regime. If this were to occur, Japan could capitalize on North Korean weakness.

On the other hand, Japan seeks more extensive security exchanges with the South Korean leadership, but must do so with little publicity. Public attention, especially in South Korea, remains focused on the unaddressed plight of Korea's World War II "comfort women." A Japanese effort to compensate these women indirectly through a significant general fund for cultural activities did not receive the positive support that Prime Minister Murayama calculated. The on-again, off-again efforts of Japan to normalize its relations with North Korea further complicate Japan's relations with South Korea.

One interesting concern of the Japanese regarding a possible reunited Korea is an "inevitable economic stagnation" that would occur in its aftermath. Such a situation could invite a renewed competition by China, Russia, the United States, and Japan for predominance.[11] The Japanese see such competition in terms of assistance to a newly reunited Korea, but the implications remain uncertain. Many Japanese recall the competition among the great powers for preeminence on the Korean peninsula in the late nineteenth century and are unnerved by the insecurity and unpredictability that would surely replace the current status quo.

The power of the Taiwanese lobby in the U.S. Congress has created another, more recent security worry for Japan. The invitation of Taiwan's president, Lee Teng Hui, to the United States enraged China's leadership at a time of considerable internal difficulties, the period of leadership transition. With the Chinese military reportedly calling for a tougher line toward Taiwan,[12] Japan finds itself increasingly at odds with the United States in maintaining that it will not stray from its policy of recognition toward the Peoples' Republic of China. Comments by President Lee after his return home and after military exercises in July which saw the firing of six Chinese missiles to within 140 kilometers of Taiwan, were especially disconcerting to the Japanese. Lee suggested that it might be time for Taiwan to look again at the nuclear option in face of China's bellicose response to his visit to the United States. He warned: "Everyone knows we had the plan before, but this issue drew international attention and affected the whole country's image...We should re-study the question from the long-term point of view."[13] He also vowed to create military forces that would "terrify and stop" a Chinese assault. This exchange and the vehemence of China's response after Lee's return encouraged many in Asia, especially in Japan, to consider building a cooperative security community in Northeast Asia.

Against this backdrop of threatening events in Asia, some negotiations towards a multilateral security community within the Asia-Pacific region has occurred. The Association of Southeast Asian Nations accepted its seventh member, Vietnam, in August, 1995. Some Chinese observers noted that this action represented another American action in the neo-containment policy of resolving outstanding problems among states on China's periphery to isolate China. Of course, one can also see U.S. policy as the preliminary step to creation of a truly cooperative security system in Asia in which no single state would be "the enemy."

Meetings of the Association of Southeast Asian Nations' Regional Forum, dedicated to discussion of security issues, have also taken place at the ministerial level. Japan has taken an active part in such multilateral discussions, and sharply criticized France's planned resumption of nuclear testing at Brunei in August 1995.[14] The only regional initiative Japan has been reluctant to endorse has been the Malaysian-inspired East Asia Economic Caucus, which pointedly excludes the United States.[15]

While there is little hope for multilateral dialogue among states without working infrastructures, this represents an area that needs attention. Northeast Asia, the most heavily armed locale on the globe, requires creation of a cooperative regional or sub-regional security system to insure a safe transition to the post-Cold War world. The question is whether Japan will assume a position of constructive leadership in partnership with the United States to achieve such a new security arrangement, or have recent bilateral arguments driven Japan to consider an all-Asian approach that eliminates the United States? We must now examine the Japanese course in a more formal way to see if an *atarashi kase* (fresh breeze) might reinvigorate U.S.-Japanese relations, permitting Japan to continue on a course minimizing the role of military power as an instrument of state policy. Or is Japan destined to develop the military might that befits a superpower?

## Japan's Evolving Security Policy

Japan has enjoyed relative stability with its security policy since 1976 when the Miki government issued the National Defense Program Outline (sometimes shortened to its Japanese nickname of *Taiko* which settled the previous defense question of "how much is enough?"). *Taiko* defined clear planning ceilings for equipment and personnel strengths for the Japanese Self Defense Forces. It stabilized an internal debate that had focused on a series of five-year defense build-up plans and budgets. [Refer to Figure 1, the NDPO] In fact, a week after announcing the *Taiko*, the government introduced another supplementary restraint to ease the worries of opponents of continuous defense increase. The restraint placed a cap of 1 percent of GNP for any defense budget. These two developments permitted the Japanese military to focus on efforts to improve U.S.-Japanese cooperation.

From 1976 until the end of the Cold War, Japanese efforts concentrated on enhancing the bilateral security relationship with the United States as a guarantee of significant defense capability against the Soviet threat. Landmark accommodations have included the 1978 guidelines to facilitate force coordination, the 1983 Agreement on Transfer of Military Technology, efforts to build the FSX fighter aircraft, numerous exercises between military units, and the expansion of Japanese base support programs to the point that Japan now pays 70 percent of expenses. Since the end of the Cold War, Japan has explored involvement in international security issues outside the limits of the U.S.-Japanese relationship. Indeed, in June of 1990, Japan took its first formal step in recognizing "out of area" responsibilities at the Knokke Heist Conference between NATO and Japan in Belgium. At this conference, titled

## Figure 1. National Defense Program Outline: SDF Strength Guideline

|  | New | Current |
|---|---|---|
| *Ground Self-Defense* | | |
| Personnel quota | | |
|     Standing authorized strength | 145,000 | 180,000 |
|     Combat-ready reserves | 15,000 | — |
| Basic Units | | |
|     Units deployed regionally | 8 divisions & | 12 divisions & |
|       in peacetime | 6 brigades | 2 combined brigades |
|     Mobile operation units | No change | 1 armored division |
| | No change | 1 airborne brigade |
| | No change | 1 helicopter brigade |
|     Low-altitude ground-to-air | | |
|       missile units | No change | 8 antiaircraft artillery groups |
| Main equipment | Apx. 900 tanks | Apx. 1,200 |
| | Apx. 900 howitzers, and | Apx. 1,000 |
| | missile and rocket launchers | |
| *Maritime Self-Defense Force* | | |
| Basic units | | |
|     Destroyers units, | | |
|       for mobile operations | No change | 4 escort flotillas |
|     Destroyers units, | | |
|       for regional districts | 7 local destroyer units | 10 |
|     Submarine units | No change | 6 units |
|     Minesweeping units | 1 flotilla | 2 |
|     Land-based antisubmarine | | |
|       aircraft units | 13 squadrons | 16 |
| Main equipment | Apx. 50 destroyers | Apx. 60 |
| | No change | 16 submarines |
| | Apx. 170 combat aircraft | Apx. 220 |
| *Air Self-Defense Force* | | |
| Basic units | | |
|     Aircraft control and | 8 groups, 20 units, | 28 groups |
|       warning units | 1 squadron | |
|     Interceptor units | 9 squadrons | 10 |
|     Support fighter units | No change | 3 squadrons |
|     Air reconnaissance units | No change | 1 squadron |
|     Air transport units | No change | 3 squadrons |
|     Early-warning units | No change | 1 squadron |
|     High-altitude ground-to-air | | |
|       missile units | No change | 6 groups |
| Main equipment | Apx. 400 combat aircraft | Apx. 430 |
| | including 300 fighters | |

Source: Defense Agency and *The Japan Times*, 29 Nov 95, p. 3.

"Global Security: North American, European, Japanese Interdependence in the 1990s," Deputy Foreign Minister Hisashi Owada introduced the concept of *pax consortis:* a mechanism based on consultation among the major players of the system which would maintain the international order. He commented that Japan would increasingly assume greater worldwide security roles of a nonmilitary, but supportive, nature primarily in Asia and other developing regions.[16]

Shortly after those comments, Saddam Hussein invaded Kuwait. In the period between the invasion and the dispatch of Japanese minesweepers after hostilities had ended, Japan responded to requests for assistance with contributions totalling over $13 billion. The Japanese, however, did not contribute this considerable sum with grace. In fact, their gift was an international public relations disaster, as the ruling party (the Liberal Democrats) was split, and only achieved consensus on contributions with its opponents after a considerable time. However politically debilitating, the contributions marked another threshold for Japan's involvement on the international scene outside the relationship of the U.S.-Japan Security Treaty. Although the coalition complained about the tardiness of the Japanese response, in relative historic terms, Japan's action was revolutionary. Dispatch of maritime self defense force minesweepers to the Gulf (after an earlier abortive attempt to involve the air self defense force) marked another significant milestone in Japan's new global engagement.

By 1992, after intense internal political debate, the Diet passed a Peace-Keeping Law that allows the dispatch of limited noncombative support forces to approved United Nations peace-keeping operations. Since then, Japanese Self Defense Force personnel have played a significant role in UN-sponsored elections in Cambodia and in UN efforts in Mozambique and Zaire to cope with the Rwanda refugee crisis.[17] In August 1995, the Japanese socialists approved, albeit with major restrictions, the sending of an army transportation unit to the Golan Heights to replace Canadians as UN observers. Nevertheless, restrictions forbid Japanese forces from transporting either weapons or ammunition of any other nations' troops. Not surprisingly, other forces on the Heights found the Japanese conditions disruptive.[18]

This activity comes at a time when the original Peace-Keeping Law legislation undergoes a mandatory review. This review will determine whether current restrictions will remain—that only support forces can participate, not military units with an operational mission—or whether Japanese involvement will move beyond the logistical. The Socialist and Sekigake members of the coalition government will be reluctant, however, to agree to such an expansion of Japan's role. Only general elections for the Lower House scheduled for 1996 (but the House may dissolve earlier) will clarify the political situation and lead to a final decision on the scope of Japanese military action abroad.[19]

However, the Japanese Self Defense Forces have already embarked on a series of organizational reforms to prepare for a different future. The *Taiko* had placed an upper limit on the ground self defense force of 180,000 personnel, but actual serving troops only numbered approximately 150,000. In 1989, a reorganization of the ground forces placed approximately 60 percent of Japan's main battle tanks in the north. The self defense forces, ground, air, and naval, in conjunction with American forces, were preparing to deal with a Soviet attack.

## New Policy Initiatives

While strategic changes since 1989 have redefined what the self defense forces might do, the basic force structure and equipment ceilings put in place in 1976 still guide acquisition policy. The Nakasone cabinet technically removed the 1-percent-of-GNP ceiling but the government has only exceeded the guidelines twice by insignificant margins. The 1 percent budget restriction now represents a political barrier, not an administrative one and, as the threat from the Soviet Union has dissipated, so has any pressure to push budget appropriations closer to the 1 percent level. In fact, with the Socialists in the coalition government, pressure has moved in the opposite direction. However, the post-Cold War environment has provoked some important developments.

The Hosokawa cabinet (February 1994)—the first non-Liberal Democratic Party government since 1956—initiated the first serious review of Japanese security policy since the special advisory committee headed by Masataka Kosaka during the Nakasone cabinet. Headed by a noted brewer, Hirotaro Higuchi, Chairman of the Board, Asahi Breweries, Ltd., the commission had representatives from business, government, and academia. Two respected scholars, Akio Watanabe of Tokyo University and Kuniko Inoguchi of Sophia University, provided intellectual credibility, and former civil servants provided the necessary bureaucratic connections. Because of the flux in Japanese politics, the commission had a unique opportunity to receive guidance and briefings from three different sitting prime ministers: Morihiro Hosokawa on 28 February 1994; Tsutomu Hata on 11 May; and Tomiichi Murayama on 13 July. Finally, on 12 August, the committee briefed Prime Minister Murayama on its report, "The Modality of the Security and Defense Capability of Japan: The Outlook for the Twenty-first Century," and released it to the press for public review.[20]

Reacting to dynamic changes in the international system, the commission recommended that the government transform the self defense force (postured to oppose a landing by moderately heavy Soviet forces and supplemented with significant antisubmarine capabilities and a highly developed air superiority mission) into a lighter, smaller, and more mobile force. This new force would be capable of actively contributing to UN peace-keeping missions. Specific recommendations included a reduction of personnel strength by 34,000 men, scrapping heavy armor in the ground forces (too heavy for modern missions), reducing in the navy's antisubmarine and antimine roles, and a reduced air intercept role for air forces. The committee voiced interest in a theater antimissile program, greater sea and airlift (with in-flight refueling capabilities), and a shift to more "sophisticated equipment with increased mobility and high tech applications."[21] Most significantly, it recommended that Japan "must part with" the 1976 *Taiko*. The committee also made a strong commitment to controlling the spread of weapons of mass destruction, tying aid for developing states to low levels of defense expenditures, and moving toward multilateral security concepts in Asia. Not quite as an afterthought, but certainly not on page one, the committee recognized the importance of the U.S.-Japan security relationship.[22] In addressing this relationship, the committee's report found, "The Japan-U.S. Security Treaty remains an indispensable precondition for the defense of Japan even in the post-Cold War security environment." Significantly, a following statement indicated that "...the range of fields in which Japan and the United States can cooperate for the security of Asia is expected to widen."

This report, certainly the single most important indicator of Japan's future security policy, was echoed by a number of books by political figures seeking Japan's future role in the international community and articles by "observers" and "analysts." Ichiro Ozawa, secretary general of the current Shinshinto Party and possible future prime minister, called for Japan to be a "normal nation."[23] In essence, he set out a more pragmatic approach to Japanese policy in the international arena. He recommended first that Japan assume those responsibilities considered "natural" in the world community; and second, that Japan should, in conjunction with the other states, create prosperous and stable lives for its citizens.[24] Such an approach would even lead to a revision of Article 9 of the Constitution, which currently prohibits military force as an instrument of Japanese policy. Ozawa also anticipated an expanded role for the United Nations through creation and use of a UN reserve force.[25] He also endorsed more multilateral diplomacy, as well as enhanced efforts to control nuclear weapons.

The annual Defense White Paper issued in summer 1995 confirmed the general trend in Japanese security assessments to assume that the Soviet threat is dead. Here Japan faces problems. The country must undertake force-sizing efforts against nuclear threats, with the size, nature, and source of conflict all in question, but within the context of a continuing U.S.-Japanese security system. Although the stationing of U.S. troops in Japan is now cheaper than their stationing on the U.S. (and thus a major argument for Japanese tolerance of the forward presence), such costs do have a considerable impact in the Japanese defense budget. They squeeze the finances for equipment, personnel, and facilities for Japanese forces.

The *Taiko* review is not yet complete. Internal consultants to Japan's Security Council began to revise the *Taiko* in June 1995. The Security Council membership includes the prime minister, the head of the Defense Agency, the foreign minister, the home affairs minister, the minister for international trade and industry, and five others. A total of ten meetings have been proposed, one-half the number of the advisory group in 1994. Basing its work on the Advisory Report with additional input from the Defense Agency, the government hoped to complete both by the end of 1995 in time for the budget cycle. Several reported recommendations include a reduction of the ground self defense force from 180,000 to 150,000 and incorporation of high quality weapons and equipment that will ultimately cost more.[26]

The 1995 White Paper offers little additional insight into Japanese thinking. One can only conclude that if the coalition government remains in office, the new *Taiko* will be a restrictive, rather than an expansive, document as far as the self defense force. Those elements of the 1994 Advisory Report that supported downsizing and restructuring of Japanese forces will probably find favor. Recommendations about theater missile defense and active involvement in peace-keeping operations beyond logistic support are unlikely to find a voice.

If, however, the Shinshinto were to assume power, one would most likely see a more active and expansive role for defense. The notion that expenditures for security can and should—on occasion—take precedence over social priorities is gaining credibility, as is the idea that credible threats do exist in post-Cold War Northeast Asia. The notion that active confidence-building measures and arms control activities need the support of a financial commitment has also gained acceptance. Overall, six years after the collapse of the Soviet Union, Japan's emerging security policy has adjusted to an environment of increasing uncertainty and recognizes that the nation's future involvement in the international arena might take it along a wider path than in the past.

New ideas about Japan's role in the international arena include the policy espoused by the *Asahi Shimbun* that Japan should become the "national equivalent of a conscientious objector." Here, Japan would behave as an international activist in nonmilitary activities. To facilitate such a role, new legislation to support international cooperation with a peace support corps would be required.[27] The *Asahi*, representing the traditional political left in Japanese media, holds Article 9 of the Constitution sacrosanct and attracts those who support the 1947 Constitution. The *Yomiuri Shimbun*, taking a more pragmatic approach, calls for Japan's participation in UN peace-keeping activities and has even drafted and published a revised Constitution. The *Sankei Shimbun* also favors revision of the Constitution and advocates that it allow Japan to deal with the "realities" of the world and its position. This normally conservative newspaper cited its own opinion poll, which showed that 72 percent of respondents favored a revision of the Constitution. The *Nikkei Shimbun*, the prestigious economic journal, favors a course of "re-interpretation" rather than revision. On the other hand, the *Mainichi Shimbun* notes that its polling indicates that only 28 percent support changes in the Constitution, while 27 percent oppose.[28] Regional newspapers commenting on the issue of the Constitution called for a careful review before any action (Hokkaido), for caution as the current constitution had brought peace and prosperity (Okinawa), and for an understanding of the hidden agendas of those who advocate revising the constitution, (Kyoto).[29]

Professor Kazuo Yoshida of Kyoto University is typical of Japanese security experts motivated by an impression that the decline of the *Pax Americana* requires formation of a new system in which international cooperation will play a larger role. They believe Japan "will have to bear its share of responsibility for the maintenance of international order."[30] In order to meet its obligations, Yoshida calls for a Japanese seat on the UN Security Council and a thorough discussion of the Constitution. While there is no perceptible rush to revise the Constitution, the call for a more pragmatic reinterpretation of basic law in light of changes in the international environment is the most probable course Japan will follow over the next decade.

## Development and Redefinition of Japanese Security Policy

In the near-term, Japan is likely to broaden its relationship with the United States while at the same time increasing independent participation in regional and international affairs. The Japanese will not accomplish this through legislative action, but by a quiet shifting of their emphasis on the relationship. They could achieve their goals by turning away from this strict "defense of Japan" orientation to an expanded role that would include broad support for U.S. military presence in the East Asian and Pacific area,[31] a movement suggested by Japanese Defense Agency May 1995 public releases that the Japanese prepared for a visit by U.S. Secretary of Defense William Perry. Reportedly, the Defense Agency director was ready to state that the U.S.-Japanese security relationship was an indispensable framework for Japan to support U.S. activities and to maintain world stability.[32] Political difficulties, of course, bar the path to such a redefinition, but bureaucratic efforts, as well as unofficial military-to-military dialogue, can facilitate the ultimate objective.

During 1995 the Japanese have resolved or addressed a number of problems preventing closer U.S.-Japan cooperation. Negotiators reached agreement in mid-July on the level of support Japan would provide for the U.S. presence. Japan has agreed to maintain current support for salaries and allowances for Japanese employees, as well as utility costs. While the agreement did represent an increase, as the U.S. desired, support still does not broach the current 70 percent contribution to the total cost of stationing U.S. forces in Japan. That figure ran to approximately 453 billion yen in fiscal year 1995—more than $4.7 billion.[33]

Continuation of base support at mid-1995 levels is a powerful indication of Japan's continued commitment to its relationship with the United States. In July, however, Japan indicated that it might increase that support to the U.S. as a corollary to the idea of an expanded international role for Japan. Apparently, moves are afoot to complete an acquisition and cross-servicing agreement under which the military services of the two countries could exchange fuel, food, and transport services. Food, fuel, and spare parts would be paid for on an annual basis, but services would be provided reciprocally, free of charge. The agreement would exclude ammunition and would remain valid in peacetime only for, or during, joint exercises.[34] Reportedly, the actual signing of the agreement will occur in March 1996 and take effect on 1 April, the beginning of the Japanese fiscal year. This agreement was in line with a public announcement in May 1995, of the Defense Agency Director General, Tokuichiro Tamazawa. He informed the Pentagon that Japan would conclude the acquisition and cross-servicing agreement that would cover items such as food, petroleum products, clothing, troop accommodation services, transportation, communications, and other features such as base support, storage, spare parts, repair and maintenance, and harbor and air facilities.[35]

It is still not clear if this agreement will extend to UN peace-keeping operations, but it could, if extended to such missions, facilitate the dispatch of self defense force units worldwide, as U.S. facilities could be available for support. Whatever the outcome of the UN question, completion of the agreement in March 1996 represents a major step toward integrating the two nations' defense forces. At this point, the applicability of such missions remains to be settled. But U.S. forces in Japan are expected to benefit more from the arrangement than the Japanese. In August 1995, the United States requested an increase of 3,000 (to a total of 25,600) in the number of Japanese workers on its bases.[36] The Japanese were not pleased to see that increased productivity within the newly implemented forty-hour work week would not satisfy the Americans. With a budget increase of 2.9 percent, the Japanese Defense Agency argued for a phased introduction of the increase, or some other compromise to dampen the budgetary impact of 3,000 new employees. Since these costs come from the self defense forces' budget, opposition was considerable, but the Japanese eventually settled for the increase in personnel.

One can find concrete indications of Japan's future defense policy in its budgetary commitments and in the annual White Paper issued each July. In 1995 the White Paper noted the generally uncertain nature of the post-Cold War environment with special attention paid to China and North Korea. The Japanese saw the fact that North Korea is still dedicating 20-25 percent of its GNP to the military as a "factor that could bring instability not only to Northeast Asia...but...to the entire international community."[37] Reportedly, this concern surfaced in June meetings in the Finance Ministry, always a key player in the distribution of resources in Japan. As the Defense Agency seeks to draw up a new *Taiko*, it wants forces that would allow it to counter the North Korean special forces threat to the Home Islands. Moreover, the Japanese see an immediate and all-too-close potential enemy developing missiles with ranges that exceed 1,000 kilometers, specifically the No-dong II.[38] The fact that one of their F-4s intercepted a Chinese fighter over the disputed Senkaku Islands in late August was also not lost on Japanese planners.[39] Although the White Paper does reflect the confused nature of the region, it fails to shed much light on the final version of the national defense review. In particular, it does not reveal how far the recommendations of the August 1994 special advisory commission's report will be integrated into the basic planning document for the next decade.

Budget developments for FY 1996 reveal the concrete obligations that create force posture. The 1996 draft reflects pressures for meeting ever-increasing out-year obligations with a budget that falls at every turn. Installment payments on one Aegis-class destroyer, four AWACS aircraft, and other expensive equipment purchases require a defense budget at least 150 billion yen higher than the 1995 version. Thus, the Japanese Defense Agency argues for a figure of 192 billion yen, a 4 percent growth over last year's budget, while the Socialists, especially Prime Minister Murayama, have called for a ceiling of .855 percent growth at most.[40]

Since obligatory payments account for 35.5 percent of the defense budget, while personnel and support costs account for another 44 percent, there is little room for maneuver. In FY 1995, to find such money, the self defense forces cut back on military exercises.[41] Reports in August 1995 indicated a possible budget increase of 2.9 percent for the Defense Agency. Thus, further cuts will have to be made. Over the next several years, barring a remarkable change in the political and bureaucratic situation in Japan or the emergence of a significant threat, the Japanese Self Defense Forces will face personnel cuts, organizational restructuring, and budgetary reductions imposed under the authority of a new *Taiko* that captures many of the recommendations of the 1994 Defense Advisory Commission Report. However, in the context of a healthy and developing relationship between Japanese and American forces in Japan, the coming years could see slow, but steady, progress in learning how to work as a team in an uncertain and potentially dangerous period.

The 4 September 1995 rape of a twelve-year-old Okinawan girl by three U.S. servicemen underlines, however, the fundamental ambiguity of Japanese-U.S. relations. With Okinawans obviously angry at the continued presence of American troops on their islands, the incident catalyzed intense opposition to the continued presence of U.S. Forces. Immediate apologies from the president, secretary of defense, U.S. ambassador, and the local commanding officers dampened, but did not dissipate, the furor. Furthermore, demands for the immediate transfer of the accused marines and sailor soon gave way to calls for a fundamental review of the status of forces agreement with Japan, as well as demands for the removal of all U.S. forces and termination of the Security Treaty.[42] Okinawa's governor, Masahide Ota, used this unfortunate incident to maximize the case for reducing U.S. troops in his southern prefecture. Refusing to force landowners to renew leases for land used by U.S. forces, he embarked on a significant confrontation with Prime Minister Murayama and the Tokyo bureaucracy. Ultimately, his stance probably played a major role in Murayama's decision to step down on 5 January 1996.

Actually, the shock of the Okinawan rape incident coming only several months after the U.S.-Japanese confrontation over automobile trade issues did force attention on the details regarding the alliance. The Murayama Cabinet reportedly accomplished a serious review and update of the 1978 Guidelines for Security Cooperation in late November 1995.[43] The importance of the guidelines lies in its principle role in defining the nature of joint actions that U.S. and Japanese armed forces can take in the event of natural disaster or international conflict. The guidelines will supplement the new National Defense Program Outline (*Shin Taiko*) that the Cabinet approved in late November.

The draft guidelines note that one cannot dismiss "the possibility" of regional crises" in this unsettled era. In the event of a direct invasion of Japan, it provides for joint operations with the United States to "repel the invasion at the outset of hostilities." This is much clearer than the original version, now almost twenty years old, and it notes that in the event of regional situations threatening the peace and safety of Japan, "appropriate measures should be taken" in a smooth and effective manner. More importantly, it stresses a smooth and effective implementation of the U.S.-Japan security system. On an official level, at least, 1995 ended with a real attention to the details of the alliance. The U.S.-Japan security system had received a jolt from trade disputes and the irresponsible act of individuals, but it had not collapsed.

Koji Kakizawa, former Minister of Foreign Affairs during the Hata cabinet, compared the reaction of the Japanese electorate to the "no" delivered by Hosokawa to Clinton during the summit on trade issues to the general support the Imperial government received after its 1933 withdrawal from the League of Nations and the 1937 statement by Prime Minister Fuminaro Konoe that Japan would not deal with Chiang Kai-Shek.[44] Instead of building barriers with a "no," he believes Japan has a critical intermediary role in the international arena. He advocates that Japan "must make acting as a bridge between Asia and the West a basic plank of its foreign policy."

Not surprisingly in the post-Cold War environment, some Japanese, active in defining their country's future security course, place greater emphasis on the United Nations than on the U.S. relationship. In fact, some believe that only through active participation in the Security Council can Japan achieve its place as a "normal" nation. In speaking about Japan's future world role, Yasushi Akashi, special representative of the secretary general for UN operations in Yugoslavia noted: "Japan should no longer be content with living peacefully under the U.S. security umbrella. For the first time, Japan is faced with the tough task of finding its proper place in the international community."[45] In Akashi's opinion, Japan could find this proper place, alone or with a great deal less dependence on the United States. While support for the United Nations remains strong in Japan and is even a part of the 1947 Constitution, it is not clear that either the socialists or Sakigake would favor the elevation to permanent status in the Security Council. The United Nations itself has not reached consensus on Japan's elevation and the question of Security Council membership will probably remain unresolved.

How can Japan react to its imprecise and unpredictable environment, act in its own interests, and still maximize its international leverage? Increasing support for a meaningful multilateral organization in Northeast Asia may be one way. However, such an organization must have a definable mission, an operationally functioning infrastructure, and innovative leadership. The United States must also clearly be a supportive, engaged player. One approach would involve Japan in the assumption of a dynamic leadership role within

Northeast Asia, in an issue that involves all its neighbors, but especially those on the Korean Peninsula. Such an issue must meet a number of requirements. It cannot be militarily threatening to Japan's neighbors (or any state); it should be positive in all respects to reinforce Japan's image as a state concerned with the region's stability and security; it should involve an issue upon which most Japanese can agree; and, finally, if at all possible, it should involve an issue on which Japan has a unique perspective. Such an issue might be found in the controversy over nuclear proliferation facing all the states of Northeast Asia or in the need to foster a cooperative security regime for the region.

## Creating a Cooperation Security Regime in Northeast Asia: A Possible Framework for Japan's Creative Involvement in Asia

It is clear that Japan is increasingly interested in exploring possible missions for multilateral initiatives in Asia. Talks between ministry of foreign affairs and defense agency officials in Tokyo in July 1995 had turned to such areas. Within these organizations, the Japanese were forming cadres of key personnel. One such office within the internal bureau of the Japanese Defense Agency had received the charge to examine future multilateral options, including confidence-building measures to examine future multilateral options, including arms control initiatives. A commitment of such resources is not just a key indicator of a serious policy review, but indicates a willingness to act. Japan could assume a leadership role in implanting a limited nuclear-free zone in Northeast Asia in light of the need to reinforce and realize the nuclear accord with North Korea and ensure that Taiwan does not seek a nuclear option. That agreement could form the basis for a cooperative security community for Northeast Asia. Indeed, Prime Minister Murayama, in his 15 August statement apologizing for Japan's actions in World War II, clearly noted that Japan had no higher calling than contributing to the removal of nuclear weapons from the earth.[46]

### *Description of a Possible Initiative*

There have been many recommendations for nuclear-free zones in Northeast Asia. All too often these suggestions have reflected the tensions and confrontations of the Cold War and were advanced for self-serving reasons in the global contest between the Soviet Union and the United States. Most aimed at keeping the U.S. Seventh Fleet safely away from the Asian continent. Some, such as the proposal by the leader of the Japanese Socialist Party,

Takako Doi, incorporated vast areas of the North Pacific and would have been too extreme as a starting point. In any event, all these ideas were still-born because U.S. policy required at least the threat that it might use nuclear weapons in the region.

In September 1991, however, to facilitate the North-South nuclear talks on the Korean peninsula, and recognizing that the strategic needs for such weapons had waned, President George Bush withdrew tactical nuclear weapons from the American surface fleet and from operational land forces throughout the world. Not only did this gesture facilitate progress in demili-tarization talks on the Korean peninsula but it also then became feasible to address the question of further restriction on nuclear weapons in Northeast Asia. Hopes for involving China in serious arms control activities even sur-faced.

In early 1992, a proposal for a limited nuclear-free zone structured with a 1,200 NM radius centered on the DMZ of the Korean peninsula was pre-sented first in Washington, D.C. and then in Beijing. The proposal required removal of all nuclear weapons from within the zone, a pledge by non-nuclear states within the zone not to develop nuclear weapons, and creation of an agency with a verification force that would monitor all commitments. Thus, those states with nuclear weapons (Russia, China, the United States) would withdraw their nuclear weapons from the zone, while the non-nuclear area (Japan, South Korea, North Korea, Mongolia, and Taiwan) would not develop nuclear weapons themselves. All were to participate in a regional agency that would mutually inspect and verify the treaty's accords. In the process, daily working-level contacts between administrators and inspectors of the agency would create the trust required to carry out the program with a spirit of cooperation. A new security community would begin to emerge. The concept, in essence, would become a confidence-building measure leading to a degree of regional cooperation historically unprecedented in Asia. It would also remain a focused endeavor using nuclear weapons to tie together former adversaries. The prospect for gradual expansion would exist, but the overall concept would be limited in all respects.

Japan's special nuclear experiences, the existing public infrastructure to encourage nonproliferation, the nuclear-free zone commitments of the Mayor of Hiroshima, and the special role then played by Prime Minister Murayama in updating the role of the Socialist Party all argue well for Japan's leadership. Throughout 1993 and 1994 the proposal has been presented to almost 1,000 government officials, military officers, academics, and the press in all areas within the region except North Korea. Furthermore, members of the North Korean delegation to the United Nations have been briefed and kept "in the loop" to insure that all possible parties are fully informed of this initiative.

## Major Review

In January 1995, a group of security experts assembled in Atlanta to address this issue and consider all aspects of the existing nuclear-free zone proposal. Five specialists in Northeast Asian security matters, General Jae Chang Kim (former vice chairman of the South Korean JCS), Lt. General Toshiyuki Shikata (former commander of the Northern Army, Japan), Maj. General V. Bunin (former director of the Center for Japanese and Korean Studies at the Institute of Far Eastern Studies of the Russian Academy of Sciences), Dr. Xue-tong Yan, (deputy director, Chinese Institute for Contemporary Affairs), and the author (former director, Institute for National Strategic Studies, Washington, D.C.) met for five weeks to discuss the concept and draw up recommendations for its implementation. The group represented individuals with significant experience in the strategic field who remain actively involved in the policy process of their respective countries.

The senior panel recommended that a major international conference with participants from the area meet as an interim agency to decide on various aspects of the initiative. The senior panel also made several significant recommendations on the size of the zone, the weapons included, the verification system to be employed, and the location of the agency that it hoped would be endorsed during official negotiations. Discussions indicated, though, that a zone that included approximately 75 percent of all of China's deployed nuclear weapons would, at the outset, impose too great a restriction on the Chinese, while relieving the U.S. mainland of any nuclear threat from China. The participants also argued that any system that includes the United States as a major partner would have to be linked to U.S. territory. The panel created a modified zone that would move its western boundary eastward—still retaining a portion of Chinese territory—and its eastern boundary across the Sea of Lkhotsk to include a portion of Alaska. With no agreement on weapons with significant range, the senior panel examined the other end of the weapons spectrum and recommended that tactical nuclear warheads should fall under the ban. Such items as mines, artillery-fired nuclear shells, and short-range ballistic missiles or bombs dropped by tactical aircraft were weapons about which the participants could agree.

In order to create a verification system for tactical weapons under the observation of the Agency of the Limited Nuclear Free Zone, the senior panel traveled to the Sandia National Laboratory in New Mexico. There, experts recommended a simple system with off-site monitoring that would serve as a way to start the process of inspection and control. The senior panel also agreed that an administrative body, responsible for oversight, would be required. Indeed, this body, probably located in Japan at Hiroshima or another suitable site, would be the most significant contribution to the building of a cooperative security community. This organization would assume special significance as it would become the first operational regional institution in Northeast Asia with a permanent infrastructure, such as a secretariat and a professional verification force. While the specifics of the zone would need resolution by international dialogue (hopefully by an interim agency), such an organization would represent a major step in the realization of a security community. Nor would the economic repercussions be negligible. With such a community, economic development programs such as the Tumen River Project might make the progress development specialists had originally desired.

Japan is central to the success of such a concept. The Limited Nuclear Free Zone becomes more than just another commitment by Japan to a future free from nuclear weapons; it becomes the bridge, not only to the West, but to those neighbors once so alienated from Japan that full trust is still elusive. Its participation would end the speculation in Asia that Japan will create nuclear weapons from the more than eight tons of plutonium to which it has access. There are few events that would be so destablizing to East Asia as a Japanese decision to build a nuclear weapon. Even though its reprocessing program is under full safeguards, leaders of the region still fear Japanese power. Japan's leadership in a Limited Nuclear-Free Zone would demonstrate its good intentions, while providing the necessary start-up facilities and funding for further measures. Fundamental to the success of such a measure is the active participation of the United States. In the deliberations of the senior panel, the participants adamantly agreed that U.S. participation and continued U.S. bilateral commitments to South Korea and Japan were necessary. Its members saw the United States as vital to regional stability during the transition to an actual cooperative security regime in Northeast Asia. Those who point to historical political differences in the region and predict failure for such a concept must recognize that reducing the threat of nuclear war was what finally brought the United States and the Soviet Union into serious negotiations.

Much work has been done to realize a Limited Nuclear-Free Zone in Northeast Asia, but as all recognize, much more remains to be done.[47] Ultimately, there is no insurmountable reason why nuclear arms control, nuclear arms reduction, and, eventually, nuclear arms elimination should not appear on the official agendas of all the nations of East Asia. Japan has a unique duty among states to begin the process for the eventual elimination of nuclear weapons. However, in addressing this duty it must realize that only in a step-by-step manner can it achieve the goal. The region still harbors too much distrust, maintains too much animosity, and has too many unresolved security issues to remove all nuclear weapons in the immediate future. A gradual process must begin with a narrowly focused program in which all parties learn to trust over time. Then, and only then, will it be possible to put out the flame of Hiroshima.

As Japan looks to the future, it must grasp this concept of gradual regional confidence building. It will likewise be up to the other states to acknowledge that all stand to gain from such an enterprise. With ever-increasing interest in the security opportunities achieved by regional multilateralism, one may be optimistic that such an initiative may indeed be the way Japan defines its role in the twenty-first century. Japan will continue to honor its Peace Constitution, its partnership with the United States, its role with the United Nations, and its contribution to the world by being a developed techno-industrial superpower dedicated to peace.

# Endnotes

## Introduction
## Learning Nothing From the Past

1. *The Economist,* January 27–February 2, 1996, p.19.

2. Unless, of course, one believes that even Saddam Hussein would be so stupid as to repeat the errors that he made so egregiously in the 1990–1991 period.

3. See Gérard Prunier, *The Rwanda Crisis: History of a Genocide* (New York, 1995) and Alain Destexhe, *Rwanda and Genocide in the Twentieth Century* (New York, 1995) See also David Rieff, "An Age of Genocide," *The New Republic,* 29 January 1996. We might note that the same thing that happened in Rwanda is about to break out in Burundi.

4. The United States may not have another 1983 Beriut on its hands, but do not be surprised if it does.

5. See Brian R Sullivan, "American Strategic Policy for an Uncertain Future," *Brassey's Mershon American Defense Annual, 1995–1996,* ed. by Williamson Murray (Washington, DC, 1995), pp. 34–35. See also Paul Kennedy, *Preparing for the Twenty First Century* (London, 1994).

6. Allan R Millett and Williamson Murray, "Lessons of War," *The National Interest,* Winter 1988/1999, p. 85.

7. The contrast between the assessments in 1990 of US. intelligence and diplomatic on one side (based largely on ahistorical conceptualizations of the Middle East arena) and Samir al-Khalil's book, *The Republic of Fear, The Politics of Modern Iraq* (Berkeley, 1989) suggests the gulf between U.S. knowledge of the external world and the reality. But then al-Khalil obviously knows and understands western and Arab cultures, literature, ideologies, and histories so that he possessed insight into what was going on in Iraq. The failure to topple Saddam since the Gulf War and the Clinton administration's response to Iraq's attempt to blow up a former president of the United States—a response that aimed at killing janitors rather than perpetrators—

underlines our lack of understanding. For Iraq's efforts to achieve other great deeds against America see Laurie Mylroie, "The World Trade Center Bomb—Who is Ramzi Yousef? Why It Matters," *The National Interest*, Winter 1995/1996.

8. For the actual situation in Bosnia see Samantha Power, "River Phoenix," *The New Republic*, 26 February 1996, pp. 11–12.

9. For that history, see among others Iro Andric, *The Bridge on the Driwa* (Chicago, 1977).

10. For an excellent short survey of East Asia's prospects and perils see, "Asian Security, Asia's Wobble," *The Economist*, 23 December 1995–5 January 1996, pp.35–37.

11. See in particular Harold Moore and Joseph Galloway, *We Were Soldiers Once..and Young* (New York, 1994).

12. The words are a direct quote from Admiral William Owens' column, "System-of-Systems, US' Emerging Dominant Battlefield Awareness Promises to Dissipate the 'Fog of War,'" *Armed Forces Journal International*, January 1996.

13. Off the record conversation, fall 1995.

14. For the factors and parameters within which states develop strategy see Williamson Murray and MacGregor Knox, *The Making of Strategy: Rulers, States, and War* (Cambridge, 1994).

15. For a sense of the immensity of the literature see the footnotes in Gerhard Weinberg's *A World at Arms: A Global History of World War II* (Cambridge, 1994) as well as the bibliography in my *The Change in the European Balance of Power: The Path to Ruin* (Princeton, NJ, 1984).

16. There are, of course, exceptions. Christopher Thorne, after his perceptive and thorough examination of the origins of the European war in the late 1960s (Christopher Thorne, *The Approach of War, 1938–1939* [London, 1969]) turned his attention to the origins and the course of the war in Asia in a series of masterful works: Christopher Thorne, *The Limits of Foreign Policy, The West, the League, and the Far Eastern Crisis of 1931–1933* (New York, 1972) and *Allies of a Kind, The United States, Britain, and the War against Japan, 1941–1945* (New York, 1978). One should also mention that the dean of strategic historians, Gerhard Weinberg, has managed to put the Pacific and European wars and their origins into a brilliantly researched and thought out whole. See Weinberg, *A World at Arms*.

17. For a fascinating look at a portion of the deeper, more complex causes of the War in Asia see Authur Waldron, *From War to Nationalism: China's Turning Point, 1924–1925* (Cambridge, 1995).

18. This factor represents a long tradition in Chinese history. See in particular Authur Waldron, "Chinese Strategy from the Fourteenth to the Seventeenth Centuries," in *The Making of Strategy*.

19. See the article by Arthur Waldron on China's difficulties and possibilities in this issue.

20. See "Don't Even Think about It," *The Economist*, 3 February 1996, p. 13.

21. Conversation with Andrew Marshall, Director of Net Assessment, summer 1992.

22. For the line that international trade will fix all the difficulties between the United States and China—just as it did those between Britain and Germany in the period before World War I—see Jeffrey E. Garten, "Power Couple," *The New York Times*, January 15, 1996. Garten was Under Secretary of Commerce in the Clinton administration's early days and is presently the Dean of the Yale School of Management—an institution where undoubtedly history has never appeared.

23. The paper presented by Christopher Donnelly on the future of Russia's defense policy is particularly good in this regard. Christopher Donnelly, "The Future of Russian National Security Policy and Military Strategy: The Nuclear and Conventional Dimension," unpub-

lished paper presented at the Tri-Service Defence Conference on "British Security in 2010—The Role of the British Armed Forces in the First Decade of the 21st Century," Church House, 16–17 November 1996. See also Michael Specter, "Red Flag Aloft, a Russian City Defiantly Upholds Soviet Ways," *The New York Times*, 3 February 1996, pp. 1A, 4A.

24. See John Gaddis, "International Relations Theory and the End of the Cold War," *International Security*, Winter 1992/1993.

25. For comments on these issues see MacGregor Knox, "What History Can Tell Us About the 'New Strategic Environment,'" *The Brassey's Mershon American Defense Annual, 1995–1996* (Washington, DC, 1995), pp. 5–6.

26. Clausewitz was certainly not read by the Germans. See the comment made by the panzer general and member of the general staff, Leo Geyer von Schweppenburg, to Liddell Hart after World War II in Williamson Murray, *German Military Effectiveness* (Baltimore, MD, 1992), p. 11.

27. See Barry Watt's chapter "Friction in Future War" in this volume.

28. See in particular: Allan Beyerchen, "Clausewitz, Nonlinearity, and the Unpredictability of War," *International Security*, Winter 1992/1993.

29. Owens, "System-of-Systems," p. 47.

30. Even if the technocrats are right and we can—in Admiral Owens' words—"destroy[our enemy] or his operational scheme from greater and greater distances with finer and finer precision," they miss entirely the political penalty that may well come from a world in which public opinion molded by CNN pictures of Americans slaughtering Iraqis from outer space at no danger to themselves would turn entirely against the United States. We have already seen the American reaction to such a situation in the Gulf War, where even a senior American airman remarked that the war had degenerated into "beating a tethered goat." We make war not as we would like to, but rather as the political context dictates.

31. See the essay by Barry Watts in this volume.

32. Off the record conversation with Department of Defense official, January 1996.

33. CJCSI 180001, 3 January 1996, Chairman of the Joint Chiefs of Staff Instruction.

34. Department of the Air Force, "New World Vistas, Air and Space Power for the 21st Century," Summary Volume, USAF Scientific Board, 15 December 1995, p. 6.

35. Ibid., p. 11.

36. For a discussion of the intellectual content of that relatively short iteration of AFM 1-1 see Williamson Murray, *German Military Effectiveness* (Baltimore, MD, 1992), chapt 5.

37. Carl von Clausewitz, *On War*, ed. and trans. by Michael Howard and Peter Paret (Princeton, NJ, 1976), p. 141.

38. Ibid., p. 168.

39. Ibid., p. 134.

40. Ibid., p. 136. As Clausewitz suggested a few pages later in his discussions about theory: "[Theory] is an analytic investigation leading to a close *acquaintance* with the subject; applied to experience—in our case military history—it leads to thorough *familiarity* with it. The closer it comes to that goal, the more it proceeds from the objective form of a science to the subjective form of a skill, the more effective it will prove in areas where the nature of the case admits no arbiter but talent." (Ibid., p. 141.)

41. Owens, "Systems of Systems," p. 47.

42. See Williamson Murray, *Operations*, report 1, *Gulf War Air Power Survey*, vol 2, *Operations and Effectiveness* (Washington, DC, 1993), pp. 30–31. See also Williamson Murray with Wayne Thompson, *Air War in the Persian Gulf* (Baltimore, MD, 1995), pp. 28–29.

43. See in particular, Lt Gen. John H. Cushman, "The Military Owes the President(s) More," *Proceedings*, July 1995, pp. 8–10 for the importance of military insight.

44. On the problem of strategic surprise see Michael Handel, "Intelligence and the Problem of Strategic Surprise," *Journal of Strategic Studies*, September 1984, pp. 229–281.

45. In the immediate aftermath of the Gulf War a group of marine generals stood on an Iraqi bunker that remained largely undamaged, but which had fallen with few casualties. One general, like the others a veteran of the Vietnam War quietly commented: "We were lucky we were not fighting North Vietnamese." Conversation with Lt. Gen. Paul Van Riper, Commander Marine Corps Combat Development Command, October 1995.

46. See among others on deception in World War II, Michael Handel, ed., *Strategic and Operational Deception in the Second World War* (London, 1987). For the best overall account of intelligence on the Allied side see F. H. Hinsley, et al., *British Intelligence in the second World War: Its Influences on Strategy and Operations*, five vols. (London, 1979–1990).

47. I am indebted to Lt. Col. Jim Rodgers, USAF, a student at the Marine Corps War College, for extending my thinking on the implications of the World War II experience for information war.

48. See in particular Gordon Welchman, *The Hut Six Story, Breaking the Enigma Codes* (New York, 1982), especially pp. 163–169.

49. This was particularly true in regards to the war at sea. See Hinsley, *British Intelligence in the Second World War*, vol. 2, pp. 177, 179, 230, 553; and especially Patrick Beesley, *Very Special Intelligence: The Story of the Admiralty's Operational Intelligence Centre, 1939–1945* (New York, 1978), pp. 168–169.

50. See particularly Beesley, *Very Special Intelligence*; and John Winton, *Ultra at Sea: How Breaking the Nazi Code Affected Allied Naval Strategy During World War II* (New York, 1988).

51. See J.C. Masterman, *The Double-Cross System in the War of 1939 to 1945* (New Haven, CT, 1972); and Hinsley, *British Intelligence in the Second World War*, vol. 5, Michael Howard, *Strategic Deception* (New York, 1990).

52. The memoirs on the British intelligence effort in World War II are particularly good on this point. On the works already cited see among many others: Peter Calvocoressi, *The Ultra Secret* (New York, 1980); Aileen Clayton, *The Enemy is Listening* (London, 1980); and particularly R.V. Jones, *The Wizard War: British Scientific Intelligence, 1939–1945* (New York, 1978).

53. For a clear warning in this regard see: Charles J. Dunlop, Jr., "How We Lost the High Tech War of 2007, A Warning from the Future," *The Weekly Standard*, 29 January 1996.

54. Murray, *Air War in the Persian Gulf*, pp. 298–301.

55. Dale Eisman, "Navy Brass Shows Off First 'Super Hornet,'" *The Virginian Pilot*, 19 September 1995, p. 1.

56. Colonel David Deptula, "Background Paper on the F/A-18E/F," Commission on Roles and Missions, January 1995.

57. Ibid.

58. Ibid.

59. Steve Uehling, "The Latest F–18 Could Hurt the Navy," *Air Force Times*, 2 October 1995, p. 36.

60. Ibid.

61. Deptula, "Background Paper on the F/A-18E/F." There is an additional reason why the E/F with its more powerful engines is attractive over the C/D. Under most conditions the latter cannot hack landing back on carriers with bombs on board. This means dumping them in the sea; with dumb bombs the costs do not mean a great deal. But in an era of pgms, which cost a great deal more, the navy cannot afford to dump them in the sea when targets are obscure.

62. James P. Stevenson, "The F/A-18E/F: Scamming the Acquisition System," Business Executives for National Security Issue Brief, February 1996.

63. Uehling, "The Latest F-18 Could Hurt the Navy," *Air Force Times*, 2 October 1995, p. 36.

64. Stevenson, "The F/A-18E/F: Scamming the Acquisition System."

65. Uehling, "The Latest F-18 Could Hurt the Navy," p. 36.

66. Ibid.

67. Senator John McCain, Business Executives for National Security Forum, Washington, DC, 4 May 1994.

68. That was certainly the feeling among a number of RAF officers that this author talked to at the "Tri-Services Defence Conference" in London, November 1995.

69. Deptula, "Backgound Paper on F/A-18E/F."

# Chapter 1
# The Great 1996 Non-Debate on National Security

1. *Democratic Fact Book: Issues for 1992*, June 1992, p. 318.

2. "Threats to American Goals and Interests: When Is a Military Response Necessary?," *The Defense Monitor*, 4, 1995, p. 2.

3. David C. Morrison, "Defense Deadlock," *National Journal*, 4 February 1995, p. 276.

4. Dick Amery, "The National Security Restoration Act: HR. 7," HRC *Legislative Digest*, 27 September 1994.

5. Dick Cheney, "Defense: Inadequate Strategy, Inadequate Resources," *The Washington Times*, 4 November 1994, p. 21.

6. Richard K Betts, *Military Readiness* (Washington, DC, 1995), p. 205.

7. Les Aspin, "National Security in the 1990s: Defining a New Basis for US. Military Forces," speech and paper presented to the Atlantic Council, 6 January 1992, p. 2.

8. Ibid., p. 4.

9. Ibid., p. 4.

10. Ibid., p. 7.

11. Mike Moore, "More Security for Less Money," *Bulletin of the Atomic Scientists*, 25 August 1995, p. 33.

12. Lauren Spain, "The Competition has Bowed Out," *Bulletin of the Atomic Scientists*, 25 August 1995, p. 37.

13. "Is More Money Needed for New Weapons?," *The Defense Monitor*, 24: 6 July 1995, p. 6.

14. Lawrence J Korb. "The Overstuffed Armed Forces," *Foreign Affairs*, November/December 1995, p. 23.

15. Ibid.

16. Ibid.

17. Ibid., p. 117.

18. Ibid.

19. David C Morrison, "Defense Deadlock," p. 276.

20. Lauren Spain, "The Competition Has Bowed Out," p. 37.

21. David C Morrison, "Ready for What?," *National Journal*, 20 May 1995, p. 1221.

22. Ibid.

23. Bradley, Graham, and Harris, "Army's Combat Readiness Is Overstated, Perry Admits," *The Washington Post*, 16 November 1995, p. 1A.

24. Morrison, "Ready for What?," p. 1221.

25. Pat Towell, "Concerns About Readiness Fuel Battle Over Budget," *Congressional Quarterly*, 3 January 1995, p. 3614.

26. David Isenberg, "The Misleading Military Readiness Crisis," *Foreign Policy Briefing*, The Cato Institute, no. 35, 25 July 1995, p. 2.

27. Morrison, "Ready for What?," p. 1219.

28. Isenberg, "The Misleading Military Readiness Crisis," p. 3.

29. Tony Cappaccio, "A Battle Over the Readiness Crisis," *Defense Week*, 27 February 1995, p. 5.

30. Ibid.

31. Morrison, "Ready for What?," p. 1220.

32. Ibid., p. 1222.

33. Ibid., p. 1221.

34. Ibid., p. 1220.

35. Caleb Baker, "Fund Contingencies, Save Training," *Defense News*, 6–12 March 1995, p. 19.

36. Isenberg, "The Misleading Military Readiness Crisis," p. 10.

37. Bradley Graham, "Pentagon Leaders Urge Accelerated 50 Percent Bonus in Procurement," *The Washington Post*, 11 November 1995, p. A12.

38. Steven M Kosiak, "Analysis of the Fiscal Year 1996 Defense Budget Request," *The Defense Budget Project*, March 1995, p. 13.

39. James Kitfield, "The Last Superpower," *Government Executive*, December 1994, p. 19.

40. Senator Richard G. Lugar, "Opening Statement," Committee on Foreign Relations, 22 August 1995.

41. "Lugar for President," World Wide Web, http://www.iquest.net/lugar/security/htm.

42. Senator Sam Nunn, "Opening Statement," Senate Permanent Subcommittee on Investigation, 31 October 1995.

43. Samuel P. Huntington, "The Clash of Civilizations," *Foreign Affairs*, 72: 3, 1993.

44. Paul Kennedy, *Preparing for the 21st Century* (New York, 1993).

45. Staff Statement, Senate Permanent Subcommittee on Investigations, "Hearings on Global Proliferation of Weapons of Mass Destruction," 31 October 1995.

46. Kyle B Olson, "Statement Before Senate Permanent Subcommittee on Investigations," Hearings on Global Proliferation of Weapons of Mass Destruction, 31 October 1995.

47. Staff Statement, "Hearings on Global Proliferation of Weapons of Mass Destruction."

48. "Russian Security Inadequate for Chemical Weapons Storage," Agency France Presse, 2 August 1995, p. 4.

49. Vil S. Mirzayanov, Statement before Senate Permanent Subcommittee on Investigations, 1 November 1995.

50. U.S. Department of Energy, Office of Intelligence and National Security, Office of Threat Assessment, "The Russian Mafia," 15 November 1993.

51. "The High Price of Freeing Markets," *The Economist*, 19 February 1994, citing Jonathan Dean, "The Fine State of Arms Control," Union of Concerned Scientists, 21 May 1994.

52. Dr David Osias, Statement before the Senate Foreign Relations Committee, 22 August 1995.

53. Amanda Bichsel, "How the GOP learned to Love the Bomb," *The Washington Monthly*, October 1995, p. 27.

54. John Barry, "Future Shock," *Newsweek*, 24 July 1995, p. 33.

55. Dr. David Oehler, Director, Non-Proliferation Center, Central Intelligence Agency, Statement before the Senate Armed Services Committee, 31 January 1995.

56. Dr. Thomas B. Cochran, Statement before the Senate Committee on Foreign Relations, 23 August 1995.

57. Ibid., p. 3.

58. Graham T Allison, et al., Statement before Senate Committee on Foreign Relations, 22 August 1995.

59. Ibid., p. 3.

60. Barry, "Future Shock."

61. Matthew McCandless, Business Executives for National Security, "White Paper," November 1995.

62. Ibid., p. 4.

63. Dr. Thomas B. Cochran, Speech Given to the American Bar Association Conference on Non-Proliferation of Weapons of Mass Destruction, 11 June 1994.

64. Dunbar Lockwood, "The Nunn-Lugar Program: No Time to Pull the Plug," *Arms Control Today*, June 1995, p. 8.

65. Associated Press, "Russia Needs More Nuclear Arms Control, Panel Says," *The Washington Post*, 24 August 1995, p. 22.

66. Tara Sonenshine, "US Swipe at Terrorism Misses the Mark," *The Boston Globe*, 23 March 1995, p. 19.

67. Allison, et al., Statement before the Senate Committee on Foreign Relations, p. 7.

68. "The Cost of a Vote," *The Economist*, 2 September 1995, p. 26.

69. Council for a Livable World, "Defense Appropriations Conference Report," 14 November 1995.

70. Col. Dave Deptula, "Still No Bomber Strategy," White Paper for the Commission on Roles and Missions, 11 May 1995.

71. Jeff Record, "B-2 Smells of Rancid Pork," *Defense Week*, 6 November 1995, p. 8.

72. Council for a Livable World, "Senate Armed Services Fiscal 1996 DoD Authorization Bill," 31 July 1995.

73. David Evans, "The FY 1996 Military Construction Budget," Business Executives for National Security Point Paper, 28 July 1995.

74. David Evans, "Business as Usual," *Proceedings*, October 1995, p. 13.

75. Ibid.

76. Senator John McCain, "Cut the Pork and Beef up Defense," *The Wall Street Journal*, 9 March 1995, p. 18.

77. Senator John McCain," Defense Pork, Even a Hawk Would Choke on It," *The Washington Post*, 26 October 1995, p. A16.

78. David C. Morrison, "Defense Deadlock," *The National Journal*, 4 February 1995, p. 277.

79. Associated Press, "Chechens Say They Planted Radioactive Lode in Moscow," *The Washington Post*, 24 November 1995, p. A34.

80. Ibid., p. A1.

## Chapter 2
## Reengineering U.S. Intelligence

1. The discussion of recent and future trends in the business world comes from the author's experiences as a management consultant and four recent books: Michael Hammer and James Champy, *Reengineering the Corporation* (New York, 1993), Gary Hamel and C.K. Prahalad, *Competing for the Future, Breakthrough Strategies for Seizing Control of Your Industry and Creating the Markets of Tomorrow* (Cambridge, MA, 1994), Hamish McRae, *The World in 2020, Power, Culture, and Prosperity* (Cambridge, MA, 1994), and Charles Hardy, *The Age of Paradox* (Cambridge, MA, 1994).

2. This is the main theme of Hamel and Prahalad's book, *Competing for the Future*. See also Deborah Dougherty and Edward N. Bowman, "The Effects of Organizational and Downsizing on Product Innovation," *California Management Review*, 37:4, Summer 1995. This article stresses the damage done by radical, unfocused downsizing to the informal networks in companies that often promote innovation.

3. One example of the philosophy behind this approach is a methodology developed by Stephen M. Millett, Andrew Messina, and others for use by Battelle Memorial Institute's Technology Management Group in support of commercial projects. It stresses that for a technology to be strategic, customers must see and value it in the products they buy; it must contain some sustainable technical or other advantage (patents, skilled personnel, proprietary processes); and it must support the company's broader strategic goals. See Stephen M Millett, "STEPUP, The Strategic Technology Evaluation, Planning, and Utilization Procedure," Battelle paper, 1994.

4. Joseph N. Nye, "Estimating the Future," in Roy Godson et al., eds., *US Intelligence at the Crossroads: Agendas for Reform*, (Washington, DC, 1995), p. 90.

5. For the World War II SIGINT effort, start with F. H. Hinsley, et al., *British Intelligence in the Second World War*, 5 vols. (London, 1979–1992). Christopher Andrew, *For the President's Eyes Only* (New York, 1995), highlights the key role SIGINT has played in top level decision making since World War II. For an overview of current U.S. intelligence collection capabilities and Cold War intelligence relationships between Washington and its allies see Jeffrey Ritchelson, *The US Intelligence Community*, 3rd edition (Washington, 1995), and *The Ties That Bind* (Washington, 1988).

6. For information on the Corona program see Kevin C. Ruffner, *Corona: America's First Satellite Program* (Washington, DC, 1995). For a good overview of the warning problem prior to the Gulf War and IMINT's role, see the first chapter, "War by Miscalculation," of Michael Gordon and Bernard E. Trainor, *The Generals' War: The Inside Story of the Conflict in the Gulf* (New York, 1995).

7. Recent revelations that the previously super-secret National Reconnaissance Office (NRO) has been hoarding large amounts of cash and has built itself a palatial headquarters in Washington's Virginia suburbs will not make the defense of future budgets for overhead reconnaissance systems any easier.

8. Following the Gulf War, even some friendly powers, desirous of breaking the U.S. monopoly on overhead reconnaissance information, accelerated their own programs. In summer 1995, a French-Italian-Spanish consortium launched an imaging satellite (Helios-IA) which reportedly could provide images with a resolution of about three feet. According to press sources, Helios' lack of all-weather and near real-time transmission capabilities makes it less sophisticated than the latest U.S. systems but France is attempting to obtain German support for a new generation of satellites with infra-red and radar imaging systems. See "Arianespace

Successfully Orbited Europe's First Spy Satellite, Helios-IA, and Two Secondary Payloads Friday from the Guiana Space Center in Kourou," *Defense Daily*, 188, 4, p. 32, 10 July 1995, and "France: Seeking German Involvement with Helios and Horus Reconnaissance Programs," *Defense News*, 10 July 1995, p. 1.

9. See Roger Hilsman, "Does the CIA Still Have a Role?," *Foreign Affairs*, September/October, 1995, pages 104–116. See also Stansfield Turner, *Secrecy and Democracy: The CIA in Transition* (New York, 1985).

10. For a fascinating account of the Iraqi deception effort, see David Kay, "Denial and Deception, The Lessons of Iraq," in *US Intelligence at the Crossroads*.

11. Statement by David Christian, CIA Public Affairs Office, to author, August 1995.

12. Gordon and Trainor, *The Generals' War*, chapter 1. Nye, "Estimating the Future," notes many of these failures. See also, Richard Betts, *Surprise Attack*, (Washington, DC, 1982). For an interesting assessment of the Reagan/Bush policy toward Iraq, see Bruce W. Jentileson, *With Friends Like These: Reagan, Bush and Saddam, 1982–1990* (New York, 1994).

13. Ibid.

14. Greater suspicion of Iraqi motives among intelligence analysts might have led to more detailed scrutiny of Baghdad's continued conventional buildup as well as the state of its program to develop weapons of mass destruction, and the impact of a deteriorating economy on Saddam's willingness to take risks. For an excellent overview of how a determined and ruthless totalitarian regime can upset such wishful thinking, again see David Kay, "Denial and Deception: The Lessons of Iraq," in Godson, *US Intelligence at the Crossroads*.

15. The author recalls trudging into the Agency on several occasions to write a piece for the current publications simply because someone had seen something interesting in the overnight *Post* or *Times* and thought CIA had better comment on it. Whether the agency had anything unique to add seemed incidental.

16. For additional comments on current intelligence, see Jay T. Young, "US Intelligence Assessment in a Changing World: The Need for Reform," *Intelligence and National Security*, April 1993, pp. 125–139.

17. See Young, "US Intelligence Assessment in a Changing World," for a more detailed description of this process as it existed in 1991, when the author left the agency. Another analyst who left soon after had similar comments on DI's bizarre practices: Richard J. Russell, "CIA: A Cold War Relic?," *International Journal of Intelligence and Counterintelligence*, Spring 1995, pp. 11–18.

18. Douglas J. MacEachin, "The Tradecraft of Analysis," in Godson, et. al., *US Intelligence at the Crossroads*.

19. Nye, "Estimating the Future."

20. See Mark P. Lagon, "The Illusion of Collective Security," in *The National Interest*, 40, 1995, pp. 51–55, for a trenchant critique of some of the stranger intellectual excesses of those who accept the broader definition of security.

21. The Japanese case was far more serious than the French fiasco. According to the press, the intelligence community mounted a major effort to determine Japanese intentions during automobile import negotiations in early 1995. This effort included substantial eavesdropping on Japanese Foreign Ministry communications, and, presumably, extensive tapping of human sources. According to one senior US official, however, the intelligence received was of little value: "But in the end did it help much? Beyond some valuable detail we could have not gotten elsewhere, did it tell us much about which way Hashimoto (the Japanese Foreign Minister) would go? It would be hard to make that case." See David E. Sanger and Tim Weiner, "Emerging Role for the CIA: Economic Spy," *New York Times*, 2 October 1995, page A1.

22. For an intelligent discussion, see Randall M. Fort, "Economic Espionage," in Godson, *US Intelligence at the Crossroads*.

23. John H. Hedley, *Checklist for the Future of Intelligence* (Washington, DC, 1995).

24. Ibid.

25. For commentary on the RMA, see James R. Fitzsimmons, "Intelligence and the Revolution in Military Affairs," in Godson, *US Intelligence at the Crossroads*, pp. 265–287; "The Software Revolution: A Survey of Defence Technology," *The Economist*, 10 June 1995; and a series of articles on defense and technology in *National Review*, 31 July 1995, especially Eliot A. Cohen, "Come the Revolution," pp. 26–30. For an overview of OSD Net Assessment's work, see Thomas E. Ricks, "Warning Shot: How Wars are Fought Will Change Radically, Pentagon Planner Says," *Wall Street Journal*, 15 July 1994, p. 1.

26. Thomas A. Keaney and Eliot A. Cohen, *Gulf War Air Power Survey Summary Report* (Washington, DC, 1993), p. 248. For some interesting commentary on what the vastly improved intelligence now available may do to the nature of war and the role of the commander, see John Ferris and Michael I. Handel, "Clausewitz, Intelligence, Uncertainty, and the Art of Command in Military Operations," in *Intelligence and National Security*, January 1995, pp. 1–58.

27. The preceding draws heavily on Fitzsimmons, "Intelligence and the Revolution in Military Affairs." See the *Gulf War Air Power Survey Summary Report*, chapter 4, for discussion of the problems caused by an inadequate prewar database on Iraq.

28. Ibid.

29. Recent reporting suggests that systems with some of these capabilities may now be emerging. For example, to support operations in Bosnia, NSA has organized SIGINT information into a central database that permits local commanders quickly to retrieve data on electronic transmissions in areas where their troops may be operating. What is not clear is what, if any, analysis accompanies this information. See "All Eyes Are Set on Bosnia: Spying Prowess at a High Level, US Officials Say," *Navy Times*, 5 February 1996, p. 27.

30. *Gulf War Airpower Survey*, Chapter 4.

31. Edward Luttwak, "Post Heroic Warfare," *Foreign Affairs*, May/June 1995, pp. 109–122.

32. On Ames, see David Wise, *Nightmover: How Aldrich Ames Sold the CIA to the KGB for $4.6 million* (New York, 1995). For Angleton's bizarre story and its effect on the Agency see Tom Mangold, *Cold Warrior: James Jesus Angleton, The CIA's Master Spy Hunter* (New York, 1991).

33. CIA spokesman David Christian to author, August 1995. For the report of a recent DOD commission on security see *Redefining Security, A Report by the Joint Security Commission*, 28 February 1994.

34. The Georgetown group also made this recommendation.

35. Roy Godson, "Covert Action: Neither Exceptional Tool Nor Magic Bullet," in *US Intelligence at the Crossroads*, p. 156.

36. May commentary on Godson paper in *US Intelligence*, pp. 173–177.

38. See Patrick Neil Mescall, "A Creature of Compromise: The Establishment of the DIA," *International Journal of Intelligence and Counterintelligence*, Fall 1994, pp. 251–274.

38. In one instance, however, improved coordination by CIA with the military appears to have helped ensure more timely delivery of HUMINT to the field. According to a recent report, "A CIA agent in Bosnia...recently obtained information spelling out the procedures used by one of the warring parties when laying mines...The CIA has astonished military intelligence officials with a new willingness to cooperate with the Defense Department in Bosnia...." *Navy Times*, 5 February 1996. If the main thrust of Deutch's efforts is to improve

delivery of sensitive HUMINT to field commanders, then they may prove worthwhile. What remains unclear is exactly what other roles the new liaison offices are performing and whether they might be more properly (and effectively) carried out by service intelligence elements.

39. Hedley, *Checklist for the Future of Intelligence*, pp. 10–13.

40. See Tim Weiner, "Tainted Items Sent By CIA Are Put At 95," *New York Times*, 10 November 1995.

41. See Tim Weiner, "Breaking With the Past," *New York Times*, 28 September 1995, p. A1.

42. See "Spooking the Director," *Newsweek*, 6 November 1995, p. 42.

43. For example, during the 1980s, CIA offered only one introductory course in military analysis whose length and rigor progressively declined following the course's inception in 1984.

44. The degree of substantive expertise varies greatly from office to office. During the author's time in the Office of African and Latin American Analysis, there was a fairly large number of trained historians and other specialists—but also many junior personnel, especially economists, with little understanding of regional socio-political peculiarities. The office did not, however, always place a high value on some of its best specialists, while others rapidly evolved into astute bureaucratic careerists once they realized that promotion depended far more on volume of production than on further substantive development and unique analysis.

45. On the economy, see, for example, Georges Sokoloff, "Sources of Soviet Power: Economy, Population, Resources," in *Prospects for Soviet Power in the 1980s*, part I, Adelphi Paper 151 (London, 1979) pp. 30–36; and William Hyland, "Soviet Security Concerns in the 1980s," in part 2, pp. 18–23. Both cite an influential CIA report issued in April 1977, *Soviet Economic Problems and Prospects*, ER 77–10436U, which indicated that the USSR would face major economic problems in the 1980s, to bolster their own assessments that, "...the Soviet Union faces grave economic problems in the 1980s..." (Sokoloff, p. 35). For assessments on Soviet Military Power, see Donald P. Steury, ed., *Estimates on Soviet Military Power, 1954–1984: A Selection*, CIA Center for the Study of Intelligence, December 1994.

46. "CIA and the Fall of the Soviet Empire: The Politics of `Getting It Right'," Kennedy School of Government, Case Program, Case C16-94-1251.0, 1994, pp. 38–41.

47. Ibid., pp. 66–67.

48. Ibid., p. 12.

49. Nye, "Estimating the Future," and especially Angelo Codeveilla, *Informing Statecraft: Intelligence for a New Century* (New York, 1992). Walter Lacquer, *The Dream That Failed: Reflections on the Soviet Union* (New York, 1994) and Abbot Gleason, *Totalitarianism: The Inner History of the Cold War* (New York, 1995) respectively dissect the failures of Sovietology and analyze the mental gymnastics performed by Western intellectuals about whether the USSR was truly totalitarian. See also Robert Conquest, "The Useful Idiots: How Communism Collapsed and How Its Converts Were Deceived and Deceiving," *Times Literary Supplement*, 2 June 1995, p. 5.

50. Recently, DI took an important first step by abolishing its current training courses, but what will replace them is unclear.

51. A recent, extended conversation with an old friend who is now a branch chief at CIA sparked some of these thoughts. This individual, who appears to be one of the few people at CIA aware of the extent of the managerial/technology revolution underway in the commercial world, is worried that recent efforts to reform the system, especially the training program, may be slowing down.

## Chapter 3
## Friction in Future War

1. Hans Rothfels quoted in Peter Paret, *Clausewitz and the State: The Man, His Theories, and His Times* (Princeton, NJ, 1976), p. 124, note 3.

2. Carl von Clausewitz, *On War*, trans. by Peter Paret and Michael Howard (Princeton, NJ, 1976), p. 119.

3. See, for example, the March 1992 edition of *Air Force Manual 1-1: Basic Aerospace Doctrine of the United States Air Force*, vol. 1, p. 2; and U.S. Marine Corps, *Warfighting*, FMFM 1, March 1989, pp. 4–7.

4. See: "[Admiral William A.] Owens Says Technology May Lift 'Fog of War': Breakthroughs Could Give Forces Total Command of Future Battlefield," *Inside the Navy*, 23 January 1995, p. 3. Also see Admiral William A. Owens, "System-of-Systems: US Emerging Battlefield Awareness Promises to Dissipate the 'Fog of War'." *Armed Forces Journal International*, January 1996, p. 47.

5. Michael J. Mazarr, et al., "The Military Technical Revolution: A Structural Framework," Center for Strategic and International Studies, March 1993, p. 58.

6. Paret, *Clausewitz and the State*, p. 124.

7. Michael Howard, *Clausewitz* (Oxford, 1983), pp. 14 and 16; and Carl von Clausewitz, *Historical and Political Writings*, ed. and trans. Peter Paret and Daniel Moran (Princeton, NJ, 1992), pp. 63 and 73–75.

8. Quoted in Paret, *Clausewitz and the State*, p. 71; see also Clausewitz, *Historical and Political Writings*, p. 90.

9. Quoted in Paret, *Clausewitz and the State*, p. 191.

10. Ibid., *Clausewitz and the State*, pp. 197–198.

11. Ibid., p. 202.

12. Ibid., p. 256; Clausewitz, *On War*, p. 119.

13. Clausewitz, *On War*, p. 65.

14. Paret, *Clausewitz and the State*, p. 202. Chapters 5–8, *On War*, indicate the diverse factors that distinguish real war from war on paper and include war's intense physical demands, its mortal danger, pervasive uncertainties, and the play given to chance in battlefield processes.

15. Clausewitz, *On War*, p. 70.

16. Ibid., p. 77.

17. Ibid., p. 78.

18. Ibid., p. 86.

19. Ibid., p. 119.

20. Ibid., pp. 120 and 579.

21. Ibid., p. 104.

22. Ibid., p. 122.

23. Ibid., pp. 114, 115, 117, and 119.

24. See Lt. Gen. Harold G. Moore and Joseph L. Galloway, *We Were Soldiers Once...And Young* (New York, 1992); and Avigdor Kahalani, *The Heights of Courage: A Tank Leader's War on the Golan* (Westport, CT, 1984).

25. Clausewitz, *On War*, p. 117.

26. Ibid., pp. 84–85.

27. Paret, *Clausewitz and the State*, p. 373.

28. John G. Hines and Daniel Calingaert, "Soviet Strategic Intentions, 1973–1985: A Preliminary Review of U.S. Interpretations," RAND Working Draft WD-6305-NA, December 1992, pp. 4–7.

29. Clausewitz, *On War*, pp. 139 and 149.

30. Ibid., pp. 605–608.

31. Quoted in Charles Edward White, "The Enlightened Soldier: Scharnhorst and the *Militärische Gesellschaft* in Berlin, 1801–1805," Ph.D. Dissertation, Duke University, 1986, pp. 43–44.

32. Clausewitz, *On War*, pp. 100–103 and 122.

33. Clausewitz, *On War*, pp. 17, 167, 198, 407–408, and 560. John Boyd has long criticized Clausewitz for focusing almost exclusively on reducing one's own (internal) friction and failing to explore the rich possibilities for "magnifying [the] adversary's friction/uncertainty" (John R. Boyd, "Patterns of Conflict," briefing dated April/June/July 1979, Slide 24; in the December 1986 version of this briefing, see slide 41). Boyd is right.

34. Clausewitz, *On War*, pp. 119 and 120.

35. The author was the task-force chief for the operations and effects volume of the Gulf War Air Power Survey. The survey was commissioned by Secretary of the Air Force Donald B. Rice in August 1991 and directed by Eliot A. Cohen.

36. Gulf War Air Power Survey, "Missions" Database, ATO [Air Tasking Order] Day 3, entries for the 48th Fighter Wing.

37. Thomas A. Keaney and Eliot A. Cohen, *Gulf War Air Power Survey: Summary Report* (Washington, DC, 1993), p. 16.

38. See Richard J. Blanchfield, et al., *The Gulf War Air Power Survey*, vol. 4, *Weapons, Tactics, and Training and Space Operations* (Washington, DC, 1993), Part I, *Weapons, Tactics, and Training*, p. 86.

39. Clausewitz, *On War*, p. 120.

40. Barry D. Watts and Thomas A. Keaney, *The Gulf War Air Power Survey*, vol. 2, *Operations and Effects and Effectiveness* (Washington, DC, 1993), Part II, *Effects and Effectiveness*, pp. 388–389.

41. Major General Buster C. Glosson, Gulf War Air Power Survey interview, 14 April 1992.

42. Haywood S. Hansell, Jr., *The Air Plan that Defeated Hitler* (Atlanta, GA, 1972), p. 121.

43. Watts and Keaney, Part II, *Effects and Effectiveness*, p. 111.

44. Ibid., p. 109.

45. Major Lewis D. Hill, et al., *The Gulf War Air Power Survey*, vol. 5, *A Statistical Compendium and Chronology* (Washington, DC, 1993), Part I, *A Statistical Compendium* p. 241.

46. Watts and Keaney, Part II, *Effects and Effectiveness*, pp. 125–126.

47. Ibid., p. 129.

48. Norman Cigar, "Iraq's Strategic Mindset and the Gulf War: Blueprint for Defeat," *The Journal of Strategic Studies*, March 1992, pp. 3–5, 14–16, and 18–20.

49. Watts and Keaney, Part II, *Effects and Effectiveness*, pp. 239–240.

50. George Bush, "Address to the Nation Announcing the Deployment of United States Armed Forces to Saudi Arabia," 8 August 1990, in *Public Papers of the Presidents of the United States: George Bush, 1990*, vol. 2, book II, *1 July to 31 December 1990* (Washington, DC, 1991), p. 1108.

51. DoD, *Conduct of the Persian Gulf War* (Washington, DC, 1992), p. 95.

52. Watts and Keaney, Part II, *Effects and Effectiveness*, vol. 2, p. 79.

53. In fact the Iraqis were very close to having a bomb, but this was only discovered *after the war*. See particularly David A. Kay, "Denial and Deception Practices of the WMD Proliferators: Iraq and Beyond," *The Washington Quarterly*, Winter 1995, p. 85.

54. Postwar inspections eventually uncovered some thirty-nine nuclear facilities at nineteen different geographic locations in Iraq, while as late as 27/28 February U.S. Intelligence was holding only eight nuclear targets, of which supposedly five were destroyed and two damaged. See United Nations Security Council, "Report of the Seventh IAEA On-Site Inspection in Iraq under Security Council Resolution 687 (1991): 11–22 October 1991," Report S/23215, 14 November 1991, pp. 8 and 63; and "J-2/JCS Daily Briefing BDA Assessment: Operation Desert Storm," GWAPS NA 353, briefing slides for 27/28 February 1991.

55. Watts and Keaney, Part II, *Effects and Effectiveness*, pp. 314–315.

56. Rolf Ekeus, United Nations Security Council, Report S/23165, 25 October 1991, "Annex: Report by the Executive Chairman of the Special Commission Established by the Secretary General Pursuant to Paragraph 9 (b)(i) of Security Council Resolution 687 (1991)," p. 4.

57. Kay, "Denial and Deception Practices of WMD Proliferators: Iraq and Beyond," pp. 87–98.

58. David Kay, letter to Barry D. Watts, 20 October 1992, GWAPS, NA-375.

59. Revealing insofar as general friction's persistence is concerned, General H. Norman Schwarzkopf still believed as of the publication date of his memoirs in 1992 that the coalition had destroyed the Iraqi nuclear program during Desert Storm. See H. Norman Schwarzkopf with Peter Petre, *The Autobiography: It Doesn't Take a Hero* (New York, 1992), p. 499.

60. Michael R. Gordon and General Bernard E. Trainor, *The General's War: The Inside Story of the Conflict in the Gulf* (New York, 1995), pp. 304, 371, and 376.

61. Brigadier General Robert H. Scales, Jr., *Certain Victory: The United States Army in the Gulf War* (Washington, DC, 1993), pp. 216–223.

62. Richard M. Swain, *"Lucky War:" Third Army in Desert Storm* (Leavenworth, KS, 1994), p. 230; see also Schwarzkopf, *The Autobiography*, pp. 453–454.

63. Gordon and Trainor, *The General's War*, p. 379; Swain, *"Lucky War,"* pp. 236–237.

64. Swain, *"Lucky War,"* p. 238.

65. Lieutenant General John H. Cushman, "Desert Storm's End Game," *Proceedings*, October 1993, p. 76.

66. As of 1 March 1991, some 840 tanks (at least 365 of which were Republican Guard T-72s), 1,412 other armored vehicles (mostly armored personnel carriers), and 279 artillery pieces of various types were still in Iraqi hands. Central Intelligence Agency, Office of Imagery Analysis, "Operation Desert Storm: A Snapshot of the Battlefield," IA 93-10022, September 1993.

67. Swain, *"Lucky War,"* p. 250.

68. CIA, "Operation Desert Storm: A Snapshot of the Battlefield," IA 93-10022.

69. Op. cit. Cushman, pp. 76 and 80.

70. See BDM Corporation, "Generals Balck and von Mellenthin on Tactics: Implications for NATO Military Doctrine," BDM/W-81-399-TR, 1 July 1981, pp. 26, 31–32, and 39; also, Hanson W. Baldwin, *Tiger Jack* (Fort Collins, CO, 1979), pp. 39–46 and 61–69.

71. Schwarzkopf, *The Autobiography*, pp. 384 and 499.

72. For accounts of friction in the campaign, see Robert Allen Doughty, *The Breaking Point: Sedan and the Fall of France, 1940* (Hamden, CT, 1990); and Telford Taylor, *The March of Conquest* (New York, 1958).

73. Jules Henri Poincaré was perhaps the first to develop a rigorous basis for believing that physical systems could exhibit long-term unpredictability (Ian Stewart, *Does God Play Dice? The Mathematics of Chaos* [Oxford, 1989], pp. 64–72). However, the significance of Poincaré's work "was fully understood only in 1954, as a work of the Russian academician A. N. Kolmogorov, with later additions by two other Russians, Vladimir Arnold and J. Moser" (John

Briggs and F. David Peat, *Turbulent Mirror: An Illustrated Guide to Chaos Theory and the Science of Wholeness* [New York, 1990], pp. 41–42).

74. "The greatest obstacle to the establishment of the theory of evolution was the fact that evolution cannot be observed directly like the phenomena of physics...or any other process that takes place in seconds, minutes, or hours during which the ongoing changes can be carefully recorded." (Ernst Mayr, *The Growth of Biological Thought: Diversity, Evolution, and Inheritance* [Cambridge, MA, 1982], p. 310).

75. The terms "adaptive" and "adaptation" are used in John Holland's expansive sense of encompassing the algorithmic information processing and search problems that "occur at critical points in fields as diverse as evolution, ecology, psychology, economic planning, control, artificial intelligence, computational mathematics, sampling, and inference." John H. Holland, *Adaptation in Natural and Artificial Systems: An Introductory Analysis with Applications to Biology, Control, and Artificial Intelligence* (Cambridge, MA, 1992), p. 1.

76. F.A. Hayek, *The Collected Works of F.A. Hayek*, ed. by W.W. Bartley III, vol. 1, *The Fatal Conceit: The Errors of Socialism* (Chicago, 1988), p. 7.

77. "In Praise of Hayek," *The Economist*, 28 March 1992, p. 75.

78. Hayek, *The Fatal Conceit*, p. 14.

79. Ibid., pp. 29–30.

80. Ibid., p. 31.

81. Ibid., p. 42.

82. Ibid., p. 77.

83. Ibid., p. 84.

84. Ibid., p. 71.

85. Hayek did not, of course, claim that the extended order associated with capitalist or market economies produced anything approaching a *perfect* allocation and use of resources, only that the "order generated without design can far outstrip plans men consciously contrive." (*The Fatal Conceit*, p. 8).

86. Ibid., p. 62. For additional evidence that definite limits to human knowledge exist in a variety of fields, see: Kurt Gödel, "On Formally Undecidable Propositions in *Principia Mathematica* and Related Systems I," *From Frege to Gödel: A Source Book in Mathematical Logic, 1879–1931*, ed. Jean van Heijenoort (Cambridge, MA, 1967), pp. 595–616; Ian Stewart, "The Ultimate in Undecidability," *Nature*, 10 March 1988, p. 115; G.J. Chaitin, *Information, Randomness, and Incompleteness: Papers on Algorithmic Information Theory* (London, 1990), especially pp. 14–19 and 307–313; Edward N. Lorenz, "Deterministic Nonperiodic Flow," in Hao Bai-Lin, *Chaos* (Singapore, 1984), particularly pp. 282–293; and Philip E. Ross, "Lorenz's Butterfly: Weather Forecasters Grapple with the Limits of Accuracy," *Scientific American*, September 1990, p. 42.

87. Hayek, *The Fatal Conceit*, p. 98.

88. Ibid., p. 97.

89. Daniel C. Dennett, *Darwin's Dangerous Idea: Evolution and the Meanings of Life* (New York, 1995), p. 97.

90. Ibid., p. 98.

91. Ibid., pp. 99 and 103. "Species have an extension in space and time; they are structured and consist of populations which, at least in part (when they are isolated), are independent of each other" (Mayr, *The Growth of Biological Thought*, p. 408). Put another way, the boundaries between species are surprisingly fuzzy, spatially as well as temporally (Richard Dawkins, *The Blind Watchmaker: Why the Evidence of Evolution Reveals a Universe without Design* (New York, 1987), pp. 262–267).

92. For lucid introductions to the structure, dimensionality, and vastness of biological "design space," see Dennett, *Darwin's Dangerous Ideas*, chapter 5, pp. 104–123; also Dawkins, *The Blind Watchmaker*, chapters 3 and 4, pp. 43–109.

93. R. Jeffrey Smith, "U.N. Says Iraqis Prepared Germ Weapons in Gulf War," *The Washington Post*, 26 August 1995, p. A1.

94. See Colonel James G. Burton, "Pushing Them Out the Back Door," *Proceedings*, June 1993, pp. 37–42; Lt. Gen. Ronald H. Griffith, "Mission Accomplished—In Full," *Proceedings*, August 1993, pp. 64–65; Maj. Gen. Paul E. Funk, *Proceedings*, September 1993, pp. 22 and 24; and Col. James G. Burton, *Proceedings*, November 1993, pp. 19–25.

95. As philosopher Daniel Dennett has noted regarding the nuclear incident at Three Mile Island, we cannot yet say whether the meltdown was a good thing or a bad thing The problem is not one "of insufficiently *precise* measurement, we can't even determine the *sign*, positive or negative, of the value to assign to the outcome" (*Darwin's Dangerous Idea*, p. 498).

96. John Boyd has been especially clear that the orientation following observation in his observation-decision-action cycle is "shaped by genetic heritage, cultural tradition, previous experiences, and unfolding circumstances" ("Organic Design for Command and Control," May 1987, Slide 13).

97. See Michael Polanyi, *Knowledge and Being*, ed. by Marjorie Grene (Chicago, 1969), pp. 123, 133–134, 164, 212, and 218.

98. For a recent account of how the brain works based on current research, see Daniel Dennett, *Consciousness Explained* (Boston, 1991), pp. 253–256.

99. Charles Darwin, *The Origins of the Species by Means of Natural Selection* in *Great Books of the Western World*, ed. Robert M. Hutchins (Chicago, 1952), vol. 49, p. 239.

100. Dennett, *Darwin's Dangerous Idea*, p. 19.

101. Stephen Jay Gould, "The Evolution of Life on Earth," *Scientific American*, October 1994, p. 85.

102. Richard Dawkins, "Darwin Triumphant: Darwinism as Universal Truth," in *Man and Beast Revisited*, eds. Michael H. Robinson and Lionel Tiger (Washington, 1991), p. 38.

103. Swain, *"Lucky War,"* p. 300.

104. Ibid., pp. 300–301.

105. The loss of focus, particularly on leadership targets, that became evident toward the end of the first week of the air campaign among coalition air planners in (then) Brig. Gen. Glosson's planning cell indicates that the frictional problems Swain highlighted in the case of coalition ground operations surfaced among airmen as well.

106. John Boyd deserves credit for reminding the author that mechanized forces such as German panzer units in World War II were able to sustain offensive operations longer than four days by allowing participants to "cat nap" at every opportunity.

107. Lionel Tiger, "The Cerebral Bridge from Family to Foe," in *Sociobiology and Conflict: Evolutionary Perspectives on Cooperation, Violence, and Warfare*, ed. by J. Von Der Dennan and V. Flager (London, 1990), p. 103.

108. This formulation was consciously patterned on John Boyd's observation-orientation-decision-action "cycle" or "loop."

109. Robin Fox, "Aggression: Then and Now," in *Man and Beast Revisited*, p. 89.

110. Isaac Newton, *Mathematical Principles of Natural Philosophy*, in *Great Books of the Western World*, vol. 34, p. 14.

111. Mayr, *The Growth of Biological Thought*, p. 33. In key instances in which biological and physical thought conflicted, as in William Thomson's calculation that the age of the earth had to be several orders of magnitude less than the "several thousand million years" postulated

by Darwin, the biologists turned out to be right and the physicists wrong (ibid., p. 428). As Mayr has also noted, the skepticism about evolution expressed to him by physicists as prominent as Niels Bohr and Wolfgang Pauli seems to have been based in no small part on an "oversimplified understanding of the biological processes involved in evolution." (ibid., p. 429).

112. For a summary of the main facts and generalizations that constituted Darwin's original theory of evolution by natural selection, see Mayr, *The Growth of Biological Thought*, pp. 479–480. For the main principles of neo-Darwinian population genetics, see ibid., p. 551.

113. Michael Scriven, "Explanation and Prediction in Evolutionary Theory," *Science*, 28 August 1959, p. 477.

114. Henri Poincaré, *Science and Method*, trans. Francis Maitland (New York, 1952), pp. 15–24.

115. Stewart, *Does God Play Dice?*, pp. 116–118.

116. Ibid., p. 87.

117. Alan Beyerchen, "Clausewitz, Nonlinearity, and the Unpredictability of War," *International Security*, Winter 1992/1993, pp. 87–88.

118. Heinz-Otto Peitgen, et al., *Chaos and Fractals: New Frontiers of Science* (New York, 1992), pp. 585–587; also Stewart, *Does God Play Dice?*, pp. 155–164. For a rigorous treatment of the logistic mapping (alias the "quadratic iterator"), see chapter 11 in Peitgen, et al., *Chaos and Fractals*. As Peitgen and his colleagues note, the final-state or "Feigenbaum diagram" (after the physicist Mitchell Feigenbaum) for the logistic mapping "has become the most important icon of chaos theory" (Ibid., p. 587). *Mathematica*'s built-in function Nestlist renders the research mathematics needed for a basic understanding of the logistic mapping almost trivial. However the same calculations can be carried out on a calculator like the Hewlett Packard HP-48SX.

119. For a discussion of Boscovich, see John D. Barrow, *Theories of Everything: The Quest for the Ultimate Explanation* (New York, 1991), pp. 24–27 and p. 54.

120. R. Harré, "Laplace, Pierre Simon de," *The Encyclopedia of Philosophy*, ed. by Paul Edwards (New York, 1967), vol. 4, p. 392.

121. Isaac Newton, *Optics in Great Books of the Western World*, vol. 34, p. 542; also, Richard S. Westfall, *Never at Rest: A Biography of Isaac Newton* (New York, 1980), pp. 777–778.

122. Harré, "Laplace, Pierre Simon de," p. 392.

123. Pierre Simon de Laplace, "Concerning Probability," *The World of Mathematics: A Small Library of the Literature of Mathematics from A'h-mosé the Scribe to Albert Einstein* (Redmond, WA, 1988), vol. 2, p. 1301.

124. David Ruelle, *Chance and Chaos* (Princeton, NJ, 1991), pp. 45–47.

125. Westfall, *Never at Rest*, p. 430.

126. Ibid., p. 540.

127. Ibid., p. 543.

128. The history of mathematics is littered with impossible problems. For example, see Howard DeLong, *A Profile of Mathematical Logic* (New York, 1970), pp. 29, 69, 195, and 200. The "impossibility" associated with Newton's three-body problem is somewhat different from mathematical cases such as the logical impossibility of trisecting an angle with ruler-and-compass constructions. The impossibility Newton faced with the three-body problem is not that there are no solutions at all, or even no stable ones, but that in certain regimes the dynamics become so unstable that future states of the system cannot be predicted even approximately.

129. Laplace in James R. Newman, "Commentary on Pierre Simon de Laplace," *The World of Mathematics*, vol. 2, p. 1293.

130. Tony Rothman, "God Takes a Nap: A Computer Finds that Pluto's Orbit Is Chaotic," *Scientific American*, October 1988, p. 20.

131. Gerald Jay Sussman and Jack Wisdom, "Numerical Evidence that the Motion of Pluto Is Chaotic," *Science*, 22 July 1988, p. 433; also Sussman and Wisdom, "Chaotic Evolution of the Solar System," *Science*, 3 July 1992, p. 56.

132. Stewart, *Does God Play Dice?*, pp. 70–72.

133. James P. Crutchfield, et al., "Chaos," *Scientific American*, December 1986, p. 46.

134. Bai-Lin, *Chaos*, pp. 67–71.

135. Clausewitz, *On War*, pp. 85 and 86.

136. Ibid., p. 119.

137. John R. Boyd, "Conceptual Spiral," unpublished briefing, July–August 1992, Slides 14 and 31. Boyd details nine features of the various systems and processes we use to make sense of the world that, unavoidably, generated mismatches or differences, whether large or small, in initial or later conditions. These futures include: the numerical imprecision inherent in using the rational and irrational numbers in calculations and measurement; mutations arising from replication errors or other unknown influences in molecular and evolutionary biology; and the ambiguities of meaning built into the use of languages like English or German, as well as the interactions between them through translations (Ibid., Slide 32).

138. Clausewitz, *On War*, p. 139.

139. See J.A. Dewar, J.J. Gillogly, and M.L. Juncosa, "Non-Monotonicity, Chaos, and Combat Models," RAND Corporation, R-3995-RC, 1991, p. iii.

140. Roberta Wohlstetter, *Pearl Harbor: Warning and Decision* (Stanford, CA, 1962), p. 397.

141. Lt. Col. Ed Felker, "Information Warfare: A View of the Future," *A Common Perspective: Joint Warfighting Center's Newsletter*, September 1995, p. 18.

142. Larry Lynn, "Battlefield Dominance and ARPA Focus," Advanced Research Projects Agency (ARPA) memorandum, 29 June 1995, p. 2.

143. Paul Carrol, *Big Blues: The Unmaking of IBM* (New York, 1993), pp. 217–222, 325–328, and 347. IBM executives had ample warning of the changes that would restructure their industry. "They commissioned months-long task forces with loads of smart people and forecasted the changes in the market that would cripple IBM, but IBMers couldn't quite bring themselves to do anything about those cataclysmic changes" (Ibid., p. 3).

144. Andrew Marshall provided this anecdote.

145. "A Survey of Telecommunications: The Death of Distance," *The Economist*, 30 September, 1995, p. 28.

146. Martin van Creveld, *The Transformation of War* (New York, 1991), pp. ix–x, 2, 29, 62, and 224–225.

147. Ibid., p. 245.

148. Richard Simpkin, *Race to the Swift: Thoughts on Twenty-First Century Warfare* (London, 1985), p. 106.

149. Rudolf Clausius formulated the second law as the principle that "No process in which the *sole result* is the transfer of energy from a cooler body to a hotter body" (Peter W. Atkins, *The Second Law* [New York, 1984], p. 25). Entropy, whose unit of measurement is energy/temperature, was introduced to label the manner in which energy is stored in thermodynamic systems (ibid., p. 38). A more modern statement of the second law is that if an isolated system in thermodynamic equilibrium has a state function, $S$, which is the entropy or degree of disorder of the system, then $dS/dt \geq 0$ (Grégoire Nicolis and Ilya Prigogine, *Exploring Complexity: An Introduction* [New York, 1989], pp. 61–62). In the 1940s, Claude Shannon's early work on infor-

mation theory revealed that information, understood as a measure of one's freedom of choice when selecting a message, has the same form as Boltzmann's famous equation for entropy (Claude E. Shannon and Warren Weaver, *The Mathematical Theory of Communication* [Urbana, IL, 1949], pp. 9, 27, and 48–53). Perhaps more than anything else, it was John Boyd's appreciation of this connection between information (in the sense of uncertainty) and entropy (of disorder) that led him to connect Clausewitzian friction with the second law of thermodynamics.

# Chapter 4
# Rethinking the "Ould" Alliance: Europe and the United States after the Cold War

1. William Wallace, "British Foreign Policy after the Cold War," *International Affairs*, 68:3, 1992, p. 427.

2. Raymond G H. Seitz, "Britain and America: toward Strategic Coincidence," *The World Today*, 49:5, 1993, p. 88.

3. François Heisbourg, "The European-US. Alliance: Valedictory Reflections on Continental Drift in the post-Cold War Era," *International Affairs*, 68:4, 1993, p. 88.

4. Michael Smith, "The Devil You Know: the United States and a Changing European Community," *International Affairs*, 68:1, 1992, pp. 103–120.

5. Michael Brenner, "The EC in Yugoslavia: a Debut Performance," *Security Studies*, 1:4, 1992, p. 604.

6. James E Goodby, "Collective Security in Europe after the Cold War," *Journal of International Affairs*, 146:2, 1993, p. 300.

7. The development of the Victory Programme in 1941 is instructive in tracing the definition of America's national interest. See Mark S. Watson, *Chief of Staff: Prewar Plans and Preparations* (Washington, DC, 1974), pp. 338–357; Charles E. Kirkpatrick, *An Unknown Future and a Doubtful Present: Writing the Victory Plan of 1941* (Washington, DC, 1990), pp. 61–63.

8. For Atlanticist definitions, see Zbigniew Brzezinski, "A Plan for Europe," *Foreign Affairs*, 74:1, 1995, p. 26; Richard Holbrooke, "America, A European Power," *Foreign Affairs*, 74:2, 1995, p. 38.

9. Peter Rudolf, "The Strategic Debate in the USA—Implications for the American Role in Europe," *Aussenpolitik*, 44:2, 1993, p. 113.

10. Seitz, "Britain and America: towards Strategic Coincidence," p. 88.

11. Pierre Shostal, "Reviewing the US-European Relationship," *Parameters*, 24:4, 1994, p. 49.

12. Linda Miller, "The Clinton Years: Reinventing US. Foreign Policy," *International Affairs*, 70:4, 1994, p. 631.

13. Charles L Glaser, "Why NATO is Still Best," *International Security*, 18:1, 1993, pp. 5–50

14. Michael Mandelbaum, "Preserving the New Peace: The Case Against NATO Expansion," *Foreign Affairs*, 74:3, 1995, p. 12.

15. Brzezinski, "A Plan for Europe," p. 27.

16. George Szamuely, "Clinton's Clumsy Encounter with the World," *Orbis*, 38:3, 1994, pp. 281–283.

17. Jeff Newnham, "New Constraints for US. Foreign Policy," *The World Today*, 51:4, 1994, pp. 72–74.

18. Arthur Schlesinger, Jr, "Back to the Womb? Isolationism's Renewed Threat," *Foreign Affairs*, 74:4, 1995, p. 6.

19. Quoted in Szamuely, "Clinton's Clumsy Encounter with the World," p. 376.

20. Michael Smith and Stephen Woolcock, "Learning to Cooperate: The Clinton Administration and the European Union," *International Affairs*, 70:3, 1994, p. 461.

21. Miller, "The Clinton Years: Rewriting US. Foreign Policy," pp. 629–30.

22. Georg Schild, "America's Foreign Policy Pragmatism," *Aussenpolitik*, 46:1, 1995, p. 37.

23. Glaser, "Why NATO is Still Best," p. 47.

24. Heisbourg, "The European-US. Alliance: Valedictory Reflections of Continental Drift in the post-Cold War Era," pp. 667–668.

25. Edward Mortimer, "European Security after the Cold War," Adelphi Paper 271, 1992, p. 52.

26. Johan Jorgen Holst, "European and Atlantic Security in the Period of Ambiguity," *The World Today*, 48:12, 1992, p. 220.

27. For what follows, see Mathias Jopp, "The Strategic Implications of European Integration," Adelphi Paper 290, 1994, pp. 26–30.

28. Mortimer, "European Security after the Cold War," p. 63.

29. William T Johnson and Thomas-Durrell Young, "France and NATO: The Image and the Reality," *Parameters*, 24:4, 1994, pp. 26–30.

30. Reinhand Meier-Weiser, "Germany, France and Britain on the Threshold to a New Europe," *Aussenpolitik*, 43:4, 1992, p. 338.

31. Michael Sutton, "Chirac's Foreign Policy: Continuity—with Adjustment," *The World Today*, 51:7, 1995, p. 138.

32. Christoph Bluth, "Germany: Defining the National Interest," *The World Today*, 51:3, 1995, p. 54.

33. Lothar Guttjahr, "Stability, Integration, and Global Responsibility: Germany's Changing Perspectives on National Interest," *Review of International Studies*, 21:3, 1995, p. 316.

34. Quoted in Beatrice Heuser, "European Defense before and after the 'Turn of the Tide'," *Review of International Studies*, 19:4, 1993, p. 416.

35. Guttjahr, "Stability, Integration, and Global Responsibility," p. 316.

36. Douglas Hurd, "Deepening the Common and Foreign Security Policy," *International Affairs*, 70:3, 1994, pp. 421–429.

37. Christopher Coker, "Britain and the New World Order," *International Affairs*, 68:3, 1992, p. 413.

38. William Wallace, "British Foreign Policy after the Cold War," *International Affairs*, 68:3, 1992, p. 429.

39. Beatrice Hauser, "Containing Uncertainty—Options for British Nuclear Strategy," *Review of International Studies*, 19:3, 1993, pp. 245–269.

40. Lawrence Freedman, "Alliance and the British Way in Warfare," *Review of International Studies*, 21:2, 1995, pp. 145–148.

## Chapter 5
## The United States and Asian Security

1. Although the author is a specialist in the history of American military policy, he has familiarized himself with Asian security affairs for the last decade and is now writing a comprehensive history of the Korean War. Since 1986 he has visited India, Singapore, Australia, Thailand, Vietnam, Hong Kong, the Republic of Korea, and Japan. In 1991 he was a Fulbright Distinguished Visiting Professor at the Korean National Defense University and has returned to Seoul every year since then. In 1995 he also served as a visiting professor at the Australian Defence Academy, Canberra. In 1993 and 1995 he received command briefings at Headquarters, U.S. Pacific Command and has discussed Korean contingencies with three different J-5s, Combined Forces Command, Korea. The views expressed in this essay, however, do not represent the official positions of any organization or individual within any of the military establishments the author has visited, but he wants to thank his military friends of many nations for contributing to his education.

2. Rear Adm. John Rodgers, USN, to Secretary of the Navy George M. Robeson, "Capture and Destruction of Corean Forts," 5 July 1871, *Reports of the Secretary of the Navy 1871* (Washington, DC, 1871), pp. 279–284; Magistrate of Kanghwa, *Cultural Properties of Kanghwa-do Island* (Kanghwa Magistrate, Republic of Korea, 1989). The American casualties on Kanghwa-do were not the first in the Asia-Pacific region. One Marine (Pvt. Benjamin T. Brown) and one sailor (Seaman William P. Smith) died in a punitive expedition against Malay pirates at Quallah Battoo, Sumatra, on 7 February 1832, thus winning the distinction of becoming America's first combat deaths in Asia. Another sailor died in action in a raid on Shanghai, China, on 5 April 1854, and another at Fiji on 25 September 1855. In an engagement with forts barring the harbor of Canton, an American squadron lost six sailors killed in action 20–22 November 1856. In a similar engagement between three ships and six batteries of the Prince of Nagato, Shimonoseki Straits, Honshu, Japan, the steam frigate *Wyoming* (Commander D. MacDougall) lost one Marine and four sailors in combat on 16 June 1863. The most notable fatality was Lt. Cmdr. Alexander Slidell MacKenzie, USN, the son of a famous naval officer, who died leading a raiding party on Formosa on 13 June 1867. The action was supposed to avenge the murder of the crew of an American merchantmen, *Rover*. The navy and marine corps thus had lost one officer and fourteen enlisted men before the Kanghwa-do action in 1871.

3. *New York Times* and *Washington Post*, 17–31 December 1994.

4. Compiled from Department of Defense, *Defense 94: Almanac* (Washington, DC, 1994) and a casualty analysis compiled from US. military reports and summarized in Allan R. Millett and Peter Maslowski, *For the Common Defense: A Military History of the United States of America*, (rev. ed., New York, 1994), pp. 653–654.

5. For one attempt to catch all the nuances of the relationship, see Akira Iriye, *Across the Pacific: An Inner History of American-East Asia Relations* (rev. ed., Chicago, 1992).

6. Andrew C Nahm, *Korea: Tradition and Transformation: A History of the Korean People* (Seoul, 1993), pp. 150–152.

7. For a summary of the political development of the Asia-Pacific region since World War II, see International Institute for Strategic Studies, *Strategic Review*, issued annually since 1966 For a perceptive recent interpretation, see Paul Dibb, *Towards a New Balance of Power in Asia*, Adelphi Paper 295, 1995.

8. The official position on US. security concerns in Asia may be found in William J. Clinton, *A National Security Strategy of Engagement and Enlargement, 1994–1995* (London and Washington, DC, 1996); Office of International Security Affairs, Department of Defense, *United States Security Strategy for the East Asia-Pacific Region* (Washington, DC, 1995); Institute for National Strategic Studies, National Defense University, *Strategic Assessment 1995* (Washington, DC, 1995) and Adm. Richard C. Macke, USN, "A Commander in Chief Looks at East Asia," *Joint Forces Quarterly*, 7, Spring 1995, pp. 8–15. The author has also profited from CINCPAC plans and operations briefings at Camp H. M. Smith in 1991 and 1994. See also Dora Alves, ed., *New Perspectives for U.S.-Asia Pacific Security Strategy, Proceedings of the 1991 Pacific Symposium* (Washington, DC, 1992).

9. US. Pacific Command, *Asia-Pacific Economic Update, 1994*, provided the author by the Strategic Planning and Policy Directorate, Research and Analysis Division, J-5, USAPACOM, Camp H.M. Smith, Oahu, Hawaii. For the fundamentals of the argument of the "Japan First" argument, see Joseph S. Nye, Jr., "The Case for Deep Engagement," and Chalmers Johnson and E.B. Keehn, "The Pentagon's Ossified Strategy," *Foreign Affairs*, 74, July/August 1995, pp. 90–102 and 103–114.

10. Barry Buzan and Gerald Segal, "Rethinking East Asian Security," and Harry Harding, "On the Four Great Relationships: The Prospects of China," *Survival*, 36, Summer 1994, pp. 3–21 and 22–42. Ron Montaperto, "Managing U.S. Relations with China," *Strategic Forum*, 42, August 1995, Institute for Strategic Studies, National Defense University.

11. For contrasting views on the influence of ROK-US relations on Asian security issues, see Chalmers Johnson, "Korea and Our Asia Policy," *The National Interest*, 41, Fall 1995, pp. 66–67; Sang Hoon Park, "North Korea and the Challenge to the US-South Korean Alliance," *Survival*, 36, Summer 1994, pp. 78–91; George H. Quester, "America, Korea and Japan: The Crucial Triangle," *Journal of East Asian Affairs*, 9, Summer/Fall 1995, pp. 228–251.

12. The demographic analysis is drawn from the 1990 statistics summarized in Robert Famighetti, et al., *The World Alamanac and Book of Facts 1995* (Mahwah, NJ, 1995), pp. 374–378. The opinion data is drawn from "The World," *The New York Times*, 1 October 1995 and Chicago Council of Foreign Relations, *American Public Opinion and U.S. Foreign Policy 1995* (Waukegan, IL, 1995).

13. Mark J Valencia, *China and the South China Sea Disputes*, Adelphi Paper 298, 1995; Michael Mandelbaum, ed., *The Strategic Quadrangle: Russia, China, Japan, and the United States in East Asia* (New York, 1995).

14. Dibb, *Towards a New Balance of Power in Asia*, pp. 39–69; John Laffin, *The World in Conflict*, War Annual 6 (London and Washington, DC, 1994); Michael Kidron and Dan Smith, *The New State of War and Peace* (New York, 1991); PLA Senior Col. and Prof. Zhang Jingyi, "Korea to Kampuchea: The Changing Nature of Warfare in East Asia, 1950–1986," 28th Annual Conference, IISS, Kyoto, Japan, September 1986; Ruth Leger Sivard, *World Military and Social Expenditures, 1993* (Washington, DC, 1993), p. 21; Stockholm International Peace Research Institute, *SIPRI Yearbook 1994* (London, 1994), pp. 551–562; International Institute for Strategic Studies, *The Military Balance, 1995-1996* (London, 1995), pp. 168–198, 270–275.

15. International Institute for Strategic Studies, *Strategic Survey 1993–1994* (London and Washington, DC, 1994), pp. 145–190.

16. For one analysis, see Bruce W. Bennett, "The Prospects for Conventional Conflict on the Korean Peninsula," *Korean Journal of Defense Analysis*, 7, Summer 1995, pp. 95–127.

17. *New York Times*, 8 October 1995.

18. *Defense Almanac 94*, pp. 44–46; J-5 PACOM, "IMET," 1994 briefing paper; U.S. Department of Commerce, *Statistical Abstract of the United States 1994* (Washington, DC, 1994), pp. 183–187; Sivard, *World Military and Social Expenditures 1993*, pp. 42–51; Jeff Cole and Sarah Lubman, "Global Arms Market—Bombs Away," *Wall Street Journal*, 28 January 1994; Robert S. Greenberger, "Politics and Policy as Congress Sharpens Knives to Cut Foreign Aid," *Wall Street Journal*, 18 May 1995.

19. John W. Lewis and Hua Di, "China's Ballistic Missile Programs: Technologies, Strategies, Goals," and John R. Harvey, "Regional Ballistic Missiles and Advanced Strike Aircraft: Comparing Military Effectiveness," *International Security*, 17, Fall 1992, pp. 5–40 and 41–83; Bill Gerta, "Scud's Bigger Brothers," *Air Force*, June 1994, pp. 52–57; Robert Shuey, "Missile Proliferation," Congressional Research Service Report 90-120F, 21 February 1990, Congressional Research Service.

20. Jerome H. Kahan, *Nuclear Threats from Small States* (Carlisle, PA, 1994); Robert Blackwill and Albert Carnesale, eds., *Coping with New Nuclear Nations* (New York, 1994); Andrew Mack, "A Nuclear Free Zone for Northeast Asia," *Journal of East Asian Affairs*, 9, Summer/Fall 1995, pp. 288–322; Paul Brachen, "Nuclear Weapons and State Survival in North Korea," *Survival*, 35, Autumn 1993, pp. 137–151; Mark D. Mandeles, "Between a Rock and a Hard Place: Implications for the U.S. of Third World Nuclear Weapons and Ballistic Missile Proliferation," *Security Studies*, 1, Winter 1991, pp. 235–261; Jed C. Synder, "South Asian Security," Strategic Forum No.43, Institute for Strategic Studies/National Defense University; William C. Potter, "Before the Deluge? Assessing the Threat of Nuclear Leakage from the Post-Soviet States," *Arms Control Today*, 25, October 1995, pp. 9–16.

# Chapter 6
# China

1. This essay presents the personal views of the author and in no way represents the official position of the United States government.

2. For these see Arthur Waldron and Edward O'Dowd, eds., *Mao Tse-tung on Guerrilla Warfare*, trans. by Samuel B. Griffith (Baltimore, MD, 1992).

3. See Sun Tzu, *Sun Tzu: The Art of War*, trans. by Samuel B. Griffith (Oxford, 1963), p. 77.

4. See John Wilson Lewis and Xue Litai, *China Builds the Bomb* (Stanford, CA, 1988).

5. See Paul Beaver, "China Plans Its Great Leap Forward," *Jane's Navy International*, July–August 1995, p. 11.

6. See Michael Richardson, "East Asian Nations Race to Stock Up on an Array of High-Tech Weaponry," *International Herald-Tribune*, 13 October 1995, p. 4.

7. An excellent summary is provided by Kenneth W. Allen, Glenn Krumel, and Jonathan D. Pollack, *China's Air Force Enters The 21st Century* (Santa Monica, CA, 1995).

8. See ibid., pp. 130–131.

9. See David A Fulghum, "New Chinese Fighter Nears Prototyping," *Aviation Week & Space Technology*, 13 March 1995, pp. 26–27.

10. Allen, *China's Air Force Enters the 21st Century*, pp. xix–xx.

11. Patrick E Tyler, "China–U.S. Ties Warm a Bit as China-Taiwan Relations Chill," *New York Times*, 18 November 1995, p. A3.

12. For example, K C. Chang, *Art, Myth, and Ritual: the Path to Political Authority in Ancient China* (Cambridge, MA, 1983).

13. Mark Edward Lewis, *Sanctioned Violence in Early China* (Albany, NY, 1990), p. 65.

14. Jaroslav Prucek, *Chinese Statelets and the Northern Barbarians in the Period 1400–300 BC* (New York, 1971), p. 223.

15. I have treated these issues in "Chinese Strategy from the Fourteenth to the Seventeenth Centuries," in *The Making of Strategy: Rulers, States, and War,* eds. Williamson Murray, Macgregor Knox, and Alvin Bernstein (New York, 1994), pp. 85–114, as well as *The Great Wall of China: From History to Myth* (Cambridge, 1990).

16. *Conference on the Limitation of Armament: Washington November 12, 1921–February 6, 1922* (Washington, DC, 1922), pp. 876–886. See also Arthur Waldron, ed., *How the Peace Was Lost* (Stanford, CA, 1992), pp. 17–20, 52–55.

17. Edgar Snow, *Red Star Over China* (New York, 1961), p. 131.

18. A good introduction is Ralph D Sawyer with Mei-chün Sawyer, *The Seven Military Classics of Ancient China* (Boulder, 1993). For wei, see Waldron, The Great Wall of China, pp. 76, 90.

19. Moss Roberts, trans., *Three Kingdoms: A Historical Novel,* attributed to Luo Guanzhong (Berkeley, CA, 1991), p. 292.

20. Ibid., p. 293.

21. For this concept, see Roger T. Ames, *The Art of Rulership: a Study of Ancient Chinese Political Thought* (Honolulu, 1983), esp. pp. 65–103.

22. See Harro Von Senger, *The Book of Stratagems: Tactics for Triumph and Survival,* ed. and trans. by Myron B. Gubitz (New York, 1991).

23. A good example is Kenneth Lieberthal, *Governing China: From Revolution through Reform* (New York, 1995).

24. See John K. Fairbank, ed., *The Chinese World Order: Traditional China's Foreign Relations* (Cambridge, MA, 1968). The idea of a "tributary system" was laid out sixty years ago in two related articles, one from the Chinese side and the other from the West: T. F. Tsiang, "China and European Expansion," *Politica,* 1936, pp. 1–18, and John K. Fairbank and S. Y. Teng, "On the Ch'ing Tributary System," *Harvard Journal of Asiatic Studies,* 1942, pp. 135–246.

25. See Morris Rossabi, *China Among Equals: The Middle Kingdom and its Neighbors, 10th–14th Centuries* (Berkeley, CA, 1983); indirect light on the topic in a more recent period is cast by Ronald P. Toby's excellent *State and Diplomacy in Early Modern Japan: Asia in the Development of the Tokugawa Bakufu* (Stanford, CA, 1991).

26. See Immanuel C Y. Hsü, *China's Entrance into the Family of Nations: The Diplomatic Phase, 1858–1880* (Cambridge, MA, 1960); also L. Tung, *China and Some Phases of International Law* (Oxford, 1940). Waldron, *How the Peace Was Lost* surveys Chinese approaches to international diplomatic practice and law in the 1920s and 1930s.

27. The Soviet and American cases are well-known; for the World War II diplomacy, see Youli Sun, *China and the Origins of the Pacific War, 1931–1941* (New York, 1993).

28. On the Tiananmen massacre, see Timothy Brook, *Quelling the People: The Military Suppression of the Beijing Democracy Movement* (New York, 1992).

29. Thus at the meeting in early August 1995 in Brunei between Qian Qichen and Warren Christopher, the United States "reaffirmed in specific terms" recognition of Beijing as the sole legitimate government of China, including Taiwan. *International Herald Tribune,* 2 August 1995, pp. 1, 6.

30. See in particular Shu Guang Zhang, *Deterrence and Strategic Culture: Chinese-American Confrontations, 1949–1958* (Ithaca, NY, 1992) and King C. Chen, *China's War With Vietnam, 1979: Issues, Decisions, and Implications* (Stanford, CA, 1987).

31. See, for example, Jacob Heilbrunn, "How to Deal With China: The Next Cold War," *The New Republic*, 20 November 1995, pp. 27–30.

32. See Waldron, *How the Peace Was Lost*, esp. pp. 1–56.

# Chapter 7
# America and India: A New Approach

1. For two books of this genre see Stephen P. Cohen and Richard L. Park, *India: Emergent Power?* (New York, 1978) and John W. Mellor, ed., *India: A Rising Middle Power* (Boulder, CO, 1979).

2. For the most coherent statement of the "Cold War First" position, and its impact on American relations with the nonwestern world by a close associate of Henry Kissinger, see Peter Rodman, *More Precious than Peace: The Cold War and the Struggle for the Third World* (New York, 1994). Before the Cold War the compulsions of the Anglo-American alliance against Imperial Japan shaped Washington's South Asian policy. Indian politicians and academics still recall, with some asperity, the shift in American policy from encouragement of Indian nationalism to full support for the British in the early 1940s.

3. For the figures see A Martin Wainwright, *Inheritance of Empire: Britain, India and the Balance of Power in Asia, 1938–1945* (Westport, CT, 1994).

4. The following section is based on a book-in-progress which examines the different theories of regional conflict as held by all of the major regional states and extra-regional powers.

5. For the perspective of a clinical psychologist who has studied the origins of such paired ethnic conflicts and wars see Vamik D. Volkan, *The Need to have Enemies and Allies: From Clinical Practice to International Relationships* (New York, 1988).

6. For an overview see David Little, *Sri Lanka: The Invention of Enmity* (Washington, 1993).

7. For a discussion of recent developments see Wang Hongyu, "Sino-Indian Relations: Present and Future," *Asian Survey*, 35:6, June 1995.

8. Shekhar Gupta, describing the view of India's Hindu community, in "The Gathering Storm," in Marshall M Bouton and Philip Oldenberg, eds., *India Briefing, 1990* (Boulder, CO, 1990), p. 31.

9. Samuel Huntington's argument about a "clash of civilizations" was anticipated by a number of Indian commentators, especially Girilal Jain, but is also embedded in the writings of Jawaharlal Nehru on the left, and the conservative, Hindu-oriented political party, the Bharatiya Jan Sangh, on the right.

10. The most insightful thinker on how hostile groups, or crowds, are generated is Elias Canetti, whose book, *Crowds and Power* (New York, 1978) is a modern classic.

11. Kautilya, *The Arthashastra*, ed. and trans. L. N. Rangarajan (New Delhi, 1987), p. 555.

12. Ibid., p. 553.

13. Sandy Gordon, *India's Rise to Power in the Twentieth Century and Beyond* (New York, 1995).

14. Referred to and discussed in Stephen P. Cohen, *The Indian Army: Its Contribution to the Development of a Nation* (Delhi, 1990).

15. The alarming exception to this is the treatment, within Pakistan, of certain Islamic sects and minority groups, which have been declared to be non-Muslim, and thus heretical.

16. There are many exceptions to this characterization. Perhaps the best-known is Jagat S. Mehta, who worked closely with Nehru as a young foreign service officer, and who eventu-

ally rose to the position of Foreign Secretary under both the Janata and Indira Gandhi governments. See Jagat S. Mehta, *Rescuing the Future: Coming to Terms With Bequeathed Misperceptions* (forthcoming, 1996).

17. For a survey of the many recent unofficial and Track II regional dialogues see Sundeep Waslekar, "Track-Two Diplomacy in South Asia," second edition, Occasional Paper, Program in Arms Control, Disarmament, and International Security, University of Illinois, 1995, especially the Appendix. This includes a list of over forty recent Track II activities.

18. Of course, nearly ten years before that, in 1962, the *Enterprise* sailed in the Bay of Bengal to demonstrate American support for India against China.

19. The leading opposition party, the moderate-conservative Bharatiya Janata Party (BJP), has a somewhat different view of Kashmir; it seeks to create an India that is not free of Muslims, but one in which Indian Muslims are no longer given special privileges, are loyal and patriotic, and acknowledge that they share in the larger Indian (essentially Hindu-origin) cultural experience, and that they do nothing that is alien to Hindu sentiments. This view is not that dissimilar, in some ways, from that of Nehru, who also wrote and spoke of a special Indian civilizational identity.

20. For the best discussion of these issues see Robert Wirsing, *Pakistan, and the Kashmir Dispute: On Regional Conflict and Its Resolution* (New York, 1994).

21. Then-deputy National Security Advisor Robert Gates has been quoted extensively on the dangers of nuclear war in South Asia in Seymour Hersh's provocative article, "On the Nuclear Edge," *The New Yorker*, 29 March 1993. Hersh's account is flawed in many details, but recent studies of non-nuclear and nuclear crises in South Asia bear out the seriousness of the events of 1987 and 1990. See Kanti Bajpai, et al., *Beyond Brasstacks: Perception and Management of Crisis in South Asia* (New Delhi, 1995).

22. For examples of this scenario-building see the testimony of the Director of the Central Intelligence Agency, R. James Woolsey, before the Senate Select Committee on Intelligence, "Nomination of R. James Woolsey, Hearing," 103rd Congress, First Session (Washington, DC, 1993), and the exaggerated analysis by William E. Burrows and Rovert Windrem in their *Critical Mass: The Dangerous Race for a Superweapon in a Fragmented World* (New York, 1994).

23. S. Rashid Naim, "Aadhi Raat Ke Baad, " [ "After Midnight"], in Stephen P. Cohen, ed., *Nuclear Proliferation in South Asia: The Prospects for Arms Control* (Boulder, CO, 1991).

24. The capacity/capability distinction is currently in vogue among Indian strategists. It serves a number of purposes, including that of being able to claim to be a nuclear or missile power, without accepting the responsibilities of being one.

25. See George Perkovich, "A Nuclear Third Way in South Asia," *Foreign Policy*, 91, Summer 1993, and also the report of an Asia Society Study Group, *Preventing Nuclear Proliferation in South Asia* (New York, 1995). Other terms that have been used to describe this not-quite-nuclear situation include "recessed," "ambiguous" and "opaque" deterrence. There is a striking similarity between this situation and the hypothesized relationship between former major nuclear weapons states should they ever eliminate their arsenals, described as "virtual" deterrence by American strategists.

26. India's latent, or potential, nuclear deterrent may have influenced Beijing's calculations vis à vis New Delhi.

27. See Bajpai, *Beyond Brasstracks*, appendix 1.

28. Richard Harass, *Conflicts Unending: The United States and Regional Disputes* (New Haven, CT, 1990).

29. See Waslekar, *Track-Two Diplomacy in South Asia.*

# Chapter 8
# Korean Security in a Post-Cold War Northeast Asia

1. U.S. Pacific Command (U.S. PACOM), *Asia-Pacific Economic Update* (Honolulu, 1994), p. viii. U.S. trade with the European Union in 1993 was $218 billion. (*Asia 1995 Yearbook* [Hongkong, 1994], p. 28.) According to the U.S. Commerce Department, the 1992 trade volume between the United States and the Asia-Pacific region was $343 billion and that between the United States and the European Union was $206 billion. (See Roger Cohen, "Like the U.S., West Europe Steps Up Its Asia Trade," *The New York Times*, 24 November 1993, p. A17.) Trade data from both sides, however, often do not correspond with each other due to the usage of different methodologies and criteria.

2. As cited in U.S. PACOM, *Asia-Pacific Economic Update*, p. v.

3. Unless noted otherwise, defense statistics on Northeast Asia are drawn from *The Military Balance 1994–1995* (London 1994), pp. 164–193.

4. This argument has been advanced by Gerald Segal. See his "The Consequences of Arms Proliferation in Asia: II," Adelphi Paper, 276, April 1993, pp. 50–61.

5. Desmond Ball, "Arms and Affluence: Military Acquisitions in the Asia-Pacific Region," *International Security*, 18:3, Winter 1993/1994, pp.78–112; Andrew Mack and Desmond Ball, "The Military Build-Up in Asia-Pacific," *The Pacific Review*, 5:3, 1992, pp. 197–208.

6. During the same period 1984–1993, however, five Northeast Asian countries (China, Japan, North Korea, South Korea, and Taiwan) accounted for 73 percent of the region's total imports, as measured by SIPRI trend-indicator values. See Bates Gill, "Arms Acquisitions in East Asia," in Stockholm International Peace Research Institute, *SIPRI Yearbook 1994: World Armament and Disarmament* (Oxford, 1994), p. 552.

7. United States Department of Defense, *A Strategic Framework for the Asian Pacific Rim: Looking Toward the 21st Century* (Washington, DC, 1990) and *A Strategic Framework for the Asian Pacific Rim: Report to Congress* (Washington, DC, 1992).

8. United States Department of Defense, *United States Security Strategy for the East Asia-Pacific Region* (Washington, DC, 1995), p. i.

9. For a comprehensive overview of China's arms acquisitions from abroad, including Russia, see Bates Gill and Taeho Kim, *China's Arms Acquisitions from Abroad: A Quest for "Superb and Secret Weapons"* (Oxford, 1995); Taeho Kim, *The Dynamics of Sino-Russia Military Relations: An Asian Perspective* (Taipei, 1994).

10. The comments were made by Russian President, Boris Yeltsin, during his trip to China in December 1992. Foreign Broadcast Information Service, *Daily Report—China*, 18 and 21 December 1992, pp. 9–10 and p. 9 respectively.

11. However, a recent appreciation of the Japanese yen and high labor costs made the Japanese defense budget look larger than it really is.

12. See, for example, William T. Tow, "Post-Cold War Security in East Asia," *The Pacific Review*, 4:2, 1993, pp. 97–108, especially pp. 103–105. For an account of the Spratly issue, see Mark J. Valencia, "Spratly Solution Still at Sea," *Pacific Review*, 6:2, 1993, pp. 155–170; Hamzah Ahmad, "The South China Sea Conflict: The Need for Policy Transparency," *Asian Defence Journal*, January 1993, pp. 122–125.

13. Richard F Grimmett, *CRS Report to Congress: Conventional Arms Transfers to the Third World, 1985–1992*, Congressional Research Service, No. 93-656 F (1993); Richard A. Bitzinger, "Arms to Go: Chinese Arms Sales to the Third World," *International Security*, 17:2,

Fall 1992; Gordon Jacobs and Tim McCarthy, "China's Missiles Sales: Few Changes for the Future," *Jane's Intelligence Review*, December 1992, pp. 559–563.

14. Denny Roy has made a major theoretical contribution to the debate about the consequences of China's economic growth for Asian security. See his "Consequences of China's Economic Growth for Asia-Pacific Security," *Security Dialogue*, 24:2, 1993, pp. 181–191; "Singapore, China and the 'Soft Authoritarian' Challenge," *Asian Survey*, 34:3, 1994; "Hegemon on the Horizon: China's Threat to East Asian Security," *International Security*, 19:1, 1994, pp. 149–168. For a rosy view on the prospects for China's economic success with its destabilizing implications, see Nicholas D. Kristof, "The Rise of China," *Foreign Affairs*, 72:5, 1993, pp. 59–74. David Shambaugh has provided a well-balanced analysis on the role of major internal and external factors, including the economy, in shaping its security policy. See his "China's Security Policy in the Post–Cold War Era," *Survival*, 34:2, 1992, pp. 88–106.

15. Robert Gilpin, *War and Change in World Politics* (Cambridge, 1987), pp. 208–209; A. F. K. Organski and Jacek Kugler, *The War Ledger* (Chicago, 1980).

16. A. W. Grazebrook, "More Regional Naval Growth," *Asia-Pacific Defence Reporter*, 1995 Annual Reference Edition, pp. 12–17; Bilweer Singh, "ASEAN's Arms Procurement: Challenge of the Security Dilemma in the Post–Cold War Era," *Comparative Strategy*, April–June 1993, pp. 199–223, especially pp. 212–213; Jim Hoagland, "An Arms Race in East Asia," *The Washington Post*, 14 July 1992, p. A13.

17. The North Korean economy has continuously registered negative growth rates since 1990. They were –3.7 percent in 1990, –5.2 percent in 1992, –7.6 percent in 1993, –4.3 percent in 1993, and –1.7 percent in 1994. Bank of Korea data.

18. For a first-rate analysis on the motivations behind North Korea's decision to develop nuclear weapons, see Andrew Mack, "The Nuclear Crisis on the Korean Peninsula," *Asian Survey*, April 1993 and "A Nuclear Korea: The Choices are Narrowing," *World Policy Journal*, Summer 1994; and Paul Bracken,"North Korea: Warning and Assessment," Testimony Prepared for the Armed Services Committee of the US. House of Representatives, 24 March 1994.

19. For a full English text, see *The Korea Times*, 22 October 1994, p.5; *The Pyongyang Times*, 22 October 1994, p. 8. See also Walter B. Slocombe, "The Agreed Framework with the Democratic People's Republic of Korea: Implications for Northeast Asia," *Strategic Forum*, 23, March 1995. For a Korean text, see The ROK Ministry of National Defense, *Defense White Paper 1995–1996* (Seoul, 1995), pp. 255–257.

20. Samuel S. Kim, "North Korea in 1994: Brinkmanship, Breakdown, and Breakthrough," *Asian Survey*, January 1995, p. 13.

21. *The Chosun Ilbo (Seoul)*, 16 June 1993; *The New York Times*, 1 June 1994.

22. Korean Institute for Defense Analyses, *Defense White Paper 1994–1995* (Seoul 1995), p. 70. See also Young Koo Cha and Kang Choi, "South Korea's Defense Posture," *Joint Force Quarterly*, 7, Spring 1995, pp. 27–28.

23. For an analysis of Kim Jong Il's profile and the prospects for his political survival, see Taeho Kim, "Kim Jong Il: North Korea's New Leader," *Janes's Intelligence Review*, September 1994, pp. 421–422. The death of Marshall Oh Jin U on 24 February 1995 could further complicate the prospects for the younger Kim's political survival. Marshal Oh had been the loyal supporter of the Kim family and the third most powerful man in North Korea after Kim Il Sung and Kim Jong Il.

24. See Mack, *"The Nuclear Crisis,"* p. 32; Richard K. Betts, "Wealth, Power, and Instability: East Asia and the United States after the Cold War," *International Security*, 18:3, 1994, pp. 34–77, especially pp. 66–67; Michael T. Klare. "The Next Great Arms Race," *Foreign Affairs*, 72:3, Summer 1993, pp. 136–152, especially p. 149.

25. William T Tow, "Changing US Force Levels and Regional Security," *Contemporary Security Policy*, 15:2, August 1994, pp. 10–43, especially pp. 12–13.

26. Susumu Awanohara and Shim Jae Hoon, "Win, Hold, Confuse," *Far Eastern Economic Review*, 15 July 1993, p. 12.

27. Les Aspin, *The Bottom-Up Review: Forces for a New Era* (Washington, DC, 1993), p. 14; see also "Bottom-Up Review Heralds Leaner Hi-Tech U.S. Military," *International Defense Review*, October 1993, pp. 756–757.

28. For a discussion of this issue see a number of the articles in *The Brassey's Mershon American Defense Annual, 1995–1996* (Washington, DC, 1995).

29. Richard D. Fisher, "The Clinton Administration's Early Defense Policy Towards Asia," *The Korean Journal of Defense Analysis*, Summer 1994, pp. 109–111; William T. Tow, "Changing US Force Levels and Regional Security," pp. 14–18 and "The Folly of Clinton's Defense Plans for Korea," Heritage Foundation Backgrounder Update, 28 June 1994, pp. 3–5.

30. "Clinton May Add GI.s in Korea While Remaining Open to Talks," *The New York Times*, 17 June 1994.

31. Jim Adams, "US. Air Force Chief Skeptical of Clinton's '2-War' Strategy," *The Korean Herald*, 17 March 1994.

32. David A. Fulghum, "Lawmakers Criticize USAF Budget Priorities," *Aviation Week & Space Technology*, 7 March 1994, p. 24; *The Bottom-Up Review*, pp. 11–12.

33. For a useful discussion on various proposals for multilateral security regimes, see Patrick M. Cronin, "Pacific Rim Security: Beyond Bilateralism?" *The Pacific Review*, 5:3, 1992, pp. 209–220; Andrew Mack, "Security Cooperation in Northeast Asia: Problems and Prospects," *Journal of Northeast Asian Studies*, Summer 1992, pp. 21–34; and James A. Winnefeld, "A Framework for Realistic Dialogue on Arms Control for Northeast Asia," *The Korean Journal of Defense Analysis*, Summer 1991, pp. 21–47.

34. For an analysis on the Chinese view on multilateral security mechanisms, see Banning Garret and Bonnie Glaser, "Multilateral Security in the Asia-Pacific Region and Its Impact on Chinese Interests: Views from Beijing," *Contemporary Southeast Asia*, June 1994, pp. 14–34; Luo Renshi, "Arms Control and Disarmament in the Asia-Pacific Region," in Malcolm Chalmers, et al., *Asia Pacific Security and the UN* (West York, 1995), pp. 77–84.

35. For an excellent analysis on the impact of Japan's historical legacies on its current defense policy and perceptions, see Barry Buzan, "Japan's Defense Problematique," *The Pacific Review*, 1995, pp. 25–43.

# Chapter 9
# Security Issues in Southeast Asia

1. Michael Leifer, "The Paradox of ASEAN: A Security Organization without the Structure of an Alliance," *The Round Table*, 271, July 1978.

2. J.N. Mak, *ASEAN Defense Reorientation 1975–1992: The Dynamics of Modernization and Structural Change* (Canberra 1993), p. 13.

3. Ian Macfarling, *Military Aspects of the West New Guinea Dispute, 1958–1962* (Canberra 1990), especially, pp. 21–46.

4. Mahathir speech, 15 July 1986, cited in Mak, *ASEAN Defense Reorientation 1975–1992*, p. 12.

5. Aaron Karp, "Military Procurement and Regional Security in Southeast Asia," *Contemporary Southeast Asia*, 11:4, March 1990, pp. 334–335.

6. Jun Zhan, "China Goes to the Blue Waters: The Navy, Seapower Mentality, and the South China Sea," *Journal of Strategic Studies*, 17:3, September 1994, p. 180.

7. Mak, *ASEAN Defense Reorientation 1975–1992*, p. 46.

8. Jun, "China Goes to the Blue Waters," p. 202.

9. Tim Huxley, "The ASEAN States' Defense Policies: Influences and Outcomes," *Post–Cold War Security Issues in the Asia-Pacific Region*, ed. by Colin McInnes and Mark G. Rolls (London 1994), p. 138.

10. Bob Lowry, *Indonesian Defense Policy and the Indonesian Armed Forces* (Canberra 1993), p. 44.

11. Peter Dennis and Jeffrey Grey, *Emergency and Confrontation: Australian Military Operations in Malaya and Borneo, 1950–1966* (Sydney 1966).

12. Karp, "Military Procurement and Regional Security in Southeast Asia."

13. Ibid.

14. Mak, *ASEAN Defense Reorientation 1975–1992*, pp. 97, 102.

15. Ibid., p. 81.

16. Carlyle Thayer, *Vietnam's Developing Military Ties with the Region: The Case for Australian Defense Contacts* (Canberra 1995), p. 39.

17. The above is based on a reading of Carlyle Thayer, *Beyond Indochina*, Adelphi Paper 297, London, 1995.

18. Huxley, "The ASEAN States' Defense Policies," pp. 151–152.

19. Thayer, *Beyond Indochina*; Mark G. Rolls, "Security Cooperation in Southeast Asia: An Evolving Process," in *Post–Cold War Security Issues in the Asia-Pacific Region*, pp. 65–77.

20. *The Policy of the State Defense and Security of the Republic of Indonesia* (Jakarta 1995), p. 6.

21. William T. Tow, "Changing U.S. Force Levels and Regional Security," in *Post–Cold War Security Issues in the Asia-Pacific Region*.

22. See Hikmahanto Juwana, "Japan's Defense Conception and Its Implications for Southeast Asia," *The Indonesian Quarterly*, 1993, pp. 483–494; Paridah Abdul Samad and Mokhtar Muhammad, "Japan in Southeast Asia: Its Diplomatic, Economic, and Military Commitment," *The Indonesian Quarterly*, 1994, pp. 260–269.

23. Sandy Gordon, "India and Southeast Asia: A Renaissance in Relations?" in *India Looks East: An Emerging Power and Its Asia-Pacific Neighbors*, ed. by Sandy Gordon and Stephen Henningham (Canberra, 1995), pp. 212–218.

24. Brahma Chellaney, "India and Its Asian Neighbors: Nuclear and other Defense Aspects," in *India Looks East*, p.114.

25. Paul Dibb, *The Political and Strategic Outlook, 1994–2003: Global, Regional, and Australian Perspectives* (Canberra 1994).

26. The Indonesian Defense White Paper notes "the potential for military conflict...with subsequent disturbance to regional stability," *Policy of State Defense and Security*, p. 5.

27. Rizal Sukma, "China's Defense Policy and Security in the Asia Pacific," *The Indonesian Quarterly*, 1995, pp. 85–87.

28. Jusuf Wanandi, "Security Cooperation in the Asia-Pacific," *The Indonesian Quarterly*, 1994, pp. 198–204; J. Soedjati Djiwandono, "Cooperative Security in the Asia-Pacific Region: An ASEAN Perspective," ibid., pp. 205–214.

# Chapter 10
# Japan's Emerging International Security Policy

1. *The Japan Times*, 14 July 1995, p. 1.

2. Ibid., 28 July 1995, p. 3.

3. Subsequent events in late 1995 led the Tokyo governor to reverse his position as the general state of the Japanese banking system continued to decline.

4. *The Japan Times*, 25 July 1995, p. 1.

5. Ibid., 2 July 1995, p. 1.

6. LCDR Tesuro Doshita, JMSDF, "Regional Threat Perceptions in the Post-Cold War Era: A Japanese View," Unpublished Paper, presented at KIDA, Seoul, Korea, 6 June 1995.

7. Professor Toshiyuki Shikata, "Japan's Security Strategy in a New Era," Unpublished paper presented to the Trilateral Conference: Germany-USA-Japan, entitled "Challenges of the 21st Century," Berlin, Germany, 12 June 1995, pp. 10–11.

8. Statement made by Maj. General V. Bunin, Soviet Army, (Ret.) in a lecture to students of the course "Pacific Security Issues," Georgia Institute of Technology, February 1995, Atlanta, Georgia.

9. *The Japan Times*, 5 June 1995, p. 1.

10. Discussions in August 1995 in Seoul with various Korean and American participants of the bilateral relationship. Severe floods that ravaged North Korea in late summer resulted in an unprecedented appeal to the United Nations for assistance, accompanied, however, by a verbal blast at Japan and the United States for causing changing weather patterns because of continued disregard for environmental concerns.

11. Shitata, "Japan's Security Strategy in a New Era," p. 10.

12. *The Japan Times*, 18 July 1995, p. 4.

13. Ibid., 29 July 1995, p. 4.

14. Ibid., 2 August 1995, p. 1.

15. *The Nikkei Weekly*, 3 July 1995, p. 15.

16. The author was present at the referenced conference in June 1990.

17. Isaka Satoshi, "Clear Sailing Seen for Rwanda Mission," *Nikkei Weekly*, 22 August 1994, p. 1, and Toshiyuki Skikata, "By the Sweat of Our Brows," *By The Way*, November/December, 1992, p. 14.

18. *The Japan Digest*, 24 August 1995, p. 1.

19. MITI Minister Ryutaro Hishimoto replaced Foreign Minister Yohei Kono as President of the Liberal Democratic Party in the September 1995 party elections. The scenario for a "snap" general election for the Lower House in late 1995 or 1996 becomes an increasing likelihood. With Hashimoto the leader of the Liberal Democratic Party, the prime minister and head of the current coalition, Tomiichi Murayama, will find less in common with Hashimoto than he had with Kono; this relationship may lead to "snap" elections before 1996.

20. Advisory Group on Defense Issues, "The Modality of the Security and Defense Capability of Japan: The Outlook for the Twenty-First Century," 12 August 1995, Tokyo, Japan.

21. Ibid., pp. 21–23.

22. Ibid., p. 16.

23. Ichiro Ozawa, *Blueprint for a New Japan* (Tokyo 1994). See especially Book II, "Becoming a 'Normal Nation,'" pp. 91–150.

24. Ibid., pp. 94–95.

25. Ibid., p. 110.

26. *The Japan Times,* 10 June 1995, p. 2.

27. Ibid., 21 May 1995, p. 18.

28. Ibid., 21 May 1995, p. 18.

29. Ibid., 21 May 1995, p. 18.

30. Kazuo Yoshida, "Japan's Security Needs Require Reassessment," *The Nikkei Weekly,* 3 July 1995, p. 2.

31. See especially *The Japan Times,* 24 June 1995, p. 4.

32. Ibid., 23 June 1995, p. 4.

33. *The Japan Digest,* 21 August 1995, p. 3.

34. *The Nikkei Weekly,* 10 July 1995, p. 4.

35. *The Nikkei Weekly,* 10 July 1995, p. 4.

36. *The Japan Digest,* 23 August 1995, p. 3.

37. *The Japan Times,* 1 July 1995, p. 1.

38. See especially ibid., 9 July 1995, p. 2.

39. *The Japan Digest,* 25 August 1995, p. 1.

40. *The Japan Times,* 29 July 1995, p. 2.

41. Ibid., 12 July 1995, p. 3.

42. See the Japanese daily newspapers from 5 September onward. Even as late as 4 October *The Japan Times* the matter was receiving significant press attention.

43. Hisayoshi Ina, "New Defense Guidelines Hinge on Continental U.S. Role," *The Nikkei Weekly,* 8 January 1996, p. 7.

44. Koji Kakizawa, "Multilateral Concerns," *By The Way,* May/June 1994, p. 22.

45. Yasushi Akashi, "Active Participation in UN. Necessary for Japan's Growth," *Nikkei Weekly,* 15 June 1994.

46. *The Japan Times,* 14 July 1995, p. 1.

47. Specifically, the next steps will involve two meetings of a review group consisting of five distinguished individuals from each of the five states represented in the senior panel. Their task will be to review the sixteen-page agreement of principles developed by the five-man senior panel in February 1995 and come to a new consensus on the specifics of the limited nuclear free zone. Each country's team will consist of a retired diplomat, retired flag officer, nuclear specialist, academic, and businessman. The American team will consist of a former assistant secretary of state, a former deputy assistant secretary of defense, a former director of the Los Alamos Nuclear Lab, a CEO and president of one of the nation's leading banks, and the author. All teams include such individuals who continue to have a demonstrated impact on the policies of their governments. The Russian team, for example, will include a former foreign minister, a former commander of the Pacific Fleet, and a former deputy director general of the general staff, among others.

This expanded senior panel is currently scheduled to meet twice before turning over its work to the respective governments. They will assemble once in Buenos Aires to discuss the experiences of the Latin American Nuclear Free Zone with members of the Argentine Foreign Ministry, and once in Bordeaux to reach final consensus and turn the product over to official government representatives. Having meetings in spring and fall of 1996 will permit the individual members to return to their respective countries and receive feedback and reaction from appropriate colleagues before the final meeting in Bordeaux.

It is hoped that the process will benefit from the elections scheduled in many of the member nations during the coming year. Interjecting this policy consideration into the public debate will result in improvements to the concept itself and likely incorporation of the concept into the campaign planks of contending political groups. It is difficult to predict the outcome of such activity, but it becomes crucial to the development in the region as a whole of the image of an area security community which, of course, is the long-term strategic objective of the entire enterprise.

# Index

# About the
# Contributors

**Stephen P. Cohen** is the Director of the Program of Arms Control, Disarmament, and International Security and holds appointments as Professor of History and Political Science at the University of Illinois at Urbana-Champaign. He was scholar-in-residence at the Ford Foundation, New Delhi in 1992–1993. Professor Cohen was a member of the policy planning staff of the U.S. Department of State from 1985 to 1987, advising on matters of security and weapons proliferation in South and Southwest Asia. He has written or edited seven books, most recently *Nuclear Proliferation in South Asia* and *South Asia After the Cold War: International Perspectives* (1993). Professor Cohen has served as a consultant to the RAND Corporation, the Departments of Defense and State, Lawrence Livermore National Laboratory, and various foundations.

**John Endicott** is the Director, Center for International Strategy, Technology, and Policy and a professor of international affairs, Georgia Institute of Technology. He went to his present position from the National Defense University, where he served as the Director, Institute for National Strategic Studies, National Defense University. A former air force officer, Professor Endicott was on the faculties of the National War College and Air Force Academy. He has consulted and advised several government agencies and private sector boards. He is currently the co-chair of the Council for U.S.-Japan Security Relations. A keen student of Asian security issues, with an emphasis on Japan, Professor Endicott's last book was *Regional Security Issues* (1990).

**Robert W. Gaskin** is the former Vice President for Policy and Programs at Business Executives for National Security, a defense-oriented, public policy organization in Washington, D.C. and is currently a private sector advocate. He served in the air force for twenty-eight years, retiring in 1992 as a colonel. As chief of doctrine on the Air Staff from 1985–1988, Mr. Gaskin created the concept of the joint force air component commander (JFACC) and played a key role in firmly establishing this into joint doctrine. Then-Colonel Gaskin also served as the Assistant Director of Net Assessment under Dr. Andrew Marshall where he wrote the definitive assessment of the military balance on the Korean Peninsula. He has lectured at the Air War College, the army's School for Advanced Military Science, Army War College, National War College, Navy College, as well as at Harvard and Georgetown Universities.

**John Gooch** is professor of international history at the University of Leeds, United Kingdom. He is joint editor of the *Journal of Strategic Studies* and the chairman of the Army Records Society. Professor Gooch is also a vice-president of the The Royal Historical Society. Until 1991, he was department head and professor of history at Lancaster University. Appointed the founding Secretary of the Navy senior research fellow at the United States Naval War College in 1985–1986, Professor Gooch taught in the College of Naval Warfare as a member of the strategy department. In 1988, he was Visiting Professor of Military History at Yale University. Professor Gooch has published eleven books on British and European military history. His most recent works are *Military Misfortunes: The Anatomy of Failure in War* (with Eliot A. Cohen) and *Air Power: Theory and Practice*.

**Jeffrey Grey** is senior lecturer in history at the University College, Australian Defence Force Academy in Canberra. He has taught in the Australian staff colleges and at the National College for Defence and Strategic Studies, and is currently writing a book on the Royal Australian Navy in Southeast Asia, 1955–1975. Professor Grey is the author or editor of nine books, including *A Military History of Australia* (1990), several volumes on the Vietnam War, and most recently (with Peter Dennis), *Emergency and Confrontation: Australian Military Operations in Malaya and Borneo, 1950–1966* (1996).

**Taeho Kim** is a senior China analyst in the policy planning directorate at the Korea Institute for Defense Analyses, Seoul, Korea and a research associate (not in residence) of the Mershon Center, The Ohio State University. He is a former associate editor of *The Korean Journal of Defense Analysis*. Dr. Kim is the author and co-author of several works on Asian security issues including most recently *China's Arms Acquisitions from Abroad: A Quest for "Superb and Secret Weapons"* (1995). His most recent English language article appeared in *Jane's Intelligence Review*, "Kim Jong Il: North Korea's New Leader" (October, 1994).

**Arthur Waldron** is professor of strategy at the Naval War College and adjunct professor of East Asian Studies at Brown University. Trained at Harvard and in Europe and Asia, he is the author or editor of numerous articles and of six books, including publications in Italian, Japanese, and Chinese. Professor Waldron's latest book is *From War to Nationalism: China's Turning Point, 1924–1925*.

**Barry Watts** is senior analyst at Northrop Grumman Corporation. He has been with Northrop since retiring from the air force as a lieutenant colonel in 1986. His varied career included flying assignments in Vietnam and Japan, teaching (philosophy and mathematical logic), mentoring, and leading at the Air Force Academy, Soviet threat specialist with the Air Staff, and two tours with the Pentagon's Office of Net Assessment. Mr. Watts' analyses in the private sector have dealt with U.S. operational capabilities, doctrine, military strategy for corporate headquarters and operating divisions, as well as work on corporate long-range strategies. A regular lecturer at the Air War College on strategic bombing and the 1991 Gulf War, he played a significant role in the Gulf War Air Power Survey. Mr. Watts continues to do *pro bono* work for the Office of Net Assessment dealing with military innovation and the revolution in military affairs. He collaborated with Williamson Murray on the forthcoming *Military Innovations During the Interwar Years* (1996).

**Jay T. Young** is a management consultant with Battelle Memorial Institute, Columbus, Ohio, in the Technology Management Group. He directs competitive analysis and other business research studies. Mr. Young is a former senior military analyst for the Central Intelligence Agency. He is also an officer in the United States Naval Reserve and a Ph.D. candidate in military history at The Ohio State University.

# About the Editors

**Williamson Murray** is the Matthew C. Horner Professor of Military Theory at the Marine Corps University and Professor Emeritus of History from Ohio State University. He has also taught at the Air War College and the United States Military Academy at West Point and served as a Secretary of the Navy Fellow at the Naval War College in Newport. He is the author of a number of books, including *Luftwaffe* (Nautical and Aviation Press, 1984), *The Change in the European Balance of Power: The Path to Ruin* (Princeton University Press, 1985), *German Military Effectiveness* (Nautical and Aviation Press, 1992), and *The Air War in the Persian Gulf* (Nautical and Aviation Press, 1995). He has edited or coedited a number of books to include: *Military Effectiveness* (with Allan Millett), vol. I, *The First World War*, vol. II, *The Interwar Period*, and vol. III, *The Second World War* (Alan and Unwin, 1988), *Calculations, Net Assessment and the Coming of World War II* (with Allan Millett) (The Free Press, 1992), *The Making of Strategy, Rulers, States, and War* (with MacGregor Knox) (Cambridge University Press, 1994), and *Military Innovation in the Interwar Period* (with Allan Millett) (Cambridge University Press, 1996).

**Allan R. Millett** is the Raymond E. Mason, Jr. Professor of Military History and Associate Director, Mershon Center, The Ohio State University. A specialist in the history of American military policy and institutions, he has written numerous articles and published four books: *The Politics of Intervention: The Military Occupation of Cuba, 1906–1909* (1968); *The General: Robert L.*

*Bullard and Officership in the United States Army, 1881–1925* (1975); *Semper Fidelis: The History of the United States Marine Corps* (1980, revised edition 1991); and *In Many a Strife: General Gerald C. Thomas and the U.S. Marine Corps, 1917–1956* (1993). Professor Millett has collaborated with other scholars on several books. One of these books was *For the Common Defense: A Military History of the United States, 1607–1983* with Dr. Peter Maslowski (1984, revised edition 1994). In two other very successful projects, Professor Millett collaborated with Professor Williamson Murray to produce *Military Effectiveness* (1988) and *Calculations: Net Assessment and the Coming of World War II* (1992). His current work-in-progress is a history of the Korean War. Professor Millett has lectured at the National War College, Army War College, Air War College, Naval War College, each service academy, both the Korean Military Academy and National Defense College, and Belgian Royal Military Academy. He is a four-term trustee and former two-term president of the Society of Military History. Professor Millett retired from the USMC Reserves in 1990 as a colonel. His service—which culminated with his command of an infantry battalion—included numerous tactical assignments as well as a posting as an adjunct faculty member at the Marine Corps Command and Staff College.